Also by the Editors at America's Test Kitchen

100 Recipes: The Absolute Best Ways to Make the True Essentials

The New Family Cookbook

The Complete Vegetarian Cookbook

The Complete Cooking for Two Cookbook

The America's Test Kitchen Cooking School Cookbook

The Cook's Illustrated Meat Book

The Cook's Illustrated Baking Book

The Cook's Illustrated Cookbook

The Science of Good Cooking

The America's Test Kitchen Menu Cookbook

The America's Test Kitchen Quick Family Cookbook

The America's Test Kitchen Healthy Family Cookbook

The America's Test Kitchen Family Baking Book

THE AMERICA'S TEST KITCHEN LIBRARY SERIES AND THE TEST KITCHEN HANDBOOK SERIES

The How Can It Be Gluten-Free Cookbook

The Best Mexican Recipes

The Make-Ahead Cook

Healthy Slow Cooker Revolution

Slow Cooker Revolution Volume 2: The Easy-Prep Edition

Slow Cooker Revolution

The Six-Ingredient Solution

Pressure Cooker Perfection

Comfort Food Makeovers

The America's Test Kitchen D.I.Y. Cookbook

Pasta Revolution

Simple Weeknight Favorites

The Best Simple Recipes

THE COOK'S COUNTRY SERIES

Cook's Country Eats Local

From Our Grandmothers' Kitchens

Cook's Country Blue Ribbon Desserts

Cook's Country Best Potluck Recipes

Cook's Country Best Lost Suppers

Cook's Country Best Grilling Recipes

The Cook's Country Cookbook

America's Best Lost Recipes

THE TV COMPANION SERIES

The Complete Cook's Country TV Show Cookbook

The Complete America's Test Kitchen TV Show Cookbook 2001–2015

America's Test Kitchen: The TV Companion Cookbook (2009 and 2011–2015 Editions)

AMERICA'S TEST KITCHEN ANNUALS

The Best of America's Test Kitchen (2007–2015 Editions)

Cooking for Two (2010–2013 Editions)

Light & Healthy (2010–2012 Editions)

THE BEST RECIPE SERIES

The New Best Recipe

More Best Recipes

The Best One-Dish Suppers

Soups, Stews & Chilis

The Best Skillet Recipes

The Best Slow & Easy Recipes

The Best Chicken Recipes

The Best International Recipe

The Best Make-Ahead Recipe

The Best 30-Minute Recipe

The Best Light Recipe

The Cook's Illustrated Guide to Grilling and Barbecue

Best American Side Dishes

Cover & Bake

Steaks, Chops, Roasts & Ribs

Baking Illustrated

Italian Classics

American Classics

FOR A FULL LISTING OF ALL OUR BOOKS

CooksIllustrated.com

AmericasTestKitchen.com

Praise for Other America's Test Kitchen Titles

"The sum total of exhaustive experimentation . . . anyone interested in gluten-free cookery simply shouldn't be without it."
NIGELLA LAWSON ON *THE HOW CAN IT BE GLUTEN-FREE COOKBOOK*

"Even ultra-experienced gluten-free cooks and bakers will learn something from this thoroughly researched, thoughtfully presented volume."
PUBLISHERS WEEKLY ON *THE HOW CAN IT BE GLUTEN-FREE COOKBOOK*

"The 21st-century *Fannie Farmer Cookbook* or *The Joy of Cooking*. If you had to have one cookbook and that's all you could have, this one would do it."
CBS SAN FRANCISCO ON *THE NEW FAMILY COOKBOOK*

"This book upgrades slow cooking for discriminating, 21st-century palates—that is indeed revolutionary."
THE DALLAS MORNING NEWS ON *SLOW COOKER REVOLUTION*

"One bag, 3 meals? Get the biggest bang for your buck."
FOX NEWS ON *THE MAKE-AHEAD COOK*

"The go-to gift book for newlyweds, small families, or empty nesters."
ORLANDO SENTINEL ON *THE COMPLETE COOKING FOR TWO COOKBOOK*

"Some 2,500 photos walk readers through 600 painstakingly tested recipes, leaving little room for error."
ASSOCIATED PRESS ON *THE AMERICA'S TEST KITCHEN COOKING SCHOOL COOKBOOK*

"Ideal as a reference for the bookshelf . . . will be turned to time and again for definitive instruction on just about any food-related matter."
PUBLISHERS WEEKLY ON *THE SCIENCE OF GOOD COOKING*

"A one-volume kitchen seminar, addressing in one smart chapter after another the sometimes surprising whys behind a cook's best practices. . . . You get the myth, the theory, the science, and the proof, all rigorously interrogated as only America's Test Kitchen can do."
NPR ON *THE SCIENCE OF GOOD COOKING*

"Carnivores with an obsession for perfection will likely have found their new bible in this comprehensive collection."
PUBLISHERS WEEKLY (STARRED REVIEW) ON *THE COOK'S ILLUSTRATED MEAT BOOK*

"This encyclopedia of meat cookery would feel completely overwhelming if it weren't so meticulously organized and artfully designed. This is Cook's Illustrated at its finest."
THE KITCHN ON *THE COOK'S ILLUSTRATED MEAT BOOK*

"This book is a comprehensive, no-nonsense guide . . . a well-thought-out, clearly explained primer for every aspect of home baking."
THE WALL STREET JOURNAL ON *THE COOK'S ILLUSTRATED BAKING BOOK*

"Buy this gem for the foodie in your family, and spend the extra money to get yourself a copy too."
THE MISSOURIAN ON *THE BEST OF AMERICA'S TEST KITCHEN 2015*

"The perfect kitchen home companion. . . . The practical side of things is very much on display . . . cook-friendly and kitchen-oriented, illuminating the process of preparing food instead of mystifying it."
THE WALL STREET JOURNAL ON *THE COOK'S ILLUSTRATED COOKBOOK*

"If this were the only cookbook you owned, you would cook well, be everyone's favorite host, have a well-run kitchen, and eat happily every day."
THECITYCOOK.COM ON *THE AMERICA'S TEST KITCHEN MENU COOKBOOK*

"There are pasta books . . . and then there's this pasta book. Flip your carbohydrate dreams upside down and strain them through this sieve of revolutionary, creative, and also traditional recipes."
SAN FRANCISCO BOOK REVIEW ON *PASTA REVOLUTION*

"Further proof that practice makes perfect, if not transcendent. . . . If an intermediate cook follows the directions exactly, the results will be better than takeout or Mom's."
THE NEW YORK TIMES ON *THE NEW BEST RECIPE*

THE HOW CAN IT BE

GLUTEN FREE

COOKBOOK

VOLUME 2

THE EDITORS AT
America's Test Kitchen

AMERICA'S TEST KITCHEN

17 Station Street, Brookline, MA 02445

The How Can It Be Gluten Free Cookbook Volume 2

ISBN 978-1-936493-98-2

ISSN 2379-8300

Paperback: US $26.95 / $34.95 CAN

Manufactured in the United States of America

10 9 8 7 6 5 4 3 2 1

Distributed by Penguin Random House Publisher Services

Tel: 800.733.3000

EDITORIAL DIRECTOR: Jack Bishop

EDITORIAL DIRECTOR, BOOKS: Elizabeth Carduff

EXECUTIVE FOOD EDITOR: Julia Collin Davison

SENIOR EDITORS: Debra Hudak, Suzannah McFerran, and Stephanie Pixley

ASSOCIATE EDITORS: Sara Mayer, Sebastian Nava, and Anne Wolf

EDITORIAL ASSISTANTS: Kate Ander and Samantha Ronan

TEST COOK: Meaghen Walsh

ASSISTANT TEST COOK: Amanda Rumore

DESIGN DIRECTOR: Greg Galvan

ART DIRECTOR: Carole Goodman

DEPUTY ART DIRECTOR: Taylor Argenzio

DESIGNER: Allison Boales

PHOTOGRAPHY DIRECTOR: Julie Cote

ASSOCIATE ART DIRECTOR, PHOTOGRAPHY: Steve Klise

STAFF PHOTOGRAPHER: Daniel J. van Ackere

ADDITIONAL PHOTOGRAPHY: Carl Tremblay

FOOD STYLING: Catrine Kelty, Marie Piraino, and Sally Staub

PHOTOSHOOT KITCHEN TEAM:

    ASSOCIATE EDITOR: Chris O'Connor

    TEST COOK: Daniel Cellucci

    ASSISTANT TEST COOKS: Allison Berkey and Matthew Fairman

ILLUSTRATIONS: Jay Layman

PRODUCTION DIRECTOR: Guy Rochford

SENIOR PRODUCTION MANAGER: Jessica Quirk

PRODUCTION MANAGER: Christine Walsh

IMAGING MANAGER: Lauren Robbins

PRODUCTION AND IMAGING SPECIALISTS: Heather Dube, Sean MacDonald, Dennis Noble, and Jessica Voas

PROJECT MANAGER: Britt Dresser

COPY EDITOR: Jeff Schier

PROOFREADER: Ann-Marie Imbornoni

INDEXER: Elizabeth Parsons

PICTURED ON FRONT COVER: Yeasted Doughnuts (page 66)

PICTURED ON BACK COVER: Rosemary Polenta Cake with Clementines (page 288), Whole-Grain Sprouted Bread (page 151), Black Rice Salad with Snap Peas and Ginger-Sesame Vinaigrette (page 82), Bagels (page 161), Baked Raspberry Tart (page 258), Hamburger Rolls (page 174)

CONTENTS

Welcome to America's Test Kitchen

This book has been tested, written, and edited by the folks at America's Test Kitchen, a very real 2,500-square-foot kitchen located just outside of Boston. It is the home of *Cook's Illustrated* magazine and *Cook's Country* magazine and is the Monday-through-Friday destination for more than four dozen test cooks, editors, food scientists, tasters, and cookware specialists. Our mission is to test recipes over and over again until we understand how and why they work and until we arrive at the "best" version.

We start the process of testing a recipe with a complete lack of preconceptions, which means that we accept no claim, no theory, no technique, and no recipe at face value. We simply assemble as many variations as possible, test a half-dozen of the most promising, and taste the results blind. We then construct our own hybrid recipe and continue to test it, varying ingredients, techniques, and cooking times until we reach a consensus. The result, we hope, is the best version of a particular recipe, but we realize that only you can be the final judge of our success (or failure). As we like to say in the test kitchen, "We make the mistakes, so you don't have to."

All of this would not be possible without a belief that good cooking, much like good music, is indeed based on a foundation of objective technique. Some people like spicy foods and others don't, but there is a right way to sauté, there is a best way to cook a pot roast, and there are measurable scientific principles involved in producing perfectly beaten, stable egg whites. This is our ultimate goal: to investigate the fundamental principles of cooking so that you become a better cook. It is as simple as that.

If you're curious to see what goes on behind the scenes at America's Test Kitchen, check out our daily blog, The Feed, at AmericasTestKitchenFeed.com, which features kitchen snapshots, exclusive recipes, video tips, and much more. You can watch us work (in our actual test kitchen) by tuning in to *America's Test Kitchen* (AmericasTestKitchen.com) or *Cook's Country from America's Test Kitchen* (CooksCountryTV.com) on public television. Tune in to *America's Test Kitchen Radio* (ATKradio.com) on public radio to

listen to insights, tips, and techniques that illuminate the truth about real home cooking. Want to hone your cooking skills or finally learn how to bake—from an America's Test Kitchen test cook? Enroll in a cooking class at our online cooking school at OnlineCookingSchool.com. And find information about subscribing to *Cook's Illustrated* magazine at CooksIllustrated.com or *Cook's Country* magazine at CooksCountry.com. Both magazines are published every other month. However you choose to visit us, we welcome you into our kitchen, where you can stand by our side as we test our way to the best recipes in America.

FACEBOOK.COM/AMERICASTESTKITCHEN

TWITTER.COM/TESTKITCHEN

YOUTUBE.COM/AMERICASTESTKITCHEN

INSTAGRAM.COM/TESTKITCHEN

PINTEREST.COM/TESTKITCHEN

AMERICASTESTKITCHEN.TUMBLR.COM

GOOGLE.COM/+AMERICASTESTKITCHEN

Preface

Bagels? Baguettes? Brioche? Whole-Grain Blueberry Muffins? Currant Scones? Blondies? Chicken Parmesan? These are just a few of the recipes that you thought you would never make (or eat) again if you are gluten-free. Gluten-free bagels and baguettes usually have no chew, scones and blondies turn out greasy, and bread crumbs for chicken Parmesan are not crisp.

And gluten-free recipes are often anything but wholesome. So for *The How Can It Be Gluten-Free Cookbook Volume 2*, in addition to a new repertoire of recipes using our all-purpose blend, we invented a whole new whole-grain gluten-free flour blend (teff flour works wonders). It is great in Chocolate Chip Cookies, Brown Sugar Cookies, Gingersnaps, and Pecan Bars. We also developed many recipes with alternatives to dairy since many folks who are gluten-free also appreciate dairy-free recipes as well.

As is the custom here at the test kitchen, we dug deep to come up with techniques for solving a myriad of gluten-free baking problems. We found a way to jump-start rising for gluten-free breads to avoid dense loaves that do not rise properly. We discovered that while extended baking times solved many problems, including drying out high-liquid doughs, the bottoms of the baked goods often burned as a result. (Our answer was simple: Double up on the baking sheets to provide extra insulation to prevent burning.) Foil collars came to the rescue so that breads rose tall and rolls held their shape during baking. Plus, we found a way to take store-bought gluten-free bread and turn it into crispy bread crumbs by toasting them and adding cornstarch.

Some of my favorite recipes? Fluffy Oat Pancakes, Whole-Grain Blueberry Muffins, Currant Scones (you would never know that they are gluten-free), New York–Style Crumb Cake, Oatmeal Cookies with Chocolate Chunks and Dried Cherries, and Chocolate Angel Pie.

I have tried a wide range of gluten-free supermarket products in the process of developing this book and the pickings are slim. There are a few items—one brand of spaghetti, a multigrain sandwich bread, and the odd breakfast bar—that are acceptable, but cookies taste dry and chalky and muffins are dense and greasy. And, every time I eat store-bought gluten-free bread, I need a large glass of water nearby so I don't choke to death! The question that comes to mind is, "Why am I eating this?" (It reminds me of playing guitar badly—the silence when you stop playing is so much nicer!)

The How Can It Be Gluten-Free Cookbook Volume 2 is a game-changer. It's food that you really want to cook and eat. It has put the pleasure and the wholesomeness back into a category of recipes that have been sorely lacking in both. And, truth be told, it required fresh thinking; just using a gluten-free flour blend in your everyday recipe does not yield good results.

That reminds me of a Vermont story about fresh thinking (or the lack thereof). A long time ago, when Vermont voted almost entirely Republican, a gentleman ran for the legislature on the Democratic ticket. As expected, he lost. His background was unusual. He had been a Christian missionary to Japan before converting to Buddhism, and when he returned to Vermont he built a Buddhist temple on a small knoll near his house and brought over a pair of Buddhist monks. After the election, two locals were chatting about this gentleman's failed campaign. One of them asked, "Do you think that he would have been a good man for the legislature?" The other replied, "Yes. He is educated, well-traveled, and a man of wisdom and virtue." The other old-timer thought a bit and then said, "Yes, I think that he is a good man, and I wouldn't have minded voting for a Buddhist, but, by God, I couldn't bring myself to vote for a Democrat!"

Enjoy a whole new world of gluten-free cooking and baking.

CHRISTOPHER KIMBALL
Founder and Editor,
Cook's Illustrated and *Cook's Country*
Host, *America's Test Kitchen* and
Cook's Country from America's Test Kitchen

GLUTEN-FREE BASICS

Introduction

Our first gluten-free cookbook was published to a groundswell of support from our fans and supporters around the country, as well as from many who had never bought a book developed by our test kitchen but who were desperate for gluten-free recipes that were foolproof and tasted great. We asked for and got lots of feedback on our first book, from ideas for recipes to develop for this new collection (bagels were often mentioned) to pleas for dairy-free recipes and nutritional information for every recipe. Based on this input, we identified these goals when we started this project.

CREATE a new whole-grain gluten-free flour blend with just a handful of ingredients that would allow us to create earthy, wheaty-tasting baked goods that rivaled those made with traditional whole-wheat flour, including recipes for pancakes and waffles, sandwich bread, a rustic boule, pecan bars, and free-form tart dough. The ATK Whole-Grain Gluten-Free Flour Blend features teff flour, which adds both a nutritional boost and robust flavor to baked goods.

EXPAND our repertoire of gluten-free recipes using the ATK All-Purpose Gluten-Free Flour Blend created for our first book; among the new recipes are those for yeasted doughnuts, focaccia, baguettes, pan pizza, lemon layer cake, and chicken and dumplings.

DEVELOP dairy-free variations for a high percentage of the recipes in this book and summarize our findings so readers can tailor their own recipes to be dairy-free.

RATE key gluten-free supermarket products and ingredients that would make cooking—and eating—easier, including the wide variety of gluten-free pasta and sandwich breads now on the market.

TEACH readers about the wide range of gluten-free grains (everything from amaranth to black rice) now sold in supermarkets. Many cooks are unfamiliar with these grains, and our test kitchen explains how to buy them and offers up approachable, appealing recipes for the most versatile grains.

As the test kitchen was working on this book, we sent the most important (and most difficult) recipes out to volunteer recipe testers—home cooks like you. In all, we received more than 2,500 written reports from this army of gluten-free testers. Thank you. Your feedback helped identify techniques that needed to be described in more detail, as well as recipes that needed to be reworked.

If you have comments or questions about the recipes in this book, visit **howcanitbeglutenfree.com**, where we have posted answers to the most frequently asked questions. If your questions aren't answered there, you can email us at glutenfree@americastestkitchen.com.

The Science of Gluten

Before you attempt to cook without gluten, it's helpful to understand what gluten does in various recipes. Let's start with the most common source of gluten—wheat flour—which is the main ingredient in everything from pasta and pizza to cakes and cookies.

WHEAT FLOUR 101

Flour is milled from wheat berries, which contain starches, proteins, and fats. There are two main proteins in wheat flour—glutenin and gliadin. Glutenin is a very large, loosely coiled protein, while gliadin is a much smaller and tightly coiled sphere. Glutenin provides most of the strength and elasticity in dough, allowing it to bounce back after it has been stretched. Gliadin, on the other hand, provides the stretch.

DEFINING GLUTEN

In dry flour, these proteins are basically lifeless strands wrapped around granules of starch. But they begin to change shape when they come in contact with water, a process called hydration. Once moistened, the individual protein molecules (the glutenin and gliadin) begin to link up with one another to form long, elastic chains called gluten. These strands of gluten combine to form a membrane-like network. The network engulfs swollen starch granules and gas bubbles (created by yeast, chemical leaveners like baking powder, or foams like whipped egg whites), stretching as the batter or dough rises and then bakes, giving the finished cake or loaf its structure and chew.

GLUTEN DEVELOPMENT

There are several factors that can affect gluten development. The first is the flour itself. Bread flour is milled from high-protein wheat, which means it's capable of developing more gluten, or structure, which is perfect for chewy artisan loaves. In contrast, cake flour is made from soft wheat with a low protein content. As a result, cake flour produces less gluten, making it perfect for tender cakes. All-purpose flour has a relatively high protein content of 10 to 12 percent, depending on the brand. Bread flours have even more protein, generally 12 to 14 percent. Cake flour has just 6 to 8 percent protein.

Second, the amount of water can affect gluten development. Basically, the more water in a dough or batter, the stronger and more elastic the gluten strands. Why does this matter? If the gluten strands are strong and elastic, they can support the starch granules and air bubbles that hydrate and swell as the dough rises and bakes, producing an airier bread with good chew.

The third variable is the mixing time. A muffin batter that is gently stirred will develop less gluten than a bread dough beaten in a stand mixer for 10 minutes. More stirring equals more gluten, which equals more structure and chew.

What Is Gluten?

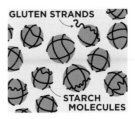

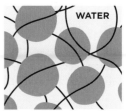

Wheat flour contains two types of protein strands, glutenin and gliadin, wrapped around starch granules.

When flour is combined with water, the protein strands unwind and link together to form a membrane-like network, which is called gluten.

Strategies for Replacing Wheat Flour

The cook who wants to remove the flour from favorite recipes needs to consider the role the flour is playing in that recipe in order to devise a successful substitute. Remember that flour contains both protein and starch, and the kind of substitute you will need when trying to convert a recipe to be gluten-free will vary because some recipes rely on one but not the other element. Let's look at the three most common roles played by wheat flour.

FLOUR THICKENS

In sauces, gravies, soups, and stews, wheat flour plays the role of thickener. When the starch granules in the flour are heated in these dishes, they absorb water, swell, and eventually burst, releasing a starch molecule called amylose that diffuses throughout the solution, trapping additional water and forming a gelatinous network. This is how a few tablespoons of flour turn chicken stock into gravy.

Some thickeners, like cornstarch, are pure starches and contain more amylose than other thickeners, like flour, that contain components other than starch molecules. (Remember, flour also contains proteins and fats, and the starch content is about 75 percent.) Purity affects not only thickening power but performance.

Cornstarch is actually more fickle than flour. For instance, overwhisking pastry cream can break the bonds of the starch gel and thin out the custard. In contrast, the proteins and lipids in flour dilute its capacity to form starch gels, so that more flour is needed for thickening. But these nonstarch compounds also act as binders, ensuring that the liquid not only thickens but also stays that way.

For these reasons, simply replacing flour with a pure starch doesn't always work. Large quantities of pure starch can impart a gritty texture to dishes. We had this problem when developing our recipe for clam chowder—the amount of cornstarch needed to thicken the soup to the proper consistency gave it a slimy and gritty mouthfeel. Luckily, there are other gluten-free starches besides cornstarch, including arrowroot (derived from a tropical tuber of the same name), potato starch, and tapioca starch (derived from cassava, another tropical tuber). In the end, we didn't find a single replacement for flour as a thickener, but given all the options we had no trouble finding an excellent work-around in varied recipes.

FLOUR COATS

In addition to its use as a thickener, flour can also be used as a coating in dishes like fried chicken or pan-fried pork chops. The starches in the flour are responsible for most of the browning and crisping, while the proteins in the flour help the coating cling to the surface of the food. The proteins also create chew or texture in the fried or baked coating.

When looking for a replacement for wheat flour, it's easy enough to deal with the starch component. Cornstarch is traditionally used as a coating in many recipes, everything from tempura to onion rings. Replacing the wheat flour with cornstarch was a start in many recipes. However, since cornstarch contains almost no protein, we had to rely on other ingredients to help the coating adhere and/or to create a chewy texture in the coating.

For our batter-fried fish, the starches in our flour blend made for an unpleasant dense and soggy coating. We found that a combination of brown rice flour and cornstarch, rested to eliminate grittiness, plus a double battering and frying method were keys to success.

Finally, in recipes that rely on a bread-crumb coating, like chicken Parmesan and breaded pork cutlets, we were able to use gluten-free sandwich bread (dried in the oven first to make the crumbs less sticky) in combination with cornstarch (which improved overall coverage and increased browning and crispness). In the end, we didn't find a single replacement for flour as a coating ingredient, but here, too, given all the options we had no trouble finding a solution.

FLOUR BUILDS STRUCTURE

Finally, the main use for flour in the home kitchen is as a structural agent in baked goods. It's here that the gluten performs an essential function; the ability of the proteins in wheat flour to expand and trap gas bubbles is key in many baked goods. In contrast to our efforts to come up with substitutions for wheat flour's other uses as a thickener or a coating, finding a replacement to replicate these structural functions using gluten-free ingredients was especially challenging because most options contain less protein.

In a baked good such as a muffin, the starch granules in the flour absorb moisture and swell as the batter is being prepared. The strands of gluten bond together and surround the starch granules. Gluten is particularly elastic and strong, especially when heated. This highly organized and strong network of gluten gives the muffin its structure and shape. Compared with wheat flour, gluten-free flours generally contain less protein, so they don't do as good of a job of organizing and holding the swollen starch granules. These proteins are also less elastic than gluten. In order to replace wheat flour with a lower-protein flour, such as rice flour, you must boost the effectiveness of that protein.

Xanthan gum acts like glue, helping cement the protein network in gluten-free flour. Another option is something that can help the flour to hydrate more readily, something that will promote the swelling of the starch granules and the bonding of the protein strands. An emulsifier such as nonfat milk powder can be used for this task. Emulsifiers can also make gluten-free flour more compatible with fat—something that wheat flour does better than other flours. Why is this important? Many baked goods (think cookies, cakes, even muffins) contain a lot of fat for flavor and moistness. If the flour doesn't absorb fat well, the baked good can be greasy (from the unabsorbed fat) and dry (because the starches are not properly coated with fat).

There's one more issue to consider when replacing wheat flour in baked goods. Wheat flour contains a starch content of roughly 75 percent. Most gluten-free flours contain an even higher starch content,

TIPS FOR SUCCESSFULLY MAINTAINING A GLUTEN-FREE DIET

If you're new to a gluten-free diet, you will want to pick up some good resources to help teach you how to read a product label and find hidden sources of gluten. Here are the key challenges, in brief.

Check Ingredients: Many foods are made with an ingredient that contains gluten. This list includes the obvious (traditional sandwich bread and Italian pasta) and the less obvious (such as soy sauce—which is typically made with soybeans and wheat—and some brands of baking powder). You will need to learn which ingredients are typically made with wheat-based ingredients, and then to read labels carefully.

Review Processing: Other foods can be processed in facilities that also handle wheat and as a result may contain trace amounts of gluten—even though the food contains no wheat. This can be an issue with foods like cornmeal or oats. If you have celiac disease or some other reason to avoid foods with even trace amounts of gluten, you need to read labels carefully to make sure naturally gluten-free foods, like oats, have not been processed in the same machines used to grind wheat.

Separate and Safe: Likewise, as a cook, you need to think about cross-contamination if you're trying to eliminate all gluten, even trace amounts, from your diet. If you're preparing dishes with wheat as well as gluten-free recipes in the same kitchen, you need to be vigilant about washing measuring tools, bowls, cutting boards, and your hands.

which means they can impart a gritty texture to baked goods. In effect, there's too much starch and not enough protein. As we developed baked goods for this book, much of our testing was aimed at solving both grittiness and weak structure.

The ATK All-Purpose Gluten-Free Flour Blend

ALL-PURPOSE
GLUTEN FREE BLEND

G-F TESTING LAB

RICE FLOURS	We had the best results using Bob's Red Mill white rice flour and brown rice flour. See page 24 for more information.
POTATO STARCH	Be sure to use potato starch, not potato flour. Alternatively, 7 ounces (1¼ cups plus 2 tablespoons) sweet white rice flour, or 7 ounces (1¾ cups) arrowroot starch/flour/powder can be substituted for the potato starch. We had better results using sweet rice flour in quick breads, cakes, and cookies, and using arrowroot starch in yeast breads.
TAPIOCA STARCH	Tapioca starch is also sold as tapioca flour; they are interchangeable.
MILK POWDER	You can omit the milk powder, but baked goods won't brown as well and they will taste less rich. Alternatively, you can substitute soy milk powder.

WHY THIS RECIPE WORKS

The decision to develop our own all-purpose blend came about after we tested a variety of other published recipes and store-bought blends, none of which worked universally well in all types of baked goods. Our ideal blend would have a rich, round flavor with enough protein to provide baked goods with a good chew and decent browning, and we wanted the ingredients to be easy to find. We also decided to leave out any binders, such as xanthan or guar gum, so that we could add them as needed to individual recipes. Most blends are based on one of three ingredients: rice, sorghum, or bean flour. We didn't like the bean- or sorghum-based flour blends; they worked well structurally but had off-flavors. Rice flour was clearly the best choice for building our own versatile flour blend, and white rice flour was ideal because of its neutral flavor and smooth texture. In addition to white rice flour, we knew that the blend would need a few other ingredients. Individual gluten-free flours and starches absorb water, swell, and gel at different temperatures and to different degrees, creating more or less structure, more or less readily. Combining white rice flour with other types of starch essentially combined the properties of each to make the blend work better in a wide array of recipes. We added brown rice flour because it has an earthy flavor and gave the baked goods some welcome heft. Cornstarch didn't work well because it made the baked goods taste very starchy. Instead we liked tapioca starch, because it provided chew and elasticity, as well as potato starch, which helped with tenderness and binding. To find the ideal ratio of white rice flour, brown rice flour, tapioca starch, and potato starch, we baked many batches of muffins and cookies (upward of a thousand) with slightly altered flour and starch proportions. In the end, we found that too much brown rice flour made baked goods gritty, too much tapioca starch made them dense, and too much potato starch

gave them crumbly textures. We liked a basic ratio of 4 parts white rice flour, 1 part brown rice flour, 1 part potato starch, and ½ part tapioca. Tinkering with these amounts a bit further helped us land closer to the final proportions, but we were still having some structural problems. Suspecting that our flour blend needed a protein boost, we considered adding one of the following three ingredients: calcium carbonate, powdered egg whites, or nonfat milk powder. Calcium carbonate (also known as the active ingredient in Tums) is added to many gluten-free breads, so we tried crushing and adding some tablets, but ultimately the hassle factor outweighed the slight tenderness it added. Powdered egg whites added a big boost in terms of structure but imparted an unpleasant meringue-like flavor. The nonfat milk powder, however, helped with structure, tenderness, and browning and added rich and caramel-like flavor; it also helped temper the starchiness. Now we had a balanced and versatile blend that would perform well in many different types of recipes.

ATK All-Purpose Gluten-Free Flour Blend

MAKES 42 OUNCES (ABOUT 9⅓ CUPS)

If you don't bring the flour to room temperature before using, the recipe may not work as expected.

- **24 ounces (4½ cups plus ⅓ cup) white rice flour**
- **7½ ounces (1⅔ cups) brown rice flour**
- **7 ounces (1⅓ cups) potato starch**
- **3 ounces (¾ cup) tapioca starch**
- **¾ ounce (3 tablespoons) nonfat milk powder**

Whisk all ingredients together in large bowl until well combined. Transfer to airtight container and refrigerate for up to 3 months, or freeze for up to 6 months. Bring to room temperature before using.

The ATK Whole-Grain Gluten-Free Flour Blend

G-F TESTING LAB

TEFF FLOUR	We used teff flour made by Bob's Red Mill during our testing. We also tested several other brands of teff flour and found that they all worked equally well.
RICE FLOURS	We had the best results using Bob's Red Mill brown rice flour and sweet white rice flour. See page 24 for more information.
GROUND GOLDEN FLAXSEEDS	We used Flax USA 100% Natural Flax, Cold Milled Ground Golden Flax Seed during our testing. We don't recommend using Bob's Red Mill ground golden flaxseeds because it is too coarsely ground and will taste gritty in the baked goods. Do not substitute ground brown flaxseeds because its flavor will be too strong. Do not attempt to grind flaxseeds yourself because you will not be able to grind them fine enough.

✓ WHY THIS RECIPE WORKS

In addition to our ATK All-Purpose Gluten-Free Flour Blend, we wanted a whole-grain flour blend that loosely mimicked the flavor, color, and texture of whole-wheat flour. We started by testing a variety of store-bought blends and published blend recipes to get the lay of the land. Surprisingly, most whole-grain blends we tested produced decent baked goods, but none of them had a deep, hearty, "wheaty" flavor. In fact, when we set up a blind taste test and pitted baked goods made with these whole-grain blends against our own all-purpose blend, most tasters could not tell the difference. We knew we could do better. As with our all-purpose blend, we wanted the whole-grain blend to use five ingredients or less, and we didn't want to include any binders such as xanthan or guar gum. Also, we wanted to keep this blend as allergen-friendly as possible and avoid milk powder, oat flour, and potato starch. Finally, we wanted whole-grain flours to make up more than 50 percent of our blend. The world of gluten-free whole-grain flours is fairly large, but we quickly narrowed it down to just eight options—amaranth, brown rice, buckwheat, coconut, millet, quinoa, sorghum, and teff. We ran these flours through a series of tests to help identify their flavors and textures and confidently eliminated buckwheat, quinoa, and coconut flours from the race because they all tasted too distinctive for a blend. Moving forward with teff, brown rice, sorghum, millet, and amaranth, we began a series of tests that paired them together in various configurations, round-robin style, to see what worked best. We also added some tapioca starch into the mix, knowing that we'd finesse the type and amount of starch later. As we moved through this intense round of testing (during which time we produced over 600 muffins), teff flour consistently came out on top for its hearty chew, darker color, and wheatlike flavor. Brown rice flour also ranked well because its mild flavor and texture smoothed out the rough edges of the teff. Sorghum, millet, and amaranth all fell out of the testing along the way—the sorghum consistently made muffins taste dry and tough, while the millet and amaranth added an unwelcome aftertaste and a grainy texture. Working with a ratio of 3 parts teff flour to 1 part brown rice flour, we put the tapioca under the spotlight and tested it against a few other starches including arrowroot, sweet white rice flour, and cornstarch. Tasters unanimously preferred the clean flavor and smooth, nongritty texture of sweet white rice flour over the others, and we settled on 3 parts teff flour and 1 part brown rice flour to ⅔ part sweet white rice flour. Finally, we turned our attention to a somewhat random group of secret ingredients that are sometimes added to blends in small amounts to add flavor, help with browning, or boost the protein content to make the blend stronger. Our secret list included ground flax, chia, and hemp seeds and pea powder isolate. We loved ground golden flaxseeds because they added a well-rounded, wheaty flavor and richness to both muffins and cookies. After 126 tests and more cookies and muffins than any one person could consume in a year, we nailed down the ingredients in our whole-grain blend: 3 parts teff flour, 1 part brown rice flour, 1 part ground golden flaxseeds, and ⅔ part sweet white rice flour.

ATK Whole-Grain Gluten-Free Flour Blend

MAKES 45 OUNCES (ABOUT 10 CUPS)

If you don't bring the flour to room temperature before using, the recipe may not work as expected.

- **24 ounces (5¼ cups) teff flour**
- **8 ounces (1¾ cups) brown rice flour**
- **8 ounces (2⅓ cups) ground golden flaxseeds**
- **5 ounces (1 cup) sweet white rice flour**

Whisk all ingredients together in large bowl until well combined. Transfer to airtight container and refrigerate for up to 3 months, or freeze for up to 6 months. Bring to room temperature before using.

What About Store-Bought Flour Blends?

In traditional baking recipes, the brand of flour isn't terribly important. That's because all brands of all-purpose flour (as well as bread flour) contain the same single ingredient—wheat flour. Yes, protein levels in the wheat will vary among different brands, but this has minimal impact on the finished product.

In gluten-free baking recipes that call for a gluten-free flour blend, the brand of flour will have significantly more impact on the final baked good. That's because each brand of flour blend, whether all-purpose or whole-grain, relies on a mix of different ingredients, yielding cookies, cakes, breads, and muffins with varying textures, colors, and flavors.

TESTING ALL-PURPOSE FLOUR BLENDS

To get a sense of the range of possible outcomes, we tested 10 store-bought all-purpose gluten-free flour blends in three well-vetted recipes—chocolate chip cookies, blueberry muffins, and sandwich bread—from our first gluten-free book. Twenty tasters from our test kitchen participated in these blind taste tests, which also included samples of each recipe made with the ATK flour blend (the control). Tasters were asked to rate how close each sample came to the control.

THE RESULTS

For the most part, all of the blends worked in these recipes—that is, they made cookies, muffins, and loaves of bread that at least looked the part. However, there were significant textural and flavor differences (see the charts on pages 11 and 12). Our two favorite brands are made with neutral-tasting rice flour. Brands that ended up at the bottom of the rankings tend to include ingredients with more personality, such as sorghum or bean flours, which were detectable in the baked goods. Based on these tastings, we divided these 10 flour blends into two groups: recommended replacements for the ATK flour blend and those recommended with reservations.

RECOMMENDED ALL-PURPOSE FLOUR BLENDS

For the best results with recipes in this book (as well as our previous book), we recommend that you use the ATK flour blend. It was designed especially for these recipes. It's also cheaper than store-bought blends and more convenient, since you can make it in bulk rather than buying little boxes.

If shopping for five ingredients and spending less than 5 minutes to combine them is too much

bother, we recommend that you use King Arthur Gluten-Free Multi-Purpose Flour in recipes that call for an all-purpose flour blend. Our second choice is Betty Crocker All-Purpose Gluten Free Rice Flour Blend. (This product wasn't available when we developed recipes for our first book; based on our experience testing the Betty Crocker blend in all the recipes in this book, we can say with confidence that it will also work in the recipes in our first book.)

Finally, we tested recipes in this book (as well as our first gluten-free book) with Bob's Red Mill GF All-Purpose Baking Flour, the most widely available brand in the United States. While we don't love its beany, earthy notes, it can be the only choice in many markets, and therefore we deemed it important to understand how this flour blend worked in our recipes. It's an acceptable choice in nearly all of our recipes, with the exception of Yeasted Doughnuts (page 67), Popovers (page 71), Baguettes (page 155), Bagels (page 161), and Rugelach (page 207).

REMEMBER TO WEIGH

If you decide to use a store-bought all-purpose flour blend, we strongly recommend that you weigh it. Because each blend is made with different ingredients, it packs into dry cup measures differently. A scale ensures that you have the right amount of flour—no matter the brand.

A WORD ON WHOLE-GRAIN FLOUR BLENDS

We could not find a store-bought whole-grain flour blend that delivered the same earthy, "wheaty" flavor as our blend (see page 13 for details on this testing). We don't recommend using any store-bought blends in recipes that call for our whole-grain blend.

Evaluating All-Purpose Flour Blends

We tested these 10 store-bought blends in three of our own gluten-free recipes—blueberry muffins, chocolate chip cookies, and sandwich bread—and compared them to baked goods made using the ATK All-Purpose Gluten-Free Flour Blend. Here are the results:

RECOMMENDED

These two blends performed very similarly to the ATK All-Purpose Gluten-Free Flour Blend in most of the recipes throughout this book. Look for more details in the G-F Testing Lab notes that accompany each recipe.

BRAND	INGREDIENTS	TASTERS' COMMENTS
KING ARTHUR Gluten-Free Multi-Purpose Flour PRICE: $7.95/1.5-lb box ($5.30/lb)	White Rice Flour, Tapioca Flour, Potato Starch, Brown Rice Flour, Calcium Carbonate, Niacinamide (a B vitamin), Reduced Iron Thiamin Hydrochloride (vitamin B1), Riboflavin (vitamin B2)	Across the board this blend performed well in terms of both delivering good structure and having a neutral, not-too-starchy flavor. It finished in the top for all three tests. A few tasters found it too sweet in cookies and muffins, but overall it won out for its superior flavor. Many noted a grainy, gritty texture, but not enough to push it to the bottom of any tastings.
BETTY CROCKER All-Purpose Gluten Free Rice Flour Blend PRICE: $3.75/1-lb box	Rice Flour, Potato Starch, Tapioca Starch, Guar Gum, Salt	In all three of our tests this blend was ranked highly, particularly in the chocolate chip cookies. Overall the blend won out for having a flavor very similar to our homemade blend. In terms of texture, a handful of tasters noted a "bouncy" texture in muffins and a "gummy" crumb in breads. However, the overall versatility of the blend kept it near the top in all of our tastings.

RECOMMENDED WITH RESERVATIONS

These eight blends (listed alphabetically and not in order of performance) all produced edible baked goods in the tasting; however, some worked better than others. We cannot guarantee that these blends will work as a replacement for the ATK All-Purpose Gluten-Free Flour Blend with the exception of Bob's Red Mill, which we tested in the recipes in this book and found to be an acceptable substitute with a few exceptions (see page 10); it will add a noticeable bean flavor in most instances.

BRAND	INGREDIENTS	TASTERS' COMMENTS
AUTHENTIC FOODS GF Classical Blend PRICE: $15.79/3-lb bag ($5.26/lb)	Brown Rice Flour, Potato Starch, Tapioca Flour	This blend fared well in producing muffins, but failed to satisfy tasters when baked into cookies and bread. Due to the relatively high proportion of potato starch in the mix, tasters found the bread and cookies to be "doughy" and "pasty." The blend also changed the way the baked goods performed in the oven, producing "squat" muffins and cookies that "didn't spread."
BOB'S RED MILL GF All-Purpose Baking Flour PRICE: $4.29/1.5-lb bag ($2.86/lb)	Garbanzo Bean Flour, Potato Starch, Tapioca Flour, Sorghum Flour, Fava Bean Flour	Our tasters did not like the distinctive taste of bean flour in their baked goods. There were complaints that items tasted "stale," and most panelists picked up strong "earthy" notes. Structurally speaking, muffins were "dense" and "crumbly," cookies spread into very thin crisps, and while bread had a "good structure," many noted that it was "dry."

RECOMMENDED WITH RESERVATIONS (continued)

BRAND	INGREDIENTS	TASTERS' COMMENTS
CUP4CUP Gluten Free Flour PRICE: $19.95/3-lb bag ($6.65/lb)	Cornstarch, White Rice Flour, Brown Rice Flour, Nonfat Milk Powder, Tapioca Flour, Potato Starch, Xanthan Gum	Made up primarily of cornstarch, this blend left a starchy coating on the tongue and produced a "tight" texture in baked goods. Many tasters complained about the samples being "gummy." The cookies fared better than the muffins, in part because the sugar seemed to mask the presence of the cornstarch.
GLUTINO Gluten Free Pantry All Purpose Flour PRICE: $4.55/1-lb box	White Rice Flour, Potato Starch, Tapioca Starch, Pea Hull Fiber, Acacia Gum, Rice Protein	Since this blend includes some of the most unique ingredients we've seen in any blend (pea hull fiber, acacia gum, and rice protein), we were interested to see how it would perform in our recipes. Unfortunately the added ingredients came along with additional flavors that weren't appreciated by tasters. Muffins had a "bitter vegetal" note, cookies had a distinct "bean" flavor, and the bread tasted "sour."
LIVING NOW Gluten-Free All-Purpose Flour PRICE: $4.49/1-lb box	White Rice Flour, Brown Rice Flour, Tapioca Flour, Potato Starch, Potato Flour, Cellulose	Producing muffins that were "heavy" and "dusty," cookies that tasters called "gritty" and "biscuit-y," and bread with an "odd flavor" and "lemon-like after-taste," this blend fell short in flavor and texture. The blend produced "almond-y" and "nutty" tastes in the finished products that many found to be welcome in muffins and cookies, but out of place in bread.
PAMELA'S All-Purpose Artisan Flour Blend PRICE: $7.98/1.5-lb bag ($5.31/lb)	Brown Rice Flour, Tapioca Flour, White Rice Flour, Potato Starch, Sorghum Flour, Arrowroot Flour, Sweet Rice Flour, Xanthan Gum	Although tasters were partial to the muffins made with this blend, chocolate chip cookies and sandwich bread fared poorly in our testing. Many noted the samples had a "grainy" quality and the bread had an "off vegetal flavor."
PILLSBURY Best Multi-Purpose Gluten Free Flour Blend PRICE: $9.42/2-lb bag ($4.71/lb)	Rice Flour, Potato Starch, Pea Fiber, Tapioca Starch, Xanthan Gum	While tasters were partial to the "sweet buttery flavor" of baked goods made with this flour blend, the "gritty" texture of the flour distracted from the taste. Cookies were "crunchy," while muffins had a "strange coarse-ness," and loaves of bread were "tough and chewy." All of the samples failed to rise as much as the control, resulting in squat breads and muffins.
TRADER JOE'S Baker Josef's Gluten Free All Purpose Flour PRICE: $3.99/1-lb bag	Brown Rice Flour, Potato Starch, Rice Flour, Tapioca Flour	Bread made with the Trader Joe's blend was one of the favorites of the tasting panel; the chocolate chip cookies and blueberry muffins, however, didn't stand up against the rest. Our bread loaves had a "good structure," "tall rise," and a "tender" crumb. Cookies and muffins "lacked structure," "spread" during bak-ing, and had an "off aftertaste" that bothered tasters.

Evaluating Whole-Grain Flour Blends

We wanted to find a store-bought whole-grain flour blend that we could recommend as a suitable alternative to the ATK Whole-Grain Gluten-Free Flour Blend (page 9), but unfortunately we didn't find any. In fact, there are very few whole-grain blends on the market at all, never mind a brand that is widely available in supermarkets. We tracked down five whole-grain blends (mostly online) and gave them each a turn in Whole-Grain Chocolate Chip Cookies (page 187) and Whole-Grain Blueberry Muffins (page 47). Although all of the blends produced edible cookies and muffins (some more edible than others), none of them came close to delivering the deep, hearty, "wheaty" flavor of the ATK blend. Below are the five blends we tested, along with our tasting notes; note that they are listed alphabetically, not in order of preference.

BRAND	INGREDIENTS	TASTERS' COMMENTS
CUP4CUP Wholesome Flour Blend PRICE: $23.99/2-lb bag ($12.00/lb)	Brown Rice Flour, White Rice Flour, Ground Golden Flaxseed, Rice Bran, Xanthan Gum	Our tasters were partial to the complex "nutty" and "oatmeal"-like flavors of this blend, particularly when baked into chocolate chip cookies. However, the coarse ground flaxseeds added to the mix left tasters picking their teeth long after they were done enjoying the cookies. Putting the blend to the test in our muffins resulted in "squat" blueberry muffins with a texture that tasters called "spongy," "tough," and "rubbery."
HODGSON MILLS Multi Purpose Baking Mix PRICE: $4.19/12-oz box ($5.59/lb)	Whole Grain Millet Flour, Whole Grain Sorghum Flour, Whole Grain Brown Rice Flour, Xanthan Gum	The high level of millet flour (the number one ingredient in this blend) left a bitter aftertaste and produced "dense" cookies and "dry" muffins. Many tasters complained about an "odd bitterness" that masked the flavor of the baked goods, while others noted that the blend was distinctively whole-grain in flavor. The blueberry muffins fared better than the cookies, as the cookies tended to be "hard" and "crumbly."
KING ARTHUR Gluten Free Ancient Grain Blend PRICE: $10.95/2-lb bag ($5.48/lb)	Amaranth, Millet, Sorghum, Quinoa	This flour mix had a very assertive grain flavor in muffins and cookies, which tasters found to be off-putting. In cookies tasters labeled the blend as being "bitter" and "bean-y," while the muffins were "earthy" and had an "unpleasant grain flavor." In terms of texture, both baked goods were notably "dry," "crunchy," and "dense." Tasters noticed baked goods had a tendency to stick to their teeth after chewing.
KING ARTHUR Gluten Free Whole Grain Blend PRICE: $9.95/2-lb bag ($4.98/lb)	Sorghum, Brown Rice, Amaranth, Quinoa, Millet, Teff, Tapioca Flour	This blend was deemed to have a superior but neutral flavor. The muffins were praised as having a "nice crumb," while the cookies had "great chew" and a "crisp edge." Although tasters enjoyed the texture and consistency of the baked goods, the blend lost points because it was "not very wheaty."
SUN FLOUR MILLS Gluten Free Whole Grain All Purpose Flour PRICE: $6.99/2-lb bag ($3.50/lb)	Sweet Sorghum Flour, Brown Rice Flour, Teff Flour, and Cornstarch	Muffins and cookies made with this blend had a "dense" texture, as the baked goods "didn't spread." The consistency wasn't unwelcome in cookies, which tasters called "chewy." The muffins, however, were "dry" and "crumbly."

Gluten-Free Baking: Keys to Success

Traditional baking is an exact science with time-honored techniques. When it comes to gluten-free baking, however, many new factors come into play and often key tenets of standard baking no longer apply. From measuring flour and proofing bread to determining leaveners, baking times and temperatures, and more, we had to break from tradition to develop great-tasting and foolproof gluten-free recipes. Here is a summary of what we learned.

1 THE BLEND YOU CHOOSE MAKES A HUGE DIFFERENCE

You can't plug just any gluten-free flour blend into the recipes in this book and expect them to work. (Similarly, you can't plug one of our blends into another recipe and expect it to work there either.) No two gluten-free blends are the same; they can contain wildly different ingredients—from rice and bean flours to seeds and gums—and in varying amounts. This means that the blend and the recipe need to be matched up; if they're not compatible, you'll just be wasting your time. For those of you who just can't resist the convenience of a premade blend, we offer two store-bought alternatives to our all-purpose blend; you'll find recipe-specific information in the G-F Testing Lab attached to each recipe. We were unable, however, to find an acceptable store-bought substitute for our whole-grain gluten-free flour blend.

CUPCAKES

In simple yellow cupcakes, some gluten-free blends work better than others, but none tasted as good as the version made with the ATK blend.

ATK ALL-PURPOSE BLEND
Cupcake rises extremely well, with slight doming. Crumb is fine and very tender.

KING ARTHUR
Cupcake is denser and doesn't rise as well. Tastes slightly starchy.

BETTY CROCKER
Cupcake rises well but crumb is dry and crumbly. Tastes sightly pasty.

SANDWICH BREAD

In our Whole-Grain Sandwich Bread (page 141), no whole-grain gluten-free blend came close to the flavor and texture of bread made with the ATK blend.

ATK WHOLE-GRAIN BLEND
Bread rises tall, with just the right open texture.

KING ARTHUR WHOLE GRAIN BLEND
Dough is too weak to support loaf shape.

CUP4CUP WHOLESOME FLOUR BLEND
Bread is more squat and dense.

2 FINELY GROUND RICE FLOURS YIELD BETTER RESULTS

Throughout all of our testing, we found that different brands of white and brown rice flours (the former is in our all-purpose blend, and the latter is used in both of our flour blends) have slightly different grinds that affect how well our recipes work and taste. Note that because our all-purpose flour blend has three times more white rice flour than brown rice flour, the brand you choose (and its grind) can have a big impact on the success of your baked goods. Depending on the brand, the grind can range from very fine to a tad gritty. In the end, we found that finely ground flours work best in both our all-purpose gluten-free flour blend (page 7) and our whole-grain gluten-free flour blend (page 9). By comparison, the rice flours with coarser grinds (such as Arrowhead Mills and Hodgson Mills brown rice flour) will have trouble absorbing the liquid and fat and will retain their gritty texture. We found Bob's Red Mill rice flours (the most widely available brand of white and brown rice flour) to have the finest grind, although several other flours were acceptable, including EnerG (white and brown), Living Now (white), and King Arthur (brown). (Note that Goya brand rice flours are not gluten-free.) If using another brand of rice flour, the texture should be close to that of cornstarch, with no more than a hint of grit. In the photos below, you can see the difference that finely and coarsely ground flours make in a simple chocolate chip cookie recipe.

COOKIES MADE WITH ARROWHEAD MILLS RICE FLOURS
Cookies spread too much and seemed to fry in unabsorbed fat, resulting in a candylike texture.

COOKIES MADE WITH BOB'S RED MILL RICE FLOURS
Cookies spread nicely and had just the right balance of crisp edges and chewy centers.

3 GLUTEN-FREE FLOURS REQUIRE SPECIAL MEASURING TECHNIQUES

Most home bakers use the dip-and-sweep method when measuring flour, but this doesn't work well with gluten-free flours and starches. One reason is because these flours and starches are finer than wheat flours, making them hard to pack evenly and consistently into a measuring cup. Also, they are often sold in small bags or boxes, so it is hard to maneuver a measuring cup inside the package without creating a mess or unevenly packing the cup. The simple solution is to just use a scale and weigh the flours instead of relying on wavering volume measurements. **We strongly recommend that you use a scale when baking from this book.** If you insist on using measuring cups, we found the following method delivers the most uniform results.

1. Place sheet of paper towel on counter and set measuring cup in center.

2. Spoon flour into cup, occasionally shaking cup to settle flour, until flour is mounded over rim. Do not tap cup or pack flour.

3. Using flat edge (like back of butter knife), scrape away excess flour to level.

4. Use paper towel to help funnel excess flour back into bag/container.

4 **USING LESS BUTTER AND OIL MINIMIZES GREASINESS AND IMPROVES STRUCTURE**
Gluten-free flours don't absorb fat as readily as wheat flour does. In high-fat recipes, such as cookies, cakes, and pie dough, simply replacing the wheat flour with an equal amount of gluten-free flour doesn't work. The baked goods are often much too greasy, which not only makes them unappetizing but can affect how cookies spread in the oven or determine whether pie dough holds its shape when baked. When reworking conventional recipes with gluten-free flour, we often trimmed a few tablespoons of butter or oil. You can easily see the difference in these two double-crust pies: One has been made with a traditional amount of fat, and the other has been made with a reduced amount of fat.

PIE DOUGH MADE
WITH 20 TABLESPOONS
BUTTER

PIE DOUGH MADE
WITH 16 TABLESPOONS
BUTTER

5 **BINDERS ADD STRUCTURE**
Binders (such as egg, xanthan gum, and ground psyllium husk) are crucial in gluten-free baking because the flours and starches are not able to form the strong, elastic bonds necessary for structure and height. Almost every baking recipe in the book includes an extra egg for this reason, and we even include them in recipes that don't traditionally call for eggs, such as Baguettes (page 155). Xanthan gum is also added to most of our baking recipes for extra structure and strength. The xanthan is more important in some recipes than in others; you can omit it if making a muffin but not if making a cookie, as you can see in the photos of White Chocolate–Macadamia Nut Cookies (page 189) below. We've noted the binder's level of importance in the G-F Testing Lab that accompanies each recipe. Also, for more information on how to substitute different binders, see The Use of Binders on page 22.

COOKIES MADE WITHOUT
XANTHAN GUM

COOKIES MADE WITH
XANTHAN GUM

6 **EXTRA LEAVENERS HELP DOUGHS RISE PROPERLY**
Gluten-free batters and doughs have a weaker protein structure than those made with wheat flour. This means that they have a harder time holding on to air bubbles from yeast and baking powder, and so they often bake up heavy and dense. Adding a little extra leavener, such as baking powder or baking soda, can help prevent this. Also, we've found that yeast bread often benefits from the addition of baking powder or baking soda to give the loaves a small height boost, as you can see in the sandwich bread below.

SANDWICH BREAD
MADE WITH YEAST
ALONE

SANDWICH BREAD
MADE WITH YEAST AND
BAKING POWDER

7 MIXING BATTERS LONGER PROVIDES STRUCTURE

While traditional recipes often warn against overmixing to avoid building up excess structure in delicate batters (such as muffins and cakes) so that they don't turn rubbery, we found the opposite to be true of gluten-free batters. In fact, we often find ourselves trying to get the batters to have more structure so that they have a better rise and a nicer chew, and can support stir-ins, such as blueberries. The gluten-free blueberry muffins below show the difference between an undermixed batter and a well-mixed batter in terms of both overall height and the ability to support berries evenly throughout the muffin.

MUFFIN MADE
USING TRADITIONAL
MIXING METHOD

MUFFIN MADE
USING LONGER
MIXING METHOD

8 RESTING BATTERS AND DOUGHS HAS MULTIPLE BENEFITS

Early on in our testing, we were commonly plagued by a sandy texture in our quick-cooking baked goods. (It was not noticeable in our baked goods with long baking times.) We tested lots of theories on how to get rid of this grit (grinding the flours further in a food processor, soaking them in water, heating them up before making the batter), but nothing worked well. Then, almost by accident, we found that letting the batters sit for 30 minutes before baking made all the difference. It simply gave the flours and starches time to absorb the liquid and soften before baking. It also helped batters become thicker and doughs to firm up so that they were less sticky. You can see the dramatic difference this made in the Whole-Grain Pancakes (page 39) below. Be sure to cover the bowl of batter tightly with plastic wrap so that it doesn't dry out as it rests.

PANCAKES MADE
WITHOUT RESTED
BATTER

PANCAKES MADE
WITH RESTED BATTER

9 JUMP-START THE YEAST AND PROOF THE DOUGH IN YOUR OVEN

When working with gluten-free yeast breads, you want them to rise as quickly as possible before the starches begin to set and the dough becomes stiff. As the dough stiffens, which happens as soon as the abundant starches in gluten-free flours absorb liquid, it becomes more difficult for the air bubbles produced by the yeast to move evenly throughout the dough. As a result, breads can be dense with a gummy layer along the bottom of the loaf. We use a superfast rising technique that blooms instant yeast in warm, sweetened water before adding it to the dough, and then starts the one and only rise in a warm (but turned-off) oven; see page 142 for more information. This technique results in a taller loaf with an open, even texture versus bread made traditionally with a longer, two-stage rising technique, which results in a denser, more squat loaf with a gummy bottom.

BREAD USING
TRADITIONAL
LONG RISE

BREAD USING
SUPERFAST RISING
TECHNIQUE

10 COLLARS, WRAPS, AND PAN SPECIFICS

With many gluten-free baked goods, we needed some creative solutions to get rolls to hold their shape and breads to rise tall, and to keep cookies from burning. For our Hamburger Rolls (page 175), we made our own aluminum foil collars, much like professional ring molds, to help the rolls stay round; for Honey-Millet Sandwich Bread (page 143), we used a slightly smaller loaf pan (8½ by 4½ inches) but then wrapped a foil collar around the top of the pan in order to get a nice tall loaf. And for some baked goods, we found that we needed to use two baking sheets (one nestled inside another) to prevent burning. Don't ignore these instructions, or else you'll likely be very unhappy with the results.

HAMBURGER ROLL
MADE WITHOUT FOIL
COLLAR

HAMBURGER ROLL
MADE WITH FOIL
COLLAR

11 VISUAL CUES ALONE ARE NOT RELIABLE; USE AN OVEN THERMOMETER AND A TIMER

Knowing when a cake or bread is perfectly done and ready to come out of the oven can be tricky. This is especially true with gluten-free baking because traditional techniques (like a clean toothpick or pressing on the top of a cake) aren't always accurate indicators. Even when fully cooked, gluten-free baked goods often look underdone, are slightly wet inside, and feel soft to the touch. Only when they cool do the starches set and firm up. We always list visual cues to help identify when something is fully baked, but we often find that timing is a more foolproof way to determine doneness. Obviously, our baking times are only as accurate as your oven. If your oven runs hot or cold, these times will not be accurate, so be sure to use a good oven thermometer.

1. A timer is often the best way to tell when your gluten-free baked goods are done because visual cues can be misleading.

2. A well-calibrated oven is crucial for gluten-free baking. Use a good oven thermometer and place it as close to the center of the oven as possible.

12 BAKE, THEN BAKE SOME MORE

We often add extra liquid to gluten-free baked goods to hydrate the flour blends, eliminate grittiness, and achieve a less dense or dry texture. However, it is very important to drive off this extra moisture during baking, or you'll wind up with a gummy texture. This is why many of our recipes have long baking times. Some of our recipes even instruct you to bake beyond the time that a toothpick inserted into the baked good comes out clean. Whole-Grain Gingerbread Coffee Cake (page 61) is such a recipe; if you pull this cake out of the oven too soon, it will have a very mushy texture.

COFFEE CAKE BAKED
UNTIL TOOTHPICK
COMES OUT CLEAN

COFFEE CAKE BAKED
20 MINUTES PAST
POINT THAT TOOTHPICK
COMES OUT CLEAN

Troubleshooting Gluten-Free Recipes

After thousands of kitchen tests, we have a sense of what problems are likely to occur when you attempt to make a conventional baked good gluten-free. The tips on this page offer advice for common problems we encountered during our recipe development. Note that every baking recipe is a unique formula, so these solutions won't work in all cases. Think of this information as a starting point when problem-solving in your kitchen.

TYPE OF RECIPE	COMMON PROBLEM	POSSIBLE SOLUTION
Pancakes	Dense, gummy texture	Lower burner or griddle temperature and extend cooking time to help pancakes cook through without getting too brown
Muffins/Quick Breads	Crumbly texture	Add extra egg and use binder, like xanthan gum
	Dense texture	Use more leavener
	Gritty texture	Let batter rest for 30 minutes before baking
	Dry texture	Add additional liquid or sour cream
	Mushy center	Lower oven temperature and extend baking time
Drop Cookies	Excessive spread	Add binder and let dough rest
	Gritty texture	Let dough rest for 30 minutes before baking
	Greasy	Use less butter and swap in a portion of almond flour
	Overly crisp texture	Use more brown sugar, less white sugar
	Overly soft texture	Use superfine sugar and leave cookies in turned-off oven after baking for several minutes to dry out
	Airy, hollow texture	Use melted butter instead of creaming it
	Burnt bottoms	Before baking, place baking sheet of cookies inside second sheet for extra insulation on bottom
Cakes	Greasy mouthfeel	Swap in sour cream, chocolate, or cream cheese for some of fat
	Dense crumb	Reduce amount of fat, use additional liquid, use additional baking powder, use additional egg
	Gummy center	Lower oven temperature and extend baking time; swap out some of liquid for sour cream
	Edges of cake are tough	Line sides and bottom of cake pan with parchment paper
	Cake doesn't release	When parchment is not an option, make paste of butter and flour blend and brush into pan
Pie/Tart Dough	Crumbly texture	Add binder, such as xanthan gum
	Not flaky	Add small amount of rice vinegar
	Dry, difficult dough	Process butter more thoroughly during mixing
Yeast Breads	Dough doesn't rise	Add extra liquid, use instant yeast and bloom yeast in warm, sweetened water, make proofing box (see page 142)
	Dense crumb	Add ground psyllium husk
	Gummy, wet crumb	Lower oven temperature and extend baking time
	Squat loaves	Use smaller loaf pan and add foil collar
	Bread sinks after baking	Leave bread in turned-off oven after baking to dry out

Making Recipes Dairy-Free

Many people on a gluten-free diet also have other food allergy issues, including the inability to digest dairy. In fact, one of the comments we heard most from gluten-free home cooks is that they'd like to know more about how to make recipes that are both gluten-free and dairy-free. So, in response, there are dairy-free variations for many of the recipes in this book. There were only two types of recipes that occasionally stumped us: recipes that used three or more types of dairy, and recipes that depended heavily on dairy for flavor and texture, such as cheesecake or pie dough. We used only the ATK gluten-free flour blends in our dairy-free testing; we don't recommend using a store-bought flour blend when making recipes dairy-free. Please note that you can omit the milk powder from our all-purpose blend, but for better results substitute soy milk powder (see page 6).

BUTTER

When it comes to dairy-free baking, we thought that replacing the butter would be the biggest hurdle since its texture and flavor play such a big role in many baked goods. To better understand this issue, we began by testing a number of dairy-free butter options in a handful of gluten-free recipes. We tried vegetable oil and coconut oil along with several Earth Balance products including Vegan Buttery Sticks, Vegan Shortening Sticks, and Coconut Spread. The vegetable oil and Earth Balance Vegan Buttery Sticks both worked quite well in the recipes. The coconut oil also worked well but had a distinctive flavor that we knew would work only in coconut-flavored baked goods, such as Coconut-Cashew Muffins (page 49). Earth Balance Shortening Sticks and Coconut Spread fell short on flavor or tasted plasticky.

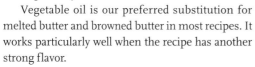

Vegetable oil is our preferred substitution for melted butter and browned butter in most recipes. It works particularly well when the recipe has another strong flavor.

Earth Balance Vegan Buttery Sticks are a good substitution for solid or softened butter. It also works well when a "buttery" flavor is important to the recipe; however, this product tastes fairly salty (so reduce or eliminate salt called for in the recipe).

Coconut oil is a good replacement for solid, softened, or melted butter in recipes, although it has a distinctive coconut flavor.

MILK

There are a number of dairy-free milks on the market today, including those made from soy, rice, hemp, oats, quinoa, almonds, hazelnuts, cashews, and coconut. Right off the bat, we took hemp, oat, quinoa, and cashew milk off our list because they were just too difficult to find. We tested the remaining milks in gluten-free muffins and cookies, and found that soy milk and almond milk worked best. Soy milk is leaner than almond milk, which makes it an ideal replacement for low-fat milk. Rice milk is more watery and gave the baked goods an overly starchy and gummy texture. The flavor of coconut milk is too specific to make it a basic milk substitute.

BUTTERMILK

We found it easy to make a buttermilk substitution by combining soy or almond milk with a dash of distilled white vinegar or lemon juice. This works best when the buttermilk is not the main flavor but rather just a background note, as in Date-Nut Bread (page 57).

TO MAKE 1 CUP OF DAIRY-FREE BUTTERMILK: Mix 1 cup of unsweetened soy or almond milk with 1 tablespoon of distilled white vinegar or fresh lemon juice.

HEAVY CREAM

There are dozens of dairy-free cream options, including coffee creamers made of hydrogenated oil as well as more natural creamers made of soy, almonds, cashews, or coconut. We tested these more natural creamers and preferred the mild flavor of plain soy creamer. None of them can be whipped.

WHIPPED CREAM

Since none of the heavy cream replacements we tried can be whipped, we tested several store-bought whipped products, including Soyatoo! Soy Whip and Soyatoo! Rice Whip, and homemade coconut whipped cream made using the thick layer of coconut fat found at the top of a can of coconut milk. Tasters didn't like Soyatoo!'s Rice Whip but found their Soy Whip to be a decent substitute for whipped cream. The homemade coconut whipped cream was also a decent substitute, although it uses a partial can of coconut milk and has a noticeable coconut flavor. Note that while soy whip is naturally gluten-free, the Soyatoo! brand is not labeled gluten-free.

TO MAKE 1 CUP OF COCONUT WHIPPED CREAM: Refrigerate a 10-ounce can of regular (not low-fat) coconut milk for a few hours, and chill a mixing bowl and beaters in the freezer for at least 20 minutes. Using a spoon, skim only the top layer of cream from the coconut milk (about ¾ cup) and combine with 1½ teaspoons sugar, ½ teaspoon vanilla, and a pinch of salt in the chilled bowl. Beat the mixture on low speed until small bubbles form, about 30 seconds, then increase the speed to high and beat until the mixture thickens and forms light peaks, about 2 minutes.

YOGURT

We tested coconut milk yogurt, soy milk yogurt, and Greek-style almond milk yogurt in several of our gluten-free recipes. The almond milk yogurt was the least successful, producing biscuits with a strong, funky flavor and a gummy texture, and muffins that were mushy. Soy milk yogurt worked fine in the muffins, but the biscuits turned out drier and crumbly. In general, however, we found soy milk yogurt to be a decent substitution for plain whole-milk yogurt even though it produced slightly dry baked goods. We prefer coconut milk yogurt, which performed well in both recipes; surprisingly, we could not taste the coconut flavor.

SOUR CREAM

A number of our recipes rely on sour cream to add richness and moisture. We found a variety of dairy-free brands on the market, including Tofutti Better Than Sour Cream, Weyfair, Vegan Gourmet, and Green Valley, and put them all to the test using some of our own gluten-free recipes. Although these products are thicker than regular sour cream, they all worked well. For this book, we used Tofutti Better Than Sour Cream for all of our testing.

CREAM CHEESE

We used cream cheese in some gluten-free cake and cookie recipes to help add structure, richness, and chew. We tested two brands of dairy-free cream cheese in our recipes: Tofutti Better Than Cream Cheese and Vegan Gourmet Cream Cheese. Both seemed more rubbery than regular cream cheese, but they worked equally well as dairy-free substitutes. In our Cream Cheese Frosting (page 270), they both produced a frosting with a slightly thinner, silkier texture. We used Tofutti Better Than Cream Cheese for all of our testing.

CHOCOLATE

Finding dairy-free chocolate is not easy if you want to make sure that it was produced in a gluten-free facility. We did find a few brands online (including Scharffen Berger and Milkless) and tested them in several of our chocolate chip cookie and chocolate cake recipes. In the end, we found that all of the dairy-free bar chocolates worked well in our cake recipes. We also found that the bars could be chopped and used in place of chips in cookies. Dairy-free chips worked well as stir-ins for the cookies but didn't work as a swap for the bar chocolate in any of the cakes. Look for dairy-free chocolate products online.

The Use of Binders

Because there is less protein in gluten-free flours than in wheat flours, gluten-free flours are not capable of forming the strong network required to stretch and surround starch granules. In our testing, we found that gluten-free flours required some help from a binder, generally in the form of xanthan gum, guar gum, or powdered psyllium husk. (See pages 25–26 for detailed descriptions of each.) These ingredients strengthen protein networks in baked goods and make them more elastic. In effect, they act as the glue that gives gluten-free baked goods the proper shape.

XANTHAN GUM AND GUAR GUM

We tested both xanthan gum and guar gum in muffins, cakes, cookies, brownies, and fresh pasta as well as in pie dough and tart dough, and we preferred xanthan gum in every application. In many cases the differences were slight, but the guar gum produced baked goods that were a bit more pasty and/or starchy. Also, baked goods made with xanthan had a longer shelf life than those made with guar. That said, guar gum produced good results in almost every case other than tart dough and fresh pasta.

CHIA SEEDS

We tested adding ground chia seeds to muffins, cookies, and pie crust in lieu of the xanthan gum. They were moderately successful in the muffins, but added a mushy texture and unwelcome flavor. In the cookies and pie crust, they didn't add enough structure to the dough; the cookies melted completely into greasy puddles, and the pie crust was very cracked and crumbly. We don't recommend them as a binder.

PSYLLIUM HUSK IN YEASTED RECIPES

Powdered psyllium husk is especially effective at creating a more open and airy crumb. In extensive kitchen tests, we found it was the only choice in yeast breads and pizza. It produced breads with a bit of chew and a better rise. And its earthy flavor (which might seem out of place in a sugar cookie) worked beautifully in bread recipes. So why does psyllium work better than either gum in yeast breads? It binds more effectively with water, and there's a lot of water in bread dough. As a result, psyllium does a better job of strengthening the protein network so it is capable of holding in lots of gas and steam during baking.

PSYLLIUM HUSK IN NONYEASTED RECIPES

We tried psyllium husk in nearly a dozen other recipes. In most cases it worked fine but not quite as well as xanthan, in part because so much more of it is required. In recipes with less moisture than bread dough (like muffins, cookies, fresh pasta, pie dough, or tart dough), the psyllium produced a drier texture and a coarser crumb, and its hearty flavor seemed a little out of place in some cases (especially Popovers and Rainbow Sprinkle Cupcakes). That said, it was a good substitute for xanthan if you want a more "natural" option.

OUR APPROACH

Other than our yeast breads, which rely on psyllium husk, the majority of the baked goods in this book call for a small amount of xanthan gum. We know that some people have a hard time digesting xanthan, so here are some guidelines for those who want to swap it with something else. You can replace xanthan with an equal amount of guar or twice as much psyllium in most recipes in this book. The one exception is drop cookies, where xanthan does a better job of controlling spread. In our cookie recipes, we suggest replacing xanthan with three times as much guar or five times as much psyllium.

Substitution Formulas

	SUBSTITUTIONS
Baked Goods (except Drop Cookies)	1 teaspoon xanthan gum =
	1 teaspoon guar gum =
	2 teaspoons psyllium powder
Drop Cookies	1 teaspoon xanthan gum =
	3 teaspoons guar gum =
	5 teaspoons psyllium powder

The Gluten-Free Pantry

If you are serious about gluten-free baking, you will want to stock your pantry with the flours and starches that make up our versatile flour blends as well as those that are used in many of our recipes. Below you will find a list of these flours and starches as well as other helpful ingredients—such as leaveners and binders, grains and seeds, and rice and gluten-free pasta—that are essential when preparing gluten-free baked goods and savory foods.

Many of the ingredients listed in this section are sold in all supermarkets. Other items (like rice flour and teff flour) are sold in natural foods stores and well-stocked supermarkets, or you can buy them online directly from manufacturers. Bob's Red Mill makes many of the flours and starches listed below and is the brand we stock in the test kitchen. Amazon also sells most of the products listed below.

FLOURS AND STARCHES

Because protein is an important component in any flour, we have included this information below. (The percentage will vary according to how the flour is processed.) Wheat flour has 6 to 13 percent protein. Like the flours, each starch behaves differently—they are not interchangeable. Most of these starches already will be familiar to you, and you'll find that you use them in a variety of roles for both cooking and baking applications.

Almond Flour: Almond flour has a mild flavor that is subtly sweet and nutty. It is high in protein and has a coarse texture. Almond flour is usually made with blanched almonds, while almond meal can be made with blanched almonds or almonds with their skins on. That said, some manufacturers, including Bob's Red Mill, use both terms on their packaging, so read labels carefully. We prefer flour (or meal) made from blanched almonds since the lighter color tends to be more versatile. Almond flour is a good choice for rustic cakes, and we have found that it is particularly helpful in cookie recipes, like our Linzer Cookies (page 201), where a small amount contributes richness, heft, and fat without adding a noticeable flavor. You can make your own almond flour by grinding blanched almonds in a food processor.
Protein: 21%
Where to Store It: Refrigerator or freezer

Cornstarch: This refined product, made from the starchy endosperm of corn, has a neutral flavor and has long been used as a thickener for sauces and gravies. Some gluten-free recipes use it in large quantities in baked goods, but we found this approach sometimes imparted a starchy texture. In addition, cornstarch isn't the most nutritious ingredient, so using it by the cupful isn't terribly appealing.
Where to Store It: Pantry

Millet Flour: This light, powdery, pale yellow flour is ground from a seed that is believed to be the first domesticated cereal grain. Millet has a sweet, cornlike flavor and is suitable in both savory and sweet applications. Millet flour has more protein than rice flour, so we often use it to help build structure in doughs; too much, however, can leave a starchy taste, so we add it in small quantities. You can grind your own millet flour from the seeds using a spice grinder; just be sure to rinse and dry the seeds before grinding, and grind in batches until it reaches a fine, powdery consistency.
Protein: 10%
Where to Store It: Refrigerator or freezer

Oat Flour: Made by grinding oats to a powder, this flour has a subtle, slightly sweet whole-grain flavor. It adds a welcome wheatiness to sandwich bread, and because it is high in protein it helps build structure in breads. You can grind old-fashioned rolled oats in a food processor or spice grinder for about 1 minute to make your own oat flour. We also tested a number of widely available brands of oat flour and found they all performed equally well in our breads, with the exception of one type, "toasted" oat flour. We do not recommend using toasted oat flour in our recipes; the dough will be more sticky and difficult to work with, and breads will be darker in color and denser in texture. Oats are a gluten-free grain, but they're often processed in facilities that also process wheat, which creates cross-contamination issues. When buying oat flour, make sure to check the label. Alternatively, you can substitute sorghum flour for oat flour in our bread recipes. We developed our recipes using Bob's Red Mill Gluten-Free Whole-Grain Oat Flour.

Protein: 17.5%
Where to Store It: Refrigerator or freezer

Potato Starch: Made by dehydrating a slurry of water and peeled potatoes, potato starch provides structure, along with tenderness and binding power. However, it requires a higher baking temperature (and thus more time and moisture) than tapioca starch (see page 25) to reach its maximum viscosity. This makes it most useful in longer-cooking baked goods that have more moisture, like muffins or quick breads (tapioca starch is more effective in cookies). Do not confuse it with potato flour, which is made from cooked unpeeled potatoes and has a definite potato flavor. If you have a nightshade allergy and cannot use potato starch, we found that sweet white rice flour or arrowroot starch is the best substitute for potato starch in our ATK All-Purpose Gluten-Free Flour Blend.

Where to Store It: Pantry

Rice Flour, Brown: Since it still contains the bran, brown rice flour has more fiber, fat, and protein than white rice flour. It has a sandy texture like white rice flour, but a nuttier, earthier flavor (just like brown rice in comparison with white rice). Because of its fat content, brown rice flour has a short shelf life and should not be stored in the pantry. Look for brown rice flour that is as finely ground as possible. For best results when making recipes in this book, we recommend using Bob's Red Mill Brown Rice Flour.

Protein: 7.5%
Where to Store It: Refrigerator or freezer

Rice Flour, White: Made from rice after the bran and germ have been removed, white rice flour has a neutral flavor, light color, and somewhat sandy texture. It is affordable and fairly easy to find, and it has a long shelf life. Look for white rice flour that is as finely ground as possible, with little or no grit. For best results when making recipes in this book, we recommend using Bob's Red Mill White Rice Flour.

Protein: 5%
Where to Store It: Pantry

Rice Flour, Sweet White: Despite its name, sweet white rice flour isn't actually sweet, but it is much starchier than white rice flour. It is ground from a variety of white rice, called glutinous rice (no, it doesn't contain gluten), that contains a higher ratio of starch than that of white rice flour. Because of its starchiness, this flour acts as an effective binder, so much so that we included a small amount of sweet rice flour in our whole-grain gluten-free flour blend. Look for sweet white rice flour that is as finely ground as possible, with little or no grit. For best results when making recipes in this book, we recommend using Bob's Red Mill Sweet White Rice Flour.

Protein: 6%
Where to Store It: Pantry

Sorghum Flour: Largely unknown in the United States, sorghum flour is a commonly used ingredient around the rest of the world, and for good reason. It is high in protein, fiber, and iron and has a mild flavor, making it a great addition to both savory and sweet applications; it is also used to make gluten-free beer. We've found that it is a good substitute for oat flour in our recipes, not only because of its mild flavor profile, but also because of the comparable protein boost it lends baked goods. There is sorghum flour and "sweet" white sorghum flour. We tested a wide variety of available brands in our recipes for Maple-Sorghum Skillet Bread (page 179) and Popovers (page 71) and found that while we noticed slight variations in grind, color, and flavor across brands, they all performed acceptably in both recipes. For best results when making recipes in this book, we recommend using Bob's Red Mill "Sweet" White Sorghum Flour.

Protein: 12%
Where to Store It: Refrigerator or freezer

Tapioca Starch: Made from the starchy tuberous root of the cassava plant, this white powder provides chew, elasticity, and structure to baked goods. Tapioca starch is sometimes labeled tapioca flour even though it contains no protein and is a pure starch. Either product can be used in our recipes.
Where to Store It: Pantry

Teff Flour: Teff is an ancient cereal grass that is predominantly grown in Ethiopia and Eritrea. The grain has a large percentage of bran and husk because it is so small, and it is considered highly nutritious. Teff flour, which anchors our whole-grain flour blend, is high in protein and therefore helps provide structure in baked goods. It has a deep brown color, similar to whole-wheat flour, and a mild, earthy, wheaty flavor with hints of molasses. We tested a number of available brands and found they all performed equally well in our whole-grain gluten-free flour blend. We developed our recipes using Bob's Red Mill Teff Flour.
Protein: 12.5%
Where to Store It: Refrigerator or freezer

BINDERS AND LEAVENERS

In the absence of gluten's structural power, leaveners become absolutely critical in creating the necessary amount of lift and browning in baked goods. Many of the recipes in this book rely on multiple leaveners and, in some cases, in comparatively large quantities. Binders such as xanthan gum, guar gum, and psyllium husk are essential for replacing structure typically provided by gluten. See page 22 for more information on our testing of these binders.

Baking Soda: Containing just bicarbonate of soda, baking soda provides lift to cakes, muffins, and other baked goods both traditional and gluten-free. When baking soda, which is alkaline, encounters an acidic ingredient (such as sour cream, buttermilk, or brown sugar), carbon and oxygen combine to form carbon dioxide. The tiny bubbles of carbon dioxide then lift up the dough. In addition to lift, baking soda helps cookies spread and improves browning in everything from cornbread to fried chicken. For information on how baking soda helps promote tender gluten-free yeast breads, see page 160.
Where to Store It: Pantry

Baking Powder: Baking powder creates carbon dioxide to provide lift to baked goods. Cooks use baking powder rather than baking soda when there is no natural acidity in the batter. The active ingredients in baking powder are baking soda and an acidic element, such as cream of tartar. It also contains cornstarch to absorb moisture and keep the powder dry. These three ingredients are naturally gluten-free, so there should be nothing to worry about in theory. However, wheat starch is sometimes used in place of the cornstarch, so make sure to check the ingredient list on the nutritional label when buying baking powder. Also note that some brands may be produced in a facility that also processes wheat, and, if this is the case, this information will also be noted on the label. We have had good luck using Rumford and Clabber Girl brands, both of which are gluten-free. As with baking soda, baking powder is sometimes added to savory breaded or fried coatings for improved texture and chew.
Where to Store It: Pantry

Guar Gum: A powder derived from the ground endosperm of guar seeds, guar gum is high in fiber so it is often sold as a laxative. It works like xanthan gum in adding structure and thickening, although it does impart a slightly starchy texture to baked goods. We prefer to use xanthan gum rather than guar gum, but the two are interchangeable in most recipes. See page 22 for information on using guar gum in place of xanthan gum.
Where to Store It: Pantry

Nonfat Milk Powder: This shelf-stable dehydrated dairy product is in our all-purpose flour blend. It is helpful in gluten-free baking because it acts as an emulsifier, which contributes to structure by helping proteins and starches hydrate more readily so that they can then swell and form networks more effectively. It also helps gluten-free flours become more compatible with fat. It also adds dairy flavor, and the lactose sugar and milk proteins help with browning.

Where to Store It: Pantry

Powdered Psyllium Husk: Psyllium seed husk powder is one of the major components of Metamucil and Colon Cleanse. Its chemical composition is similar to that of xanthan gum, but it has a higher viscosity, so it is able to bind water even more effectively. We have found that psyllium interacts strongly with the proteins in gluten-free flours, creating a sturdy network capable of holding in lots of gas and steam during baking, and it provides a strong enough structure to support highly leavened bread once the bread cools. It adds wheat flavor that works well in breads where "whole-wheat" flavor is appropriate. We tested a number of widely available brands of powdered psyllium husk and found their performance varied. Two brands, Yerba Prima and The Vitamin Shoppe, turned the breads a purplish gray; however, this did not affect the flavor of the breads. We did find that the texture of the breads varied across the brands of psyllium husk used; some breads did not rise as well and therefore were denser, while others were a bit more wet and gummy. We had the best luck using Now Foods Psyllium Husk Powder.

Where to Store It: Pantry

Xanthan Gum: Made by using the microorganism *Xanthomonas campestris* to ferment simple sugars, xanthan gum is used widely as a thickener and stabilizer in commercial products like prepared salad dressings and toothpaste. It serves many roles in gluten-free baking. Because gluten-free flours have less protein than wheat flours and are not capable of forming the same network required to stretch and surround starch granules, they need reinforcement. Xanthan gum strengthens these networks and also makes them more elastic. Essentially, adding xanthan gum is like adding glue to the proteins in gluten-free flour. It also increases the shelf life of baked goods. Yes, xanthan gum is expensive, but you only need a little bit. See page 22 for more information about substitutions for xanthan gum.

Where to Store It: Refrigerator or freezer

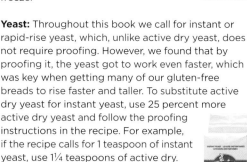

Yeast: Throughout this book we call for instant or rapid-rise yeast, which, unlike active dry yeast, does not require proofing. However, we found that by proofing it, the yeast got to work even faster, which was key when getting many of our gluten-free breads to rise faster and taller. To substitute active dry yeast for instant yeast, use 25 percent more active dry yeast and follow the proofing instructions in the recipe. For example, if the recipe calls for 1 teaspoon of instant yeast, use 1¼ teaspoons of active dry.

Where to Store It: Refrigerator (and pay attention to the expiration date)

GRAINS AND SEEDS

The world of grains is a big one—which is a great thing for those who can't eat gluten. The list below offers a wide range of options for making interesting side dishes, main dishes, and more. In chapter 2 you will find recipes using many of these gluten-free grains. In addition to grains, this list includes the seeds that can be ground into flour or used whole in baked goods and other recipes.

Amaranth: Amaranth, a staple of the Incas and Aztecs, is second only to quinoa for protein content among grains and seeds. Amaranth has a complex flavor that's very nutty and earthy. It is often dry-toasted before being cooked and can be prepared like porridge or rice. The whole seeds can also be popped like popcorn.

Buckwheat Groats and Kasha: Buckwheat, despite its name, is not related to wheat but is in fact an herb that is related to sorrel and rhubarb.

Buckwheat has an assertive flavor and can be found in several forms. Hulled, crushed buckwheat seeds are known as buckwheat groats, and because of their high carbohydrate content they are generally treated like a grain. Grayish green in color, groats have a mild, earthy flavor. They are often eaten as a staple like rice and are baked into

STORING GRAINS

To prevent open boxes and bags of grains from spoiling in the pantry, store them in airtight containers and, if you have space, in the freezer. This is especially important for whole grains, which turn rancid with oxidation.

puddings and porridges. Buckwheat's triangular seeds can also be ground to make flour.

Kasha is buckwheat groats that have been roasted. This process gives kasha a darker color and a noticeably earthier and roasty flavor that some people love, and others don't. Kasha is often served pilaf-style and as a hot cereal and is traditionally used in blintzes, com-bined with pasta to make a traditional Eastern European Jewish dish called *kasha varnishkas*, and included as part of a filling for pastries known as knishes.

Cornmeal and Polenta: For many consumers, buying cornmeal used to mean picking up a container of Quaker, or perhaps (especially if you lived in the South) a stone-ground local variety. But at most supermarkets today, you've got a lot more options to sort through: fine-, medium-, and coarse-ground; instant and quick-cooking; whole-grain, stone-ground, and regular. Whether you are making cornbread, pancakes, polenta, or a rustic Italian-style cake, different recipes require different grinds and types of cornmeal. What you use can make a big difference. Make sure to read—and buy—carefully.

Flaxseeds: Flaxseeds are similar in size to sesame seeds and have a sweet, wheaty flavor. They are naturally gluten-free and are sold in most supermarkets both whole and ground. Flaxseeds are one of the highest sources known for the omega-3 fatty acid called alpha-linolenic acid (ALA), which is found only in certain plant foods and oils and must be

supplied in our diet for good health. There are two types of flaxseeds: brown and golden. We chose to use golden flaxseeds in our whole-grain flour blend, as their milder, nutty flavor complemented the teff flour. Whole seeds have a longer shelf life, but we preferred ground flaxseeds in our whole-grain gluten-free flour blend and breads because we use them as a flour rather than as a stir-in. As an added bonus, grinding flaxseeds improves the release of nutrients.

Millet: Believed to be the first domesticated cereal grain, this tiny cereal grass seed has a long history and is still a staple in a large part of the world, particularly in Asia and Africa. The seeds can be ground into flour or used whole. Millet has a mellow corn flavor that works well in both savory and sweet applications, including breads and pan-fried cakes. It can be cooked pilaf-style, pasta-style for a grain salad, or turned into a creamy breakfast porridge. To add texture to baked goods, try incorporating a small amount of millet into the batter (see Honey-Millet Sandwich Bread on page 143).

Oats: From breakfast table to cookie jar, this nutritious cereal grass is a versatile part of the gluten-free diet. But be careful when buying oats; they're often processed in facilities that also process wheat, which creates cross-contamination issues. It's therefore critical to make sure you are buying oats that are processed in a gluten-free facility. Oats come in several forms: groats (see below), old-fashioned rolled oats, steel cut, and instant.

Oat Berries (Oat Groats): Labeled either oat berries or oat groats, this gluten-free whole grain is simply whole oats that have been hulled and cleaned. They are the least processed oat product (other forms are processed further, such as being rolled flat, cut, or ground). Because they haven't been processed, they retain a high nutritional value. They have an appealing chewy texture and a mildly nutty flavor. Oats are usually thought of as a breakfast cereal, but oat berries make a great savory side dish cooked pilaf-style or can be cooked like risotto for a rich, satisfying main dish.

Quinoa: Quinoa originated in the Andes Mountains of South America, and while it is generally treated as a grain, it is actually the seed of the goosefoot plant. Sometimes referred to as a "supergrain," quinoa is high in protein, and its protein is complete, which means it possesses all of the amino acids in the balanced amounts that our bodies require. Beyond its nutritional prowess, we love quinoa for its addictive crunchy texture, nutty taste, and ease of preparation.

White quinoa is the most commonly found variety of these tiny seeds, but red and black varieties are increasingly available. White quinoa, the largest seed of the three, has a slightly nutty, vegetal flavor with a hint of bitterness; it also has the softest texture of the three quinoas. The medium-size red seeds offer a heartier crunch, thanks to their additional seed coat, and a predominant nuttiness. Black quinoa seeds, the smallest of the three, have

the thickest seed coat. They are notably crunchy and retain their shape the most during cooking. These seeds have the mildest flavor, with a hint of molasses-like sweetness. You can use white and red quinoa interchangeably in our quinoa pilaf recipes and other side dishes or salads. However, white quinoa is best for dishes like cakes and patties because it is starchier and will hold together better. Black quinoa is better off in recipes specifically tailored to its distinctive texture and flavor. Unless labeled "prewashed," quinoa should always be rinsed before cooking to remove its protective layer (called saponin), which is unpleasantly bitter.

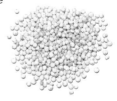

Quinoa Flakes: Quinoa flakes are simply quinoa seeds that have been rolled flat into thin flakes. They are growing in popularity as an alternative to instant oatmeal for a nutritious hot breakfast cereal. They can also be used in baked goods and granola. Quinoa flakes can be found in the cereal aisle of your grocery store, near the instant oatmeal.

RICE

In the gluten-free kitchen, rice is a lifesaver. There are many varieties on the market and many ways to prepare rice: as a simple side dish, an appealing salad, or a hearty main course when paired with multiple vegetables, or even as hearty rice cakes, as with our Miso Brown Rice Cakes (page 87).

Arborio Rice: Arborio, the variety of medium-grain rice that we use in the test kitchen to make risotto, was once grown exclusively in Italy. Now widely available, these stubby, milky grains have a high starch content, which is what enables them to make such creamy risotto.

Basmati Rice: Prized for its nutty flavor and sweet aroma, basmati rice is eaten in pilafs and biryanis and with curries. Indian basmati is aged for a minimum of a year, though often much longer, before being packaged. Aging dehydrates the rice, which translates into grains that, once cooked, expand greatly. We don't recommend American-grown basmati.

Black Rice: Like brown rice, black rice is sold unhulled. But only black rice contains anthocyanins, the same antioxidant compounds found in blueberries and blackberries. These compounds are what turn the rice a deep purple as it cooks. Note that black rice is especially easy to overcook. To keep it from turning mushy, we have found that boiling it in an abundance of water (similar to cooking pasta) is the best approach.

Brown Rice: All rice (except wild) starts out as brown rice. Each grain of rice is made up of an endosperm, germ, bran, and a protective outer hull or husk. Brown rice is simply rice that has been husked and cleaned. Considered a whole grain, brown rice has more fiber and vitamins than white rice, along with a firmer texture and a nuttier, earthier flavor. Keep in mind that the bran and germ contain oils that shorten the rice's shelf life. Brown rice takes longer to cook than white rice because it requires more time to allow water to penetrate the bran.

Brown rice comes in a variety of grain sizes: short, medium, and long. Long-grain brown rice, the best choice for pilafs, cooks up fluffy with separate grains. Medium-grain brown rice is a bit more sticky, perfect for risotto, paella, and similar dishes. Short-grain brown rice is the most sticky, ideal for sushi and other Asian dishes where getting the grains to clump together is desired.

Jasmine Rice: Native to Thailand and a staple in Southeast Asian cuisine, jasmine rice has an aroma similar to basmati rice, but the texture is stickier and moister and the grain size is much smaller. Compared with other varieties of long-grain rice, jasmine rice tends to cook up relatively soft and sticky, though it maintains a slightly firm chew. Because it clumps together when cooked, jasmine rice works well in stir-fries. It's also nice in soups.

White Rice: Like brown rice, white rice has been husked and cleaned, but then it is processed a step further by removing the germ and bran. This makes the rice cook up faster and softer, and it's more shelf-stable, but the process also removes much of the fiber, protein, and other nutrients, as well as flavor.

Like brown rice, white rice can be long-, medium-, or short-grained. Long-grain is a broad category and includes generic long-grain rice as well as aromatic varieties such as basmati and jasmine. The grains are slender and elongated and measure four to five times longer than they are wide. Long-grain white rice cooks up light and fluffy, with firm, distinct grains, making it good for pilafs and salads.

Medium-grain white rice includes a wide variety of specialty rices, including many Japanese and Chinese brands, used to make risotto and paella. The grains are fat and measure two to three times longer than they are wide. Medium-grain white rice cooks up a bit sticky, and when simmered the grains clump together, making this rice a common choice in Chinese restaurants. With the exception of sushi, we don't eat much short-grain white rice in this country. The grains are almost round, and the texture is quite sticky and soft when cooked.

Avoid converted rice, which is parboiled during processing. This tan-colored rice cooks up too separate in our opinion, and the flavor seems a bit off.

Wild Rice: Wild rice is technically not in the same family as other rices; it's actually an aquatic grass. North America's only native grain, it grows naturally in lakes and is cultivated in man-made paddies in Minnesota, California, and Canada. Its smooth grains have a remarkably nutty, savory depth and a distinct chew that make it an ideal choice for a hearty side dish or addition to soup. Cook wild rice at a bare simmer and check it often: It can go from chewy and underdone to mushy and "blown out" in a matter of minutes.

GLUTEN-FREE PASTA

Just because you're no longer eating wheat doesn't mean that pasta is off the menu. There are two routes you can take: Asian noodles that traditionally don't contain wheat and gluten-free approximations of classic Italian pasta.

Dried Italian-Style Pasta: We ran an extensive taste test of gluten-free spaghetti (see page 35). In subsequent work in the test kitchen, we had excellent results with other shapes manufactured by Jovial, winner of our spaghetti tasting. As with wheat pasta, we found that cooking times listed on packages of gluten-free pasta are often inaccurate. You must taste pasta often as it cooks. Also note that gluten-free pasta goes from al dente to mush even faster than wheat-based pasta, so err on the side of undercooking the noodles. We often call for reserving some of the starchy cooking water to help loosen sauces. Place a measuring cup in the colander so you remember not to pour all the cooking water down the drain.

Lasagna Noodles: Gluten-free lasagna noodles are available in both no-boil and boil-before-use forms. We found that no-boil gluten-free noodles varied considerably; some brands were thick and cooked up gummy, while others were thin and fragile. We had better luck using noodles that we boiled. There are just a few brands on the market. We had the most success with Tinkyada; they were tender once cooked and held up well, while other brands were incredibly fragile. Boil them for a bit less time than the package instructions indicate so they don't fall apart. After boiling and draining the noodles, toss them with a teaspoon of olive oil and spread them out in a single layer on a baking sheet to prevent sticking.

Rice Noodles: This delicate pasta, made from rice flour and water, is used in a variety of dishes in Southeast Asia and southern China. Flat rice noodles come in two widths: a medium-width (¼-inch-wide) noodle and a larger (⅜-inch-wide) noodle. Round rice noodles also come in more than one size, but we prefer the thinner rice vermicelli. Don't follow the package directions, which often call for boiling. Such treatment will turn these delicate noodles into a gummy, mushy, unappealing mess. You'll get the most reliable results by steeping these noodles in hot water. Place the noodles in a very large bowl, cover them with very hot tap water, and stir to separate the individual strands. Let the noodles soak until they are softened, pliable, and limp but not fully tender, 20 minutes for vermicelli or narrow flat noodles, or 35 to 40 minutes for wide flat noodles. Drain the noodles and use as directed.

Soba Noodles: Soba noodles possess a rich, nutty flavor and a delicate texture. They get their flavor from buckwheat flour. Be aware that many brands also contain wheat, which not only keeps the price down but gives the noodles more structure. Make sure to read the label and look for those that contain buckwheat flour only. Soba noodles should be cooked like Italian-style pasta. Since they are often used in Asian-inspired recipes that include salty ingredients like tamari, there is often no need to salt the water.

Gluten-Free Sandwich Bread

When you're avoiding gluten, it's tough to give up toast and sandwiches—and if a recipe calls for bread slices or crumbs, you're really out of luck. That's where gluten-free supermarket bread can step in. While fresh loaves are scarce, the freezer section of most supermarkets is usually packed with many gluten-free options for both white and multigrain or whole-grain breads. A few years ago, we tasted eight brands of white sandwich bread and found only one to recommend. This time around, we wanted to revisit the world of white sandwich breads and also try to find out if any of the multigrain/whole-grain options would fare any better.

GOOD NEWS/BAD NEWS

Among the new brands of white sandwich bread, two were subpar in every application. Even toasting and buttering them could not make these samples palatable. The other three breads were acceptable, though tasters still had quibbles with texture or flavor. Our previous winner (Udi's Gluten Free White Sandwich Bread), which has been reformulated since our last tasting, dropped to second place. On the multigrain front, we were pleasantly surprised by the positive response from tasters; two brands received high praise and were deemed "actually really good!" while three more fell into our Recommended with Reservations category.

TAKING A CLOSER LOOK

At first glance you might assume the multigrain breads fared so much better because they had an abundance of hearty grains and fiber. But in most instances, these breads looked like their gluten-free white bread counterparts (with the exception of those with a smattering of seeds or grains that were visible in the crust or floating within the mostly white interiors). To be labeled "multigrain," breads only have to contain more than one type of grain—and that can be in the form of refined flours, which lack the fibrous bran and nutrient-rich germ. In fact, our favorite "multigrain" gluten-free bread, Glutino Gluten Free Multigrain Bread, contains no fiber or protein at all, a sign that it contains no whole grains. By contrast, the second-place bread, Three Bakers 7 Ancient Grains Whole Grain Bread, Gluten-Free contains 4 grams of protein and 10 grams of fiber in a 100-gram serving (equivalent to about 3 slices). These two breads are our favorites from both tastings; despite being labeled as multigrain and whole-grain, in our opinion these breads are so much like white bread that they are interchangeable whether you are simply making a sandwich or using them as part of a recipe such as when making bread crumbs or a breakfast casserole.

BROWN RICE IS NICE

What was clear across both tastings was that brown rice flour, with its flavorful germ and fibrous bran, made better breads. Among the white sandwich breads, our top three breads all used brown rice flour, while the bottom-ranking breads used white rice flour, which has no fiber to help create structure, and far less flavor. All the multigrain breads we tested used brown rice flour.

WORTH ITS SALT AND FAT

Another common theme was that salt goes a long way toward enhancing flavor. Our top-ranked white sandwich bread had the second-highest level of salt; our winning multigrain bread also had plenty of salt, while the lowest-ranked breads had the least sodium. The amount of fat in these breads also mattered: more fat means more flavor (and with these gluten-free breads, it helped create an interior crumb that was fluffy and moist). Glutino Gluten Free Multigrain Bread, the winner, has 12 grams of fat per 100-gram serving, or 3.5 grams per slice.

THE BOTTOM LINE

Gluten-free breads labeled multigrain or whole-grain are a better bet than white breads. For gluten-free bread with the best flavor and texture, we recommend you reach for the breads ranked the highest in our multigrain sandwich bread tasting.

Rating Gluten-Free White Sandwich Breads

Our tasting panel tasted each sample three times: plain, then toasted with butter, and finally baked with eggs in our recipe for strata. The scores from the tastings were averaged to determine overall rankings.

RECOMMENDED WITH RESERVATIONS

CANYON BAKEHOUSE Mountain White Gluten Free Bread

PRICE: $5.00 for 18-ounce loaf
PROTEIN (100G SERVING): 3g CARBOHYDRATES: 44g
FAT: 4g SODIUM: 412mg
DIETARY FIBER: 6g SUGARS: 9g
TASTERS' COMMENTS: "I like this most of all," one taster wrote. "Amazingly close to regular bread!" agreed another. "Slightly sweet" and "nutty," it had a texture that was "softer," "the best chew of the bunch," albeit "a hint mushy," or "gummy/slimy," even when it was toasted. Baked in strata, it "holds its shape well," though some found it "spongy."

UDI'S Gluten Free White Sandwich Bread

PRICE: $6.29 for 12-ounce loaf
PROTEIN (100G SERVING): 6g CARBOHYDRATES: 45g
FAT: 7g SODIUM: 510mg
DIETARY FIBER: 2g SUGARS: 6g
TASTERS' COMMENTS: "Dry, cottony, bland," with "subtle sweetness," our former winner, newly reformulated with less sodium and less protein, didn't rock our world, but made a "nice blank canvas" as a "pretty good approximation of white sandwich bread."

THREE BAKERS Whole Grain White Bread, Gluten Free

PRICE: $6.79 for 17-ounce loaf
PROTEIN (100G SERVING): 3g CARBOHYDRATES: 44g
FAT: 4g SODIUM: 338mg
DIETARY FIBER: 7g SUGARS: 4g
TASTERS' COMMENTS: "This doesn't have much flavor," one taster wrote, which was the consensus of our panel. As for texture, it was "sandy," "crumbly," and "very chewy, not in a good way, almost marshmallow-y" when served plain; "very disappointing." Baked in strata, its flavor was "neutral, mildly sweet," but "the bread dissolved too much" and became "pasty."

NOT RECOMMENDED

KATZ White Bread, Gluten Free

PRICE: $6.19 for 21-ounce loaf
PROTEIN (100G SERVING): 3g CARBOHYDRATES: 43g
FAT: 9g SODIUM: 0mg
DIETARY FIBER: 3g SUGARS: 3g
TASTERS' COMMENTS: With "no structure," this "crumbly," "spongelike," "starchy" bread "disintegrates quickly" in the mouth: "It starts off moist but fades to gritty," a taster wrote. Some tasters complained of "fishy" or "fake butter" off-flavors. In strata, it was too "firm" and "absorbed liquid unevenly," and tasters noted a "weird, almost plastic" flavor.

THE ESSENTIAL BAKING COMPANY Sunny Seeded White Bread, Gluten Free

PRICE: $5.50 for 14-ounce loaf
PROTEIN (100G SERVING): 3g CARBOHYDRATES: 36g
FAT: 18g SODIUM: 273mg
DIETARY FIBER: 6g SUGARS: 9g
TASTERS' COMMENTS: "Sweet, incredibly dry, so weird for white bread"—tasters agreed about this loaf whose crust is solidly studded with whole sunflower seeds. While tasters felt the seeds gave the crust a pleasing nutty flavor, they gave thumbs-down to the interior crumb. "Hack! I need the Heimlich maneuver. So sandy and dusty." In strata, it was "wet" and "pasty."

Note: In a previous tasting, we tried and did not recommend the following breads (manufacturers confirmed that the formulations have not changed): Kinnikinnick Soft White Bread, Gluten Free; Schar Classic White Bread Gluten-Free Wheat-Free; Genius by Glutino Gluten Free White Sandwich Bread; Rudi's Gluten Free Organic Original (Rudi's bread was about to be reformulated at the time of this tasting); Food For Life Gluten Free White Rice Bread; EnerG Gluten Free Tapioca Loaf, Thin Sliced.

Rating Gluten-Free Multigrain Sandwich Breads

Our tasting panel tasted each of these breads twice: plain and then toasted with butter. The scores from both tastings were averaged to determine overall rankings.

RECOMMENDED

GLUTINO Gluten Free Multigrain Bread
PRICE: $5.49 for 14.1-ounce loaf
PROTEIN (100G SERVING): 0g   CARBOHYDRATES: 45g
FAT: 12g   SODIUM: 586mg
DIETARY FIBER: 0g   SUGARS: 3g
TASTERS' COMMENTS: With the most salt of all the breads, and with one of the highest fat contents (at 3.5 grams per slice), this loaf had a flavor advantage. "It has chew and some structure," with an interior that was "fluffy and light, almost like challah," though some noted that it "doesn't seem very multigrain." Overall, as one taster wrote, "Miles better than the others."

THREE BAKERS 7 Ancient Grains Whole Grain Bread, Gluten-Free
PRICE: $5.99 for 17-ounce loaf
PROTEIN (100G SERVING): 4g   CARBOHYDRATES: 63g
FAT: 4g   SODIUM: 412mg
DIETARY FIBER: 10g   SUGARS: 6g
TASTERS' COMMENTS: With "a yeasty, rich flavor," "crust that is very chewy," and "seeds and grains that add interest," this bread was appealing to tasters. Toasted, this loaf had "nice crunch" but became "gummy in the middle."

RECOMMENDED WITH RESERVATIONS

CANYON BAKEHOUSE 7-Grain Bread, Gluten-Free
PRICE: $5.49 for 18-ounce loaf
PROTEIN (100G SERVING): 6g   CARBOHYDRATES: 41g
FAT: 4g   SODIUM: 309mg
DIETARY FIBER: 6g   SUGARS: 6g
TASTERS' COMMENTS: "Nutty" and "slightly sweet," this loaf had "normal bread flavor." Toasted, it was much less successful: "a little off—sort of sweet and turns mushy quickly in my mouth."

KINNIKINNICK Soft Multigrain Bread, Gluten-Free
PRICE: $4.99 for 16-ounce loaf
PROTEIN (100G SERVING): 5g   CARBOHYDRATES: 35g
FAT: 11g   SODIUM: 316mg
DIETARY FIBER: 9g   SUGARS: 2g
TASTERS' COMMENTS: This bread was deemed "very light" with "no chew" to the interior but a "substantial" crust.

RECOMMENDED WITH RESERVATIONS (continued)

UDI'S Gluten Free Whole Grain Bread
PRICE: $5.99 for 12-ounce loaf
PROTEIN (100G SERVING): 8g   CARBOHYDRATES: 45g
FAT: 8g   SODIUM: 531mg
DIETARY FIBER: 4g   SUGARS: 6g
TASTERS' COMMENTS: "Woof. Dry," wrote one taster, who summed up the comments of many. "No chewy pull; it just breaks," with a flavor that is "nice, but not very complex." Toasted, it was dry, with a texture "like Styrofoam."

NOT RECOMMENDED

SCHAR Gluten-Free Hearty Grain Bread
PRICE: $4.99 for 15-ounce loaf
PROTEIN (100G SERVING): 7g   CARBOHYDRATES: 53g
FAT: 3g   SODIUM: 413mg
DIETARY FIBER: 7g   SUGARS: less than 1g
TASTERS' COMMENTS: "Dry, dry, dry," complained a taster. "Leaves pasty coating of sand/mud in my mouth." "Dense," "stiff," and "compact," the bread had "no chew or air," and tasters found it "a bit sour," "like old beer." Toasted, it was much the same.

THE ESSENTIAL BAKING COMPANY Super Seeded Multi-Grain Bread
PRICE: $5.99 for 14-ounce loaf
PROTEIN (100G SERVING): 6g   CARBOHYDRATES: 36g
FAT: 12g   SODIUM: 424mg
DIETARY FIBER: 12g   SUGARS: 12g
TASTERS' COMMENTS: Many tasters noted "overly sweet," "molasses-y" flavors, "like bad cinnamon raisin bread." It also featured "lots and lots of sunflower seeds," which contributed to its high fat content. As toast, it still had problems: It was "very sweet—off-putting."

KATZ Whole Grain Bread, Gluten-Free
PRICE: $6.19 for 21-ounce loaf
PROTEIN (100G SERVING): 3g   CARBOHYDRATES: 43g
FAT: 7g   SODIUM: 0mg
DIETARY FIBER: 3g   SUGARS: 3g
TASTERS' COMMENTS: Tasters disliked this bread's "dry, rocklike texture." It was "stiff," "brittle," and "foamy." "Truly awful," wrote one. "I would give up bread if this were my only option."

Italian-Style Dried Gluten-Free Pasta

For people who are avoiding gluten in their diets, finding good wheat-free pasta with the right texture and flavor is a challenge, one which has been met in a variety of ways by pasta manufacturers. We first evaluated gluten-free pasta several years ago, and the results were grim. The majority were gritty and grainy or dissolved into a mushy, gummy mess. Only one product, Jovial Organic Brown Rice Spaghetti, offered chewy yet tender noodles with a pleasant, neutral flavor.

We hoped that, given the number of new companies jumping on the gluten-free bandwagon recently, we might have better luck this time around. To find out, we pitted our top two scorers against six new products, tasting them cooked in salted water and tossed with canola oil, and a second time served with our favorite tomato sauce.

NEW BRANDS, SAME PROBLEMS

To our dismay, the majority of the brands again failed to meet our expectations. As before, many products were unpleasantly "pasty" and "gummy" with "zero chew." Even when we closely monitored their cooking time and strained them promptly, some of them practically disintegrated. But our old runner-up fell into the other end of the texture spectrum. Last time, we'd noticed a slight "rubbery" quality that we were willing to overlook due to its neutral flavor. But now that some brands are hitting the mark, our standards are higher. This time around, our tasters deemed it unacceptably "firm" and "chewy."

CORN WORTH EATING

A newcomer, made with a combination of corn and rice flours, joined our brown rice favorite at the top. When pasta is boiled, the starch granules absorb water and swell. If the protein network is not strong enough to hold those swollen granules in place, starch will leach out of the pasta as it cooks, resulting in soggy and sticky noodles (and very cloudy cooking water). The proteins in corn are more water-soluble than those in rice and therefore more likely to escape the pasta. We'd nixed corn flour pastas in our earlier testing because they had been especially clumpy and gummy, but this pasta remained "intact" and had an "al dente" texture. How had they done it?

We knew that the rice flour was helping, but we'd had poor results with a similar blend in our first tasting. A closer look revealed that this pasta also contains mono- and diglycerides. Corn pastas can be brittle, and these stabilizers help hold the starches together and keep the pasta tender.

THE RIGHT RATIO

For all types of pasta, protein is the most important factor in determining texture. More protein is generally better than less, but all of our spaghetti contained between 4 and 6 grams per serving, and those numbers didn't correlate with our rankings. However, gluten-free pastas don't behave in exactly the same ways as pastas made with white or whole-wheat flour. Most get their strength from rice flour—in fact, it's a primary ingredient in every brand we tasted—and it's much lower in protein than either white or whole-wheat flour. Although particles of fiber can interfere with the protein bonds in wheat pasta and cause it to weaken during cooking, rice fiber plays a helpful role in gluten-free pasta—to a point. The ideal combination turns out to be a relatively high amount of protein (at least 4 grams) and a fiber content that's less than half that amount. Our two favorite brands have a relatively high amount of protein that is at least double their amount of fiber; both remained intact but tender after cooking, earning praise for their ability to pass as "regular" pasta. The rest of the samples, all of which had been soft and mushy or gritty and grainy, had a near-equal ratio of protein and fiber.

THE BOTTOM LINE

Many products are still disappointing, but it is possible to find good-quality gluten-free spaghetti made entirely from brown rice flour or with a combination of corn and rice flour. In both, a relatively large amount of protein and very little fiber is the key to pasta that doesn't disintegrate during cooking.

Rating Italian-Style Dried Gluten-Free Pastas

Our panel tasted each sample twice—cooked in salted water and tossed with canola oil, then again served with our favorite tomato sauce. The scores from the two tastings were averaged to determine overall rankings.

The following products were not recommended in our original tasting and have not been reformulated: Bionaturae Organic Gluten Free Spaghetti; Ancient Harvest, Gluten Free, Spaghetti Style; Tinkyada Pasta Joy Ready Brown Rice Pasta, Spaghetti Style; Rustichella d'Abruzzo Organic Corn Spaghetti; DeLallo Gluten Free Corn & Rice Spaghetti; DeBoles Gluten Free Rice Spaghetti Style Pasta.

RECOMMENDED

JOVIAL Organic Gluten Free Brown Rice Spaghetti

PRICE: $3.49 for 12oz ($0.29 per oz)
INGREDIENTS: Organic Brown Rice Flour, Water
TASTERS' COMMENTS: Our original favorite again emerged at the top of our rankings, thanks to a high ratio of protein to fiber. These delicate and thin strands had a "neutral, pleasant" flavor and "al dente texture" that combined for gluten-free spaghetti that was deemed "just like regular pasta."

BARILLA Gluten Free Spaghetti

PRICE: $2.69 for 12oz ($0.22 per oz)
INGREDIENTS: Corn Flour, Rice Flour, Mono- and Diglycerides
TASTERS' COMMENTS: With four times more protein than fiber and helpful emulsifiers, this spaghetti boasted a cohesive and "springy" texture much like traditional pasta. Some astute tasters identified a cornlike sweetness, but since the corn flour is combined with rice flour, its flavor was deemed pleasantly "neutral."

RECOMMENDED WITH RESERVATIONS

DELALLO Gluten Free Whole Grain Rice Spaghetti

PRICE: $5.19 for 12oz ($0.43 per oz)
INGREDIENTS: 100% Brown Rice Flour
TASTERS' COMMENTS: The texture of these small, skinny noodles was pleasant enough, but our panel was ambivalent about the flavor. While some described it as having an "earthy" or "whole wheat flavor," many tasters thought this spaghetti tasted "stale" or even "cardboard-y."

NOT RECOMMENDED

ANDEAN DREAM Gluten/Corn Free Quinoa Pasta, Spaghetti

PRICE: $4.49 for 8oz ($0.56 per oz)
INGREDIENTS: Organic Rice Flour, Organic Quinoa Flour
TASTERS' COMMENTS: Our old runner-up took a tumble in the rankings, thanks to stronger competitors and a "chewy" and "rubbery" texture that reminded tasters of Asian rice noodles.

LUNDBERG Organic Brown Rice Spaghetti Pasta

PRICE: $3.99 for 10oz ($0.40 per oz)
INGREDIENTS: Organic Brown Rice Flour
TASTERS' COMMENTS: These skinny strands broke into short fragments during cooking; no surprise since this pasta has a 1:1 ratio of protein to fiber that couldn't properly protect the starches for good cohesion. They also felt "gritty" and "grainy."

RONZONI Gluten Free Spaghetti

PRICE: $2.40 for 12oz ($0.20 per oz)
INGREDIENTS: White Rice Flour, Brown Rice Flour, Corn Flour, Quinoa Flour, Mono- and Diglycerides
TASTERS' COMMENTS: Although these noodles kept their shape during cooking and looked appealing to our tasters (probably thanks to the emulsifiers), they felt "chalky" and "sandy" even when tossed with pasta sauce. Tasters identified subtle corn and rice flavor.

DEBOLES Gluten Free Multigrain Spaghetti Style Pasta

PRICE: $3.30 for 8oz ($0.41 per oz)
INGREDIENTS: Whole Grain Brown Rice Flour, White Rice Flour, Rice Bran, Organic Amaranth Flour, Organic Quinoa Flour, Rice Bran Extract, Xanthan Gum, Vitamin & Mineral Mix (Niacin, Ferrous Sulfate, Thiamin Mononitrate, Riboflavin, Folic Acid)
TASTERS' COMMENTS: Stabilizers and other added ingredients weren't enough to save this "limp" and "mushy" pasta, which has a low ratio of protein to fiber and felt like it had "no substance." The noodles clumped into unappetizing "globs" of spaghetti and tasted "musty" and unpleasantly "earthy."

A GOOD START

■ DAIRY FREE OR INCLUDES A DAIRY-FREE VARIATION

Whole-Grain Pancakes

G-F TESTING LAB

FLOUR SUBSTITUTION	Do not substitute other whole-grain blends for the ATK Whole-Grain Gluten-Free Flour Blend; they will not work in this recipe.
BAKING POWDER	Not all brands of baking powder are gluten-free; see page 25 for more information.
RESTING TIME	Do not shortchange the batter's 30-minute rest or else the pancakes will be dense.

WHY THIS RECIPE WORKS

Whole-grain pancakes are often overly virtuous and not well balanced in terms of richness and whole-grain flavor. We set out to make a pancake that was earthy-tasting but that also had a rich, buttery flavor. Our whole-grain flour blend has a lot of teff flour, which adds a robust flavor much like traditional whole-wheat flour. But in a simple pancake the flavor was a little too robust, so to balance it we tested a variety of sweeteners including honey, brown sugar, and granulated sugar. The honey and brown sugar added too much moisture and resulted in gummy pancakes, but granulated sugar provided the best balance of sweetness while also helping with the structure, making airier pancakes. As for the dairy, we are fans of buttermilk in pancakes for its characteristic tang but in combination with our whole-grain blend it made pancakes that were a bit sour. We tried using whole milk but it made our pancakes too dense. Low-fat milk, however, hydrated the starches in the blend perfectly and lightened up the pancakes. Typically, pancake recipes include just one egg, but an additional egg helped with structure and richness here. Processing the eggs along with the other liquid ingredients helped us get additional lift from the eggs. We found that a combination of butter and oil worked best in these pancakes; butter alone, while adding flavor, made the pancakes gummy because it also includes water. Swapping out some of the butter for vegetable oil, which is a pure fat, gave us the best of both worlds: buttery flavor and a crisp exterior and moist interior. Finally, letting the batter rest for 30 minutes ensured that the starch granules in the flour softened uniformly, eliminating grittiness and also allowing the flours to become fully hydrated for pancakes that were not dense or gummy. Do not substitute skim or whole milk in this recipe.

Whole-Grain Pancakes

MAKES EIGHTEEN 3-INCH PANCAKES; SERVES 4 TO 6

- 12   ounces (2⅔ cups) ATK Whole-Grain Gluten-Free Flour Blend (page 9)
- 1¾   ounces (¼ cup) sugar
- 2¼   teaspoons baking powder
- ¾   teaspoon salt
- 2½   cups 1 or 2 percent low-fat milk, plus extra as needed
- 2   large eggs
- 2   tablespoons unsalted butter, melted and cooled
- ¼   cup vegetable oil
- 1   teaspoon vanilla extract

1. Set wire rack in rimmed baking sheet. Adjust oven rack to middle position, place prepared sheet on rack, and heat oven to 200 degrees.

2. Whisk flour blend, sugar, baking powder, and salt together in large bowl. Process milk, eggs, melted butter, 2 tablespoons oil, and vanilla in blender until frothy, about 1 minute. Whisk milk mixture into flour mixture until well incorporated and no lumps remain, about 1 minute. Cover bowl with plastic wrap and let batter rest at room temperature for 30 minutes.

3. Heat 1 teaspoon oil in 12-inch nonstick skillet over medium-low heat until shimmering, 3 to 5 minutes. Using paper towels, wipe out oil, leaving thin film in pan. Using ¼-cup measure, portion pancakes into pan, spreading each immediately into 3-inch round using back of spoon; you will fit about 3 pancakes in pan. Cook until first side is golden and bubbles on surface begin to break, 2 to 3 minutes.

4. Flip pancakes and cook until second side is golden, 1 to 2 minutes. Serve or transfer to wire rack in oven. Repeat with remaining oil and batter, whisking extra milk into batter as needed to loosen.

VARIATION

Dairy-Free Whole-Grain Pancakes

We prefer the flavor and texture of these pancakes made with soy milk but almond milk will also work; do not use rice milk.

Substitute unsweetened soy milk for milk, and vegetable oil for melted butter.

Fluffy Oat Pancakes

G-F TESTING LAB

OAT FLOUR	Oats are a gluten-free grain, but they're often processed in facilities that also process wheat, which creates cross-contamination issues. When buying oats or oat flour, make sure to check the label. We use Bob's Red Mill Gluten-Free Whole-Grain Oat Flour. For more information on oat flour, see page 23.
BAKING POWDER	Not all brands of baking powder are gluten-free; see page 25 for more information.

WHY THIS RECIPE WORKS

The beauty of these hearty oat pancakes is that they don't require a gluten-free flour blend, plus they are supereasy to make—all you need is store-bought oat flour, a blender, and a few pantry ingredients. We first tried grinding our own gluten-free oats but found that we just couldn't get the grind fine enough—our pancakes were turning out rather heavy and dense. We switched to store-bought oat flour (which is ground very fine), and the texture improved dramatically. For lift, we needed 2½ teaspoons of baking powder because of the high protein content and heaviness of the oat flour; for flavor we added cinnamon and nutmeg, which paired nicely with the hearty oat flavor. We started out using whole milk, but it had too much fat and weighed down our pancakes; switching to low-fat milk kept them light and airy. We knew we wanted eggs and a little butter for richness. Just one egg did not create enough structure to provide lift for our pancakes, so we added an extra yolk, which also gave them more flavor. To get lift from the eggs, we whipped them until frothy in a blender along with the other liquid ingredients. We tried brown sugar, maple syrup, and honey as alternative sweeteners, but they all made the texture too dense. Plain old granulated sugar gave us the best combination of sweetness and structure. Do not substitute skim or whole milk in this recipe.

Fluffy Oat Pancakes
MAKES SIXTEEN 3-INCH PANCAKES; SERVES 4

- 9 ounces (3 cups) oat flour
- 2½ teaspoons baking powder
- 2¼ teaspoons ground cinnamon
- ¾ teaspoon salt
- ¼ teaspoon ground nutmeg
- 1½ cups 1 or 2 percent low-fat milk, plus extra as needed
- ¼ cup (1¾ ounces) sugar
- 3 tablespoons unsalted butter, melted and cooled
- 1 large egg plus 1 large yolk
- 2¼ teaspoons vanilla extract
- 5 teaspoons vegetable oil

1. Set wire rack in rimmed baking sheet. Adjust oven rack to middle position, place prepared sheet on rack, and heat oven to 200 degrees.

2. Whisk oat flour, baking powder, cinnamon, salt, and nutmeg together in large bowl. Process milk, sugar, melted butter, egg and yolk, and vanilla in blender until frothy, about 1 minute. Whisk milk mixture into flour mixture until well incorporated and no lumps remain, about 1 minute.

3. Heat 1 teaspoon oil in 12-inch nonstick skillet over medium-low heat until shimmering, 3 to 5 minutes. Using paper towels, wipe out oil, leaving thin film in pan. Using ¼-cup measure, portion pancakes into pan, spreading each immediately into 3-inch round using back of spoon; you will fit about 3 pancakes in pan. Cook until first side is golden and bubbles on surface begin to break, about 3 minutes.

4. Flip pancakes and cook until second side is golden, about 3 minutes. Serve or transfer to wire rack in oven. Repeat with remaining oil and batter, whisking extra milk into batter as needed to loosen.

VARIATION
Dairy-Free Fluffy Oat Pancakes
We prefer the flavor and texture of these pancakes made with soy milk but almond milk will also work; do not use rice milk.

Substitute unsweetened soy milk for milk, and vegetable oil for melted butter.

Johnnycakes

G-F TESTING LAB

CORNMEAL	The test kitchen's favorite cornmeal for most applications, including this recipe, is finely ground Whole-Grain Arrowhead Mills Cornmeal. This brand has been processed in a gluten-free facility, but not all brands are. Make sure to read the label. See page 27 for more information.
RESTING TIME	Do not shortchange the batter's 15-minute rest or else the pancakes will be gritty.

✓ WHY THIS RECIPE WORKS

Johnnycakes, a Rhode Island specialty, are rich, crisp corn cakes that are a naturally gluten-free alternative to pancakes. Made from little more than cornmeal and water, they should be crisp on the outside and creamy in the middle. To avoid a gritty or sandy texture, we found that, after we combined the dry ingredients and then whisked them into boiling water and stirred in some butter, we needed to let the batter sit for 15 minutes to soften the grains for a consistently smooth interior. To ensure that they didn't fall apart when flipped in the pan, we let the johnnycakes set completely on the first side before gently turning and flattening them so they would be evenly cooked throughout. Johnnycakes are best served warm with maple butter (or maple syrup) for breakfast, or as a side dish for soups and stews. Do not try to turn the johnnycakes too soon or they will fall apart. If you prefer crispier johnnycakes, press them thinner in step 5.

Johnnycakes

MAKES TWELVE 3-INCH JOHNNYCAKES; SERVES 3 TO 4

- 1   cup (5 ounces) stone-ground cornmeal
- 2   teaspoons sugar
- ¾   teaspoon salt
- 2¾ cups water, plus extra as needed
- 2   tablespoons unsalted butter
- 2   tablespoons vegetable oil

1. Set wire rack in rimmed baking sheet. Adjust oven rack to middle position, place prepared sheet on oven rack, and heat oven to 200 degrees.

2. Whisk cornmeal, sugar, and salt together in bowl. Bring water to boil in large saucepan. Slowly whisk in cornmeal mixture until no lumps remain, and cook until thickened, about 30 seconds. Off heat, whisk in butter. Pour batter into bowl, cover with plastic wrap, and let batter rest at room temperature until slightly firm, about 15 minutes.

3. Rewhisk batter until smooth. Batter should be consistency of mashed potatoes; if not, whisk in 1 to 2 tablespoons extra hot water as needed.

4. Heat 1 tablespoon oil in 12-inch nonstick skillet over medium heat until shimmering. Using greased ¼-cup measure, portion 6 cakes into pan. Cook until edges are crisp and golden brown, 6 to 8 minutes.

5. Carefully flip cakes and press with spatula to flatten into 2½- to 3-inch rounds. Cook until well browned on second side, 5 to 7 minutes. Serve or transfer to wire rack in oven. Repeat with remaining oil and batter, whisking extra hot water into batter as needed to loosen.

VARIATION

Dairy-Free Johnnycakes

Substitute 1 tablespoon Earth Balance Vegan Buttery Sticks for both tablespoons of butter.

Maple Butter

MAKES ¼ CUP

If using salted butter, omit the salt.

- 4   tablespoons unsalted butter, softened
- 1   tablespoon maple syrup
- ¼   teaspoon salt

Whisk all ingredients together in bowl. (Butter can be refrigerated for up to 1 week.)

TEST KITCHEN TIP **Shaping Johnnycakes**

1. Use greased ¼-cup dry measuring cup to carefully portion 6 mounds of batter into hot pan.

2. When edges are crisp and brown, carefully flip cakes and gently flatten with spatula.

Whole-Grain Waffles

G-F TESTING LAB

FLOUR SUBSTITUTION	Do not substitute other whole-grain blends for the ATK Whole-Grain Gluten-Free Flour Blend; they will not work in this recipe.
BAKING POWDER	Not all brands of baking powder are gluten-free; see page 25 for more information.
RESTING TIME	Do not shortchange the batter's 30-minute rest or else the waffles will be dense.
COOKING TIME	These waffles may require a longer cooking time than usual.
ADDING FRUIT	For berry waffles, sprinkle 1 tablespoon berries (chopped if large) over surface of each waffle immediately after adding batter to waffle iron, and cook as directed.

WHY THIS RECIPE WORKS

We wanted a gluten-free whole-grain waffle recipe that produced crisp-on-the-outside, moist-on-the-inside waffles. We liked the idea of a classic buttermilk waffle, but unfortunately buttermilk tasted harsh in combination with our hearty whole-grain blend. We swapped out the buttermilk for low-fat milk, preferring the leaner, thinner batter along with the milder flavor. However, removing the buttermilk, the acidic component of this recipe, altered the effectiveness of the baking soda, which is acid-activated. This led to doughy, dense waffles. After numerous tests of combinations of baking powder and baking soda, we found that we liked baking powder alone the best. It gave the waffles a lighter structure and a fluffy rise. But we still noticed a slightly gritty texture. Letting the batter sit at room temperature for 30 minutes allowed the starch granules to hydrate and soften before hitting the waffle iron. Although this step made for a less gritty waffle, the starches absorbed much of the moisture, so we increased the amount of milk to allow the starches to fully hydrate without turning our batter to cement. Our last challenge was to create a crisp exterior. Even straight out of the waffle iron, our waffles were soft. It turns out the interior moisture was making its way to the surface, causing our waffles to feel doughy from edge to edge. Since butter contains some water, and since fat repels moisture, we traded the butter for pure fat in the form of vegetable oil. Waffles made with oil were significantly crispier than those made with butter, but we missed the rich, buttery flavor that complemented the whole-grain blend so well. So instead we swapped in vegetable oil for only half of the butter, and this resulted in waffles that had a crisp exterior encasing a light interior, plus rich flavor. We prefer the crisper texture provided by a Belgian waffle iron, but a classic waffle iron will also work, though it will make more waffles. Do not substitute skim or whole milk in this recipe.

Whole-Grain Waffles

MAKES FOUR 7-INCH BELGIAN WAFFLES; SERVES 4

- 12 ounces (2⅔ cups) ATK Whole-Grain Gluten-Free Flour Blend (page 9)
- 1¾ ounces (¼ cup) sugar
- 1 teaspoon baking powder
- ½ teaspoon salt
- 2 cups 1 or 2 percent low-fat milk, plus extra as needed
- 3 large eggs
- 2 tablespoons unsalted butter, melted and cooled
- 2 tablespoons vegetable oil
- 1 teaspoon vanilla extract

1. Set wire rack in rimmed baking sheet. Adjust oven rack to middle position, place prepared sheet on oven rack, and heat oven to 200 degrees.

2. Whisk flour blend, sugar, baking powder, and salt together in large bowl. In separate bowl, whisk milk, eggs, melted butter, oil, and vanilla together until combined. Whisk milk mixture into flour mixture until well incorporated, batter has thickened, and no lumps remain, about 1 minute. Cover bowl with plastic wrap and let batter rest at room temperature for 30 minutes.

3. Heat waffle iron and cook waffles according to manufacturer's instructions, until each waffle is deep golden brown and has crisp, firm exterior (use about 1 cup batter for Belgian waffle iron and scant ¾ cup for 7-inch round iron). Serve or transfer to wire rack in oven. Repeat with remaining batter, whisking extra milk into batter as needed to loosen.

VARIATION

Dairy-Free Whole-Grain Waffles

We prefer the flavor and texture of these waffles made with almond milk but soy milk will also work; do not use rice milk.

Substitute unsweetened almond milk for milk, and vegetable oil for melted butter.

Whole-Grain Blueberry Muffins

FLOUR SUBSTITUTION	Do not substitute other whole-grain blends for the ATK Whole-Grain Gluten-Free Flour Blend; they will not work in this recipe.
BAKING POWDER	Not all brands of baking powder are gluten-free; see page 25 for more information.
XANTHAN GUM	The xanthan can be omitted, but the muffins will be crumbly and more difficult to get out of the pan.
RESTING TIME	Do not shortchange the batter's 30-minute rest or else the muffins will be gritty.

WHY THIS RECIPE WORKS

We set out to create a tender blueberry muffin using our whole-grain gluten-free flour blend to deliver earthy, nutty flavor. Our starting point was testing types and amounts of liquid, as we knew this would significantly affect the texture of the muffins. We settled on yogurt, which added moisture without making the batter too loose. We needed a full cup, but it added a sour flavor. Instead we swapped in a little heavy cream for some of the yogurt, which nicely hydrated the flours and made the texture more substantial. However, the muffins were still a bit gritty and dense. To fix this, we needed to make the batter more loose, because the flours in the whole-grain blend absorbed more liquid as the batter sat. And while we typically use two eggs in a muffin recipe, this thick batter needed three to achieve the proper richness and structure. To get an open crumb we quickly learned that we needed both baking powder and baking soda; muffins made with both leaveners were lighter in texture, and they had a domed top and were more golden brown than muffins made with just baking powder. This was because the baking soda helped neutralize the acid in the yogurt, which in turn allowed the baking powder to function more effectively. You can substitute frozen berries, rinsed well and blotted dry with paper towels; however, they will bleed slightly into the batter. See page 65 for tips on how to portion the muffin batter into the prepared tin and how to store the muffins after baking to preserve freshness.

Whole-Grain Blueberry Muffins
MAKES 12 MUFFINS

- 12 ounces (2⅔ cups) ATK Whole-Grain Gluten-Free Flour Blend (page 9)
- 4 teaspoons baking powder
- ¾ teaspoon baking soda
- ¾ teaspoon salt
- ¾ teaspoon ground cinnamon
- ¼ teaspoon xanthan gum
- 7 ounces (1 cup) granulated sugar
- 10 tablespoons unsalted butter, melted and cooled
- ½ cup plain whole-milk yogurt
- ⅓ cup heavy cream
- 3 large eggs
- 1½ teaspoons vanilla extract
- 7½ ounces (1½ cups) blueberries
- 2 tablespoons turbinado sugar

1. Whisk flour blend, baking powder, baking soda, salt, cinnamon, and xanthan gum together in large bowl. In separate bowl, whisk granulated sugar, melted butter, yogurt, cream, eggs, and vanilla together until well combined. Using rubber spatula, stir butter mixture into flour mixture until thoroughly combined and no lumps remain, about 1 minute (batter will be thick). Gently fold in blueberries. Cover bowl with plastic wrap and let batter rest at room temperature for 30 minutes.

2. Adjust oven rack to middle position and heat oven to 375 degrees. Spray 12-cup muffin tin with vegetable oil spray. Portion batter evenly into prepared muffin tin. Sprinkle turbinado sugar over top. Bake until muffins are golden and toothpick inserted in center comes out clean, 20 to 22 minutes, rotating pan halfway through baking.

3. Let muffins cool in pan for 10 minutes, then remove from pan and let cool on wire rack for 10 minutes longer. Serve.

VARIATION
Dairy-Free Whole-Grain Blueberry Muffins
We prefer the flavor and texture of these muffins made with coconut milk yogurt but soy milk yogurt will also work. We had good luck using Silk Soy Creamer.

Increase baking powder to 5 teaspoons. Substitute ½ cup vegetable oil for melted butter, plain coconut milk yogurt for whole-milk yogurt, and plain soy creamer for heavy cream.

Coconut-Cashew Muffins

G-F TESTING LAB

FLOUR SUBSTITUTION	King Arthur Gluten-Free Multi-Purpose Flour 9 ounces = **1½ cups plus 2 tablespoons**	Betty Crocker All-Purpose Gluten Free Rice Blend 9 ounces = **1½ cups plus ⅓ cup**
	Muffins made with King Arthur will have a tighter crumb and not rise as well; muffins made with Betty Crocker will have a slightly pasty texture.	
BAKING POWDER	Not all brands of baking powder are gluten-free; see page 25 for more information.	
XANTHAN GUM	The xanthan can be omitted, but the muffins will be crumbly and more difficult to get out of the pan.	
RESTING TIME	Do not shortchange the batter's 30-minute rest or else the muffins will be gritty.	

WHY THIS RECIPE WORKS

We set out to create a golden-domed coconut-cashew muffin with a moist, tender interior and rich, nutty flavor. For our basic muffin base, we found that, as with many of our other gluten-free muffins, it benefited from the additional structure, moisture, and richness gained by using three eggs instead of two; the extra egg boosted the flavor (the starch granules in gluten-free flour absorb so much flavor) and provided moisture, which this thick batter needed for a proper rise. To infuse our muffins with coconut flavor we started by mixing sweetened flaked coconut into the batter, but we didn't like the texture their long strands created. Pulsing the coconut in a food processor created smaller bits that distributed evenly throughout the batter. As for the cashews, tossing chopped cashews into the batter weighed it down, and the nut flavor was lackluster. Since we already had the food processor out, we tried processing the cashews into a nut flour that we could add to the flour blend. We liked the soft, light texture this gave us, but the muffins had an underwhelming cashew flavor. Increasing the amount of cashews from ½ cup to 1¼ cups provided the ideal balance of toasted coconut flavor and rich nuttiness. Finally, sprinkling the muffins with untoasted coconut and chopped cashews before baking gave them an appealingly crunchy top. Be sure to grease the muffin tin thoroughly, as these muffins tend to stick. See page 65 for tips on how to portion the muffin batter into the prepared tin and how to store the muffins after baking to preserve freshness.

Coconut-Cashew Muffins
MAKES 12 MUFFINS

1⅔   cups sweetened flaked coconut
8   tablespoons unsalted butter, melted and cooled
3   large eggs
½   cup plain whole-milk yogurt
2   tablespoons water
½   teaspoon vanilla extract
5¼   ounces (¾ cup) sugar
1¼   cups roasted cashews, chopped
9   ounces (2 cups) ATK All-Purpose Gluten-Free Flour Blend (page 7)
1   tablespoon baking powder
½   teaspoon salt
¼   teaspoon xanthan gum

1. Adjust oven rack to middle position and heat oven to 375 degrees. Spread 1⅓ cups coconut over rimmed baking sheet and bake, stirring frequently, until lightly golden, 7 to 10 minutes. Let coconut cool for 15 minutes, then pulse in food processor until finely chopped, about 10 pulses; transfer to bowl. In separate bowl, whisk melted butter, eggs, yogurt, water, and vanilla together.

2. Process sugar and 1 cup cashews in now-empty food processor to coarse sand, 10 to 15 seconds. Add flour blend, baking powder, salt, and xanthan gum and pulse until well combined, 5 to 10 pulses. Add butter mixture and process until thoroughly combined and no lumps remain, about 30 seconds. Transfer mixture to large bowl and fold in toasted, chopped coconut (batter will be thick and stiff). Cover bowl with plastic wrap and let batter rest at room temperature for 30 minutes.

3. Spray 12-cup muffin tin thoroughly with vegetable oil spray. Portion batter evenly into prepared muffin tin. Combine remaining ¼ cup cashews with remaining ⅓ cup untoasted coconut and sprinkle over muffins. Bake until muffins are golden and toothpick inserted in center comes out clean, 18 to 20 minutes, rotating pan halfway through baking.

4. Let muffins cool in pan for 10 minutes, then remove from pan and let cool on wire rack for 10 minutes longer. Serve.

VARIATION
Dairy-Free Coconut-Cashew Muffins
We prefer the flavor of these muffins made with coconut milk yogurt but soy milk yogurt will also work.

Substitute vegetable oil for butter, and ⅔ cup plain coconut milk yogurt for whole-milk yogurt.

Corn Muffins

G-F TESTING LAB

FLOUR SUBSTITUTION	King Arthur Gluten-Free Multi-Purpose Flour 7½ ounces = **1¼ cups plus 2 tablespoons**	Betty Crocker All-Purpose Gluten Free Rice Blend 7½ ounces = **1½ cups**
	Muffins made with King Arthur will have a tighter crumb; muffins made with Betty Crocker will have a tighter crumb and the edges will be less crisp.	
CORNMEAL	Not all brands of cornmeal are gluten-free; see page 27 for more information.	
BAKING POWDER	Not all brands of baking powder are gluten-free; see page 25 for more information.	
XANTHAN GUM	The xanthan can be omitted, but the muffins will be more crumbly.	
RESTING TIME	Do not shortchange the batter's 30-minute rest or else the muffins will be gritty.	

WHY THIS RECIPE WORKS

For gluten-free corn muffins with a tender crumb, we started with the classic corn muffin ratio of two parts flour to one part cornmeal using our all-purpose gluten-free flour blend, but we found ourselves with crumbly, starchy, and bland muffins. By tipping the scale to use almost equal parts cornmeal and flour blend, we were able to create a moister crumb with a more powerful corn flavor. Unfortunately, we still had a slightly dry and lean muffin on our hands. We tried adding an extra egg, but that resulted in an overwhelming eggy flavor that overpowered the sweet corn-flavored base. Instead, we increased the milk and sour cream amounts to provide the necessary moisture and emulsified fats. In order to get an appealingly crisp edge, we brushed the tops of the muffin batter with melted butter and started baking them at 500 degrees. Halfway through baking, we reduced the oven temperature to 400 degrees, which allowed the interiors time to fully cook while the tops finished crisping up. Now we had rustic-looking gluten-free corn muffins with crisp, buttery edges, a soft but firm interior crumb, and a bold, sweet corn flavor. See page 65 for tips on how to portion the muffin batter into the prepared tin and how to store the muffins after baking to preserve freshness.

Corn Muffins

MAKES 12 MUFFINS

7½ ounces (1⅔ cups) ATK All-Purpose
     Gluten-Free Flour Blend (page 7)
6⅔ ounces (1⅓ cups) stone-ground cornmeal
1½ teaspoons baking powder
 1 teaspoon baking soda
 ½ teaspoon salt
 ¼ teaspoon xanthan gum

1⅓ cups sour cream
5¼ ounces (¾ cup) sugar
 ⅔ cup whole milk
 2 large eggs
10 tablespoons unsalted butter,
     melted and cooled

1. Whisk flour blend, cornmeal, baking powder, baking soda, salt, and xanthan gum together in medium bowl. In separate bowl, whisk sour cream, sugar, milk, eggs, and 8 tablespoons melted butter together until well combined. Using rubber spatula, stir sour cream mixture into flour mixture until thoroughly combined and no lumps remain, about 1 minute. Cover bowl with plastic wrap and let batter rest at room temperature for 30 minutes.

2. Adjust oven rack to middle position and heat oven to 500 degrees. Spray 12-cup muffin tin with vegetable oil spray. Portion batter evenly into prepared muffin tin. Brush remaining 2 tablespoons melted butter over top. Bake muffins for 7 minutes.

3. Reduce oven temperature to 400 degrees, rotate muffin tin, and continue to bake muffins until golden brown and toothpick inserted in center comes out clean, about 7 minutes.

4. Let muffins cool in pan for 10 minutes, then remove from pan and let cool on wire rack for 10 minutes longer. Serve.

VARIATION

Dairy-Free Corn Muffins

We prefer the flavor and texture of these muffins made with soy milk but almond milk will also work; do not use rice milk.

Use dairy-free sour cream. Substitute unsweetened soy milk for milk, and vegetable oil for melted butter. Add 2 additional tablespoons sugar to sour cream mixture in step 1.

Currant Scones

FLOUR SUBSTITUTION	King Arthur Gluten-Free Multi-Purpose Flour 7½ ounces = **1¼ cups plus 2 tablespoons**	Betty Crocker All-Purpose Gluten Free Rice Blend 7½ ounces = **1½ cups**
	Scones made with King Arthur will have a stickier dough and taste slightly chewy; scones made with Betty Crocker will be starchy and taste slightly rubbery.	
BAKING POWDER	Not all brands of baking powder are gluten-free; see page 25 for more information.	
XANTHAN GUM	Xanthan is crucial to the structure of the scones; see page 22 for more information.	
RESTING TIME	Do not shortchange the dough's 30-minute rest or else the scones will be harder to shape, they will spread, and they will taste gritty.	

✓ WHY THIS RECIPE WORKS

Even the best traditional bakeshops often come up short when they attempt to make gluten-free scones—the results are usually gritty, crumbly, and pale. We set out to make a light and tender scone with a buttery flavor and gentle sweetness. To fix the crumbly texture we found that a two-part solution worked best. A small amount of xanthan gum acted as a binding agent and provided the structure and stability we were missing, while an egg added additional structure along with moisture and elasticity. For scones with a light, not dense, texture, we added a full tablespoon of baking powder, and to eliminate grittiness we found that resting the dough for 30 minutes before shaping the scones hydrated the flour and softened its texture. The resting step also helped thicken the wet dough a bit and made it easier to shape. For our dairy component, we noticed that scones made with milk or cream spread way too much, and the dough was difficult to work with. Switching to thicker sour cream solved those problems. To achieve a golden crust and a nice rise, scones are typically baked at a high temperature, but we struggled to get a nice color on the tops of the scones without burning the bottoms. Lowering the oven temperature seemed like a natural solution, but we needed to bake them so long that they dried out. We had better luck preheating the oven at a high temperature and dropping it down slightly when putting the scones in the oven. We also found that using a second baking sheet as insulation kept the bottoms from burning. Make sure to preheat your oven before you make the dough. Other types of dried fruit, such as cranberries, apricots, or raisins, can be chopped fine and substituted for the currants if desired.

Currant Scones

MAKES 6 SCONES

- 7½ ounces (1⅔ cups) ATK All-Purpose Gluten-Free Flour Blend (page 7)
- 3 tablespoons plus 1½ teaspoons sugar
- 1 tablespoon baking powder
- ¼ teaspoon salt
- ¼ teaspoon xanthan gum
- 6 tablespoons unsalted butter, cut into ½-inch pieces and chilled
- ⅓ cup dried currants
- ⅔ cup sour cream
- 1 large egg

1. Adjust oven rack to upper-middle position and heat oven to 500 degrees. Line rimmed baking sheet with parchment paper and place in second baking sheet. Lay large sheet of parchment paper flat on counter and spray with vegetable oil spray.

2. Pulse flour blend, 3 tablespoons sugar, baking powder, salt, and xanthan gum in food processor until combined, about 5 pulses. Add butter and pulse until fully incorporated and mixture resembles very fine crumbs with no butter pieces visible, about 10 pulses. Transfer mixture to large bowl and stir in currants.

3. In separate bowl, whisk together sour cream and egg until combined. Using rubber spatula, stir sour cream mixture into flour mixture until no dry bits of flour remain. Cover bowl with plastic wrap and let dough rest at room temperature for 30 minutes. (Do not let dough rest for longer than 30 minutes.)

4. Using wet hands, transfer dough to prepared parchment on counter. Clean and wet hands again. Pat dough into 6-inch round about 1 inch thick. Spray knife with vegetable oil spray and cut dough into 6 equal wedges. Arrange scones on prepared baking sheet and sprinkle remaining 1½ teaspoons sugar over top.

5. Reduce oven temperature to 425 degrees and bake scones until golden brown, 12 to 14 minutes, rotating sheet halfway through baking. Transfer scones to wire rack and let cool for 20 minutes before serving. (Scones can be wrapped individually in plastic wrap and frozen for up to 1 month; unwrap and thaw in microwave for 20 to 30 seconds, then refresh in 350-degree oven for 10 to 15 minutes.)

VARIATION

Dairy-Free Currant Scones

We had good luck using Tofutti Better Than Sour Cream.

Omit salt and use dairy-free sour cream. Substitute Earth Balance Vegan Buttery Sticks for butter. Increase sugar to ¼ cup in step 2.

TEST KITCHEN TIP **Making Scones**

The dough for the scones is fairly sticky, so using wet hands, greased parchment, and a greased knife makes shaping the dough easier.

1. Pulse dry ingredients in food processor until combined. Add butter and pulse until fully incorporated and mixture looks like very fine crumbs with no visible butter.

2. In separate bowl, whisk together sour cream and egg until combined. Using rubber spatula, stir sour cream mixture into flour and currant mixture until no dry bits of flour remain.

3. Cover bowl with plastic wrap and let dough rest at room temperature for 30 minutes.

4. With wet hands, transfer dough to large sheet of parchment paper greased with vegetable oil spray. Clean and wet hands again, then pat dough into 6-inch round about 1 inch thick.

5. Spray knife with vegetable oil spray and cut dough into 6 wedges.

6. Arrange scones on prepared baking sheet and sprinkle remaining 1½ teaspoons sugar over top.

Currant Scones

We wanted a recipe for gluten-free scones that were sweet, but not overly so, with a fluffy and delicate interior crumb. To achieve the same high rise and delicate crumb as traditional scones, we had to rework the recipe slightly.

1. REIN IN THE SUGAR AND FAT: To keep the sweetness level in check and make the scones less chewy, we reduced the amount of sugar to just a few tablespoons. And since the starches in the gluten-free flour blend don't absorb fat as readily as traditional flour does, we swapped out the milk for sour cream. The sour cream added richness and flavor without making the scones greasy, because it contains a more emulsified fat that doesn't leach out during baking.

2. ADD XANTHAN GUM AND AN EGG FOR STRUCTURE: While traditional scones rely on gluten for structure, we had to find another source. Adding xanthan gum (as we had done in other recipes) helped reinforce the weak structure in the gluten-free flours and helped retain moisture to prevent the scones from becoming dry and crumbly. An egg provided additional structure along with moisture and elasticity.

3. DOUBLE UP ON THE SHEET PANS: Because we were placing the scones in a very hot oven, the bottoms were getting overly browned. Since we needed the hot oven for the rise, the only solution for protecting the bottom of the scones was to use a second baking sheet as insulation.

4. BAKE HIGH, THEN LOW: Hoping to get scones with good height and a tender crumb, we preheated our oven to 500 degrees to maximize "oven spring," which is the final burst of rising that happens when water vaporizes into steam and the air in the dough heats up and expands. The more oven spring, the lighter the crumb; with very little oven spring, you end up with a denser texture. After placing the scones in the oven we lowered the temperature to 425 degrees to ensure the crust would not burn before the interior cooked through.

Date-Nut Bread

G-F TESTING LAB

FLOUR SUBSTITUTION	King Arthur Gluten-Free Multi-Purpose Flour 10 ounces = **1½ cups plus ⅓ cup**	Betty Crocker All-Purpose Gluten Free Rice Blend 10 ounces = **2 cups**
	Bread made with King Arthur will be quite delicate and crumbly; bread made with Betty Crocker will be slightly wet and pasty.	
BAKING POWDER	Not all brands of baking powder are gluten-free; see page 25 for more information.	
XANTHAN GUM	The xanthan can be omitted, but the bread will be more crumbly and have less structure.	

✓ WHY THIS RECIPE WORKS

The dense texture and unmitigated sweetness of most date breads, whether gluten-free or not, can ruin an otherwise delicious breakfast treat. We wanted a lightly sweet bread, studded equally with dates and nuts, that was also moist and tender. To start, we simply swapped in our all-purpose gluten-free flour blend for regular all-purpose flour in one of our favorite recipes from our archives. Unsurprisingly, the loaf we sliced into a few hours later was dense and pasty, and it crumbled apart during slicing. The recipe we started from used buttermilk, but not enough, yet going up on buttermilk helped only to a point: As we increased the overall amount of buttermilk, the loaf became more moist, but it also became correspondingly wet and dense. We found 1 cup provided the best balance, though we were still plagued by a slightly dry, overly tender loaf. Adding an extra egg helped to add moisture and richness without weighing down the rise, and it also contributed binding power so we could easily cut clean slices from the loaf. To create a more open, tender crumb we took a closer look at the combination of baking powder and baking soda in our bread. Baking soda reacts with acidic ingredients, like buttermilk, to produce carbon dioxide, which creates rise in baked goods. Increasing the overall amount of baking soda from 1 to 1½ teaspoons created an even, open crumb, and, as added insurance against a heavy bread, we decreased the overall amount of dates from 10 ounces to just 6 ounces, resulting in a light, just slightly sweet, and tender date bread. The test kitchen's preferred loaf pan measures 8½ by 4½ inches; if you use a 9 by 5-inch loaf pan, start checking for doneness 10 minutes early.

Date-Nut Bread
MAKES 1 LOAF

- **10   ounces (2¼ cups) ATK All-Purpose Gluten-Free Flour Blend (page 7)**
- **1½   teaspoons baking soda**
- **1   teaspoon baking powder**
- **½   teaspoon salt**
- **¼   teaspoon xanthan gum**
- **1   cup buttermilk**
- **5¼   ounces (¾ cup packed) dark brown sugar**
- **6   tablespoons unsalted butter, melted and cooled**
- **2   large eggs**
- **1   cup pitted dates, chopped**
- **1   cup walnuts, toasted and chopped**

1. Adjust oven rack to middle position and heat oven to 350 degrees. Grease 8½ by 4½-inch loaf pan.

2. Whisk flour blend, baking soda, baking powder, salt, and xanthan gum together in large bowl. In separate bowl, whisk buttermilk, sugar, melted butter, and eggs together until well combined. Using rubber spatula, stir buttermilk mixture into flour mixture until thoroughly combined and no lumps remain, about 1 minute. Fold in dates and walnuts.

3. Scrape batter into prepared pan and smooth top. Bake until deep golden brown and toothpick inserted in center comes out clean, about 1 hour, rotating pan halfway through baking.

4. Let bread cool in pan for 20 minutes, then remove from pan and let cool on wire rack for 1 hour before serving. (Cooled bread can be wrapped in plastic wrap and stored at room temperature for up to 2 days; refresh in 300-degree oven for 10 to 15 minutes.)

VARIATION
Dairy-Free Date-Nut Bread
We prefer the flavor and texture of this bread made with soy milk but almond milk will also work; do not use rice milk.

Substitute 1 cup unsweetened soy milk mixed with 1 tablespoon distilled white vinegar (or lemon juice) for buttermilk. Substitute vegetable oil for melted butter.

Whole-Grain Chai Spice Bread

G-F TESTING LAB

FLOUR SUBSTITUTION	Do not substitute other whole-grain blends for the ATK Whole-Grain Gluten-Free Flour Blend; they will not work in this recipe.
BAKING POWDER	Not all brands of baking powder are gluten-free; see page 25 for more information.
XANTHAN GUM	The xanthan can be omitted, but the bread will be more crumbly and slightly denser.

✓ WHY THIS RECIPE WORKS

For a quick-bread recipe using our whole-grain flour blend, we looked to the modern flavor of chai spice to match our flour's earthy profile. It can be difficult to create harmony among the spices found in chai (cinnamon, cardamom, ginger, clove, and sometimes even black pepper), so instead we steeped chai-flavored tea bags in warm milk and then incorporated the spiced milk into the batter for well-rounded flavor. In our initial testing we used brown sugar as our sweetener but found that the rich, molasses-like flavor muddled the chai spices. Switching to granulated sugar gave our bread a cleaner flavor. To give this dense, hearty bread some lift, we ramped up the baking powder to a whopping four teaspoons. We also found it necessary to add extra liquid in order to hydrate and soften the whole-grain flours. Unfortunately, all this additional liquid left the bread with a wet, spongy texture. To dry it out, we continued to bake the bread 10 minutes beyond the point at which a toothpick inserted in the center came out clean. The downside of the increased baking time, however, was crumbly bread that didn't slice cleanly. Luckily, adding a smidgen of xanthan gum fixed this. The test kitchen's preferred loaf pan measures 8½ by 4½ inches; if you use a 9 by 5-inch loaf pan, start checking for doneness 10 minutes early.

Whole-Grain Chai Spice Bread

MAKES 1 LOAF

- 1¼ cups whole milk
- 3 chai-flavored tea bags
- 12 ounces (2⅔ cups) ATK Whole-Grain Gluten-Free Flour Blend (page 9)
- 4 teaspoons baking powder
- 1½ teaspoons salt
- ¼ teaspoon xanthan gum
- 7 ounces (1 cup) plus 1 tablespoon sugar
- 8 tablespoons unsalted butter, melted and cooled
- 2 large eggs
- 1 teaspoon vanilla extract
- ½ cup walnuts, toasted and chopped (optional)

1. Adjust oven rack to middle position and heat oven to 325 degrees. Grease 8½ by 4½-inch loaf pan. Bring milk to simmer in saucepan over medium-high heat. Remove pot from heat, add tea bags, and steep until fragrant, 4 to 6 minutes. Discard tea bags.

2. Whisk flour blend, baking powder, salt, and xanthan gum together in large bowl. In separate bowl, whisk spiced milk, 1 cup sugar, melted butter, eggs, and vanilla together until well combined. Using rubber spatula, stir milk mixture into flour mixture until thoroughly combined and no lumps remain, about 1 minute. Fold in walnuts, if using.

3. Scrape batter into prepared pan, smooth top, and sprinkle with remaining 1 tablespoon sugar. Bake until toothpick inserted in center comes out clean, 60 to 70 minutes, rotating pan halfway through baking, then continue to bake for 10 minutes longer.

4. Let bread cool in pan for 20 minutes, then remove from pan and let cool on wire rack for 1 hour before serving. (Cooled bread can be wrapped in plastic wrap and stored at room temperature for up to 2 days.)

VARIATION

Dairy-Free Whole-Grain Chai Spice Bread
We prefer the flavor and texture of this bread made with soy milk but almond milk will also work; do not use rice milk.

Substitute unsweetened soy milk for milk, and vegetable oil for melted butter.

SMART SHOPPING **Chai Tea**

Chai is a fragrant Indian black-tea blend that often includes cardamom, cinnamon, clove, ginger, and black pepper, though the exact formulation can vary from brand to brand; you can find it in any supermarket. We tested this recipe with several brands of caffeinated and decaffeinated chai, and they all worked equally well.

Whole-Grain Gingerbread Coffee Cake

G-F TESTING LAB

FLOUR SUBSTITUTION	Do not substitute other whole-grain blends for the ATK Whole-Grain Gluten-Free Flour Blend; they will not work in this recipe.
BAKING POWDER	Not all brands of baking powder are gluten-free; see page 25 for more information.
XANTHAN GUM	The xanthan can be omitted, but the cake will be crumbly and more difficult to get out of the pan.

WHY THIS RECIPE WORKS

For a wholesome version of a brunch favorite, we set our sights on developing a rich gluten-free gingerbread-flavored coffee cake using our whole-grain flour blend. The traditional creaming method yielded a gritty, gummy brick of a cake. We tried whipping the batter longer, which aerated it more, yet the cake was still dense because the sour cream we used to moisten the cake created a very thick, dense batter. Switching to a combination of ½ cup sour cream and 1½ cups milk got us closer, but our cake still wasn't rising enough—and it was also now very wet. A hefty amount of baking powder plus the addition of baking soda helped, but the extra liquid we added to hydrate the flours and loosen the batter meant that the cake would need an extended baking time. We baked it until a skewer came out clean, and then continued to bake it for an additional 20 minutes for a cake that was still moist with a tender crumb. Topped with a coffee-flavored glaze, this cake makes a satisfying morning treat. Do not substitute low-fat or nonfat milk in this recipe.

Whole-Grain Gingerbread Coffee Cake

SERVES 12 TO 16

CAKE

- 1½ cups whole milk, room temperature
- ½ cup sour cream, room temperature
- 3 large eggs, room temperature
- 12 ounces (2⅔ cups) ATK Whole-Grain Gluten-Free Flour Blend (page 9)
- 5 teaspoons baking powder
- 2 teaspoons ground ginger
- 1½ teaspoons salt
- 1½ teaspoons baking soda
- 1 teaspoon ground cinnamon
- ½ teaspoon ground allspice
- ½ teaspoon ground cloves
- ½ teaspoon ground nutmeg
- ¼ teaspoon xanthan gum
- 8¾ ounces (1¼ cups) granulated sugar
- 10 tablespoons unsalted butter, softened

GLAZE

- 3 tablespoons whole milk
- 1 tablespoon instant espresso or instant coffee
- 7 ounces (1¾ cups) confectioners' sugar

1. FOR THE CAKE: Adjust oven rack to middle position and heat oven to 350 degrees. Grease 12-cup nonstick Bundt pan. Whisk milk, sour cream, and eggs together in bowl. In separate bowl, whisk flour blend, baking powder, ginger, salt, baking soda, cinnamon, allspice, cloves, nutmeg, and xanthan gum together.

2. Using stand mixer fitted with paddle, beat sugar and butter on medium-high speed until light and fluffy, about 3 minutes. Reduce mixer speed to low and gradually add egg mixture, about 1 minute, scraping down bowl as needed (batter may look curdled). Gradually add flour mixture and mix until incorporated. Scrape down bowl, increase speed to medium-high, and beat until batter is light and fluffy, about 6 minutes.

3. Give batter final stir by hand. Transfer batter to prepared pan. Bake cake until skewer inserted in center comes out clean, 45 to 50 minutes, then continue to bake for 20 minutes longer.

4. Let cake cool in pan for 30 minutes, then remove from pan and let cool on wire rack for 1 hour.

5. FOR THE GLAZE: Whisk 2 tablespoons milk and espresso together until dissolved. Whisk in sugar until smooth. Gradually add remaining 1 tablespoon milk as needed until glaze is thick but pourable. Pour glaze over cooled cake, letting it drip down sides, and let set for 10 minutes. Serve. (Cake can be stored in airtight container for up to 2 days.)

VARIATION

Dairy-Free Whole-Grain Gingerbread Coffee Cake

Almond milk can be substituted for the soy milk; do not use rice milk.

Substitute unsweetened soy milk for milk and Earth Balance Vegan Buttery Sticks for butter. Use dairy-free sour cream. Reduce salt to 1 teaspoon.

New York–Style Crumb Cake

G-F TESTING LAB

FLOUR SUBSTITUTION	King Arthur Gluten-Free Multi-Purpose Flour 6 ounces = ¾ cup plus ⅓ cup	Betty Crocker All-Purpose Gluten Free Rice Blend 6 ounces = ⅔ cup plus ½ cup
	Cake made with King Arthur will be slightly greasy and won't rise as well, and the crumbs on top will melt together; cake made with Betty Crocker will be springy and slightly dense.	
XANTHAN GUM	The xanthan can be omitted, but the cake will be slightly drier and more crumbly, and it won't store as well.	

WHY THIS RECIPE WORKS

The essence of this cake is the balance between the tender, buttery cake and the thick layer of spiced crumbs that cover the top. To develop a gluten-free version, we knew we'd need to first focus on the cake and find a way to add structure, since gluten-free flours are lower in protein. We were after a cake with a dense, rich, and buttery crumb that could support a substantial topping. We tried just subbing in our all-purpose gluten-free flour blend in the test kitchen's original recipe, but the cake was flat and wet. To make a sturdier cake that would properly support the crumbs, we added an extra egg and yolk to the original. For buttery flavor, we stuck with the 6 tablespoons of butter in our original recipe. To solve the wetness issue, we swapped out the buttermilk for sour cream, which added richness without making our batter overly wet. Our cake issues solved, we turned to the topping, which proved to be more of a hurdle than we expected. Normally a mixture of flour, sugars, and butter, with gluten-free flour it became too sandy and was not cohesive. We tried a few options to fix this, and surprisingly an egg yolk was the winner. It kept our topping moist enough yet still distinct and crumbly like a proper crumb cake. It made large, doughlike crumbs that broke apart into little nuggets that we sprinkled over the batter. The nuggets held together when baked, giving us sturdy crumbs that remained tender on the inside.

New York–Style Crumb Cake

SERVES 8

TOPPING

8	tablespoons unsalted butter, melted and still warm
2⅓	ounces (⅓ cup) granulated sugar
2⅓	ounces (⅓ cup packed) dark brown sugar

1	large egg yolk
¾	teaspoon ground cinnamon
⅛	teaspoon salt
6	ounces (1⅓ cups) ATK All-Purpose Gluten-Free Flour Blend (page 7)

CAKE

6	ounces (1⅓ cups) ATK All-Purpose Gluten-Free Flour Blend (page 7)
3½	ounces (½ cup) granulated sugar
½	teaspoon baking soda
¼	teaspoon salt
¼	teaspoon xanthan gum
6	tablespoons unsalted butter, cut into 6 pieces and softened
½	cup sour cream
2	large eggs plus 1 large yolk
1	teaspoon vanilla extract
	Confectioners' sugar, for serving

1. FOR THE TOPPING: Whisk melted butter, granulated sugar, brown sugar, egg yolk, cinnamon, and salt in bowl to combine. Stir in flour blend with rubber spatula until mixture resembles thick, cohesive dough; set aside.

2. FOR THE CAKE: Adjust oven rack to upper-middle position and heat oven to 325 degrees. Cut 16-inch length of parchment paper (or aluminum foil) and fold lengthwise to 7-inch width. Spray 8-inch square baking pan with vegetable oil spray and fit parchment into pan, pushing it up sides; allow excess to overhang edges of pan.

3. Using stand mixer fitted with paddle, mix flour blend, granulated sugar, baking soda, salt, and xanthan gum on low speed to combine. Add butter, 1 piece at a time, and continue to mix until mixture resembles moist crumbs with no visible butter chunks remaining, 1 to 2 minutes. Add sour cream, eggs and yolk, and vanilla, increase mixer speed to medium-high, and beat until batter is light and fluffy, about 1 minute, scraping down bowl as needed.

4. Scrape batter into prepared pan and smooth top. Break topping into large pea-size pieces and sprinkle evenly over batter. Bake until crumbs are golden and wooden skewer inserted in center of cake comes out clean, 35 to 40 minutes, rotating pan halfway through baking.

5. Let cake cool in pan for 30 minutes. Remove cake from pan using parchment sling and transfer to platter. Dust with confectioners' sugar before serving. (Cake can be stored in airtight container at room temperature for up to 3 days.)

VARIATION

Dairy-Free New York–Style Crumb Cake
In topping, substitute Earth Balance Vegan Buttery Sticks for butter and omit salt. In cake, omit salt, substitute Earth Balance Vegan Buttery Sticks for butter, and use dairy-free sour cream.

TEST KITCHEN TIP **Making New York–Style Crumb Cake**

1. To make topping, whisk butter, sugars, yolk, cinnamon, and salt in bowl to combine. Stir in flour blend with rubber spatula until mixture resembles thick, cohesive dough; set aside.

2. Make cake batter, scrape into prepared pan, and smooth top.

3. Break topping into large pea-size pieces and sprinkle evenly over batter.

TEST KITCHEN TIP **Cooling and Storing Gluten-Free Muffins and Quick Breads**

Like their traditional counterparts, our gluten-free muffins, quick breads, and coffee cake should be cooled in the tin or pan for a short stint once they come out of the oven. This gives them time to set up, reducing the chance they'll break when you remove them. Then let them cool further, as directed in the recipe, before serving.

However, don't let them sit out for an extended time—our gluten-free muffins, quick breads, and coffee cake may taste as good as versions made with all-purpose flour, but their shelf life is shorter. The high starch content in gluten-free flour absorbs moisture much more quickly than traditional all-purpose flour does, making these baked goods dry and crumbly fairly quickly. Consequently, we highly recommend eating them as soon as they are cooled. Letting them sit out even a couple of hours beyond our recommended times makes a big difference in quality.

If you want to store leftovers, we found that they will all keep acceptably well for a day or two at room temperature (don't refrigerate them, as this only makes them drier). Quick breads and coffee cake don't freeze well, but muffins freeze quite nicely (and you can conveniently thaw them individually as needed). To avoid a starchy aftertaste, we also learned that reheating leftover muffins and quick breads is a must.

1. Once baked, cool in tin/pan on wire rack for time noted in recipe, then remove and let cool as directed. Serve or store immediately.

2. To store muffins for up to 1 day, immediately transfer cooled muffins to zipper-lock bag and store at room temperature. To store quick breads for up to 2 days, immediately wrap in plastic wrap and store at room temperature. To serve, warm in 300-degree oven for 10 to 15 minutes.

3. To store muffins for up to 3 weeks, wrap each cooled muffin individually in plastic wrap, transfer to zipper-lock bag, and freeze. To serve, remove plastic and microwave muffin for 20 to 30 seconds, then warm in 350-degree oven for 10 minutes.

TEST KITCHEN TIP **Pay Attention to Portioning**

Not only does portioning the muffin batter haphazardly result in muffins that are of various sizes—some may overflow the cups while others look awkwardly small—but it also means the muffins may cook unevenly. We like to use a ⅓-cup dry measuring cup, large spoon, or spring-loaded #16 ice cream scoop. Whichever tool you use to portion the batter, spray it with vegetable oil spray so that the batter slides off easily.

For neat, evenly sized muffins, portion ⅓ cup batter into each cup using measuring cup or ice cream scoop, then circle back and evenly distribute remaining batter with spoon.

Yeasted Doughnuts

G-F TESTING LAB

FLOUR SUBSTITUTION	Do not substitute other all-purpose blends for the ATK All-Purpose Gluten-Free Flour Blend; they will not work in this recipe.
PSYLLIUM HUSK	Psyllium is crucial to the structure of the doughnuts; see page 26 for more information.
BAKING POWDER	Not all brands of baking powder are gluten-free; see page 25 for more information.
XANTHAN GUM	Xanthan is crucial to the structure of the doughnuts; see page 22 for more information.

WHY THIS RECIPE WORKS

If there is one thing many people crave when they need to eat gluten-free, it's a great yeasted doughnut, one with a slightly crisp exterior and a tender interior. Using our gluten-free flour blend as the base proved to be the perfect start, as the potato starch in the blend created a tender crumb and the tapioca starch added elasticity. After our first test, we went down on fat by decreasing the amount of butter by 2 tablespoons and using low-fat milk instead of whole, which gave us a rich dairy flavor without weighing down the dough. To keep the doughnuts together, we first tried adding just xanthan gum, but we needed too much and the doughnuts became tough. A combination of xanthan gum and powdered psyllium husk gave us a nice chew. For a rich yeasty flavor we used a full tablespoon of yeast but added baking powder and baking soda to help the doughnuts rise and maintain their shape during proofing and frying. To get the quickest possible rise before the gluten-free flours absorbed all of the liquid, we jump-started the yeast in warmed milk and let the doughnuts rise in a warmed oven for the first 10 minutes. After just 30 minutes of rising (10 minutes in the oven and 20 on the counter), the doughnuts were ready to fry. We dropped them into 350-degree oil (which is a standard frying temperature), but in just 30 seconds the doughnuts' exteriors began to burn. We tried frying them for less time, but the interiors remained raw. Lowering the frying temperature to 325 degrees allowed us to fry the doughnuts longer, which ensured that the interiors and exteriors were done at the same time. Although a lower frying temperature would traditionally cause doughnuts to absorb more oil and become greasy, gluten-free flours do not absorb fat as readily as wheat flour does, so this was not a problem. If you don't have a doughnut cutter, you can improvise with two biscuit cutters: Use a standard cutter (about 2½ inches) for cutting out the doughnuts, and a smaller one (about 1¼ inches) for cutting out the holes. Do not substitute nonfat or whole milk in this recipe.

Yeasted Doughnuts

MAKES ABOUT 10 DOUGHNUTS AND 10 HOLES

- ¾ cup 1 or 2 percent low-fat milk, warmed to 110 degrees
- 1 tablespoon instant or rapid-rise yeast
- 2⅓ ounces (⅓ cup) plus 1 teaspoon granulated sugar
- 4 tablespoons unsalted butter, melted and cooled
- 2 large eggs
- 12½ ounces (2¾ cups) ATK All-Purpose Gluten-Free Flour Blend (page 7)
- 2 teaspoons powdered psyllium husk
- 1½ teaspoons baking powder
- ½ teaspoon xanthan gum
- ¼ teaspoon baking soda
- ¼ teaspoon salt
- ¼ teaspoon ground nutmeg
- 3–4 quarts peanut or vegetable oil
- 1½ cups confectioners' sugar, for coating

1. Adjust oven rack to middle position and heat oven to 200 degrees. As soon as oven reaches 200 degrees, turn it off. (This will be warm proofing box for dough. Do not mix dough until oven has been turned off.) Lay large sheet parchment paper flat on counter and grease with vegetable oil spray. Line baking sheet with parchment paper and dust with flour blend.

2. Combine milk, yeast, and 1 teaspoon granulated sugar in bowl and let sit until bubbly, about 5 minutes. Whisk in melted butter and eggs. In standing mixer fitted with paddle, mix flour blend, psyllium husk, baking powder, xanthan gum, baking soda, salt, nutmeg, and remaining ⅓ cup granulated sugar on low speed until combined. Slowly add yeast mixture and let dough come together, about 1 minute, scraping down bowl as needed. Increase speed to medium and beat until sticky and uniform, about 6 minutes.

3. Using wet hands, transfer dough to greased parchment. Clean and wet hands again, then pat dough to ½-inch thickness. Using 2½- or 3-inch floured doughnut cutter, cut out doughnuts; twist cutter to help release dough and reflour cutter as needed. Transfer doughnuts and holes to prepared baking sheet; gather and repat dough scraps as needed.

4. Cover doughnuts loosely with plastic wrap, place on middle rack in warmed oven, and let rise for 10 minutes; do not let plastic touch oven rack. Remove doughnuts from oven and continue to let rise on counter for 20 more minutes.

5. Add oil to large Dutch oven until it measures 2 inches deep and heat over medium-high heat to 325 degrees. Line wire rack with paper towels. Working with half of doughnuts at a time, fry until golden brown, about 30 seconds per side for holes and 45 to 60 seconds per side for doughnuts.

6. Transfer fried doughnuts to prepared wire rack and let cool for at least 10 minutes. Place confectioners' sugar in bowl. Dip both sides of each doughnut in sugar, then gently shake off excess. Serve.

VARIATIONS

Dairy-Free Yeasted Doughnuts

Do not substitute almond or rice milk for the soy milk.

Substitute ½ cup unsweetened soy milk mixed with ¼ cup water for milk, and Earth Balance Vegan Buttery Sticks for butter. Reduce salt to ⅛ teaspoon.

Cinnamon Sugar–Glazed Doughnuts

Substitute granulated sugar for confectioners' sugar and mix with 1 tablespoon ground cinnamon.

Vanilla-Glazed Doughnuts

Increase confectioners' sugar to 3 cups and combine with ½ cup buttermilk (or 5 tablespoons water for dairy-free) and ¼ teaspoon vanilla extract in bowl to make smooth glaze. Dip both sides of each doughnut in glaze to coat, letting excess drip back into bowl; return doughnuts to rack and let glaze set for 15 minutes before serving.

Chocolate-Glazed Doughnuts

Increase confectioners' sugar to 2 cups and combine with 4 ounces melted semisweet or bittersweet chocolate and ½ cup half-and-half to make smooth glaze. Dip both sides of each doughnut in glaze to coat, letting excess drip back into bowl; return doughnuts to rack and let glaze set for 15 minutes before serving.

TEST KITCHEN TIP **Cutting Doughnuts**

1. Using wet hands, transfer dough to greased parchment. Clean and wet hands again, then pat dough until ½ inch thick.

2. Using 2½- or 3-inch floured doughnut cutter, cut out doughnuts; twist cutter to help release dough. Reflour cutter as needed.

3. Transfer doughnuts and holes to baking sheet lined with floured parchment.

Yeasted Doughnuts

We wanted a great doughnut that was crunchy on the outside, tender yet sturdy on the inside, laced delicately with nutmeg, and lightly sweetened. To achieve the tender, light chew we were looking for we had to rely on a number of tricks. Here is what we learned.

1. USE THREE LEAVENERS: Since gluten-free flours are lower in protein, doughs can't hold on to air bubbles as well, so to achieve a nice rise for our doughnuts we needed a combination of leaveners: baking powder, baking soda, and yeast. And we needed a short proofing time because otherwise the flour blend absorbed the available liquid, creating a tough doughnut. To speed along the activity of the yeast, we dissolved it in warmed milk with a little sugar. The quick 30-minute proofing time is then helped along by the baking powder and baking soda.

2. GO LOW-FAT FOR A HIGHER RISE: Although tradition-ally we'd use whole milk to add richness to doughnuts, its fat weighed down our gluten-free doughnuts, preventing them from rising because the starches in gluten-free flours don't absorb fat as well as wheat flour does. Using low-fat milk easily solved this problem and gave us the higher-rising and moist doughnuts we were after.

3. PROOF IN THE OVEN: A drafty or cold room can extend rising times, and since our gluten-free blend does not pro-vide the luxury of a long proofing time (the flour absorbs more liquid as it sits, making the dough thick and heavy), we created a more reliable environment by heating the oven to 200 degrees and then turning it off while we prepared the dough. At this point the oven was the perfect temperature for proofing the dough without killing the yeast.

4. FRY AT A LOWER TEMPERATURE: When we deep-fry food, the oil is generally held between 350 and 375 degrees. When using our gluten-free flour blend, we have to overhy-drate the dough to accommodate the high amount of starches in the blend, and this means the doughnuts need to fry longer. We found that frying the doughnuts at the lower temperature of 325 degrees allowed the outside to crisp at the same rate that the inside cooked and dried out. If the oil crept above 350 degrees, the outside cooked way too quickly, leaving us with a raw interior.

Popovers

FLOUR SUBSTITUTION	King Arthur Gluten-Free Multi-Purpose Flour 4½ ounces = ½ **cup plus ⅓ cup**	Betty Crocker All-Purpose Gluten Free Rice Blend 4½ ounces = **1 cup**
	Popovers made with Betty Crocker will be shorter, rubbery, and lack air pockets.	
XANTHAN GUM	Xanthan is crucial to the structure of the popovers; see page 22 for more information.	
SORGHUM FLOUR	Sorghum flour and sweet white sorghum flour will both work in these popovers. The grind, color, and flavor of the sorghum flour will vary slightly from brand to brand; however, all five of the brands we tried produced decent popovers. We had good luck using Bob's Red Mill "Sweet" White Sorghum Flour.	

WHY THIS RECIPE WORKS

The perfect popover soars to towering heights, but only if you get the baking method and ingredients just right. We wanted a popover that not only was gluten-free, but also had a nice rise and a custardy interior. Classic recipes contain as few as four ingredients: flour, milk, eggs, and butter, but the structure of the popover is mostly created by a higher-protein flour (like bread flour). Protein content is especially important when making popovers to ensure their trademark high rise and crisp crust. We knew our gluten-free flour blend would need help because the starches in our blend melt during baking. After making batches of popovers by adding a variety of high-protein flours to our blend, such as oat, millet, and amaranth, we found that adding a small amount of sorghum flour provided enough protein to give us a nice rise without imparting a distinct flavor. The rise was then reinforced by the batter's high liquid content (from the eggs, milk, and butter), which created a lot of steam in the oven, but we wanted our popovers to rise even higher. Reducing the amount of milk made them dry; switching to low-fat milk made for a higher-rising and moist popover. We also decreased the amount of butter from 4 to 2 tablespoons, which was enough to give them rich, buttery flavor without weighing down the dough. Now for our mixing method. We preferred mixing the batter in a blender for its ease and convenience, as we had a very loose dough (more like a pancake batter). We had one last problem to tackle to ensure our popovers were reaching their full potential: the oven temperature. Popovers baked at a high oven temperature became too crusty on the outside before the inside had a chance to set. We had the best results baking the popovers for 35 minutes at 400 degrees to initiate the rise, then turning the oven down to 350 degrees so the interior would be done at the same time as the crust. We then poked a hole in the top of the popovers when they were done cooking to allow the steam to escape, and this kept the crisp structure intact. Do not substitute skim or whole milk in this recipe.

Popovers

MAKES 6 POPOVERS

- 1¼ cups 1 or 2 percent low-fat milk
- 4 large eggs
- 2 tablespoons unsalted butter, melted and cooled
- 4½ ounces (1 cup) ATK All-Purpose Gluten-Free Flour Blend (page 7)
- 1 ounce (¼ cup) sorghum flour
- ½ teaspoon salt
- ¼ teaspoon xanthan gum

1. Adjust oven rack to middle position and heat oven to 400 degrees. Spray 6-cup popover pan with vegetable oil spray. Process milk, eggs, and melted butter in blender until completely incorporated, about 30 seconds.

2. Whisk flour blend, sorghum flour, salt, and xanthan gum together in bowl. Add flour mixture to egg mixture in blender and process until smooth, about 1 minute. Portion batter evenly into prepared popover pan (batter will not quite reach top of cups). Bake until popovers are golden brown, about 35 minutes.

3. Without opening oven door, reduce oven temperature to 350 degrees and continue to bake until popovers are deep golden brown, about 20 minutes longer.

4. Transfer pan to wire rack, poke each popover with skewer, and let cool for 2 minutes. Remove popovers from pan and serve warm.

Three-Grain Breakfast Porridge

G-F TESTING LAB

QUINOA   We like the convenience of prewashed quinoa. If you buy unwashed quinoa (or if you are unsure if it's washed), give it a rinse before cooking to remove its bitter protective coating (called saponin). We developed this recipe using white quinoa; we do not recommend using red, rainbow, or black quinoa here. For more information on quinoa, see page 28.

✓ WHY THIS RECIPE WORKS

For this hearty three-grain porridge, we chose a blend of quinoa, millet, and amaranth. Finding a harmonious balance among these three grains posed a bit of a challenge. Equal amounts of each resulted in porridge that was completely overwhelmed by the amaranth's licorice flavor. A mix of mostly quinoa, slightly less millet, and a tiny amount of amaranth put us on the right track, but our porridge was now bitter from all of the quinoa. Equal parts quinoa and millet (½ cup), along with a ¼ cup of amaranth, gave us a harmonious balance of textures and flavors. Millet, with its mellow corn flavor and fine, starchy texture was balanced by the nutty, earthy flavors of quinoa, while the amaranth added bold anise flavor and an intriguing caviar-like texture. Since each of these grains absorbs liquid differently, our next challenge was to figure out how to cook them together perfectly. After testing numerous ratios of liquid to grains and various simmering times, we pinpointed the perfect compromise of 30 minutes of cooking and five cups liquid to 1¼ cups grains. The high amount of liquid encouraged the grains to swell and some to burst and release their starches. This delivered a porridge with a creamy texture. However, the lengthy 30-minute simmering time was off-putting for what was meant to be a quick breakfast. The solution was stirring the grains into boiling water the night before. This allowed the grains to hydrate and soften overnight. As a bonus, we found that the assertive licorice flavor of the amaranth mellowed over the course of the night and the grains released starches to create an appealing consistency. In the morning, all we had to do was add milk and simmer the mixture for about 10 minutes. Stirring in golden raisins and warm spices, and finishing with a bit of honey, accentuated the millet's sweetness, balanced the often-bitter quinoa, and tamed the somewhat assertive flavor of the amaranth.

Three-Grain Breakfast Porridge

SERVES 4

- **4 cups water**
- **½ cup millet, rinsed**
- **½ cup prewashed white quinoa**
- **¼ cup amaranth, rinsed**
- **½ teaspoon salt**
- **1 cup whole milk, plus extra as needed**
- **¾ cup golden raisins**
- **½ teaspoon ground cinnamon**
- **⅛ teaspoon ground nutmeg**
- **2 tablespoons honey**

1. Bring water to boil in large saucepan over high heat. Remove pan from heat and stir in millet, quinoa, amaranth, and salt. Cover pan and let sit at room temperature overnight.

2. Stir in milk, raisins, cinnamon, and nutmeg and bring to simmer over medium-high heat. Reduce heat to medium-low and simmer uncovered, stirring occasionally, until grains are fully tender and mixture is thickened, 8 to 10 minutes.

3. Stir in honey and adjust consistency with hot milk as needed; porridge will thicken as it sits. Serve.

VARIATIONS

Dairy-Free Three-Grain Breakfast Porridge
Substitute unsweetened soy milk, almond milk, or rice milk for milk.

Three-Grain Breakfast Porridge with Blueberries and Maple
Omit raisins. Substitute 3 tablespoons maple syrup for honey. Stir in 1½ cups fresh blueberries with maple syrup.

Three-Grain Breakfast Porridge with Tahini and Apricots
Substitute ½ cup finely chopped dried apricots for raisins and ground cardamom for nutmeg. Increase honey to 3 tablespoons. Stir in ¼ cup tahini with milk. Sprinkle each serving with 2 tablespoons chopped toasted pistachios.

Quinoa Granola

QUINOA FLAKES	Quinoa flakes can be found in the cereal aisle of your grocery store, near the instant oatmeal.
QUINOA	We like the convenience of prewashed quinoa. If you buy unwashed quinoa (or if you are unsure if it's washed), give it a rinse before cooking to remove its bitter protective coating (called saponin). You can use either white, red, rainbow, or black quinoa here. For more information on quinoa, see page 28.

WHY THIS RECIPE WORKS

Oat-free granola is the allergen-friendly answer to traditional oat granola. Most of the recipes we found were packed with supergrains and seeds like chia, flaxseed, and quinoa, and while we loved the crunch the quinoa added, we found that chia had an off-putting flavor and the slippery flaxseeds were overpowering. Quinoa flakes cut the tough texture of raw quinoa and added a more delicate crunch without tempering the earthy flavor, which we found appealing. Almonds and sunflower seeds were mild enough to pair well with quinoa, while unsweetened flaked coconut lent enough flavor without making our granola too sweet. To enhance the coconut flavor, we turned to coconut oil instead of vegetable oil, and this added nutty flavor without being cloying. Maple syrup and a hefty amount of vanilla rounded out the warm, rich flavor of our granola. We loved our new granola so much we decided to create a couple of variations. Pecans and chocolate paired well with the earthy flavor of the quinoa, while pepitas, golden raisins, and a dash of cayenne gave our granola a little spice without being overpowering. We prefer to chop the almonds by hand for large, evenly chopped pieces. You can substitute vegetable oil for the coconut oil if desired.

Quinoa Granola with Sunflower Seeds and Almonds
MAKES ABOUT 9 CUPS

- ⅔ cup maple syrup
- 4 teaspoons vanilla extract
- ½ teaspoon salt
- ¼ cup coconut oil, melted
- 2 cups whole almonds, chopped coarse
- 2 cups unsweetened flaked coconut
- 1 cup quinoa flakes
- 1 cup quinoa, rinsed
- 1 cup raw sunflower seeds
- 2 cups dried cherries or other dried fruit, chopped

1. Adjust oven rack to upper-middle position and heat oven to 325 degrees. Line rimmed baking sheet with parchment paper.

2. Whisk maple syrup, vanilla, and salt together in large bowl. Whisk in oil. Fold in almonds, coconut, quinoa flakes, quinoa, and sunflower seeds until thoroughly coated.

3. Transfer mixture to prepared baking sheet and spread into thin, even layer. Using stiff metal spatula, press on quinoa mixture until very compact. Bake until deep golden brown, 50 to 60 minutes, rotating pan halfway through baking.

4. Remove granola from oven and let cool on wire rack for about 1 hour. Break cooled granola into pieces of desired size. Stir in dried fruit and serve. (Granola can be stored in airtight container at room temperature for up to 2 weeks.)

VARIATIONS

Quinoa Granola with Pecans, Espresso, and Chocolate
To make dairy-free, use dairy-free chocolate chips.

Add 1 teaspoon instant espresso powder to maple syrup mixture in step 2. Substitute pecans for almonds, and mini chocolate chips for dried cherries.

Quinoa Granola with Pepitas, Cayenne, and Golden Raisins
Add ¼ teaspoon cayenne pepper to maple syrup mixture in step 2. Substitute raw pepitas for sunflower seeds, and golden raisins for dried cherries.

SMART SHOPPING **Coconut Oil**

Coconut oil is made by extracting oil from the meat of fresh coconut. It is a semisolid fat which means that it remains solid at room temperature; we don't recommend keeping it in the fridge, since it gets very hard. This oil has a mild, nutty flavor that adds richness to many sorts of dishes, from vegetables to baked goods. It is touted as a healthy fat because it is made up primarily of heart-healthy saturated fats. In terms of flavor, unrefined coconut oil has a stronger coconut flavor than refined coconut oil.

GRAINS

■ DAIRY FREE OR INCLUDES A DAIRY-FREE VARIATION

Coconut Rice with Bok Choy and Lime

G-F TESTING LAB

RICE   We prefer the nutty flavor and fluffy texture of basmati rice in this recipe; however, long-grain white, jasmine, or Texmati rice can be substituted with good results. For more information on basmati rice, see page 28.

WHY THIS RECIPE WORKS

Rich, creamy coconut rice is served around the globe as a cooling accompaniment to spicy curries, stir-fries, and more. This dressed-up version features baby bok choy along with aromatic lemon grass, lime, and cilantro. Following the traditional method, we cooked basmati rice in coconut milk along with lemon grass, which steeped in the liquid and lent its flavor as the rice simmered. We found that cooking our rice in straight coconut milk didn't provide enough moisture and resulted in crunchy, uncooked grains. Folding in coconut milk after cooking our rice left us with overly sticky clumps of rice that offered very little coconut flavor. By thinning our coconut milk with water we had perfectly cooked rice, with individual grains and fragrant coconut flavor. To ensure the hearty bok choy stalks turned tender by the time the rice was fully cooked, we sautéed them in the pan along with some minced shallot before adding the rice, water, coconut milk, and lemon grass. When the rice was mostly done, we stirred in bright lime zest and juice and fresh cilantro along with the delicate bok choy greens. The last 3 minutes of cooking on the stovetop gently wilted the greens and infused the rice with lime and cilantro flavors.

Coconut Rice with Bok Choy and Lime
SERVES 4 TO 6

2	teaspoons vegetable oil
2	heads baby bok choy (4 ounces each), stalks sliced ½ inch thick and greens chopped
1	shallot, minced
1½	cups basmati rice, rinsed
1½	cups water
¾	cup canned coconut milk
1	lemon grass stalk, trimmed to bottom 6 inches and bruised with back of knife
	Salt and pepper
2	tablespoons minced fresh cilantro
1	teaspoon grated lime zest plus 2 teaspoons juice

1. Heat oil in large saucepan over medium-high heat until shimmering. Add bok choy stalks and shallot and cook, stirring occasionally, until softened, about 2 minutes.

2. Stir in rice, water, coconut milk, lemon grass, and 2 teaspoons salt and bring to boil. Reduce heat to low, cover, and simmer gently until liquid is absorbed, 18 to 20 minutes.

3. Fold in cilantro, lime zest and juice, and bok choy greens, cover, and cook until rice is tender, about 3 minutes. Discard lemon grass. Season with salt and pepper to taste and serve.

TEST KITCHEN TIP **Preparing Lemon Grass**

1. After trimming top and bottom of each stalk, peel and discard dry outer layer until moist, tender inner stalk is exposed.

2. Smash peeled stalk with back of chef's knife or meat pounder to release maximum flavor.

TEST KITCHEN TIP **Rinsing Rice and Grains**

Rinse rice or grains in fine-mesh strainer under cool water until water runs clear, occasionally stirring rice or grains around lightly with your hand. Let drain in strainer until needed.

Indonesian-Style Fried Rice

G-F TESTING LAB

RICE   We prefer the delicate, perfumed flavor of jasmine rice in this recipe; however, long-grain white, basmati, or Texmati rice can be substituted with good results. For more information on jasmine rice, see page 29.

WHY THIS RECIPE WORKS

Nasi Goreng is an Indonesian version of fried rice seasoned with chile paste and sweet soy sauce, and garnished with fried shallots, egg, and vegetables. Since sweet soy sauce is made using wheat, we needed a substitute. Simply switching out the soy sauce for gluten-free tamari left much to be desired in terms of flavor. But a mixture of molasses, dark brown sugar, tamari, and fish sauce was the perfect alternative. To get distinct grains of rice, this dish is traditionally made with day-old rice, but we were able to mimic this effect by rinsing the rice thoroughly, sautéing it with oil before cooking, and chilling the cooked rice in the fridge before finishing the dish. For the vegetables, we liked broccoli florets, steamed in the skillet until crisp-tender. Finally, we created a few garnishes by making a simple omelet and frying thinly sliced shallots until golden. If Thai chiles are unavailable, substitute two serranos or two medium jalapeños. To make this dish less spicy, use fewer chiles. Serve with wedges of cucumber, tomato, and lime.

Indonesian-Style Fried Rice

SERVES 6

RICE

- 2 tablespoons vegetable oil
- 2 cups jasmine rice, rinsed
- 2⅔ cups water

STIR-FRY

- 7 large shallots, peeled
- 5 green or red Thai chiles, stemmed
- 4 garlic cloves, peeled
- 3 tablespoons packed dark brown sugar
- 3 tablespoons molasses
- 3 tablespoons gluten-free tamari
- 3 tablespoons fish sauce
-   Salt
- 4 large eggs
- ½ cup vegetable oil
- 1 pound broccoli florets, cut into 1-inch pieces
- ¼ cup water
- 4 scallions, sliced thin

1. FOR THE RICE: Cook oil and rice in large saucepan over medium heat until hot, 1 to 2 minutes. Stir in water and bring to boil. Reduce heat to low, cover, and simmer gently until rice is tender and water is absorbed, 16 to 18 minutes. Remove pot from heat, lay clean folded dish towel underneath lid, and let sit for 10 minutes. Spread cooked rice onto rimmed baking sheet and let cool for 10 minutes, then chill in refrigerator for 20 minutes.

2. FOR THE STIR-FRY: Coarsely chop 4 shallots and add to food processor with chiles and garlic. Pulse mixture into coarse paste, about 15 pulses; transfer to bowl. In separate bowl, combine sugar, molasses, tamari, fish sauce, and 1¼ teaspoons salt. In third bowl, whisk eggs and ¼ teaspoon salt together.

3. Thinly slice remaining 3 shallots and combine with oil in 12-inch nonstick skillet. Cook shallots over medium heat, stirring constantly, until golden and crisp, 6 to 10 minutes. Using slotted spoon, transfer shallots to paper towel–lined plate and season with salt. Pour off oil and reserve.

4. Wipe out now-empty skillet with paper towels, add 1 teaspoon reserved oil, and heat over medium heat until shimmering. Add half of eggs and tilt pan to coat bottom. Cover and cook until top is just set, about 1½ minutes. Slide omelet onto cutting board, roll up into tight log, and cut crosswise into 1-inch-wide segments; leave segments rolled. Repeat with 1 teaspoon reserved oil and remaining eggs.

5. Combine broccoli and water in now-empty skillet, cover, and cook over medium-high heat until broccoli is crisp-tender and water is absorbed, 4 to 6 minutes; transfer to small bowl. Remove rice from refrigerator and break up any large clumps.

6. Heat 3 tablespoons reserved oil in now-empty skillet over medium heat until just shimmering. Add chile mixture and cook until golden, 3 to 5 minutes. Stir in molasses mixture and bring to simmer. Fold in rice and broccoli and cook, stirring constantly, until heated through and evenly coated, about 3 minutes. Stir in scallions. Transfer to platter and garnish with omelet rolls and fried shallots. Serve.

Black Rice Salad

G-F TESTING LAB

BLACK RICE Do not substitute other types of rice for the black rice in this recipe. For more information on black rice, see page 29.

✓ WHY THIS RECIPE WORKS

Black rice, also known as purple rice or forbidden rice, is an ancient grain that was once reserved for the emperors of China. It has a delicious roasted, nutty taste and is used in anything from salads to dessert puddings. We decided to use it in a simple salad, and to stick with its decidedly Asian roots we paired it with crunchy snap peas, peppery radishes, cilantro, and a ginger-sesame vinaigrette. Our major obstacle was finding the right method for cooking the rice, as it is easy to overcook. We discovered that the best way to keep it evenly cooked was to cook it like pasta, in lots of boiling water, giving it space to move around. Once it was cooked and drained, we drizzled it with a little vinegar for a boost of flavor and let it cool completely on a rimmed baking sheet. This ensured perfectly cooked grains that had the expected chew of black rice, and without any mushiness. Once the rice had cooled, we tossed it with our vinaigrette, peas, radishes, and peppers. A bit of minced cilantro brought a fresh vibrancy to the finished salad.

Black Rice Salad with Snap Peas and Ginger-Sesame Vinaigrette

SERVES 4 TO 6

- 1½ cups black rice
  Salt and pepper
- 3 tablespoons plus 1 teaspoon rice vinegar
- 2 teaspoons minced shallot
- 2 teaspoons honey
- 2 teaspoons Asian chili-garlic sauce
- 1 teaspoon grated fresh ginger
- ¼ cup extra-virgin olive oil
- 1 tablespoon toasted sesame oil
- 6 ounces sugar snap peas, strings removed and halved
- 5 radishes, trimmed, halved, and sliced thin
- 1 red bell pepper, stemmed, seeded, and chopped fine
- ¼ cup minced fresh cilantro

1. Bring 4 quarts water to boil in large pot over medium-high heat. Add rice and 1 teaspoon salt and cook until rice is tender, 20 to 25 minutes. Drain rice, spread onto rimmed baking sheet, drizzle with 1 teaspoon vinegar, and let cool for 15 minutes.

2. Whisk remaining 3 tablespoons vinegar, shallot, honey, chili-garlic sauce, ginger, ¼ teaspoon salt, and ⅛ teaspoon pepper together in large bowl. Whisking slowly, drizzle in olive oil and sesame oil until combined. Add cooled rice, snap peas, radishes, bell pepper, and cilantro and toss to combine. Season with salt and pepper to taste and serve.

TEST KITCHEN TIP

Trimming Snow and Snap Peas

Using paring knife and thumb, snip off stem end of pea, then pull stem end along flat side of pod to remove string.

SMART SHOPPING **Black Rice**

Also sold under the name purple rice, black rice is sold unhulled and has a high fiber content similar to that of brown rice. But only black rice contains anthocyanins, the same antioxidant compounds in blueberries and blackberries. These compounds turn the rice a deep purple as it cooks.

Brown Rice Bowls

G-F TESTING LAB

RICE	We prefer the fluffy texture of long-grain brown rice in this recipe; however, short- or medium-grain brown rice can be substituted with good results. For more information on brown rice, see page 29.

✓ WHY THIS RECIPE WORKS

We were after a version of the now popular rice bowls that pair nutty brown rice with roasted vegetables. To start, we tossed sweet carrots with *za'atar* and roasted them, first covered and then uncovered, until they were tender and spotty brown. When we uncovered the carrots, we also spread sliced kale over the top of them. Briefly roasting the kale gave it great flavor and an appealingly crisp texture. While the vegetables were roasting, we baked the rice alongside them in the oven, a hands-off method that delivered distinct grains of rice. After portioning the rice and vegetables into bowls, we drizzled everything with a shallot vinaigrette and topped each bowl with a fried egg. For an accurate measurement of boiling water, bring a full kettle of water to a boil and then measure out the desired amount.

Brown Rice Bowls with Roasted Carrots, Kale, and Fried Eggs

SERVES 4

- 2 **cups boiling water**
- 1 **cup long-grain brown rice, rinsed**
  Salt and pepper
- 5 **carrots, peeled, halved crosswise, then halved or quartered lengthwise to create uniformly sized pieces**
- ⅓ **cup extra-virgin olive oil**
- 2 **teaspoons za'atar**
- 8 **ounces kale, stemmed and sliced into 1-inch-wide strips**
- 2 **tablespoons red wine vinegar**
- 1 **small shallot, minced**
- 4 **large eggs**

1. Adjust oven racks to upper-middle and lower-middle positions and heat oven to 375 degrees. Combine boiling water, rice, and ¾ teaspoon salt in 8-inch square baking dish and cover tightly with aluminum foil. Bake rice on lower rack until tender, 45 to 50 minutes. Remove rice from oven, uncover, and fluff with fork. Cover with dish towel and let sit for 5 minutes.

2. Meanwhile, toss carrots, 1 tablespoon oil, za'atar, ¼ teaspoon salt, and ⅛ teaspoon pepper together in bowl. Spread carrots onto parchment paper–lined baking sheet, cover with foil, and roast on upper rack for 20 minutes.

3. Toss kale, 1 tablespoon oil, ¼ teaspoon salt, and ⅛ teaspoon pepper together in bowl. Remove foil from carrots and spread kale over top. Continue to roast vegetables, uncovered, until carrots are spotty brown and tender and edges of kale are lightly browned, about 15 minutes.

4. Portion brown rice into individual bowls and top with roasted vegetables. Whisk vinegar, shallot, and 3 tablespoons oil together in bowl and season with salt and pepper to taste. Drizzle vinaigrette over rice and vegetables; cover and set aside.

5. Heat remaining 1 teaspoon oil in 12-inch nonstick skillet over low heat for 5 minutes. Crack eggs into 2 small bowls (2 eggs per bowl) and season with salt and pepper. Increase heat to medium-high and heat until oil is shimmering. Working quickly, pour eggs into skillet, cover, and cook for 1 minute. Remove skillet from burner and let sit, covered, 15 to 45 seconds for runny yolks, 45 to 60 seconds for soft but set yolks, and about 2 minutes for medium-set yolks. Top each bowl with fried egg and serve immediately.

TEST KITCHEN TIP **Frying Eggs**

While skillet heats, crack eggs into 2 small bowls (2 eggs per bowl) and season with salt and pepper. Working quickly, position bowls on either side of skillet and add eggs simultaneously.

SMART SHOPPING **Za'atar**

This spice mixture is used frequently in the Middle East and the Mediterranean region to season meats and vegetables. It traditionally includes ground dried herbs such as thyme and oregano, spices such as cumin, and sumac, salt, and toasted sesame seeds.

Miso Brown Rice Cakes

G-F TESTING LAB

RICE	We prefer the fluffy texture of long-grain brown rice in this recipe; however, short- or medium-grain brown rice can be substituted with good results. For more information on brown rice, see page 29.
MISO	We prefer the rich, hearty flavor of red miso here; however, white miso can be substituted with good results. Do not substitute "light" miso. Also, note that not all types of miso are gluten-free; read the label.

WHY THIS RECIPE WORKS

For these hearty rice cakes we paired long-grain brown rice with red miso and shiitake mushrooms for depth of flavor and meatiness. Although we usually cook brown rice in the oven to ensure fluffy grains, we wanted stickier rice for making the cakes. So we turned to the stovetop method, which ensured the rice released starches that helped bind the patties. Once the rice was cool, we pulsed it in a food processor to help break down the starches for even better binding. Then we mixed the rice with egg, toasted sesame oil, and the miso, plus scallions for some freshness, before forming the mixture into patties and chilling them briefly until firm. Just a few minutes in a hot skillet gave us crisp, browned rice patties. We like to serve these cakes with spicy Sriracha Mayonnaise.

Miso Brown Rice Cakes

SERVES 4

- 3   tablespoons vegetable oil
- 8   ounces shiitake mushrooms, stemmed and chopped
- 2   teaspoons grated fresh ginger
- 2   garlic cloves, minced
- 1½ cups long-grain brown rice
- 3¾ cups water
-     Salt and pepper
- 4   scallions, chopped fine
- 1   large egg plus 1 large yolk, lightly beaten
- 3   tablespoons gluten-free red miso
- 1½ teaspoons toasted sesame oil

1. Heat 1 tablespoon vegetable oil in large saucepan over medium heat until shimmering. Add mushrooms and cook until lightly browned, about 5 minutes. Stir in ginger and garlic and cook until fragrant, about 30 seconds. Add rice, water, and ½ teaspoon salt and bring to simmer. Reduce heat to low, cover, and cook, stirring occasionally, until rice is tender and liquid is absorbed, about 50 minutes. Spread rice mixture onto rimmed baking sheet and let cool for 15 minutes.

2. Pulse cooled rice mixture in food processor until coarsely ground, about 10 pulses; transfer to large bowl. Stir in scallions, egg and yolk, miso, sesame oil, ½ teaspoon salt, and ¼ teaspoon pepper until combined.

3. Line rimmed baking sheet with parchment paper and spray with vegetable oil spray. Using wet hands, divide rice mixture into 8 equal portions and pack firmly into 3½-inch-wide patties; lay on prepared sheet. Refrigerate patties, uncovered, until chilled and firm, about 30 minutes.

4. Adjust oven rack to middle position and heat oven to 200 degrees. Set wire rack in rimmed baking sheet. Heat 1 tablespoon vegetable oil in 12-inch nonstick skillet over medium-high heat until shimmering. Lay 4 rice cakes in skillet and cook until crisp and browned on both sides, about 4 minutes per side. Transfer cakes to prepared rack and keep warm in oven. Repeat with remaining 1 tablespoon vegetable oil and remaining cakes.

Sriracha Mayonnaise

MAKES ABOUT ¾ CUP

The mayonnaise can be refrigerated for up to 5 days.

- ½   cup mayonnaise
- 1   scallion, chopped fine
- 2   tablespoons Sriracha sauce
- 1   tablespoon lime juice

Combine all ingredients in bowl and serve.

SMART SHOPPING **Miso**

An essential ingredient in the Japanese kitchen, miso paste is made by fermenting soybeans and sometimes grains (such as rice, barley, or rye) with a mold called *koji*. Packed with savory flavor, miso is used to season everything from soups and braises to dressings and sauces. Although countless variations of the salty, deep-flavored ingredient are available, three common types are white *shiro* (despite its name, this miso is light golden in color), red *aka*, and brownish-black *hatcho*. Since not all types of miso are gluten-free, you must read the labels carefully.

Buckwheat Bowls with Lemon-Yogurt Sauce

G-F TESTING LAB

BUCKWHEAT GROATS	Do not substitute kasha (roasted buckwheat groats) for the buckwheat groats in this recipe. For more information on buckwheat groats, see page 26.

WHY THIS RECIPE WORKS

For a fresh, whole-grain take on rice bowls, we swapped out the rice for whole buckwheat groats and paired the grain with snow peas, chunks of ripe avocado, and toasted, spiced sunflower seeds. We first tried kasha, which is the roasted form of buckwheat groats. But its deep earthiness overwhelmed the delicate flavor profile of the finished dish. Turning to buckwheat (the same kernels as kasha but raw) lent a mild, appealing earthiness to our grain bowl that didn't dominate the other ingredients. To keep the cooking method easy, we simply boiled the buckwheat in a large pot of water until it was tender, then tossed it with a bright lemon-mint dressing. While the buckwheat cooked, we sautéed the snow peas with some coriander and toasted the sunflower seeds with lots of warm spices. Lastly, we made a quick yogurt sauce to drizzle over the top.

Buckwheat Bowls with Lemon-Yogurt Sauce
SERVES 4

YOGURT SAUCE
- ½ cup plain whole-milk yogurt
- 1 tablespoon minced fresh mint
- ½ teaspoon grated lemon zest plus 1 tablespoon juice
- ¼ teaspoon salt
- ⅛ teaspoon pepper

BUCKWHEAT AND VEGETABLES
- 1½ cups buckwheat groats
  Salt and pepper
- ¼ cup extra-virgin olive oil
- ¾ teaspoon ground coriander
- 8 ounces snow peas, strings removed and halved
- ¼ cup raw sunflower seeds
- ⅛ teaspoon ground cumin
- 1 teaspoon grated lemon zest plus 2 tablespoons juice
- 1 tablespoon minced fresh mint

- ½ teaspoon Dijon mustard
- 1 avocado, halved, pitted, and cut into ½-inch pieces

1. FOR THE YOGURT SAUCE: Whisk all ingredients together in bowl, cover, and refrigerate until needed.

2. FOR THE BUCKWHEAT AND VEGETABLES: Bring 2 quarts water to boil in large pot. Add buckwheat and 1 teaspoon salt and cook until tender, 10 to 12 minutes; drain and transfer to large bowl.

3. Meanwhile, heat ½ tablespoon oil in 12-inch nonstick skillet over medium-high heat until just smoking. Stir in ½ teaspoon coriander and cook until fragrant, about 20 seconds. Add snow peas and ¼ teaspoon salt and cook until peas are spotty brown, about 3 minutes; transfer to bowl with buckwheat.

4. Add ½ tablespoon oil, sunflower seeds, cumin, remaining ¼ teaspoon coriander, and ¼ teaspoon salt and cook over medium heat until seeds are toasted, about 2 minutes; transfer to plate and let cool.

5. In separate bowl, whisk lemon zest and juice, mint, and mustard together. Whisking constantly, drizzle in remaining 3 tablespoons oil. Season with salt and pepper to taste, pour over buckwheat mixture, and toss to coat. Portion buckwheat into individual bowls, top with avocado and spiced sunflower seeds, and drizzle with yogurt sauce. Serve.

VARIATION

Dairy-Free Buckwheat Bowls with Lemon-Yogurt Sauce
In sauce, substitute plain soy milk yogurt or coconut milk yogurt for whole-milk yogurt.

SMART SHOPPING **Buckwheat**

Despite its name, buckwheat is not related to wheat. It is actually an herb. In addition to being ground to make buckwheat flour, the kernels of its triangular seeds can be hulled and crushed to make groats. These groats have a relatively mild, grassy flavor, making them a good side dish to a variety of entrées. Buckwheat groats cook relatively quickly, making them a good option for weeknight meals. Buckwheat products can be found in natural food stores and well-stocked supermarkets.

Oat Berry and Mushroom Risotto

G-F TESTING LAB

OAT BERRIES   Oat berries may also be labeled oat groats. Not all oat berries are processed in a gluten-free facility; read the label. For more information on oat berries, see page 27.

WHY THIS RECIPE WORKS

We set out to create a satisfying whole-grain version of risotto using hearty oat berries, which we thought would be a good stand-in for Arborio rice. Once cooked, the oat berries released just enough starch to lightly thicken our cooking liquid to the perfect risotto-like consistency even without the addition of butter or cheese. We wanted a satisfying risotto with hearty add-ins, and mushrooms seemed like the perfect match for our oat berries. We began by browning onions and mushrooms. Using both cremini and dried porcini mushrooms added a meaty richness to the finished risotto. Then we added oat berries, toasting them to reinforce their naturally nutty flavor. A bit of fresh thyme and garlic provided the aromatic backbone as we built the flavorful base of the dish. Chicken broth complemented the flavor of the mushrooms and seasoned the oat berries as they cooked; using all broth resulted in a salty risotto, but cutting the broth with some water was an easy fix. Once the grains were tender and the risotto thickened, we stirred in lemon juice to brighten the flavor, while parsley gave our risotto the freshness it needed. White mushrooms can be substituted for the cremini. Serve with grated Parmesan cheese.

Oat Berry and Mushroom Risotto

SERVES 4 TO 6

- 1 tablespoon extra-virgin olive oil
- 1 onion, chopped fine
  Salt and pepper
- 8 ounces cremini mushrooms, trimmed and quartered
- ½ ounce dried porcini mushrooms, rinsed and minced
- 3 garlic cloves, minced
- 1 teaspoon minced fresh thyme or ¼ teaspoon dried
- 1½ cups oat berries
- 2½ cups chicken broth
- 1½ cups water
- 2 tablespoons chopped fresh parsley
- 2 teaspoons lemon juice

1. Heat oil in large saucepan over medium heat until shimmering. Add onion and ½ teaspoon salt and cook until onion is softened, about 5 minutes. Stir in cremini and porcini mushrooms, increase heat to medium-high, and cook until cremini begin to brown, about 4 minutes. Stir in garlic and thyme and cook until fragrant, about 30 seconds.

2. Stir in oat berries and cook until lightly toasted, about 2 minutes. Stir in broth and water, scraping up any browned bits, and bring to simmer. Reduce heat to low and simmer, stirring often, until oat berries are tender and liquid is mostly evaporated and thickened, 30 to 40 minutes.

3. Off heat, stir in parsley and lemon juice. Season with salt and pepper to taste and serve.

TEST KITCHEN TIP

Making Oat Berry Risotto

Reduce heat to low and simmer, stirring often, until oat berries are tender and liquid is mostly evaporated and thickened, 30 to 40 minutes.

SMART SHOPPING **Oat Berries**

Oats are usually thought of as a breakfast cereal, but oat berries make for a great savory side dish. Labeled either oat berries or oat groats, this gluten-free whole grain is simply whole oats that have been hulled and cleaned. They are the least processed oat product (other forms are processed further, such as being rolled flat, cut, or ground). Because they haven't been processed, they retain a high nutritional value. They have an appealing chewy texture and a mildly nutty flavor.

Rainbow Quinoa Pilaf

QUINOA   We like the convenience of prewashed quinoa. If you buy unwashed quinoa (or if you are unsure whether it's washed), give it a rinse under cold water to remove its bitter protective coating (called saponin) and spread the seeds out over a dish towel to dry before cooking. We developed this recipe using rainbow quinoa, which is also sometimes labeled tricolor quinoa. You can substitute white or red quinoa for the tricolor quinoa without changing the cooking time; do not substitute black quinoa. For more information on quinoa, see page 28.

✓ WHY THIS RECIPE WORKS

Quinoa, often called a "supergrain" because of its great nutritional profile, has an appealingly firm bite and a nutty flavor, and it is easy to prepare, generally requiring 15 to 20 minutes of hands-off cooking. For a pilaf-style side dish, we toasted the quinoa prior to adding liquid; this ensured plump individual grains and also brought out its nutty flavor. We opted to include brightly colored vegetables, such as carrots and rainbow chard, to echo the vibrant colors found in the quinoa. After the quinoa had simmered, we pulled the pan off the heat and let it sit. This resting time gave us the opportunity to gently cook our chard leaves by spreading them out over the quinoa before covering the pan and allowing the grains' heat to soften the leaves. The result was evenly cooked, fluffy quinoa with just the right bite. We then stirred in fresh citrus juice for a bright punch of acidity.

Rainbow Quinoa Pilaf with Swiss Chard and Carrots

SERVES 4 TO 6

- 1½   cups prewashed rainbow quinoa
- 10   ounces rainbow Swiss chard, stems sliced thin, leaves cut into 1-inch pieces
- 2   carrots, peeled and cut into ¼-inch pieces
- 1   shallot, minced
- 2   tablespoons vegetable oil
-     Salt and pepper
- 1   garlic clove, minced
- 1   teaspoon minced fresh thyme or ¼ teaspoon dried
- 1¾   cups water
- 4   teaspoons lemon juice

1. Toast quinoa in large saucepan over medium-high heat, stirring often, until fragrant and makes continuous popping sounds, 5 to 7 minutes; transfer to bowl.

2. Add chard stems, carrots, shallot, oil, and ¾ teaspoon salt to now-empty pot and cook over medium-low heat until vegetables are softened, 5 to 7 minutes. Stir in garlic and thyme and cook until fragrant, about 30 seconds.

3. Stir in water and toasted quinoa, increase heat to medium-high, and bring to simmer. Reduce heat to low, cover, and simmer gently until grains are just tender and liquid is absorbed, 18 to 20 minutes, stirring once halfway through cooking.

4. Off heat, place chard leaves over top, cover, and let sit until chard is wilted, about 10 minutes. Add lemon juice, season with salt and pepper to taste, and fluff gently with fork to combine. Serve.

VARIATION

Rainbow Quinoa Pilaf with Red Bell Pepper, Lime, and Cilantro

Omit chard. Substitute 1 red bell pepper, cut into ½-inch pieces, for carrots; add to pot with shallot and cook until softened, 3 to 5 minutes. Let pilaf rest off heat as directed in step 4. Substitute 1 tablespoon lime juice for lemon juice. Stir in 3 tablespoons chopped fresh cilantro before serving.

TEST KITCHEN TIP **Preparing Swiss Chard**

1. Cut away leafy portion from stem using chef's knife, and slice stems thin.

2. Stack several leaves, slice crosswise, then cut into 1-inch pieces.

Quinoa, Black Bean, and Mango Salad

G-F TESTING LAB

QUINOA   We like the convenience of prewashed quinoa. If you buy unwashed quinoa (or if you are unsure whether it's washed), give it a rinse under cold water to remove its bitter protective coating (called saponin) and spread the grain out over a dish towel to dry before cooking. You can substitute red quinoa for the white quinoa without changing the cooking time; do not use black quinoa. For more information on quinoa, see page 28.

WHY THIS RECIPE WORKS

We wanted to feature the delicate texture and nutty flavor of quinoa in a fresh-tasting salad hearty enough for a main course. We started by toasting the quinoa to bring out its flavor before adding liquid to the pan and simmering the seeds until nearly tender. We then spread the quinoa over a rimmed baking sheet so that the residual heat would finish cooking it gently as it cooled, giving us perfectly cooked, fluffy grains. Black beans, mango, and bell pepper lent the salad heartiness, bright flavor, and color. A simple but intense dressing with lime juice, jalapeño, cumin, and cilantro gave this dish the acidity needed to keep its flavors fresh. We also added scallions and avocado for bite and creaminess.

Quinoa, Black Bean, and Mango Salad with Lime Dressing

SERVES 4 TO 6

1½   cups prewashed white quinoa
2¼   cups water
      Salt and pepper
5   tablespoons lime juice (3 limes)
½   jalapeño chile, stemmed, seeded, and chopped
¾   teaspoon ground cumin
½   cup extra-virgin olive oil
⅓   cup fresh cilantro leaves
1   red bell pepper, stemmed, seeded, and chopped
1   mango, peeled, pitted, and cut into ¼-inch pieces
1   (15-ounce) can black beans, rinsed
2   scallions, sliced thin
1   avocado, halved, pitted, and sliced thin

1. Toast quinoa in large saucepan over medium-high heat, stirring often, until fragrant and makes continuous popping sounds, 5 to 7 minutes. Stir in water and ½ teaspoon salt and bring to simmer. Reduce heat to low, cover, and simmer gently until most of water has been absorbed and quinoa is nearly tender, about 15 minutes. Spread quinoa onto rimmed baking sheet, let cool for 20 minutes, then transfer to large bowl.

2. Process lime juice, jalapeño, cumin, and 1 teaspoon salt in blender until jalapeño is finely chopped, about 15 seconds. With blender running, add oil and cilantro and process until smooth and emulsified, about 20 seconds.

3. Add lime-jalapeño dressing, bell pepper, mango, beans, and scallions to cooled quinoa and toss to combine. Season with salt and pepper to taste. Serve, topping individual portions with avocado.

TEST KITCHEN TIP **Cutting Up a Mango**

1. After trimming both ends of mango, stand mango on end and cut off remaining skin in thin strips from top to bottom.

2. Cut down along each side of flat pit to remove flesh.

3. Trim any remaining flesh off sides of pit. Once removed from pit, flesh can be cut into pieces as desired.

Millet Salad with Corn and Queso Fresco

✓ WHY THIS RECIPE WORKS

The mellow corn flavor and fine texture of tiny millet seeds make them extremely versatile in savory applications. We set out to feature the small seeds in a grain-style salad that would enhance the sweet flavor of the millet. The seeds release starch as they cook, which can create large clumps. We found that using 3 quarts of boiling water to quickly cook the millet resulted in distinctive individual pieces of the cooked seeds. Spreading out the millet in a single layer on a baking sheet allowed it to cool and prevented any further clumping. With our cooking method nailed down, we set out to build the flavors of our salad. We stirred in corn to complement the millet's natural flavor and to add texture, while the addition of cherry tomatoes, *queso fresco,* and a minced jalapeño gave the salad a Southwestern flavor profile that paired well with the corn. We whipped up a quick vinaigrette using lime zest and juice to dress our salad and add brightness. A small amount of mayonnaise helped to emulsify the dressing and more evenly coat the millet. Chopped fresh cilantro added a bit of freshness and color in the finished salad. For more spice, reserve, mince, and add the ribs and seeds from the jalapeño.

Millet Salad with Corn and Queso Fresco
SERVES 4 TO 6

1   **cup millet**
    Salt and pepper
1   **teaspoon grated lime zest plus**
    2½ tablespoons juice (2 limes)
2   **teaspoons honey**
½   **teaspoon mayonnaise**
3   **tablespoons extra-virgin olive oil**
8   **ounces cherry tomatoes, quartered**
½   **cup frozen corn, thawed**
1½   **ounces queso fresco, crumbled (⅓ cup)**
¼   **cup chopped fresh cilantro**
1   **jalapeño chile, stemmed, seeded,**
    and minced

1. Bring 3 quarts water to boil in large pot. Add millet and 1 teaspoon salt and cook until grains are tender, about 20 minutes. Drain millet, spread onto rimmed baking sheet, drizzle with ½ tablespoon lime juice, and let cool for 15 minutes.

2. Whisk lime zest and remaining 2 tablespoons juice, honey, mayonnaise, and ¼ teaspoon salt together in large bowl. Whisking constantly, drizzle in oil. Add cooled millet and toss to combine. Fold in cherry tomatoes, corn, queso fresco, cilantro, and jalapeño. Season with salt and pepper to taste and serve.

VARIATIONS

Millet Salad with Oranges, Olives, and Almonds

Omit tomatoes, corn, queso fresco, cilantro, and jalapeño. Substitute orange zest for lime zest, and sherry vinegar for lime juice. Fold in 2 oranges, peeled and cut into ½-inch pieces, ⅓ cup chopped pitted green olives, ⅓ cup toasted sliced almonds, and 2 tablespoons chopped fresh oregano before serving.

Millet Salad with Endive, Blueberries, and Goat Cheese

Omit tomatoes, corn, queso fresco, cilantro, and jalapeño. Omit lime zest and substitute champagne vinegar for lime juice. Fold in 2 heads thinly sliced Belgian endive, 1½ cups blueberries, ¾ cup chopped toasted pecans, and 1 cup crumbled goat cheese before serving.

SMART SHOPPING **Millet**

Believed to be the first domesticated cereal grain, this tiny cereal grass seed has a long history and is still a staple in a large part of the world, particularly in Asia and Africa. The seeds can be ground into flour or used whole. Millet has a mellow corn flavor that makes it work well in both savory and sweet applications.

Millet Cakes with Spinach and Carrots

MILLET   For more information on millet, see page 27.

WHY THIS RECIPE WORKS

Millet makes a perfect base for pan-fried cakes because the seeds burst as they cook, releasing starch and becoming sticky. We liked the combination of millet and curry, and adding spinach and carrots along with shallot and garlic created a highly flavorful but nicely balanced mixture. Though millet holds together well on its own, we found that the addition of an egg and plain yogurt was helpful in keeping the cakes together during cooking. Chilling the formed cakes further ensured that they were sturdy and easy to handle. As for the cooking method, baking dried out the cakes, so we pan-fried them, which created a flavorful crust on the exterior while maintaining a moist interior. Be sure to let the uncooked cakes chill for 30 minutes or they will break apart during cooking. Serve with yogurt sauce.

Millet Cakes with Spinach and Carrots
SERVES 4

- 1 cup millet, rinsed
- 2 cups water
  Salt and pepper
- 3 tablespoons vegetable oil
- 1 shallot, minced
- 6 ounces (6 cups) baby spinach, chopped
- 2 carrots, peeled and shredded
- 2 garlic cloves, minced
- 2 teaspoons curry powder
- ¼ cup plain whole-milk yogurt
- 1 large egg, lightly beaten
- 2 tablespoons minced fresh cilantro

1. Combine millet, water, and ½ teaspoon salt in large saucepan and bring to simmer over medium heat. Reduce heat to low, cover, and simmer gently until grains are tender and liquid is absorbed, 15 to 20 minutes. Remove pot from heat and let millet sit, covered, for 10 minutes; transfer to large bowl.

2. Heat 1 tablespoon oil in 12-inch nonstick skillet over medium heat until shimmering. Add shallot and cook until softened, about 3 minutes. Stir in spinach and carrots and cook until spinach is wilted, about 2 minutes. Stir in garlic, curry powder, ½ teaspoon salt, and ¼ teaspoon pepper and cook until fragrant, about 30 seconds. Transfer to bowl with millet. Wipe out now-empty skillet with paper towels.

3. Stir yogurt, egg, and cilantro into millet mixture until well combined. Using wet hands, divide mixture into 8 equal portions, pack firmly into 3½-inch-wide patties, and place on parchment paper–lined baking sheet. Refrigerate patties, uncovered, until chilled and firm, for at least 30 minutes or up to 2 hours.

4. Adjust oven rack to middle position and heat oven to 200 degrees. Set wire rack in rimmed baking sheet. Heat 1 tablespoon oil in now-empty skillet over medium heat until shimmering. Lay 4 cakes in skillet and cook until crisp and browned on both sides, 5 to 7 minutes per side. Transfer cakes to prepared rack and keep warm in oven. Repeat with remaining 1 tablespoon oil and remaining cakes. Serve.

VARIATION

Dairy-Free Millet Cakes with Spinach and Carrots
Substitute plain soy milk yogurt or coconut milk yogurt for whole-milk yogurt.

Cucumber-Yogurt Sauce
MAKES ABOUT 2½ CUPS
Cilantro, mint, parsley, or tarragon can be substituted for the dill if desired. To make this sauce dairy-free, substitute soy milk yogurt or coconut milk yogurt.

- 1 cup plain whole-milk yogurt
- 2 tablespoons extra-virgin olive oil
- 2 tablespoons minced fresh dill
- 1 garlic clove, minced
- 1 cucumber, peeled, halved lengthwise, seeded, and shredded
  Salt and pepper

Whisk yogurt, oil, dill, and garlic together in medium bowl. Stir in cucumber and season with salt and pepper to taste. Serve. (Sauce can be refrigerated for up to 2 days.)

Polenta Fries

G-F TESTING LAB

INSTANT POLENTA This recipe uses instant polenta, which has a much shorter cooking time than traditional polenta; do not substitute traditional polenta. Also, not all types of instant polenta are processed in a gluten-free facility; read the label. We had good luck using Pastene Instant Polenta in this recipe.

For a fresh take on how to use gluten-free polenta, we found that if we cooked polenta, then chilled it until firm, we could slice it into thin sticks that would become crisp when fried. We began our testing using instant polenta, to minimize time on the stove. Stirring oregano and lemon zest into the fully cooked polenta lent an aromatic backbone to our fries and helped to brighten the flavor. We then poured our flavored polenta into a straight-sided 13 by 9-inch baking pan to set up in the refrigerator for easy slicing. Once our fries were cut, we looked at methods for cooking them. Deep frying resulted in fries that clumped together and stuck to the bottom of the pot, but pan frying resulted in perfectly crisp fries with a tender and fluffy interior. We seasoned the fries lightly with salt as they came out of the pan. We like to serve these fries with Herb Mayonnaise, but they also taste good with marinara sauce, Sriracha Mayonnaise (page 87), or even ketchup.

Polenta Fries

SERVES 4

- 4   cups water
-     Salt and pepper
- 1   cup instant polenta
- 2   teaspoons minced fresh oregano or ½ teaspoon dried
- 1   teaspoon grated lemon zest
- ½   cup vegetable oil

1. Line 13 by 9-inch baking pan with parchment paper and grease parchment. Bring water to boil in large covered saucepan and add 1 teaspoon salt. Slowly add polenta in steady stream while stirring constantly with wooden spoon. Reduce heat to low and cook, uncovered, stirring often, until polenta is soft and smooth, 3 to 5 minutes.

2. Off heat, stir in oregano and lemon zest and season with salt and pepper to taste. Pour polenta into prepared baking dish. Refrigerate, uncovered, until firm and sliceable, about 1 hour. (Polenta can be covered and refrigerated for up to 1 day.)

3. Gently flip chilled polenta out onto cutting board and discard parchment. Cut polenta in half lengthwise, then slice each half crosswise into sixteen ¾-inch-wide fries. (You will have 32 fries total.)

4. Adjust oven rack to middle position and heat oven to 200 degrees. Set wire rack in rimmed baking sheet. Heat oil in 12-inch nonstick skillet over medium heat until shimmering and edge of polenta sizzles when dipped in oil. Working in batches, fry half of polenta until crisp and beginning to brown, 6 to 7 minutes per side. Transfer to prepared rack, season lightly with salt, and keep warm in oven. Repeat with remaining polenta and serve warm.

Herb Mayonnaise

MAKES 1¼ CUPS

Mayonnaise can be refrigerated for up to 2 days.

- 1   cup mayonnaise
- 2   tablespoons minced fresh basil
- 1   tablespoon minced fresh parsley
- 1   tablespoon lemon juice
- 2   teaspoons chopped fresh chives
-     Salt and pepper

Combine all ingredients in bowl, season with salt and pepper to taste, and serve.

TEST KITCHEN TIP **Making Polenta Fries**

1. Flip chilled polenta onto cutting board and discard parchment. Cut polenta in half lengthwise, then slice each half crosswise into sixteen ¾-inch-wide fries.

2. Working in batches, fry half of polenta until crisp and beginning to brown, 6 to 7 minutes per side, and transfer to wire rack set in rimmed baking sheet.

COMFORT FOODS

■ DAIRY FREE OR INCLUDES A DAIRY-FREE VARIATION

Buffalo Chicken Wings

✓ WHY THIS RECIPE WORKS

We wanted to develop a recipe for roasted chicken wings that were crispy on the outside and moist and tender within, just like their fried counterpart—which usually relies on gluten. Instead, we tried rubbing the wings with baking powder and salt before they went into the oven. Baking powder acts like salt to draw out moisture from the surface of the poultry skin but also accelerates browning. More browning means crispier skin. This combination helped to draw moisture to the surface of the poultry skin. But the moisture drawn from the chicken sat as pasty beads on the skin instead of evaporating, preventing the skin from getting totally crispy. Simply blotting the wings dry with paper towels lifted away the rub, so that wouldn't work. Instead, we lowered the oven temperature to a mellow 250 degrees in order to evaporate this surface moisture without really cooking or drying out the meat. Then we cranked up the temperature and moved the wings to an upper oven rack to crisp the skin and maximize browning. The results were even better than we had hoped for: tender meat and skin that was crisp enough to pass for fried. One element remained: the sauce. Traditional Buffalo sauce is usually just Frank's RedHot Original Cayenne Pepper Sauce and butter, but we decided to add a little molasses for deeper flavor. The wings were juicy and tender, and their crispy skin held our sauce without becoming soggy. If you buy chicken wings that are already split, with the tips removed, you will need only 3½ pounds.

Buffalo Chicken Wings

SERVES 4 TO 6

- **4 pounds chicken wings, cut at joints, wingtips discarded**
- **2 tablespoons baking powder**
- **¾ teaspoon salt**
- **½ cup Frank's RedHot Original Cayenne Pepper Sauce**
- **4 tablespoons unsalted butter, melted**
- **1 tablespoon molasses**

1. Adjust oven racks to upper-middle and lower-middle positions and heat oven to 250 degrees. Set wire rack in aluminum foil–lined rimmed baking sheet. Pat wings dry with paper towels and place in large bowl. Combine baking powder and salt, sprinkle over wings, and toss to coat evenly. Arrange wings, meaty side up, in single layer on prepared wire rack.

2. Roast wings on lower rack for 30 minutes. Move wings to upper rack, increase oven temperature to 425 degrees, and roast until wings are golden brown and crispy, 40 to 50 minutes longer, rotating sheet halfway through baking.

3. Remove wings from oven and let stand for 5 minutes. Meanwhile, whisk hot sauce, butter, and molasses together in large bowl. Add wings to sauce, toss to coat, and serve.

VARIATION

Chicken Wings with Sweet and Spicy Thai Sauce

To make dairy-free, substitute Earth Balance Vegan Buttery Sticks for butter.

Substitute following sauce for hot sauce mixture in step 3: Simmer ½ cup packed brown sugar, ¼ cup lime juice (2 limes), 1 tablespoon toasted sesame oil, 1 teaspoon red pepper flakes, and 1 minced garlic clove in small saucepan over medium heat until slightly thickened, about 5 minutes. Off heat, whisk in 2 tablespoons fish sauce and transfer to large bowl.

TEST KITCHEN TIP **Prepping Chicken Wings**

1. Using chef's knife, cut through joint between drumette and wingette.

2. Cut off and discard wingtip.

New England Clam Chowder

G-F TESTING LAB

FLOUR SUBSTITUTION	King Arthur Gluten-Free Multi-Purpose Flour 2 ounces = **6 tablespoons**	Betty Crocker All-Purpose Gluten Free Rice Blend 2 ounces = **6 tablespoons**
	Chowder made with King Arthur will be a bit thicker; chowder made with Betty Crocker will be thicker and slightly starchy.	
CLAMS	We like to use cherrystone clams in this recipe; however, littlenecks or cockles will also work well. Avoid using clams larger than 4 to 5 inches in diameter, as they will be tough and will give the chowder a distinct "inky" flavor.	

WHY THIS RECIPE WORKS

There's nothing quite as comforting as a steaming bowl of creamy New England clam chowder, but it is commonly thickened with flour. Hoping for an easy fix, we simply omitted the flour, relying only on the heavy cream to give it the requisite rich body. But the chowder was just too thin and loose. In our next test, we pureed a portion of the simmered soup (before adding clams to the mix) and reduced the cream on the stovetop before stirring it in. While the soup was indeed thicker, it was lumpy and had a greasy, unsatisfying mouthfeel. We then turned to gluten-free thickeners: arrowroot, tapioca starch, cornstarch, potato starch, gelatin, and even xanthan gum. Gelatin and xanthan gum made the soup base goopy, while the individual starches produced slimy and gritty soups. Finally, we turned to our own gluten-free flour blend. We scattered 2 ounces of our blend over the vegetables we'd browned in the rendered bacon fat, and this thickened our chowder base into a velvety soup without grit or slime. Rather than deal with the pain of shucking raw clams, we simply steamed them, pulling out the meat when they just started to open to guard against overcooking. We started with bottled clam juice as our broth, then added some of the clam steaming liquid to cut the saltiness.

New England Clam Chowder

SERVES 6

- 3   cups water
- 6   pounds medium hard-shell clams, such as cherrystones, scrubbed
- 2   slices bacon, chopped fine
- 2   onions, chopped fine
- 2   celery ribs, chopped fine
- 1   teaspoon minced fresh thyme or ¼ teaspoon dried
- 2   ounces (7 tablespoons) ATK All-Purpose Gluten-Free Flour Blend (page 7)
- 3   (8-ounce) bottles clam juice
- 1½ pounds Yukon Gold potatoes, peeled and cut into ½-inch pieces
- 1   bay leaf
- 1   cup heavy cream
- 2   tablespoons minced fresh parsley
     Salt and pepper

1. Bring water to boil in Dutch oven over medium-high heat. Add clams, cover, and cook for 5 minutes. Stir clams well, cover, and continue to cook until they begin to open, 2 to 7 minutes. As clams open, transfer to large bowl; discard any that refuse to open.

2. Measure out and reserve 2 cups clam steaming liquid, avoiding any gritty sediment that has settled on bottom of pot. Remove clam meat from shells and chop coarse.

3. Clean now-empty Dutch oven, add bacon, and cook over medium heat until crisp, 5 to 7 minutes. Stir in onions and celery and cook until softened, 5 to 7 minutes. Stir in thyme and cook until fragrant, about 30 seconds. Stir in flour blend and cook for 1 minute.

4. Gradually whisk in reserved steaming liquid and bottled clam juice, scraping up any browned bits and smoothing out any lumps. Stir in potatoes and bay leaf and bring to boil. Reduce to gentle simmer and cook until potatoes are tender, 30 to 35 minutes.

5. Stir in cream and return to brief simmer. Off heat, discard bay leaf, stir in parsley, and season with salt and pepper to taste. Stir in chopped clams, cover, and let warm through, about 1 minute. Serve.

VARIATION

Quicker New England Clam Chowder

Skip steps 1 and 2. Substitute 4 (6.5-ounce) cans minced clams, drained and juice reserved, for steamed chopped clams and reserved clam steaming liquid. Add 1 teaspoon salt to pot with thyme.

Pecan-Crusted Chicken

G-F TESTING LAB

SANDWICH BREAD

Our favorite brand of gluten-free multigrain sandwich bread is Glutino Gluten Free Multigrain Bread (see page 33 for complete tasting). Slices of gluten-free bread can vary in size from brand to brand, so we recommend going by weight rather than by number of slices. Also, how quickly the bread toasts can vary dramatically from brand to brand; keep your eye on the crumbs as they toast in the oven. We don't recommend substituting gluten-free panko for the fresh bread crumbs in this recipe.

✓ WHY THIS RECIPE WORKS

For a twist on breaded chicken, we turned to nuts, which we thought would add a robust flavor element and appealing crunch to the breading. We started by dredging the chicken breasts in cornstarch, dipping them into an egg wash, then coating them with finely ground nuts. We then sautéed the chicken in a skillet until well browned and cooked through. Unfortunately, this didn't work. The crust tasted dense and greasy, with a gummy layer hiding underneath the breading. In addition, this heavy crust failed to stick to the chicken. To lighten up the texture of the nuts, we combined them with a handful of homemade bread crumbs. Toasting the nuts and bread crumbs together in the oven helped bring out the nut flavor and added some good crunch. We also swapped the oven for the skillet, and baked the breaded cutlets instead of sautéing them to make them less greasy. To help the breading stick better to the chicken, we employed three tricks. First, we etched a shallow crosshatch pattern into the chicken's surface which released moisture and tacky proteins from the chicken, giving the coating an exceptionally solid footing. Second, we swapped out the egg wash for buttermilk; the moisture in raw egg is bound up in its proteins, making it less available to be soaked up. Plus, we liked the subtle tang of buttermilk, along with some Dijon mustard and a little sugar, to perk up the flavor of the breading. Third, we let the breaded chicken rest, which made the coating more cohesive. Pistachios, hazelnuts, or almonds can be substituted for the pecans.

Pecan-Crusted Chicken
SERVES 4

- 1 cup pecans, chopped
- 4 ounces (4 slices) gluten-free multigrain sandwich bread, torn into quarters
- 1 tablespoon unsalted butter
- 1 shallot, minced
- Salt and pepper
- ⅓ cup cornstarch
- 1 cup buttermilk
- 1 tablespoon Dijon mustard
- 2 teaspoons sugar
- 4 (6- to 8-ounce) boneless, skinless chicken breasts, trimmed

1. Adjust oven rack to middle position and heat oven to 425 degrees. Pulse pecans and bread in food processor into coarse meal, about 30 pulses. Spread crumbs in even layer on rimmed baking sheet and bake, stirring often, until golden brown, about 5 minutes. Transfer crumbs to shallow dish and reduce oven temperature to 350 degrees.

2. Melt butter in 8-inch nonstick skillet over medium heat. Add shallot and ¼ teaspoon salt cook until softened, about 2 minutes; stir into crumbs.

3. Set wire rack in rimmed baking sheet. Place cornstarch in large zipper-lock bag. In second shallow dish, whisk buttermilk, mustard, and sugar together. With sharp knife, cut 1/16-inch-deep slits on both sides of chicken breasts, spaced ½ inch apart, in crosshatch pattern.

4. Season chicken with salt and pepper. Working with 1 piece chicken at a time, add to bag of cornstarch and shake to coat. Remove chicken from bag, shaking off excess cornstarch, then dip in buttermilk mixture, and finally coat with nut mixture, pressing gently to adhere. Lay breaded chicken on prepared wire rack and let sit for 10 minutes.

5. Bake chicken until it registers 160 degrees, 25 to 30 minutes, rotating sheet halfway through baking. Let rest 5 minutes before serving.

TEST KITCHEN TIP **Scoring Chicken Breasts**

To ensure that coating clings to chicken, use sharp knife to cut 1/16-inch-deep slits on both sides of breasts, spaced ½ inch apart, in crosshatch pattern.

Orange-Flavored Chicken

SOY SAUCE   Soy sauce is traditionally a blend of fermented wheat and soybeans, but some supermarkets stock gluten-free soy sauce. Tamari is naturally gluten-free but some brands sometimes contain some wheat so it's still important to read the label. Tamari has a more pungent flavor than soy sauce, but we've found it usually works well as a substitute.

✓ WHY THIS RECIPE WORKS

Orange-flavored chicken is a Chinese takeout classic, but most versions are more breading than chicken, and the sauce is often gloppy and lackluster. We wanted to create a gluten-free version that would be even better than the original. We started by marinating the chicken in a flavorful mixture of soy sauce, garlic, ginger, chicken broth, and fresh orange juice for bright, true orange flavor. We reserved some marinade to make our sauce, which kept our recipe streamlined. To achieve a perfect crust on our chicken—tender and yielding in places and delicately crunchy in others—we coated the chicken pieces first in egg whites, then dredged them in cornstarch. A bit of baking soda encouraged deep, flavorful browning. We prefer the flavor and texture of thigh meat for this recipe, though an equal amount of boneless, skinless chicken breasts can be used. It is easiest to grate the orange zest and remove the strips of orange zest before juicing the oranges; use a sharp vegetable peeler to remove the strips. For extra spiciness, increase the cayenne in the sauce to ½ teaspoon. The whole dried chiles are mostly for appearance, and can be omitted from the sauce with little difference in flavor. Use a Dutch oven that holds 6 quarts or more for this recipe. Sprinkle with sliced scallions and serve with white rice.

Orange-Flavored Chicken

SERVES 4

- ¾ cup chicken broth
- 1½ teaspoons grated orange zest plus 8 (2-inch) strips zest and ¾ cup juice (2 oranges)
- 6 tablespoons distilled white vinegar
- 3½ ounces (½ cup packed) dark brown sugar
- ¼ cup gluten-free soy sauce or tamari
- 3 garlic cloves, minced
- 1 tablespoon grated fresh ginger
- ½ teaspoon cayenne pepper
- 1½ pounds boneless, skinless chicken thighs, trimmed and cut into 1½-inch pieces
- 2 tablespoons water
- 5 teaspoons plus 1 cup cornstarch
- 8 small whole dried red chiles (optional)
- 3 large egg whites
- ½ teaspoon baking soda
- 3 cups peanut or vegetable oil

1. Whisk broth, grated orange zest and juice, vinegar, sugar, soy sauce, garlic, ginger, and ¼ teaspoon cayenne together in large saucepan until sugar is dissolved. Transfer ¾ cup of mixture to large zipper-lock bag, add chicken, and toss to coat; press out as much air as possible and seal bag. Refrigerate chicken for 30 to 60 minutes; do not marinate longer than 60 minutes.

2. Meanwhile, bring remaining mixture in pot to boil over high heat. Whisk water and 5 teaspoons cornstarch together in bowl, then whisk into pot and cook until mixture is thickened, about 1 minute. Off heat, stir in orange zest strips and chiles, if using; cover and set aside.

3. Set wire rack in each of 2 rimmed baking sheets and line 1 with several layers of paper towels. Beat egg whites in shallow dish until frothy. Combine remaining 1 cup cornstarch, baking soda, and remaining ¼ teaspoon cayenne in large zipper-lock bag.

4. Drain chicken and pat dry thoroughly with paper towels. Working with half of chicken at a time, coat with egg whites, then transfer to bag with cornstarch and shake to coat. Shake off excess cornstarch and place on unlined wire rack.

5. Heat oil in large Dutch oven over medium-high heat until 350 degrees. Working with 1 piece of chicken at a time, add half of chicken to oil and fry until golden brown, about 5 minutes, turning chicken as needed. Transfer to paper towel–lined wire rack. Return oil to 350 degrees and repeat with remaining chicken.

6. Reheat sauce over medium heat until simmering, about 2 minutes. Add chicken and gently toss until evenly coated and heated through. Serve.

Chicken Parmesan

G-F TESTING LAB

SANDWICH BREAD	Our favorite brand of gluten-free multigrain sandwich bread is Glutino Gluten Free Multigrain Bread (see page 33 for complete tasting). Slices of gluten-free bread can vary in size from brand to brand, so we recommend going by weight rather than by number of slices. Also, how quickly the bread toasts can vary dramatically from brand to brand; keep your eye on the crumbs as they toast in the oven.
PANKO	You can substitute 1 cup gluten-free panko for the sandwich bread in this recipe and skip the processing and toasting in step 1. Note that the panko will make a harder and slightly less flavorful coating. We had good luck using Ian's Gluten-Free Panko Bread Crumbs.

WHY THIS RECIPE WORKS

Traditional chicken Parmesan is a minefield of potential problems—a soggy crust that doesn't stick, overcooked chicken, and a chewy blanket of mozzarella—so we knew that making this recipe gluten-free was sure to pose some challenges. Typically, pounded chicken cutlets are dipped in flour, then beaten egg, and finally bread crumbs to create an even, crisp coating. After they are pan-seared, the cutlets are then covered with tomato sauce and cheese and baked. Turning to the flour coating first, we found that simply replacing the flour with cornstarch worked well for a gluten-free version. As an added bonus, the additional starch helped the coating cling well to the chicken and also contributed to creating and retaining crispness. The biggest challenge was the bread-crumb coating itself. We tried using store-bought gluten-free bread crumbs but found them to vary widely among brands, with many tasting bland, dusty, and gritty overall. So for the sake of consistency, we settled on making our own fresh crumbs in the food processor. But unlike homemade bread crumbs made with wheat bread, those made with gluten-free bread didn't coat the chicken slices evenly. Because of gluten-free bread's high starch content and lack of structure, the bread crumbs broke down into sticky pieces that clumped together. The solution was to dry them out in the oven and add cornstarch, which helped eliminate clumping. To keep the cheese topping tender, we mixed the usual shredded mozzarella cheese with an equal amount of creamy fontina. We placed the mixture directly on the fried cutlets and briefly broiled them to form a waterproof layer between the crust and the sauce. This cheese barrier delivered a juicy cutlet that kept its crunch.

Chicken Parmesan

SERVES 4

- 4 ounces (4 slices) gluten-free multigrain sandwich bread, torn into quarters
- 1 ounce Parmesan cheese, grated (½ cup)
- ½ cup plus 1 tablespoon cornstarch
- ½ teaspoon garlic powder
- ⅛ teaspoon dried oregano
- 1 large egg
- 4 (3- to 4-ounce) chicken cutlets, ½ inch thick, trimmed
  Salt and pepper
- 6 tablespoons vegetable oil
- 2 ounces whole-milk mozzarella cheese, shredded (½ cup)
- 2 ounces fontina cheese, shredded (½ cup)
- 1 cup tomato sauce, warmed
- ¼ cup chopped fresh basil

1. Adjust 1 oven rack to lower-middle position and second rack 4 inches from broiler element. Heat oven to 425 degrees. Process bread in food processor until evenly ground, about 45 seconds. Spread crumbs in even layer on rimmed baking sheet and bake on lower rack, stirring often, until golden brown, about 5 minutes. Transfer crumbs to shallow dish and break up large clumps into fine crumbs. Stir in Parmesan, 1 tablespoon cornstarch, garlic powder, and oregano.

2. Set wire rack in each of 2 rimmed baking sheets and line 1 with several layers of paper towels. Beat egg in second shallow dish. Place remaining ½ cup cornstarch in large zipper-lock bag. Pat chicken dry with paper towels and season with salt and pepper. Working with 1 piece chicken at a time, add to bag of cornstarch and shake to coat. Remove chicken from cornstarch and shake off excess, then dip in egg, and finally coat with crumb mixture, pressing gently to adhere; lay coated chicken on unlined wire rack.

3. Heat broiler element. Heat 4 tablespoons oil in 12-inch nonstick skillet over medium-high heat until shimmering. Place 2 cutlets in skillet and cook, without moving them, until bottoms are crisp and deep golden brown, 1 to 2 minutes. Flip cutlets and cook on second side until deep golden brown, 1 to 2 minutes; transfer to paper towel–lined rack. Add remaining 2 tablespoons oil to skillet and repeat with remaining cutlets, lowering heat if necessary.

4. Remove paper towels underneath chicken. Combine mozzarella and fontina and sprinkle evenly over cutlets to cover completely. Broil on upper rack until cheese is melted and beginning to brown, about 2 minutes. Transfer chicken to serving platter and top each cutlet with 2 tablespoons sauce. Sprinkle with basil and serve with remaining sauce.

Quick Tomato Sauce

MAKES ABOUT 2 CUPS

This recipe makes enough sauce to top the cutlets as well as four servings of gluten-free pasta.

- 2 **tablespoons extra-virgin olive oil**
- 2 **garlic cloves, minced**
  Salt and pepper
- ¼ **teaspoon dried oregano**
  Pinch red pepper flakes
- 1 **(28-ounce) can crushed tomatoes**
- ¼ **teaspoon sugar**
- 2 **tablespoons chopped fresh basil**

1. Heat 1 tablespoon oil in medium saucepan over medium heat until shimmering. Stir in garlic, ¾ teaspoon salt, oregano, and pepper flakes and cook until fragrant, about 30 seconds. Stir in tomatoes and sugar, increase heat to high, and bring to simmer. Reduce heat to medium-low and simmer until thickened, about 20 minutes.

2. Off heat, stir in basil and remaining 1 tablespoon oil. Season with salt and pepper to taste; cover and set aside.

TEST KITCHEN TIP **Making Chicken Cutlets**

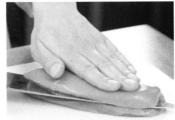

1. If tenderloin is attached to chicken breast, remove it. Also trim any excess fat, gristle, or pieces of bone where wing and ribs were attached.

2. Lay chicken breast flat on cutting board, smooth side facing up. Rest 1 hand on top of chicken and, using chef's knife, slice chicken in half horizontally.

3. Place cutlets, cut side up, between sheets of plastic wrap and pound gently to ½-inch thickness.

Chicken Parmesan

Making a gluten-free version of chicken Parmesan required finding an alternative way to coat the chicken cutlets. With some clever problem-solving, we were able to develop a technique for coating the chicken and ensuring that it stayed crunchy.

1. MAKE YOUR OWN BREAD CRUMBS AND BAKE THEM: We had the best results making our own bread crumbs using our favorite store-bought gluten-free multigrain bread. But because of its high starch content and lack of structure it didn't act like regular bread. When ground into crumbs in the food processor, it broke down into sticky clumps; the solution was to dry the crumbs out in the oven. After grinding up the bread in the food processor, we spread the crumbs onto a rimmed baking sheet and baked them until evenly golden brown.

2. BREAK UP ANY LARGE CLUMPS: After toasting our home-made bread crumbs, we found that a few large crumbs still remained. Breaking these up into finer crumbs and adding cornstarch to the mix ensured a finer, drier coating for the chicken. Stirring Parmesan cheese into the starchy (and therefore soggy-prone) bread crumbs helped give the coating more structure, added flavor, and kept it extra crispy when cooked.

3. DREDGE CHICKEN IN CORNSTARCH: Using a standard bound breading procedure (dredging in flour, then dipping in egg, then pressing in bread crumbs), we substituted cornstarch for the dredging flour. The starch granules in the cornstarch absorbed moisture and swelled, forming a sticky, thick glue that helped our bread-crumb coating adhere to the chicken cutlets. This sticky glue baked up into an ultracrisp sheath under the bread crumbs.

4. BUILD A CHEESY BARRIER: After working so hard to create a shatteringly crisp exterior, we didn't want to set our chicken cutlets into a pool of tomato sauce, which would immediately turn them soggy. After pan-frying the coated cutlets, we topped them with shredded mozzarella and fontina cheeses and set them under the broiler. This mix of cheeses kept the topping soft and appealing instead of hard and waxy. Once the cheese was bubbling and gooey, we served our chicken Parmesan with a spoonful of sauce over the top.

Chicken and Dumplings

G-F TESTING LAB

FLOUR SUBSTITUTION	King Arthur Gluten-Free Multi-Purpose Flour 9 ounces = **1½ cups plus 2 tablespoons**	Betty Crocker All-Purpose Gluten Free Rice Blend 9 ounces = **1½ cups plus ⅓ cup**
	Dumplings made with King Arthur will be slightly gummy and dense; dumplings made with Betty Crocker will taste quite rubbery.	
XANTHAN GUM	The xanthan can be omitted but the dumplings will be more crumbly and will not hold together well.	
BAKING POWDER	Not all brands of baking powder are gluten-free; see page 25 for more information.	

WHY THIS RECIPE WORKS

The best chicken and dumplings boasts dumplings that are light and tender yet substantial in a brothy stew full of concentrated chicken flavor. For a gluten-free version of this comfort food classic, we started by developing a flavorful chicken and vegetable stew that was simple enough to make on a weeknight. Right off the bat we found that boneless, skinless chicken thighs were the perfect choice here because they require very little prep and are nearly impossible to overcook. After browning them, we set them aside and focused on building the stew, first sautéing chopped carrots, onions, and celery. To thicken the stew, we added 2 tablespoons of our all-purpose gluten-free flour blend and then deglazed the pan with a little sherry, which added bright flavor. After adding some chicken broth and the reserved chicken thighs, we let the stew simmer until the chicken was tender and ready to shred. Turning our attention now to the gluten-free dumplings, we first swapped in our flour blend in the usual mixture of flour, milk, melted butter, and a hefty dose of baking powder, but these dumplings simply melted into the stew. We tried adding a little xanthan gum for binding, and while these dumplings retained their shape better, they sank into the stew and had a texture that was more akin to gnocchi than to biscuits. Switching from whole milk to low-fat lightened up the batter and got us closer, but our stew still could not support the starchier dumplings. For a thicker stew, we cut back the broth to 3 cups and added more chopped carrots and celery so the dumplings could rest on a raft of chicken and vegetables while they simmered. They cooked through properly, yielding moist, tender dumplings that soaked up the sauce perfectly.

Chicken and Dumplings

SERVES 6

STEW

- 2 pounds boneless, skinless chicken thighs, trimmed
  Salt and pepper
- 3 tablespoons vegetable oil
- 4 carrots, peeled and cut into ¾-inch pieces
- 2 celery ribs, chopped fine
- 1 onion, chopped fine
- 1 teaspoon minced fresh thyme
- 2 tablespoons ATK All-Purpose Gluten-Free Flour Blend (page 7)
- ¼ cup dry sherry
- 3 cups chicken broth
- ½ cup frozen peas
- ¼ cup minced fresh parsley

DUMPLINGS

- 9 ounces (2 cups) ATK All-Purpose Gluten-Free Flour Blend (page 7)
- 1 tablespoon baking powder
- 1 teaspoon salt
- ⅛ teaspoon xanthan gum
- ½ cup plus 1 tablespoon 1 or 2 percent low-fat milk
- ½ cup plus 1 tablespoon water
- 3 tablespoons unsalted butter, melted

1. FOR THE STEW: Pat chicken dry with paper towels and season with salt and pepper. Heat 2 tablespoons oil in Dutch oven over medium-high heat until shimmering. Add chicken and brown well on both sides, 6 to 8 minutes; transfer to plate.

2. Add remaining 1 tablespoon oil, carrots, celery, onion, and thyme to fat left in pot and cook over medium heat, stirring often, until vegetables are well browned, 5 to 7 minutes. Stir in flour blend and cook for 1 minute. Stir in sherry, scraping up any browned bits. Whisk in broth, smoothing out any lumps. Stir in browned chicken and any accumulated juices, and bring to simmer. Cover, reduce heat to medium-low, and simmer until chicken registers 175 degrees, about 15 minutes.

3. Remove pot from heat. Transfer chicken to cutting board, let cool, then shred into 1-inch pieces with 2 forks. Let broth settle for 5 minutes, then skim fat from surface. Stir in shredded meat, peas, and parsley, and season with salt and pepper to taste.

4. FOR THE DUMPLINGS: Whisk flour blend, baking powder, salt, and xanthan gum together in large bowl. Microwave milk, water, and butter in separate bowl until just warm, about 1 minute. Using rubber spatula, stir warmed milk mixture into flour mixture until incorporated and no flour pockets remain; mixture will begin to bubble immediately.

5. Return stew to vigorous simmer over medium heat. Using greased tablespoon measure, spoon portions of dumpling batter evenly over top of stew; you should have about 24 dumplings. Cover,

reduce heat to medium-low, and simmer vigorously until dumplings have doubled in size and toothpick inserted into center comes out clean, about 15 minutes. Serve.

VARIATION

Dairy-Free Chicken and Dumplings
In dumplings, substitute soy milk for milk and Earth Balance Vegan Buttery Sticks for butter.

TEST KITCHEN TIP **Making Chicken and Dumplings**

1. Brown chicken thighs well on both sides, 6 to 8 minutes; transfer to plate.

2. After sautéing aromatics and adding flour blend and sherry to pot, whisk in chicken broth, smoothing out any lumps. Return browned chicken to pot, cover, and simmer for about 15 minutes.

3. Transfer chicken to cutting board, let cool slightly, then shred into 1-inch pieces with 2 forks. Defat broth, then stir in shredded meat, peas, and parsley and season with salt and pepper to taste.

4. Using rubber spatula, stir warmed milk mixture into flour mixture until incorporated and no flour pockets remain; mixture will begin to bubble immediately.

5. Using greased tablespoon measure, spoon portions of dumpling batter evenly over top of vigorously simmering stew; you should have about 24 dumplings.

6. Cover, reduce heat to medium-low, and simmer vigorously until dumplings have doubled in size and toothpick inserted into center comes out clean, about 15 minutes. Serve.

Batter-Fried Fish

WHY THIS RECIPE WORKS

Creating batter-fried fish with a supercrisp yet light coating encasing tender, perfectly cooked fish is challenging at best; try to make it gluten-free and you better have a few tricks up your sleeve. For starters, we needed to find the right substitute for the cup of regular flour in the batter. We started by swapping in our all-purpose gluten-free flour blend for the flour, but the resulting coating was very heavy and dense. The high starch content of our blend was the reason; the starches melted when exposed to the hot oil and created a tough, unpleasant layer around our fish. We tried a variety of other flours and found we liked the flavor and texture of brown rice flour the best. We cut it with a little cornstarch, which gave us a smoother result. We also let the batter rest for a full 30 minutes to allow the flour to fully hydrate into a smooth, silky batter. Moving on to the liquid in our batter, we first tried gluten-free beer; most batters include either beer or seltzer, as the carbonation helps promote a lighter, lacier crust. But the gluten-free beers were adding a sweetness to the batter we didn't like. Seltzer, however, added the right texture but with a clean, neutral flavor. We also added baking powder to the batter to help lighten it up further, as well as some baking soda to help with the browning. But the batter wasn't sticking uniformly, and it was too thin. Dredging the fish in additional cornstarch helped the batter adhere more evenly, but our big breakthrough happened when we gave double frying a try, which allowed us to build layers of crisp coating. This technique gave us a sturdy, crunchy, golden crust without overcooking the delicate fish inside. A sweet and tangy tartar sauce was all we needed to round out the flavors of the dish. Use a Dutch oven that holds 6 quarts or more for this recipe.

Batter-Fried Fish

SERVES 4

FISH

- 1 cup brown rice flour
- ¾ cup cornstarch
- 1 teaspoon baking powder
- ½ teaspoon baking soda
- Salt and pepper
- 1¼ cups plain seltzer
- 1½ pounds cod, cut into 4-inch-long by 1-inch-thick fingers
- 3 quarts peanut or vegetable oil

TARTAR SAUCE

- ¾ cup mayonnaise
- 2 tablespoons capers, drained and minced
- 2 tablespoons sweet pickle relish
- 1 tablespoon minced shallot
- 1½ teaspoons distilled white vinegar
- ½ teaspoon Worcestershire sauce
- ½ teaspoon pepper

1. FOR THE FISH: Adjust oven rack to middle position and heat oven to 200 degrees. Set wire rack in each of 2 rimmed baking sheets and line 1 with several layers of paper towels. Whisk brown rice flour, ½ cup cornstarch, baking powder, baking soda, 1½ teaspoons salt, and ⅛ teaspoon pepper together in large bowl. Whisk in seltzer until no lumps remain, about 30 seconds. Cover bowl with plastic wrap and let sit at room temperature for 30 minutes.

2. FOR THE TARTAR SAUCE: Combine all ingredients in bowl, cover, and refrigerate until serving.

3. Spread remaining ¼ cup cornstarch in shallow dish. Pat fish dry with paper towels and season with salt and pepper. Dredge fish in cornstarch, shaking off excess, and place on unlined wire rack.

4. Heat oil in large Dutch oven over medium-high heat to 375 degrees. Working with half of fish, dip into batter, letting excess drip back into bowl, and add to hot oil. Fry fish for 1 minute, then return to unlined rack. Return oil to 375 degrees and repeat with remaining fish.

5. Return oil to 375 degrees. Working with half of fried fish, dip again in batter and fry second time until golden brown, about 2 minutes. Transfer to paper towel–lined wire rack and keep warm in oven. Return oil to 375 degrees and repeat with remaining fish. Serve with tartar sauce.

G-F TESTING LAB

BAKING POWDER	Not all brands of baking powder are gluten-free; see page 25 for more information.
RESTING TIME	Do not shortchange the batter's 30-minute rest or else the coating will be too thin and will taste gritty.

Batter-Fried Fish

We wanted a batter that coated the fish well and that also resulted in a light, airy, and extra-crispy crust. To accomplish this without traditional flour, we needed to completely rework our standard recipe.

1. USE BROWN RICE FLOUR AND CORNSTARCH: We started by swapping in our all-purpose gluten-free flour blend for the regular flour in our traditional fish-fry batter, but this didn't work because the blend contained too much starch. The starch simply melted into a heavy and gummy coating as soon as it hit the hot oil. Swapping in a whole-grain flour worked much better, and we liked the neutral flavor of brown rice flour best. Cutting the brown rice flour with a small amount of starch (cornstarch) helped the brown rice bind together and make a smooth, crisp coating.

2. ADD SELTZER, NOT BEER: Many batters for fried foods contain beer because it adds a welcome wheaty flavor, and the bubbles lighten up the texture to produce a crispier crust. Unfortunately, we found that gluten-free beers (most of which are made with sorghum) don't work well as a substitute because they have a very strong, sweet flavor. Plain water also didn't work because the lack of bubbles made the batter tough and dense. So we turned to seltzer, which produced a noticeably lighter and lacier crust without adding any off-flavors.

3. LET THE BATTER REST: We figured out early on that this batter required some extra liquid for the brown rice flour to absorb, or else it had a starchy and gritty texture. The brown rice flour also needed some extra time to sit and absorb the liquid, so we added a 30-minute resting period. As the batter rested, it became thicker and clung better to the fish.

4. BATTER FISH TWICE AND FRY TWICE: Despite all our tricks, the coating on the fish was turning out a bit thin and patchy. Dredging the fish in cornstarch before dipping it in the batter helped with the patchiness, but the batter was still too thin. So we turned to a "double-fry" method whereby we battered and fried the fish twice. A first dip in the batter and a quick fry, followed by a second dip in the batter and another brief fry, made for layers of crisp coating without overcooking the fish.

Breaded Pork Cutlets

G-F TESTING LAB

SANDWICH BREAD	Our favorite brand of gluten-free multigrain sandwich bread is Glutino Gluten Free Multigrain Bread (see page 33 for complete tasting). Slices of gluten-free bread can vary in size from brand to brand, so we recommend going by weight rather than by number of slices. Also, how quickly the bread toasts can vary dramatically from brand to brand; keep your eye on the crumbs as they toast in the oven.
PANKO	You can substitute 1 cup gluten-free panko for the sandwich bread in this recipe and skip the processing and toasting in step 1. Note that the panko will make a harder and slightly less flavorful coating. We've had good luck using Ian's Gluten-Free Panko Bread Crumbs.

✓ WHY THIS RECIPE WORKS

Since pork cutlets are so lean and mild, a flavorful coating and the right cooking method are key. To ensure the best flavor and texture, we began by making our own cutlets by cutting medallions from a pork tenderloin and then pounding them. Next we made our own bread crumbs. We had learned previously that making bread crumbs from gluten-free bread took some work, as they break down into sticky clumps when ground; the key was to toast them in the oven to dry them out. Still, there were some clumps, creating bare spots in our breading. We solved this by adding in some cornstarch to further dry out the crumbs, which helped fill in the gaps as well as boost browning and crispness. We also mixed in some grated Parmesan cheese to add more flavor to the coating.

Breaded Pork Cutlets

SERVES 4

4	ounces (4 slices) gluten-free multigrain sandwich bread, torn into quarters
1	ounce Parmesan cheese, grated (½ cup)
½	cup plus 1 tablespoon cornstarch
½	teaspoon garlic powder
⅛	teaspoon dried oregano
2	large eggs
1	(1-pound) pork tenderloin, trimmed
	Salt and pepper
6	tablespoons vegetable oil
	Lemon wedges, for serving

1. Adjust oven rack to lower-middle position and heat oven to 425 degrees. Process bread in food processor until evenly ground, about 45 seconds. Spread crumbs in even layer on rimmed baking sheet and bake, stirring often, until golden brown, about 5 minutes. Transfer crumbs to shallow dish and break up large clumps into fine crumbs. Stir in Parmesan, 1 tablespoon cornstarch, garlic powder, and oregano. Beat eggs in second shallow dish. Place remaining ½ cup cornstarch in large zipper-lock bag.

2. Set wire rack in each of 2 rimmed baking sheets and line 1 with several layers of paper towels. Cut pork crosswise into 6 pieces. Place each piece, cut side up, between sheets of plastic wrap and pound gently to ⅓-inch thickness. Season pork with salt and pepper.

3. Working with 1 piece pork at a time, add to bag of cornstarch and shake to coat. Remove pork from cornstarch and shake off excess, then dip in egg, and finally coat with crumb mixture, pressing gently to adhere; lay coated pork on unlined wire rack.

4. Heat 4 tablespoons oil in 12-inch nonstick skillet over medium heat until shimmering. Place 3 cutlets in skillet and cook, without moving them, until bottoms are crisp and deep golden brown, 2 to 4 minutes. Flip cutlets and cook on second side until deep golden brown, 2 to 4 minutes; transfer to paper towel–lined rack. Add remaining 2 tablespoons oil to skillet and repeat with remaining cutlets, lowering heat if necessary. Serve with lemon wedges.

VARIATION

Lemon-Thyme Breaded Pork Cutlets

Omit oregano. Add ½ teaspoon dried thyme and 2 teaspoons grated lemon zest to bread-crumb mixture. Add 2 sprigs fresh thyme and 2 teaspoons grated lemon zest to skillet with oil and heat oil as directed; leave thyme sprigs and lemon zest in skillet when cooking pork.

TEST KITCHEN TIP **Making Pork Cutlets**

1. Cut tenderloin crosswise into 6 equal pieces, including tapered tail end (fold tip of tail underneath before pounding).

2. Place cutlets, cut side up, between sheets of plastic wrap and pound gently to ⅓-inch thickness.

Cheesy Southwestern Meatloaf

G-F TESTING LAB

CORN TORTILLAS	Not all brands of corn tortillas are gluten-free (or processed in a gluten-free facility); read the label.
SALSA	The test kitchen's preferred brand of jarred salsa is Chi-Chi's Medium Thick and Chunky Salsa, which is gluten-free and is processed in a gluten-free facility.

WHY THIS RECIPE WORKS

For a fun twist on meatloaf, we created this South-western version. Gluten-free corn tortillas, ground in the food processor, replaced the usual panade (a mixture of bread and milk) used as the binder in meatloaf, and they added an intense corn flavor that perfectly complemented our south-of-the-border theme. The combination of ground beef and ground pork made for a tender texture and slightly sweet flavor, while a little sour cream, in addition to the eggs, helped keep the loaf moist. We flavored the meat with a combination of classic Southwestern spices and herbs: chili powder, cumin, and cilantro. Then, instead of the standard ketchup mixture, we covered the raw loaf with a little salsa mixed with brown sugar, which turned into a flavorful, sticky glaze as the loaf baked. Halfway through baking, we covered the top of the loaf with shredded pepper Jack cheese, which melted into a smooth layer. We simmered the rest of the salsa–brown sugar mixture to reduce it, and served it on the side as a sauce. To get the most flavor impact, use either medium or hot salsa. Ground pork adds tenderness and sweetness to the meatloaf, but you can use 2 pounds of ground beef if you prefer.

Cheesy Southwestern Meatloaf

SERVES 6

- 1 cup prepared tomato salsa
- 3 tablespoons packed brown sugar
- 4 (6-inch) corn tortillas, torn into small pieces
- ½ cup sour cream
- 3 large eggs
- 1 (4-ounce) can green chiles, drained and finely chopped
- ¾ cup chopped scallions
- ¼ cup minced fresh cilantro
- 1 tablespoon chili powder
- 1 teaspoon ground cumin
- 1 teaspoon salt
- ½ teaspoon pepper
- 8 ounces ground pork
- 1½ pounds 80 percent lean ground beef
- 4 ounces pepper Jack cheese, shredded (1 cup)

1. Adjust oven rack to middle position and heat oven to 350 degrees. Fold piece of heavy-duty aluminum foil into 10 by 6-inch rectangle. Place foil in center of wire rack and set in rimmed baking sheet. Grease foil, then poke holes with skewer about ½ inch apart.

2. Combine salsa and brown sugar in small saucepan; set aside. Process corn tortillas in food processor until they resemble cornmeal; transfer to large bowl. Stir in sour cream, eggs, chiles, scallions, cilantro, chili powder, cumin, salt, and pepper. Add pork and knead with hands until thoroughly combined. Add beef and continue to knead until uniform.

3. Transfer meat mixture to foil rectangle and shape into 9 by 5-inch loaf. Brush with ¼ cup salsa mixture. Bake for 40 minutes.

4. Sprinkle pepper Jack on top of meatloaf and continue to bake until loaf registers 160 degrees, 30 to 35 minutes.

5. Remove meatloaf from oven and let cool slightly. Meanwhile, simmer remaining salsa mixture over medium-high heat until thickened, 3 to 5 minutes. Serve sauce with meatloaf.

TEST KITCHEN TIP **Avoiding Greasy Meatloaf**

Set wire rack inside rimmed baking sheet and top with 10 by 6-inch rectangle of aluminum foil. Grease foil, then poke holes about ½ inch apart with skewer.

Vegetable Pot Pie with Crumble Topping

G-F TESTING LAB

FLOUR SUBSTITUTION	King Arthur Gluten-Free Multi-Purpose Flour 5 ounces = ⅔ **cup plus ¼ cup** 3 ounces = ⅓ **cup plus ¼ cup**	Betty Crocker All-Purpose Gluten Free Rice Blend 5 ounces = **1 cup** 3 ounces = ½ **cup plus 2 tablespoons**
	Pot pie made with King Arthur will have a slightly thicker filling and a somewhat starchy-tasting crumble topping. Pot pie made with Betty Crocker will have a thicker filling and the crumble topping will be less crisp and slightly chewy.	
BAKING POWDER	Not all brands of baking powder are gluten-free; see page 25 for more information.	
RESTING TIME	Do not shortchange the topping's 30-minute rest or else it will taste gritty and greasy.	

WHY THIS RECIPE WORKS

We set out to make the ultimate spring-vegetable pot pie, one that was easy and could serve a crowd. In lieu of a crust, we created a savory gluten-free crumble topping by rubbing softened butter with a mixture of our flour blend and baking powder by hand, adding Parmesan and then cream to bind it all together. For the filling, we lightly sautéed the vegetables in butter, then stirred in our flour blend for the roux, cooking it briefly before adding sherry and whisking in vegetable broth and cream. We already had prebaked the crumble to ensure that it was supercrisp before scattering it over the hot pie filling. At that point, the topped casserole needed only a mere 10 minutes to finish browning.

Vegetable Pot Pie with Crumble Topping

SERVES 6 TO 8

TOPPING

5 ounces (1 cup plus 2 tablespoons) ATK All-Purpose Gluten-Free Flour Blend (page 7)
1¼ teaspoons baking powder
¼ teaspoon salt
¼ teaspoon pepper
4 tablespoons unsalted butter, cut into ½-inch cubes and chilled
1⅓ ounces Parmesan cheese, grated (⅔ cup)
¾ cup heavy cream

FILLING

7 tablespoons unsalted butter
1½ pounds cremini mushrooms, trimmed and sliced thin
Salt and pepper
2½ pounds leeks, white and light green parts only, halved lengthwise, sliced thin, and washed thoroughly
1¼ pounds carrots, peeled and cut into ½-inch pieces
2 pounds asparagus, trimmed and cut on bias into 1-inch lengths
4 garlic cloves, minced

3 ounces (⅔ cup) ATK All-Purpose Gluten-Free Flour Blend (page 7)
⅔ cup sherry
2½ cups vegetable broth
1 cup heavy cream
3 cups frozen peas, thawed
3 tablespoons chopped fresh tarragon
2 tablespoons grated lemon zest (2 lemons)

1. FOR THE TOPPING: Adjust oven rack to middle position and heat oven to 425 degrees. Whisk flour blend, baking powder, salt, and pepper together in large bowl. Sprinkle butter pieces over top. Using fingers, rub butter into flour mixture until it resembles coarse cornmeal. Stir in Parmesan and cream until combined. Cover bowl with plastic wrap and let rest at room temperature for 30 minutes.

2. Crumble mixture into irregularly shaped ½-inch pieces on parchment paper–lined rimmed baking sheet. Bake until starting to brown, 10 to 15 minutes, rotating sheet halfway through baking. Leave oven on.

3. FOR THE FILLING: Meanwhile, melt 4 tablespoons butter in Dutch oven over medium-high heat. Add mushrooms and ½ teaspoon salt and cook until mushrooms have released their liquid and begun to brown, 15 to 20 minutes; transfer to medium bowl.

4. Melt remaining 3 tablespoons butter in now-empty pot over medium heat. Add leeks, carrots, and 2 teaspoons salt and cook for 3 minutes. Stir in asparagus and cook until carrots and leeks are softened and asparagus is crisp-tender, 3 to 5 minutes. Stir in garlic and cook until fragrant, about 30 seconds.

5. Stir in flour blend and cook for 1 minute. Stir in sherry and cook until evaporated, about 30 seconds. Slowly whisk in broth and cream until no lumps remain. Off heat, stir in cooked mushrooms, peas, 2 tablespoons tarragon, and lemon zest. Season with salt and pepper to taste.

6. Pour filling into 13 by 9-inch baking dish and sprinkle evenly with topping. Bake until filling is bubbling and topping is well browned, about 10 minutes. Let pot pie cool for 10 minutes. Sprinkle with remaining 1 tablespoon tarragon and serve.

Beef Pot Pie

G-F TESTING LAB

FLOUR SUBSTITUTION	King Arthur Gluten-Free Multi-Purpose Flour 1½ ounces = ¼ **cup**	Betty Crocker All-Purpose Gluten Free Rice Blend 1½ ounces = ⅓ **cup**
	Pot pie made with King Arthur will have a slightly thicker filling and a less-sturdy pie dough. Pot pie made with Betty Crocker will have a thicker, starchier filling.	
SOY SAUCE	Soy sauce is traditionally a blend of fermented wheat and soybeans, but some supermarkets stock gluten-free soy sauce. Tamari is naturally gluten-free but some brands sometimes contain some wheat so it's still important to read the label. Tamari has a more pungent flavor than soy sauce, but we've found it usually works well as a substitute.	

WHY THIS RECIPE WORKS

Beef pot pie hits all the marks as a comforting one-dish meal, with its flaky pastry topping and flour-thickened gravy—so it's all the more disappointing that it's typically off-limits for anyone avoiding gluten. We knew we'd be using our own gluten-free pie dough for the crust, so we moved on to finding a roux replacement that would deliver an equally velvety, rich sauce. We tested every gluten-free thickener we could think of: arrowroot, tapioca starch, potato starch, potato flour, white rice flour, gelatin, and even xanthan gum. The latter two turned the sauce gloppy and unappetizing, while most of the starches produced fillings that were slimy and oddly translucent. Finally, we turned to our own flour blend. While perhaps not as straightforward as using a single starch or flour, it amounted to minimal extra work since we needed it for the pastry anyway. We found that just 1½ ounces provided sufficient thickening power, and because the blend contains a combination of flours and starches, it didn't turn the gravy slimy, like starches alone, or gritty, like flour alone. The rest of the filling came together easily. When choosing a flavorful cut of meat, we found that chuck roast fit the bill without a high price tag. Browning just half of the beef before stewing imparted the rich, deep flavor of searing without overcrowding the pan and requiring the browning of two batches of beef. Sautéed mushrooms, tomato paste, beef broth, soy sauce, and Worcestershire added even more meaty umami flavor. Once our classic filling was prepared, we unrolled the dough over the hot filling and popped it in the oven. But instead of baking up nice and flaky, the dough turned out gummy because of all the liquid. So instead we carefully shaped, chilled, and then parbaked the pastry topping until it was golden, then slid it over the filling. All the assembled pie needed was about 10 minutes in the oven to finish cooking through and unify the flaky crust and hearty, comforting filling. If you don't have a rimless baking sheet to use for baking the crust, use an inverted rimmed baking sheet.

Beef Pot Pie

SERVES 4 TO 6

CRUST

- 3 tablespoons ice water
- 1½ tablespoons sour cream
- 1½ teaspoons rice vinegar
- 6½ ounces (¾ cup plus ⅔ cup) ATK All-Purpose Gluten-Free Flour Blend (page 7)
- 1½ teaspoons sugar
- ½ teaspoon salt
- ¼ teaspoon xanthan gum
- 8 tablespoons unsalted butter, cut into ¼-inch pieces and frozen for 10 to 15 minutes

FILLING

- 2¼ pounds boneless beef chuck-eye roast, trimmed and cut into ¾-inch pieces
  Salt and pepper
- 3 tablespoons vegetable oil
- 4 ounces cremini mushrooms, trimmed and quartered
- 2 carrots, peeled and cut into ½-inch pieces
- 1 onion, chopped fine
- 2 tablespoons tomato paste
- 4 garlic cloves, minced
- 1 teaspoon minced fresh thyme or ½ teaspoon dried
- 1½ ounces (⅓ cup) ATK All-Purpose Gluten-Free Flour Blend (page 7)
- ½ cup dry red wine
- 1¾ cups beef broth
- 1 tablespoon gluten-free soy sauce or tamari
- 1 tablespoon Worcestershire sauce
- 1 bay leaf
- 1 cup frozen peas

1. FOR THE CRUST: Combine ice water, sour cream, and vinegar together in bowl. Process flour blend, sugar, salt, and xanthan gum together in food processor until combined, about 5 seconds. Scatter butter over top and pulse until crumbs look uniform and distinct pieces of butter are no longer visible, 20 to 30 pulses.

2. Pour sour cream mixture over flour mixture and pulse until dough comes together in large pieces around blade, about 20 pulses.

3. Turn dough onto sheet of plastic wrap and flatten into 5-inch disk. Wrap tightly in plastic and refrigerate for at least 1 hour or up to 2 days. Before rolling out dough, let it sit on counter to soften slightly, about 30 minutes. (Dough cannot be frozen.)

4. Adjust oven racks to upper-middle and lower-middle positions and heat oven to 400 degrees. Roll pie dough between 2 sheets of parchment paper into 10-inch circle; discard top parchment. Fold over outer ½-inch rim of dough to create 9½-inch circle, then crimp edge of dough using fingers. Using paring knife, cut four 2-inch-long vent holes in center.

5. Transfer dough, still on parchment, to rimless baking sheet and freeze until firm, about 15 minutes. Bake on upper rack until golden and crisp, 18 to 20 minutes, rotating sheet halfway through baking; let cool. Reduce oven temperature to 350 degrees.

6. FOR THE FILLING: Meanwhile, pat beef dry with paper towels and season with salt and pepper. Heat 1½ tablespoons oil in Dutch oven over medium-high heat until just smoking. Brown half of beef on all sides, 7 to 10 minutes; transfer to bowl, along with remaining unbrowned beef.

7. Add remaining 1½ tablespoons oil, mushrooms, carrots, and onion to now-empty pot and cook over medium heat until vegetables are lightly browned, about 5 minutes. Stir in tomato paste, garlic, and thyme and cook until fragrant, about 30 seconds. Stir in flour blend and cook for 1 minute. Stir in wine and cook, scraping up any browned bits, until evaporated, about 2 minutes. Slowly whisk in broth, soy sauce, and Worcestershire until no lumps remain.

8. Add beef and any accumulated juices and bay leaf to pot and bring to simmer. Cover pot, transfer to lower oven rack, and cook until beef is tender, 1¼ to 1½ hours.

9. Remove bay leaf, stir in peas, and season with salt and pepper to taste. Pour mixture into 9½-inch deep-dish pie plate and slide parbaked pie crust on top. Bake on lower rack until crust is deep golden brown and filling is bubbly, about 10 minutes. Let pot pie cool for 5 to 10 minutes before serving.

TEST KITCHEN TIP **Making Pot Pie Crust**

1. After folding in outer ½-inch rim of dough, use index finger of 1 hand and thumb and index finger of other hand to crimp folded edge to make fluted rim. Cut 4 oval-shaped vents in dough.

2. Bake frozen crust, still on baking sheet, on upper-middle rack until golden brown, 18 to 20 minutes.

3. Carefully slide parbaked pie crust on top of warm filling.

Vegetable Lasagna

✓ WHY THIS RECIPE WORKS

We wanted a gluten-free vegetable lasagna with tender, flavorful vegetables, great cheese flavor, and a light tomato sauce. To start, we zeroed in on our choice of vegetables and settled on eggplant and yellow squash. Roasting the vegetables intensified their flavor and rid them of excess moisture. But we found that when it comes to making a gluten-free version of a classic vegetable lasagna, the biggest challenge was the noodles. As with wheat noodles, you have two options (no-boil and boil-before-use) when selecting among the various gluten-free options. No-boil noodles, a standard in the test kitchen when it comes to making traditional lasagna, failed us in the gluten-free universe. These noodles varied drastically from brand to brand. They came out unevenly cooked, gummy, starchy, or brittle, or they completely disintegrated. Old-fashioned boil-before-use noodles produced more consistent results, with tender noodles that held up in the oven. Still, our preferred noodles were more delicate than the traditional ones, so we made sure to boil them only until just tender. Typical lasagna recipes with no-boil noodles rely on extra liquid in the sauce to soften the noodles. In the case of this lasagna, our preboiled noodles would not absorb much moisture during the baking time. For this reason, we had to keep sauciness to a minimum. A bright and simple no-cook tomato sauce of crushed tomatoes, basil, and olive oil bound together the layers with minimal fuss and no excess moisture. Prepared with a classic ricotta filling, this lasagna impressed everyone in the test kitchen. You can use whole-milk or part-skim mozzarella and ricotta in this recipe. Undercooking the vegetables in step 2 is crucial, as they will continue to cook inside the lasagna. Leaving the skins on the eggplant and squash helps keep them intact and prevents them from turning mushy.

Vegetable Lasagna
SERVES 6 TO 8

NOODLES AND VEGETABLES

- 12 gluten-free lasagna noodles (10 ounces)
  Salt and pepper
- 4 tablespoons plus 1 teaspoon extra-virgin olive oil
- 1 pound eggplant, cut into ½-inch cubes
- 1 pound yellow squash, cut into ½-inch pieces
- 2 tablespoons minced fresh thyme or 1 teaspoon dried
- ¼ teaspoon red pepper flakes

TOMATO SAUCE AND CHEESE

- 1 (28-ounce) can crushed tomatoes
- ¾ cup chopped fresh basil
- 2 garlic cloves, minced
- 2 tablespoons extra-virgin olive oil
- ¼ teaspoon red pepper flakes
  Salt and pepper
- 1 pound (2 cups) whole-milk ricotta cheese
- 2½ ounces Parmesan cheese, grated (1¼ cups)
- 1 large egg, lightly beaten
- 8 ounces mozzarella cheese, shredded (2 cups)

1. FOR THE NOODLES AND VEGETABLES: Bring 4 quarts water to boil in large pot. Add lasagna noodles and 1 tablespoon salt and cook, stirring often, until just tender. Drain noodles, return them to pot, and toss with 1 teaspoon oil. Spread oiled noodles out over baking sheet.

2. Adjust oven rack 6 inches from broiler element and heat broiler. Line rimmed baking sheet with greased aluminum foil. Toss eggplant and squash with remaining 4 tablespoons oil, thyme, pepper flakes, and ¾ teaspoon salt and spread evenly over prepared baking sheet. Broil vegetables, stirring occasionally, until softened and beginning to brown

G-F TESTING LAB

LASAGNA NOODLES	We've had good luck using Tinkyada lasagna noodles (see page 30 for more details), which require boiling, but be careful not to overcook these noodles or they will fall apart when handled.

but still slightly underdone, 15 to 20 minutes; let cool slightly.

3. FOR THE SAUCE AND CHEESE: Adjust oven rack to lower-middle position and heat oven to 375 degrees. Whisk tomatoes, ½ cup basil, garlic, oil, pepper flakes, and ½ teaspoon salt together in bowl. In separate bowl, combine ricotta, 1 cup Parmesan, egg, remaining ¼ cup basil, ½ teaspoon salt, and ½ teaspoon pepper.

4. Spread ¾ cup tomato sauce evenly over bottom of 13 by 9-inch baking dish. Lay 3 noodles in dish and spread 3 tablespoons ricotta mixture over each noodle. Top evenly with ½ cup mozzarella, followed by 2 cups roasted vegetables and ¾ cup tomato sauce. Repeat layering of noodles, ricotta mixture, mozzarella, vegetables, and sauce 2 more times. For final layer, arrange remaining 3 noodles on top and spread remaining ricotta mixture over noodles. Cover completely with remaining sauce, then sprinkle with remaining ½ cup mozzarella and remaining ¼ cup Parmesan.

5. Cover dish tightly with greased aluminum foil. Bake for 20 minutes. Remove foil and bake until cheese is spotty brown and edges are just bubbling, 20 to 25 minutes longer. Let lasagna cool for 25 to 30 minutes before serving.

TEST KITCHEN TIP **Making Vegetable Lasagna**

1. Boil lasagna noodles until just tender, drain, and toss with oil. Spread oiled noodles out over baking sheet.

2. Broil eggplant and squash, stirring occasionally, until softened and beginning to brown but still slightly underdone, 15 to 20 minutes; let cool slightly.

3. Spread ¾ cup tomato sauce evenly over bottom of 13 by 9-inch baking dish. Lay 3 noodles in dish and spread 3 tablespoons ricotta mixture over each noodle.

4. Top with ½ cup mozzarella, 2 cups roasted vegetables, and ¾ cup tomato sauce. Repeat layering of noodles, ricotta mixture, mozzarella, vegetables, and sauce 2 more times.

5. For final layer, arrange remaining 3 noodles on top, and spread remaining ricotta mixture over noodles. Cover completely with remaining sauce, then sprinkle with remaining cheese.

6. Bake, covered, for 20 minutes. Uncover and bake until cheese is spotty brown and edges are just bubbling, 20 to 25 minutes longer. Let cool before serving.

Chicken Enchiladas

WHY THIS RECIPE WORKS

Chicken enchiladas offer a rich and complex combination of flavors and textures, but traditional cooking methods require hours of preparation. We wanted a streamlined recipe for this popular casserole. We created a quick but flavorful red chili sauce with onions, garlic, spices, and tomato sauce. We poached the chicken directly in the sauce, which both enhanced the flavor of the sauce and ensured moist, flavorful meat for our enchilada filling. Sharp cheddar cheese complemented the rich filling nicely, while canned jalapeños and fresh cilantro rounded out the flavors and provided tang and brightness. We brushed the tortillas with oil and microwaved them to make them pliable. After experimenting with oven temperatures and times, we found that covering the assembled enchiladas and baking them at 450 degrees for 15 minutes resulted in perfectly melted cheese and kept the edges of the tortillas from drying out. Serve with sour cream, diced avocado, sliced radishes, shredded romaine lettuce, and lime wedges.

Chicken Enchiladas
SERVES 4 TO 6

- ¼   cup vegetable oil
- 1   onion, chopped fine
- 3   tablespoons chili powder
- 3   garlic cloves, minced
- 2   teaspoons ground coriander
- 2   teaspoons ground cumin
- 2   teaspoons sugar
- ½   teaspoon salt
- 1   pound boneless, skinless chicken thighs, trimmed and cut into ¼-inch-wide strips
- 2   (8-ounce) cans tomato sauce
- 1   cup water
- ½   cup minced fresh cilantro
- ¼   cup jarred jalapeños, chopped
- 12 ounces sharp cheddar cheese, shredded (3 cups)
- 12 (6-inch) corn tortillas

1. Heat 2 tablespoons oil in medium saucepan over medium-high heat until shimmering. Add onion and cook until softened, 5 to 7 minutes. Stir in chili powder, garlic, coriander, cumin, sugar, and salt and cook until fragrant, about 30 seconds. Stir in chicken and coat thoroughly with spices. Stir in tomato sauce and water, bring to simmer, and cook until chicken is cooked through, about 8 minutes.

2. Strain mixture through fine-mesh strainer set over bowl, pressing on chicken mixture to extract as much sauce as possible. Transfer chicken mixture to separate bowl, refrigerate for 20 minutes to chill, then stir in cilantro, jalapeños, and 2½ cups cheese.

3. Adjust oven rack to middle position and heat oven to 450 degrees. Spread ¾ cup sauce over bottom of 13 by 9-inch baking dish. Brush both sides of tortillas with remaining 2 tablespoons oil. Stack tortillas, wrap in damp dish towel, and place on plate; microwave until warm and pliable, about 1 minute.

4. Working with 1 warm tortilla at a time, spread ⅓ cup chicken filling across center of tortilla. Roll tortilla tightly around filling and place seam side down in baking dish; arrange enchiladas in 2 columns across width of dish.

5. Pour remaining sauce over top to cover completely, and sprinkle remaining ½ cup cheese down center of enchiladas. Cover dish tightly with greased aluminum foil. Bake until enchiladas are heated through and cheese is melted, 15 to 20 minutes. Serve.

Strata with Spinach and Gruyère

G-F TESTING LAB

SANDWICH BREAD	Our favorite brand of gluten-free multigrain sandwich bread is Glutino Gluten Free Multigrain Bread (see page 33 for complete tasting). Slices of gluten-free bread can vary in size from brand to brand, so we recommend going by weight rather than by number of slices.
RESTING TIME	Do not shortchange the strata's 8-hour refrigerating time or else there will be pockets of raw bread in the center of the casserole.

☑ WHY THIS RECIPE WORKS

Since a classic strata breakfast casserole is all about the bread, making it gluten-free was setting the bar pretty high, especially since brands of gluten-free bread vary so widely. Also, gluten-free bread is less absorbent than regular bread, so we needed to make adjustments to the recipe because the excess liquid created a greasy, scrambled layer around the edges of the dish. We cut down overall on the amount of custard we usually use, reducing the dairy by ¼ cup and the eggs by one. We also switched from our usual half-and-half to whole milk to combat the greasiness issue. We have used white wine previously to lighten the heaviness of dairy and decided to try that here. We cut down the amount and found that reducing it in the skillet helped to concentrate the flavor as well as keep our amount of liquid in check. We thoroughly squeezed the frozen spinach to remove excess moisture, and then sautéed it to extract even more. To determine how long our strata needed to sit before baking, we started by weighing it down for an hour or two but found the gluten-free bread did not absorb the custard evenly in that amount of time. Letting it sit overnight greatly improved its texture, and we could bake it the following morning for a perfect make-ahead breakfast.

Strata with Spinach and Gruyère

SERVES 4 TO 6

2	tablespoons unsalted butter
4	shallots, minced
	Salt and pepper
10	ounces frozen chopped spinach, thawed and squeezed dry
⅓	cup dry white wine
8	ounces (8 slices) gluten-free multigrain sandwich bread
6	ounces Gruyère cheese, shredded (1½ cups)
5	large eggs
1½	cups whole milk

1. Melt butter in 10-inch nonstick skillet over medium heat. Add shallots and pinch salt and cook until shallots are softened, about 3 minutes. Stir in spinach and cook until warmed through, about 2 minutes; transfer to plate. Add wine to now-empty skillet and simmer over medium-high heat until it has reduced by half, about 3 minutes; let cool.

2. Grease 8-inch square baking dish. Arrange half of bread in single layer in dish. Sprinkle half of spinach mixture and ½ cup Gruyère over top. Repeat with remaining bread, remaining spinach mixture, and ½ cup Gruyère to make second layer.

3. Whisk eggs, reduced wine, milk, ½ teaspoon salt, and pinch pepper together in bowl, then pour evenly over top. Cover dish tightly with plastic wrap, pressing it flush to surface. Weigh strata down and refrigerate for at least 8 hours or up to 24 hours.

4. Adjust oven rack to middle position and heat oven to 325 degrees. Meanwhile, let strata sit at room temperature for 20 minutes. Unwrap strata and sprinkle with remaining ½ cup Gruyère. Bake until edges and center are puffed and edges have pulled away slightly from sides of dish, 50 to 55 minutes. Let cool for 5 minutes before serving.

VARIATION

Strata with Sausage, Mushrooms, and Monterey Jack Cheese

Chorizo, kielbasa, or hot or sweet Italian sausage can be substituted for the breakfast sausage.

Omit spinach and substitute Monterey Jack cheese for Gruyère. Before adding shallots to skillet, add 8 ounces crumbled breakfast sausage and cook for 2 minutes, then stir in 8 ounces trimmed and sliced white mushrooms and cook until lightly browned, 5 to 10 minutes.

TEST KITCHEN TIP **Weighing Down Strata**

Cover dish tightly with plastic wrap, pressing it flush to surface. Top with second casserole dish (or trimmed piece of cardboard) and weigh it down with several heavy cans.

BREAD, PIZZA, AND CRACKERS

■ DAIRY FREE OR INCLUDES A DAIRY-FREE VARIATION

Whole-Grain Sandwich Bread

G-F TESTING LAB

FLOUR SUBSTITUTION	Do not substitute other whole-grain blends for the ATK Whole-Grain Gluten-Free Flour Blend; they will not work in this recipe.
PSYLLIUM HUSK	Psyllium is crucial to the structure of the bread; see page 26 for more information.
BAKING POWDER	Not all brands of baking powder are gluten-free; see page 25 for more information.

WHY THIS RECIPE WORKS

While we were developing our whole-grain gluten-free flour blend, the idea to use it in a sandwich bread recipe was never far from our minds. Teff flour provides the backbone of the blend and lends a wheaty, earthy flavor that mimics the flavor of whole wheat, while flaxseeds add a nutty richness. Our testing had shown that, in comparison with our all-purpose blend, this high-protein flour blend absorbs more liquid, and as expected our initial loaves turned out dry and dense. We tested the addition of increasing amounts of water until we settled on the right amount. While it may seem finicky, we found that 2 cups plus 2 tablespoons of water worked perfectly. Any more made the bread slightly mushy, while less made the interior crumb taste dry. The earthy flavor of our whole-grain blend certainly made for a hearty-tasting loaf, but we noticed it tasted slightly lean. A side-by-side test of additional butter versus an extra egg yolk showed that the yolk was the winner, providing a rich, but not wet, texture. While we were happy with the flavor, we still felt that the loaf was too dense. Our other gluten-free sandwich breads all include a small amount of baking powder to help the dough rise nicely after being pressed in the loaf pan. We had initially omitted it here, thinking that the higher protein content of the whole-grain blend would translate into a more elastic dough that could rebound nicely after being pressed into the pan. We were wrong. Adding baking powder to the dough quickly fixed this problem and helped the loaf rise well, producing an open and tender crumb. We also learned that variations in kitchen temperature affected how well the loaf rose. To minimize these inconsistencies and make the recipe more foolproof, we employed two old-time baking tricks. First, we created a warm proofing box using the oven. A proofing box simply is a controlled environment with optimal conditions for letting bread rise. Second, we jump-started the yeast in warm water laced with 1 teaspoon of sugar before adding it to the dough. These two tricks also sped up the rising time substantially, from roughly 1 hour to just 30 minutes. Finally, to prevent the loaf from falling slightly as it cooled, we turned the oven off after the baking time and let the loaf cool down slowly in the oven. This gave the starches more time to set up. Note that this recipe calls for an 8½ by 4½-inch loaf pan; if using a 9 by 5-inch loaf pan, the dough will not rise as high and the bread will not be quite as tall. For information on how to shape the dough in the loaf pan, see page 145.

Whole-Grain Sandwich Bread
MAKES 1 LOAF

17	ounces (2 cups plus 2 tablespoons) warm water (110 degrees)
2¼	teaspoons instant or rapid-rise yeast
3	tablespoons plus 1 teaspoon sugar
2	large eggs plus 1 large yolk
2	tablespoons unsalted butter, melted and cooled
19½	ounces (4⅓ cups) ATK Whole-Grain Gluten-Free Flour Blend (page 9)
3	tablespoons powdered psyllium husk
2	teaspoons baking powder
1½	teaspoons salt

1. Adjust oven rack to middle position and heat oven to 200 degrees. As soon as oven reaches 200 degrees, turn it off. (This will be warm proofing box for dough. Do not begin step 2 until oven has been turned off.) Spray 8½ by 4½-inch loaf pan with vegetable oil spray.

2. Combine warm water, yeast, and 1 teaspoon sugar in bowl and let sit until bubbly, about 5 minutes. Whisk in eggs and yolk, and melted butter. Using stand mixer fitted with paddle, mix flour blend, psyllium, baking powder, salt, and remaining 3 tablespoons sugar together on low speed until combined, about 1 minute. Slowly add yeast mixture and mix until combined, scraping down bowl as needed, about 1 minute. Increase speed to medium and beat until dough is sticky and uniform, about 6 minutes. (Dough will resemble cookie dough.)

3. Using rubber spatula, scrape dough into prepared pan. Using wet hands, press dough gently into corners and smooth top. Run finger around entire edge of loaf, pressing down slightly, so that sides are about ½ inch shorter than center. Cover loosely with plastic wrap, place in warmed oven, and let rise for 10 minutes; do not let plastic touch oven rack.

4. Remove pan from oven and let sit on counter until loaf has risen ½ inch above rim of pan, about 20 minutes. Meanwhile, heat oven to 350 degrees.

5. Remove plastic and spray loaf with water. Bake until top is browned, crust is firm, and loaf sounds hollow when tapped, about 1½ hours, rotating pan halfway through baking. Turn off oven and leave bread in oven for 15 minutes longer.

6. Remove bread from oven and let cool in pan for 10 minutes. Unmold bread onto wire rack and let cool completely, about 3 hours. Serve. (Cooled bread can be wrapped in double layer of plastic wrap and stored at room temperature for up to 3 days or frozen for up to 1 month. See freezing instructions on page 145.)

VARIATION

Dairy-Free Whole-Grain Sandwich Bread
Substitute vegetable oil for melted butter.

TEST KITCHEN TIP **Ensuring a Good Rise**

Unlike traditional bread dough, which gets punched down during rising, gluten-free breads cannot be deflated once they've risen. You have only one chance to get a gluten-free bread to rise, and we've found that the best rise happens right after the dough has been mixed. Gluten-free doughs start out loose and wet but become dramatically more dense as they sit, even if for a short time. Therefore, you want the yeast to work as quickly as possible after the dough has been mixed, while it's still loose and malleable. We've also found that the temperature of the kitchen can affect how quickly and successfully these breads rise. A cold kitchen will cause the bread to rise more slowly and thus have trouble reaching its ideal height. Note that the ultimate height of a loaf isn't just for looks; it also has a substantial effect on the bread's interior texture. A shorter loaf will be much denser and harder. Given all of this, we incorporated two key tricks into all of our bread recipes to ensure a maximum, superquick rise. First, we create a warm proofing box using a warmed (but turned-off) oven. A proofing box is simply a controlled environment with optimal conditions for letting the bread rise. Second, we use instant or rapid-rise yeast (which activate more quickly than dry active yeast) and jump-start it by dissolving it in sweetened, warm water before mixing the dough.

1. Adjust oven rack to middle position and heat oven to 200 degrees. As soon as oven reaches 200 degrees, turn it off. Do not begin to mix dough until oven has been turned off. The oven will be 100 to 150 degrees when proofing the dough.

2. Combine 110-degree water, yeast, and 1 teaspoon sugar (or honey) in bowl. (Note that 1 packet of yeast equals 2¼ teaspoons.)

3. Let yeast mixture sit at room temperature until it begins to bubble and froth, about 5 minutes. Add this mixture to dough as directed in specific recipes.

Honey-Millet Sandwich Bread

✓ WHY THIS RECIPE WORKS

A seed grown in semiarid climates, millet is naturally gluten-free and highly nutritious, and it has a slightly sweet, cornlike flavor. The seed is high in fiber and protein, making it a good addition to gluten-free breads when ground into flour. We loved the idea of featuring this underutilized seed (both whole and ground) in a sandwich bread recipe. We started with a combination of our all-purpose flour blend (the flavor of the whole-grain blend would overpower the millet) and millet flour for the base of this bread. While the millet flour has a great flavor, too much of the flour made our loaf overly tacky and starchy; 6 ounces of millet flour was the right amount to lend a subtle flavor without compromising the texture. A combination of yeast and baking powder was necessary to achieve an open crumb and a higher rise, while psyllium husk and eggs guaranteed a domed loaf that didn't sink after baking. We had been using a small amount of butter but found that replacing it with vegetable oil gave our loaf a cleaner flavor, and to finish we stirred in ½ cup of rinsed millet. The seeds lent an appealing pop and enhanced the subtle flavor of the millet flour. We love this mild bread for making sandwiches, but it is also great served simply with honey butter alongside chili, soup, or stew. Note that this recipe calls for an 8½ by 4½-inch loaf pan; if using a 9 by 5-inch loaf pan, the dough will not rise as high and the bread will not be quite as tall.

Honey-Millet Sandwich Bread

MAKES 1 LOAF

- 14 ounces (1¾ cups) warm water (110 degrees)
- 2¼ teaspoons instant or rapid-rise yeast
- ¼ cup plus 1 teaspoon honey
- 3 large eggs
- 2 tablespoons vegetable oil
- 12 ounces (2⅔ cups) ATK All-Purpose Gluten-Free Flour Blend (page 7)
- 6 ounces (1⅓ cups plus ¼ cup) millet flour
- 3 tablespoons powdered psyllium husk
- 2 teaspoons baking powder
- 1½ teaspoons salt
- ½ cup millet, rinsed

1. Adjust oven rack to middle position and heat oven to 200 degrees. As soon as oven reaches 200 degrees, turn it off. (This will be warm proofing box for dough. Do not begin step 2 until oven has been turned off.) Spray 8½ by 4½-inch loaf pan with vegetable oil spray.

2. Combine warm water, yeast, and 1 teaspoon honey in bowl and let sit until bubbly, about 5 minutes. Whisk in eggs, vegetable oil, and remaining ¼ cup honey. Using stand mixer fitted with paddle, mix flour blend, millet flour, psyllium, baking powder, and salt together on low speed until combined, about 1 minute. Slowly add yeast mixture and mix until combined, scraping down bowl as needed, about 1 minute. Increase speed to medium and beat until dough is sticky and uniform, about 6 minutes. Reduce speed to low, add millet, and mix until incorporated, about 1 minute. (Dough will resemble cookie dough.)

3. Using rubber spatula, scrape dough into prepared pan. Using wet hands, press dough gently into corners and smooth top. Run finger around entire edge of loaf, pressing down slightly, so that sides are about ½ inch shorter than center. Tightly wrap double layer of aluminum foil around pan so that top edge of foil rests at least 1 inch above rim of pan; secure foil collar with staples. Cover loosely with plastic wrap, place in warmed oven, and let rise for 10 minutes; do not let plastic touch oven rack.

4. Remove pan from oven and let sit on counter until loaf has risen ½ inch above rim of pan, about 20 minutes. Meanwhile, heat oven to 350 degrees.

5. Remove plastic and spray loaf with water. Bake until top is golden, crust is firm, and loaf sounds

G-F TESTING LAB

FLOUR SUBSTITUTION	King Arthur Gluten-Free Multi-Purpose Flour 12 ounces = **1⅔ cups plus ½ cup**	Betty Crocker All-Purpose Gluten Free Rice Blend 12 ounces = **2¼ cups plus 2 tablespoons**
	Bread made with King Arthur will rise less and will be more dense; bread made with Betty Crocker will have a slightly spongy and rubbery texture.	
PSYLLIUM HUSK	Psyllium is crucial to the structure of the bread; see page 26 for more information.	
BAKING POWDER	Not all brands of baking powder are gluten-free; see page 25 for more information.	

hollow when tapped, 60 to 75 minutes, rotating pan halfway through baking.

6. Remove bread from oven and let cool in pan for 10 minutes. Unmold bread onto wire rack and let cool completely, about 3 hours. Serve. (Cooled bread can be wrapped in double layer of plastic wrap and stored at room temperature for up to 3 days or frozen for up to 1 month. See freezing instructions below.)

Honey Butter

MAKES ¼ CUP

We think this butter tastes terrific with the Honey-Millet Sandwich Bread. Store any leftovers in the refrigerator for up to 1 week.

 4   **tablespoons unsalted butter, softened**
 1   **tablespoon honey**
 ¼   **teaspoon salt**

Mix all ingredients together in bowl until combined.

TEST KITCHEN TIP **Making a Foil Collar**

Loaf breads that use the ATK All-Purpose Gluten-Free Flour Blend require a foil collar. Because this blend (as opposed to our whole-grain blend) has less protein than wheat flour, the bread has a hard time rising straight up in the oven. In many tests, loaves spilled over the sides of the pan as they baked, causing a real mess. Rather than resign ourselves to short, squat loaves (as many recipes do), we came up with a clever way to make the loaf pan taller.

Tightly wrap double layer of aluminum foil around pan so that top edge of foil rests at least 1 inch above rim of pan; secure foil collar with staples.

TEST KITCHEN TIP

Making a Nicely Domed Loaf

After baking hundreds of loaves of gluten-free bread, we uncovered a small trick to help them achieve an iconic, domed top. It is not crucial for the success of the bread, but it will make the loaf look better. If you skip this step, the loaf will taste fine, but the top might be flat or have a slightly uneven rise.

After putting dough into loaf pan, run finger around edge of loaf, pressing down slightly, so that sides are about ½ inch shorter than center.

TEST KITCHEN TIP **Freezing Gluten-Free Bread**

We have found that freezing fully cooled loaves is a good option for most gluten-free breads. For sandwich breads, we like to slice the bread before freezing so that we can pull individual slices from the freezer as needed. This applies to Whole-Grain Sandwich Bread, Honey-Millet Sandwich Bread, Flourless Nut and Seed Loaf, Brioche, and Whole-Grain Sprouted Bread. For Baguettes, Rustic Bread, Whole-Grain Walnut-Cherry Boule, and Rosemary Focaccia, freeze leftover bread in a single piece, defrost it at room temperature, and then reheat the bread in a 400-degree oven for about 10 minutes to recrisp the crust. (You can also slice these breads before freezing and then take out pieces one at a time for toasting.) Do not keep any gluten-free bread in the freezer for longer than one month.

Flourless Nut and Seed Loaf

G-F TESTING LAB

OATS	Do not use quick oats; they have a dusty texture that doesn't work in this recipe. Make sure to buy old-fashioned rolled oats that have been processed in a gluten-free facility. For more information, see page 27.
FLAXSEEDS	Both brown and golden flaxseeds will work well here.
PSYLLIUM HUSK	Psyllium is crucial to the structure of the bread; see page 26 for more information.
COCONUT OIL	Vegetable oil or olive oil can be substituted for the coconut oil.

✓ WHY THIS RECIPE WORKS

We wanted to develop a naturally gluten-free bread and set our sights on a flourless nut and seed loaf that would be high in protein and all-around nutritious with a hearty flavor. A slice of this bread, especially toasted and slathered with butter and good jam, would be all you need for breakfast. To start, we toasted the nuts and seeds to enhance their flavor. We then needed to find a way to bind all the nuts and seeds together. Since oats are a morning staple, we thought that creating a binding porridge with them would do the trick. We also used flaxseeds and powdered psyllium husk, which, when hydrated, create a gel with strong binding properties. For flavor we liked the combination of sunflower seeds, sliced almonds, and pepitas, while maple syrup added a subtle sweetness. Coconut oil complemented the nutty flavor of the loaf. To ensure the bread stayed together, we allowed everything to fully hydrate for a few hours in the loaf pan before baking. But baking this bread in a loaf pan did not allow for enough evaporation, and the inside of the loaf remained wet. To fix this, we baked the loaf for 20 minutes to allow the outside to set before turning it out onto a wire rack set in a rimmed baking sheet and returning it to the oven for 35 to 45 minutes. After letting the loaf cool for a few hours before cutting, we had a rich, nutty loaf perfect for snacking or toasting. Note that this recipe calls for an 8½ by 4½-inch loaf pan; if using a 9 by 5-inch loaf pan, the loaf will not be quite as tall.

Flourless Nut and Seed Loaf

MAKES 1 LOAF

- 1 cup sunflower seeds
- 1 cup sliced almonds
- ½ cup pepitas
- 1¾ cups old-fashioned rolled oats
- ¼ cup whole flaxseeds
- 3 tablespoons powdered psyllium husk
- 12 ounces (1½ cups) water
- 3 tablespoons coconut oil, melted and cooled
- 2 tablespoons maple syrup
- ¾ teaspoon salt

1. Adjust oven rack to middle position and heat oven to 350 degrees. Combine sunflower seeds, almonds, and pepitas on rimmed baking sheet and bake, stirring occasionally, until lightly browned, 10 to 12 minutes.

2. Line bottom of 8½ by 4½-inch loaf pan with parchment paper and spray with vegetable oil spray. Transfer toasted nut-seed mixture to bowl, let cool slightly, then stir in oats, flaxseeds, and psyllium. In separate bowl, whisk water, coconut oil, maple syrup, and salt together until well combined. Using rubber spatula, stir water mixture into nut-seed mixture until completely incorporated.

3. Scrape mixture into prepared pan. Using wet hands, press dough into corners and smooth top. Cover loosely with plastic wrap and let sit at room temperature until mixture is fully hydrated and cohesive, about 2 hours.

4. Adjust oven rack to middle position and heat oven to 350 degrees. Remove plastic and bake loaf for 20 minutes.

5. Invert loaf onto wire rack set inside rimmed baking sheet. Remove loaf pan and discard parchment. Bake loaf (still inverted) until deep golden brown and loaf sounds hollow when tapped, 35 to 45 minutes.

6. Let loaf cool completely on rack, about 2 hours. Serve. (Loaf can be stored at room temperature, uncovered, for up to 3 days; do not wrap. It can also be wrapped in double layer of plastic and frozen for up to 1 month; see freezing instructions on page 145.)

Brioche

FLOUR SUBSTITUTION	King Arthur Gluten-Free Multi-Purpose Flour 14½ ounces = **2½ cups plus 2 tablespoons**	Betty Crocker All-Purpose Gluten Free Rice Blend 14½ ounces = **2¾ cups plus 2 tablespoons**
	Brioche made with Betty Crocker will have a slightly gummy and chewy texture.	
OAT FLOUR	Not all brands of oat flour are gluten-free; read the label. Alternatively, 4 ounces (¾ cup plus 2 tablespoons) of sorghum flour can be substituted for the oat flour; we had good luck using Bob's Red Mill "Sweet" White Sorghum Flour.	
PSYLLIUM HUSK	Psyllium is crucial to the structure of the brioche; see page 26 for more information.	
BAKING POWDER	Not all brands of baking powder are gluten-free; see page 25 for more information.	

✔ WHY THIS RECIPE WORKS

We set out to create a tender and plush gluten-free brioche with the same butter-rich flavor and high rise but without the normally labor-intensive process. We looked at our traditional brioche recipe as a jumping-off point and found that it relies on higher-protein flours to help with rise, as the proteins form strong networks to support the weight of the eggs and butter. We needed to achieve a similar height in our gluten-free version, so we added 1⅓ cups of oat flour to boost the protein of our all-purpose gluten-free flour blend, along with 3 tablespoons of psyllium husk to form a strong network and trap the gas and steam formed during baking. For a rich flavor, the average brioche contains up to 50 percent butter (most butter-enriched doughs contain between 10 and 20 percent butter). The high ratio of fat lubricates the wheat proteins in flour and softens the bonds and prevents the dough from becoming tough. Since we did not have to worry about forming strong gluten bonds, we settled on 8 tablespoons of butter (half the amount used in traditional brioche), which added rich flavor without the dough becoming greasy. For our mixing method, instead of adding softened butter slowly to the dough one piece at a time, we found that simply melting the butter and adding it directly to the eggs worked just fine. We used a combination of one egg and three yolks, which added more protein and structure along with the signature eggy flavor. Since the brioche had a lot of water and fat, we needed to bake it a little longer to help dry it out and make sure it did not fall when removed from the oven. Baking the loaf for 70 minutes, then brushing it with an egg wash, allowed us to get the hallmark shiny crust without it becoming too dark. After the loaf was completely baked, we turned the oven off to allow it to dry out a little longer. Now we had a tall and beautiful brioche that was tender and rich-tasting—perfect for a sandwich or for simply slathering with butter and jam. Note that this recipe calls for an 8½ by 4½-inch loaf pan; if using a 9 by 5-inch loaf pan, the dough will not rise as high and the brioche will not be quite as tall. For information on how to shape the dough in the loaf pan and make a foil collar, see page 145.

Brioche

MAKES 1 LOAF

DOUGH

- 16 ounces (2 cups) 1 or 2 percent low-fat milk, heated to 110 degrees
- 2¼ teaspoons instant or rapid-rise yeast
- 3 tablespoons plus 1 teaspoon sugar
- 8 tablespoons unsalted butter, melted and cooled
- 1 large egg plus 3 large yolks
- 14½ ounces (3¼ cups) ATK All-Purpose Gluten-Free Flour Blend (page 7)
- 4 ounces (1⅓ cups) oat flour
- 3 tablespoons powdered psyllium husk
- 2 teaspoons baking powder
- 1½ teaspoons salt

EGG WASH

- 1 large egg
- 1 teaspoon water

1. FOR THE DOUGH: Adjust oven rack to lowest position and heat oven to 200 degrees. As soon as oven reaches 200 degrees, turn it off. (This will be warm proofing box for dough. Do not begin step 2 until oven has been turned off.) Spray 8½ by 4½-inch loaf pan with vegetable oil spray.

2. Combine warm milk, yeast, and 1 teaspoon sugar in bowl and let sit until bubbly, about 5 minutes. Whisk in melted butter and egg and yolks. Using stand mixer fitted with paddle, mix flour blend, oat flour, psyllium, baking powder, salt, and remaining 3 tablespoons sugar together on low speed until combined, about 1 minute. Slowly add yeast mixture and mix until combined, scraping down bowl as needed, about 1 minute. Increase speed to medium and beat until dough is sticky and uniform, about 6 minutes. (Dough will resemble cookie dough.)

3. Using rubber spatula, scrape dough into prepared pan. Using wet hands, press dough gently into corners and smooth top. Run finger around entire edge of loaf, pressing down slightly, so that sides are about ½ inch shorter than center. Tightly wrap double layer of aluminum foil around pan so that top edge of foil rests at least 1 inch above rim of pan; secure foil collar with staples. Cover loosely with plastic wrap, place in warmed oven, and let rise for 10 minutes; do not let plastic touch oven rack.

4. Remove pan from oven and let sit on counter until loaf has risen ½ inch above rim of pan, about 20 minutes. Meanwhile, heat oven to 350 degrees.

5. Remove plastic, spray loaf with water, and bake for 70 minutes.

6. FOR THE EGG WASH: Beat egg and water together in bowl, then brush gently over top of hot, partially baked bread. Continue to bake until top is deep golden brown, crust is firm, and loaf sounds hollow when tapped, about 20 minutes. Turn off oven and leave bread in oven for 15 minutes longer.

7. Remove bread from oven and let cool in pan for 10 minutes. Unmold bread onto wire rack and let cool completely, about 3 hours. Serve. (Cooled bread can be wrapped in double layer of plastic wrap and stored at room temperature for up to 3 days or frozen for up to 1 month. See freezing instructions on page 145.)

VARIATION

Dairy-Free Brioche

We prefer the flavor and texture of this brioche made with soy milk, but almond milk will also work; do not use rice milk.

Substitute 1 cup unsweetened soy milk and 1 cup water for milk, and Earth Balance Vegan Buttery Sticks for butter.

TEST KITCHEN TIP **Keys to Making Gluten-Free Brioche**

1. Let milk, yeast, and sugar sit until bubbly, about 5 minutes. Whisk melted butter and egg and yolks into bubbly yeast mixture.

2. After loaf has baked for 70 minutes, gently brush egg-water mixture over top and continue to bake for 20 minutes longer.

3. After brioche has finished baking, turn off oven and leave brioche in oven for 15 minutes longer to dry out.

Whole-Grain Sprouted Bread

✓ WHY THIS RECIPE WORKS

For the health-conscious, sprouted grain breads are very appealing, but good luck finding a gluten-free loaf in your local market. Given the success of our Whole-Grain Sandwich Bread (page 141), we were confident we could create a wholesome, hearty, and healthy gluten-free whole-grain sprouted grain bread. There are two common methods for incorporating sprouted grains (and often legumes) into homemade breads: either through sprouted grain flour or by sprouting grains, processing them in a food processor to a mush, and adding the mush to the bread dough. Since we couldn't find sprouted grain flour at our local grocery store, our decision was easy—we would be sprouting grains and processing them ourselves. Thinking that this recipe would need to employ the same tricks we used for our other gluten-free loaves, we put together a working recipe and made sure to include psyllium husk for binding and rise, baking powder and yeast for an open crumb and good rise, and a good amount of water to hydrate the starches and create steam for even more lift during baking. One noticeably absent ingredient was egg; all that sprouted grain mush contributed its own binding power and structure, so eggs weren't necessary. The only question that remained was which grains and/or legumes to sprout. We tested sprouting lentils, corn, oat berries, quinoa, chickpeas, millet, brown rice, and sorghum and landed on three ingredients commonly found in a gluten-free pantry: quinoa, lentils, and millet. Their flavors complemented each other, and the texture they gave the loaf wasn't too tacky or dense. We settled on ¼ cup each of lentils and quinoa and ¾ cup millet; using more of either quinoa or lentils overpowered the delicate flavor of millet, while using any more millet resulted in a loaf that was too starchy. The sprouted grains gave our bread a great flavor, but it also made the bread fairly dense. To open up the crumb a little we tested water amounts until we found the sweet spot (1⅔ cups), but we also found that 1 tablespoon of cider vinegar gave our loaf a better, more even rise. Adding ¼ cup

of roasted pepitas and sesame seeds to the dough added a nice crunch and flavor, and sprinkling some over the top before baking made our loaf even more beautiful. This bread can take up to 4 days to make, although most of the time is hands-off. Note that this recipe calls for an 8½ by 4½-inch loaf pan; if using a 9 by 5-inch loaf pan, the dough will not rise as high and the loaf will not be quite as tall. For information on how to shape the dough in the loaf pan, see page 145.

Whole-Grain Sprouted Bread
MAKES 1 LOAF

¾	cup millet
¼	cup quinoa
¼	cup brown lentils, picked over
2	cups water for soaking grains, plus 13⅓ ounces (1⅔ cups) warm water (110 degrees) for dough
¼	cup roasted, unsalted pepitas
2	tablespoons sesame seeds
2¼	teaspoons instant or rapid-rise yeast
3	tablespoons plus 1 teaspoon honey
1	tablespoon cider vinegar
14	ounces (3 cups plus 2 tablespoons) ATK Whole-Grain Gluten-Free Flour Blend (page 9)
1½	tablespoons powdered psyllium husk
1½	teaspoons salt
1	teaspoon baking powder

1. Combine millet, quinoa, lentils, and 2 cups water in bowl, cover with plastic wrap, and let soak at room temperature until quinoa starts to sprout, 12 to 24 hours. Drain through fine-mesh strainer, return to bowl, and cover with plastic. Let grains sit at room temperature, rinsing and draining them daily, until each type of grain begins to sprout, 1 to 3 days. (Each individual grain does not need to sprout.)

2. Adjust oven rack to middle position and heat oven to 200 degrees. As soon as oven reaches 200 degrees, turn it off. (This will be warm proofing

G-F TESTING LAB

FLOUR SUBSTITUTION	Do not substitute other whole-grain blends for the ATK Whole-Grain Gluten-Free Flour Blend; they will not work in this recipe.
PSYLLIUM HUSK	Psyllium is crucial to the structure of the bread; see page 26 for more information.
BAKING POWDER	Not all brands of baking powder are gluten-free; see page 25 for more information.

box for dough. Do not begin step 3 until oven has been turned off.) Spray 8½ by 4½-inch loaf pan with vegetable oil spray. Process sprouted grains in food processor to thick, sticky paste, stopping to scrape down bowl often, 2 to 3 minutes. Combine pepitas and sesame seeds in bowl.

3. Combine 13⅓ ounces warm water, yeast, and 1 teaspoon honey in bowl and let sit until bubbly, about 5 minutes. Whisk in remaining 3 tablespoons honey and vinegar. Using stand mixer fitted with paddle, mix flour blend, psyllium, salt, and baking powder on low speed until combined, about 1 minute. Slowly add yeast mixture and sprouted grain paste and mix until combined, about 1 minute, scraping down bowl as needed. Increase speed to medium and beat until sticky and uniform, about 6 minutes. (Dough will resemble cookie dough.) Reduce speed to low, add ¼ cup seed mixture, and mix until incorporated, 30 to 60 seconds.

4. Using rubber spatula, scrape dough into prepared pan. Using wet hands, press dough gently into corners and smooth top. Run finger around entire edge of loaf, pressing down slightly, so that sides are about ½ inch shorter than center. Using serrated knife, cut three ½-inch-deep slashes diagonally across top of dough. Cover loosely with plastic wrap, place in warmed oven, and let rise for 10 minutes; do not let plastic touch oven rack.

5. Remove pan from oven and let sit on counter until loaf has risen ½ inch above rim of pan, about 20 minutes. Meanwhile heat oven to 350 degrees.

6. Remove plastic, spray loaf with water, and sprinkle with remaining seed mixture. Bake until top is browned, crust is firm, and loaf sounds hollow when tapped, about 2 hours, rotating pan halfway through baking.

7. Remove bread from oven and let cool in pan for 10 minutes. Unmold bread onto wire rack and let cool completely, about 3 hours. Serve. (Cooled bread can be wrapped in double layer of plastic wrap and stored at room temperature for up to 2 days or frozen for up to 1 month. See freezing instructions on page 145.)

TEST KITCHEN TIP **Sprouting Grains for Bread**

1. Combine millet, quinoa, lentils, and 2 cups water in bowl, cover with plastic wrap, and let soak at room temperature until quinoa starts to sprout, 12 to 24 hours.

2. Drain soaked grains through strainer, return to bowl, and cover with plastic. Let grains sit at room temperature, rinsing and draining daily, until each type of grain begins to sprout, 1 to 3 days. (Every individual grain does not need to sprout.)

3. Process sprouted grains in food processor to thick, sticky paste, stopping to scrape down bowl often, 2 to 3 minutes.

Baguettes

G-F TESTING LAB

FLOUR SUBSTITUTION	Do not substitute other all-purpose blends for the ATK All-Purpose Gluten-Free Flour Blend; they will not work well in this recipe.
OAT FLOUR	Not all brands of oat flour are gluten-free; read the label. Alternatively, 2 ounces (7 tablespoons) of sorghum flour can be substituted for the oat flour.
PSYLLIUM HUSK	Psyllium is crucial to the structure of the bread; see page 26 for more information.
WATER	Using the correct amount of water is crucial for this recipe; we strongly recommend weighing the water instead of using a liquid measuring cup.
BAGUETTE PAN	This recipe requires a two-loaf perforated baguette pan with 1-inch-deep trenches.

WHY THIS RECIPE WORKS

Making traditional baguettes is daunting for all but the most practiced home bakers, so we wondered whether we could develop a relatively simple gluten-free recipe. We cobbled together a working recipe using our all-purpose gluten-free flour blend, some oat flour for flavor and structure, and ground psyllium husk as a binder. Baguettes traditionally begin with a starter—a small mixture of flour, yeast, and liquid allowed to bubble and ferment—before making the dough in order to give the bread a deeper, richer flavor. We tried two different starters in our recipe, one using our all-purpose blend and another using oat flour. Oddly, the starter made with the all-purpose blend never fermented but rather turned into a rainbow of fuzzy mold. The oat flour starter, however, worked well and added an earthy, sweet fermented flavor to the bread. When testing how long the starter needed to sit, we were happy to find that 30 minutes was long enough to give the bread plenty of flavor. Traditionally, French baguettes also include a substantial amount of water in the dough in order to achieve their hallmark chewy texture and open crumb. To mimic this in our gluten-free version, we tested various amounts of water and found that 8 ounces of water to 10 ounces of flour gave us the chewy, airy crumb we were after. We also learned that measuring the water accurately makes a big difference. If you're off by just a table-spoon or two, the shape and texture of the final loaf will vary dramatically; for accuracy, we recommend weighing the water rather than using a liquid mea-suring cup. A traditional baguette recipe would never include eggs, but we found that adding a couple of eggs to this gluten-free dough made a big differ-ence. The eggs boosted the protein in the dough to make it stronger and gave the bread a fuller, rounder flavor. We were getting closer to a good baguette, but the crumb was still a bit too dense. Wondering if an alkaline or an acidic ingredient could help open up the crumb, we tried adding them to the dough both separately and together. Adding an alkaline ingredi-ent (baking soda) gave the bread a gummy texture and turned the loaf a strange pink color. Adding an acid (vinegar), however, opened up the crumb nicely, making the airholes larger and more authentic. Testing a few different types of acid—including yogurt, buttermilk, water kefir, milk kefir, lemon juice, rice vinegar, and apple cider vinegar—we found that a mere tablespoon of cider vinegar opened up the crumb just enough without giving the bread a sour flavor. Traditional baguettes bake for only 20 minutes or so, but our gluten-free baguettes required nearly an hour in the oven in order to dry out. To prevent the crust from becoming overly thick and dense during this long baking time, we covered the loaves with a piece of foil (with holes poked into it to help release some of the steam) during the first half of the baking time. Using a very hot oven in addition to the foil gave the baguettes a nice tall oven spring. After we removed the foil, we reduced the oven temperature so that the loaves could dry out and brown evenly. Throughout all of our testing, we tried a variety of shaping methods and found that a perforated baguette pan is crucial because the dough is so wet and slack.

Baguettes
MAKES 2 LOAVES

STARTER
- 2 ounces (⅔ cup) oat flour
- 4 ounces (½ cup) warm water (110 degrees)
- 1½ teaspoons sugar
- ½ teaspoon instant or rapid-rise yeast

DOUGH
- 8 ounces (1¾ cups) ATK All-Purpose Gluten-Free Flour Blend (page 7)
- 7 teaspoons powdered psyllium husk
- 1½ teaspoons sugar
- 1 teaspoon instant or rapid-rise yeast
- ¾ teaspoon salt
- 4 ounces (½ cup) warm water (110 degrees)
- 2 large eggs
- 1 tablespoon cider vinegar

1. FOR THE STARTER: Combine oat flour, warm water, sugar, and yeast in bowl and let sit until bubbly and fragrant, about 30 minutes. Adjust oven rack to middle position and heat oven to 200 degrees. When oven reaches 200 degrees, turn it off. (This will be warm proofing box for dough. Do not begin step 2 until oven has been turned off.)

2. FOR THE DOUGH: Using stand mixer fitted with paddle, mix flour blend, psyllium, sugar, yeast, and salt together on low speed until combined, about 1 minute. Slowly add warm water, eggs, vinegar, and starter and mix until combined, scraping down bowl as needed, about 1 minute. Increase speed to medium and beat until dough is sticky and uniform, about 6 minutes. (Dough will resemble cookie dough.)

3. Scrape down bowl, then scrape half of dough onto clean counter; dough will be very sticky. Using hands, roll into rough 6-inch-long rope. Clean and dry hands, then continue to roll dough into 13-inch-long rope, working from center out to ends and pinching holes together as needed; do not taper ends. Gently transfer loaf to baguette pan. Repeat with remaining dough to form second loaf.

4. Place baguette pan on rimmed baking sheet. Cover loosely with plastic wrap, place in warmed oven, and let rise for 10 minutes; do not let plastic touch oven rack. Remove sheet from oven and let sit on counter until loaves have risen by 50 percent, about 20 minutes. Meanwhile, heat oven to 450 degrees.

5. Remove plastic and cut three 4-inch-long, ½-inch-deep diagonal slashes down length of each loaf using serrated knife. Tent baking sheet loosely with aluminum foil and crimp edges to seal; do not let foil touch top of loaves. Using sharp knife, poke 6 holes in foil. Bake baguettes until lightly browned, about 25 minutes.

6. Carefully remove foil (watch for steam), rotate sheet, and reduce oven temperature to 350 degrees; if necessary, hold oven door open for a few seconds to help it cool down. Continue to bake until baguettes are golden brown, 25 to 35 minutes. Transfer baguettes to wire rack and let cool completely, about 1 hour. Serve. (Cooled bread can be wrapped in double layer of plastic and stored at room temperature for up to 1 day or frozen for up to 1 month. See freezing instructions on page 145.)

TEST KITCHEN TIP **Making Baguettes**

1. Scrape down bowl, then scrape half of dough onto clean counter; dough will be very sticky. Using hands, roll into rough 6-inch-long rope.

2. Washing and drying your hands before continuing to roll dough into 13-inch-long rope is crucial. Dough will become less sticky as you continue to roll it.

3. After dough has risen in perforated baguette pan, cut three 4-inch-long, ½-inch-deep diagonal slashes down length of each loaf using serrated knife.

Baguettes

We wanted baguettes with a crisp, crackly top, a moist, open crumb, and a subtly sweet, earthy tang. To achieve this flavor and texture we had to employ a few unconventional tricks and ingredients. This is what we learned.

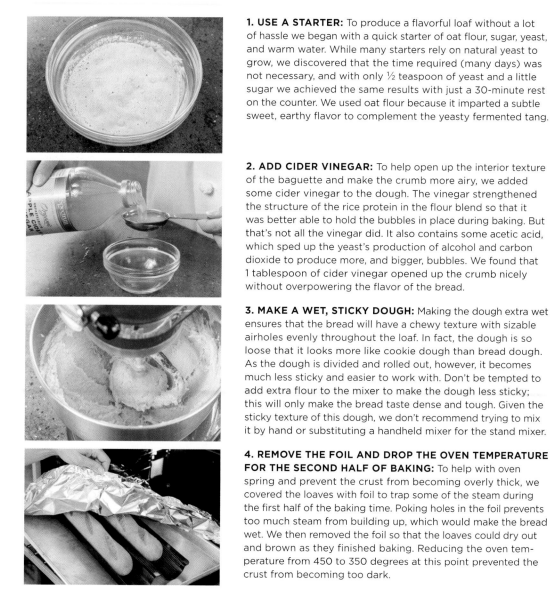

1. USE A STARTER: To produce a flavorful loaf without a lot of hassle we began with a quick starter of oat flour, sugar, yeast, and warm water. While many starters rely on natural yeast to grow, we discovered that the time required (many days) was not necessary, and with only ½ teaspoon of yeast and a little sugar we achieved the same results with just a 30-minute rest on the counter. We used oat flour because it imparted a subtle sweet, earthy flavor to complement the yeasty fermented tang.

2. ADD CIDER VINEGAR: To help open up the interior texture of the baguette and make the crumb more airy, we added some cider vinegar to the dough. The vinegar strengthened the structure of the rice protein in the flour blend so that it was better able to hold the bubbles in place during baking. But that's not all the vinegar did. It also contains some acetic acid, which sped up the yeast's production of alcohol and carbon dioxide to produce more, and bigger, bubbles. We found that 1 tablespoon of cider vinegar opened up the crumb nicely without overpowering the flavor of the bread.

3. MAKE A WET, STICKY DOUGH: Making the dough extra wet ensures that the bread will have a chewy texture with sizable airholes evenly throughout the loaf. In fact, the dough is so loose that it looks more like cookie dough than bread dough. As the dough is divided and rolled out, however, it becomes much less sticky and easier to work with. Don't be tempted to add extra flour to the mixer to make the dough less sticky; this will only make the bread taste dense and tough. Given the sticky texture of this dough, we don't recommend trying to mix it by hand or substituting a handheld mixer for the stand mixer.

4. REMOVE THE FOIL AND DROP THE OVEN TEMPERATURE FOR THE SECOND HALF OF BAKING: To help with oven spring and prevent the crust from becoming overly thick, we covered the loaves with foil to trap some of the steam during the first half of the baking time. Poking holes in the foil prevents too much steam from building up, which would make the bread wet. We then removed the foil so that the loaves could dry out and brown as they finished baking. Reducing the oven temperature from 450 to 350 degrees at this point prevented the crust from becoming too dark.

Rustic Bread

G-F TESTING LAB

FLOUR SUBSTITUTION	King Arthur Gluten-Free Multi-Purpose Flour 12 ounces = **1⅔ cups plus ½ cup**	Betty Crocker All-Purpose Gluten Free Rice Blend 12 ounces= **2¼ cups plus 2 tablespoons**
	Bread made with Betty Crocker will have a softer texture and milder flavor.	
OAT FLOUR	Not all brands of oat flour are gluten-free; read the label. Alternatively, 4 ounces (¾ cup plus 2 tablespoons) of sorghum flour can be substituted for the oat flour. We had good luck using Bob's Red Mill "Sweet" White Sorghum Flour.	
PSYLLIUM HUSK	Psyllium is crucial to the structure of the bread; see page 26 for more information.	
WATER	Using the correct amount of water is crucial for this recipe; we strongly recommend weighing the water instead of using a liquid measuring cup.	

WHY THIS RECIPE WORKS

We wanted to develop a recipe for rustic bread with good wheaty flavor, a chewy interior, and a thick, hearty crust. Classic recipes for this type of bread contain as few as four ingredients—water, yeast, salt, and flour—but they rely heavily on the protein in the flour to create an open crumb and give the loaf a nice shape that holds its own without having to bake it in a pan. Knowing that our all-purpose blend would need a protein boost in order to support this kind of loaf, we combined it with a substantial portion of oat flour along with a couple of eggs. To help open the interior crumb of the bread so that it would have large, rustic airholes, rather than the small, tight holes you'd expect in a sandwich bread, we increased the amount of water substantially and made the dough quite wet. To help the wet bread hold on to these larger airholes during rising and baking, we added two key ingredients: psyllium husk and vinegar. The psyllium made the dough stronger and more elastic, and the vinegar also made the dough stronger while speeding up the yeast activity. Focusing next on the flavor, we found our working recipe still tasted too bland. To help give it deeper flavor, we borrowed a technique from our baguette recipe and added a starter. A starter is a small mixture of flour, yeast, and liquid allowed to bubble, ferment, and develop flavor before making the actual bread dough. Using the same 30-minute oat flour starter that we used for the baguettes gave this bread the hearty, wheaty flavor we were after. Up until this point, we had been shaping the dough into one big loaf, but the finished breads were often inconsistent in terms of height and oven spring. Trying a variety of different bread shapes, we found that making two small loaves worked much better. We had one last problem to tackle—baking the bread. With so much water in the dough to provide steam, we had to bake the bread longer to dry out the inside, but this caused the bottom crust to burn. Insulating the baking sheet by placing it inside another baking sheet enabled us to bake the bread for 90 minutes and dry it out but not burn the crust.

Rustic Bread with Sesame Seeds

MAKES 2 LOAVES

STARTER

- 4 ounces (1⅓ cups) oat flour
- 8 ounces (1 cup) warm water (110 degrees)
- 1 tablespoon sugar
- 1 teaspoon instant or rapid-rise yeast

DOUGH

- 12 ounces (2⅔ cups) ATK All-Purpose Gluten-Free Flour Blend (page 7)
- 5 tablespoons powdered psyllium husk
- 1 tablespoon instant or rapid-rise yeast
- 1 tablespoon sugar
- 1½ teaspoons salt
- 9 ounces (1 cup plus 2 tablespoons) warm water (110 degrees)
- 2 large eggs
- 1 tablespoon cider vinegar
- 1 tablespoon sesame seeds

1. FOR THE STARTER: Combine oat flour, warm water, sugar, and yeast in bowl and let sit until bubbly and fragrant, about 30 minutes. Adjust oven rack to middle position and heat oven to 200 degrees. When oven reaches 200 degrees, turn it off. (This will be warm proofing box for dough. Do not begin step 2 until oven has been turned off). Line rimmed baking sheet with parchment paper and place inside of second baking sheet.

2. FOR THE DOUGH: Using stand mixer fitted with paddle, mix flour blend, psyllium, yeast, sugar, and salt on low speed until combined, about 1 minute. Slowly add warm water, eggs, vinegar, and starter and mix until combined, scraping down bowl as needed, about 1 minute. Increase speed to medium and beat until dough is sticky and uniform, about 6 minutes. (Dough will be thick and sticky.)

3. Divide dough into 2 equal pieces. Working with 1 piece of dough at a time, roll into rough 6-inch-long rope on clean counter. Dough will be sticky, so clean and dry hands, then gently continue to roll dough into 8-inch-long rope, working from center out to ends and pinching holes together as needed; do not taper ends. Gently transfer loaves to prepared sheet, spaced 4 inches apart.

4. Cover loosely with plastic wrap, place in warmed oven, and let rise for 10 minutes; do not let plastic touch oven rack. Remove from oven and let sit on counter until loaves have risen by 50 percent, about 20 minutes. Meanwhile, heat oven to 350 degrees.

5. Remove plastic and cut three 2-inch-long, ½-inch-deep diagonal slashes down length of each loaf using serrated knife. Spray loaves with water and sprinkle with sesame seeds. Bake until tops are deep golden brown, crusts are firm, and loaves sound hollow when tapped, about 90 minutes, rotating pan halfway through baking.

6. Transfer sheet with baguettes to wire rack and let bread cool for 10 minutes. Remove loaves from sheet and let cool completely on rack, about 3 hours. Serve. (Cooled bread can be wrapped in double layer of plastic and stored at room temperature for up to 3 days or frozen for up to 1 month. See freezing instructions on page 145.)

TEST KITCHEN TIP **5 Key Ingredients for Great Gluten-Free Bread**

We've baked well over a thousand loaves of gluten-free bread in search of perfection. Here are the five key ingredients without which good gluten-free bread is just not possible.

GROUND PSYLLIUM HUSK All of our breads call for ground psyllium husk for two reasons. First, it reinforces the protein structure in the dough, much like a glue, so that the dough is stronger and better able to hold on to air bubbles. Second, it helps bind water into the dough, making the crumb more moist. Note that psyllium darkens as it ages, which can discolor the bread.

INSTANT YEAST All of our breads call for instant yeast (aka rapid-rise). Instant yeast is different from active dry yeast because it has been processed more gently, which in turn makes it work faster. Rather than add the instant yeast to the dough in its dried, granular form, we first dissolve it in warm, sweetened water to help speed it up even more. This ensures that the bread has a swift rise with lots of airholes evenly dispersed throughout the loaf.

VINEGAR Our Baguettes and Rustic Bread recipes have a little vinegar added to the dough to help them develop large, airy pockets and a hearty chew. The vinegar has an acidic pH and works on a molecular level to make the rice proteins in the flour blend stronger so that they can hold on to large gas bubbles better. We like cider vinegar because the flavor isn't noticeable in the final bread.

BAKING POWDER Most of our recipes call for baking powder, which is a leavener made of baking soda, an acid (such as cream of tartar), and buffering agents that prevent any reaction from happening until liquid or heat is added. Once activated, it produces gas bubbles that, in addition to the yeast, help bread rise. It is a stronger leavener than baking soda alone because it activates itself twice: once when combined with liquid and a second time when heated. That's why baking powder is often called "double-acting."

BAKING SODA Two of our whole-grain breads call for baking soda, which is a leavener with an alkaline pH. As a leavener, it reacts with any acidity in the dough (including acid created by the fermenting yeast) to create gas that, in addition to the yeast, helps bread rise. Even more important, however, the alkaline pH of the baking soda dissolves some of the proteins in the dough, which makes the bread more tender and soft. This is especially useful in our whole-grain breads (which have a very high protein content) to help soften their tougher texture. We don't add it to any of our breads that use the all-purpose blend, because it makes them mushy and turns them an unappealing purple-pink color.

Bagels

✓ WHY THIS RECIPE WORKS

All too often, the best part of a gluten-free bagel is the cream cheese smeared on top. We knew developing a really good gluten-free bagel with a crisp crust and substantial chew was setting the bar high since even traditional bagels rely on lots of tricks. To start, we compiled a variety of recipes and substituted our all-purpose gluten-free flour blend. The first round of bagels were like small, dense hockey pucks. Despite their problems, bagels that were boiled before baking had a nice crisp crust. The slightly alkaline water (due to the baking soda) cooked the exterior starches on the bagels, giving them a glossy sheen, while the baking soda also helped the bagels brown. We got rid of the multiple proofing steps because with multiple rising steps we were deflating the dough, so we shaped the bagels right out of the mixer and proofed them for just 30 minutes. We then drastically increased the amount of water in the dough from the traditional 55 percent hydration (in glutenous bagels) to 85 percent in hopes that it would open the crumb. The bagels rose high, but when they hit the boiling water they started to fall apart. Psyllium husk powder and xanthan gum made the dough easier to work with and keeping the boiling time to 10 seconds also helped. Next we swapped some of our flour blend for high-protein oat flour, which produced a uniform interior crumb. We missed the nutty flavor that malt syrup usually adds to bagels and found that molasses was the perfect substitute. We learned that baking the bagels at 425 degrees for the first half of the baking time ensured a nice rise, then turning down the oven to 350 degrees dried out the interiors without the exteriors getting too dark.

Bagels
MAKES 6 BAGELS

- 13.3 ounces (1⅔ cups) warm water (110 degrees) for dough, plus 4 quarts for boiling bagels
- 1 tablespoon instant or rapid-rise yeast
- 1 tablespoon sugar
- 3 tablespoons unsalted butter, melted and cooled
- 1 teaspoon molasses
- 13½ ounces (3 cups) ATK All-Purpose Gluten-Free Flour Blend (page 7)
- 2 ounces (⅔ cup) oat flour
- 1½ tablespoons powdered psyllium husk
- 2 teaspoons baking powder
- 1½ teaspoons salt
- ½ teaspoon xanthan gum
- 1 tablespoon baking soda

1. Adjust oven rack to middle position and heat oven to 200 degrees. As soon as oven reaches 200 degrees, turn it off. (This will be warm proofing box for dough. Do not begin step 2 until oven has been turned off.) Line rimmed baking sheet with parchment paper and spray with vegetable oil spray.

2. Combine 13.3 ounces warm water, yeast, and sugar in bowl and let sit until bubbly, about 5 minutes. Whisk in melted butter and molasses. Using stand mixer fitted with paddle, mix flour blend, oat flour, psyllium, baking powder, salt, and xanthan gum on low speed until combined, about 1 minute Slowly add yeast mixture and mix until combined, about 1 minute, scraping down bowl as needed. Increase speed to medium and beat until dough is sticky and uniform, about 6 minutes. (Dough will be quite stiff.)

3. Divide dough into 6 equal pieces (5¼ ounces each). Working with 1 piece of dough at a time, roll into 9-inch-long rope (do not taper ends). Bring ends of rope together to form circle, overlapping ends by 1 inch. Gently pinch ends of dough together to seal. Pick up bagel, and using two fingers, gently roll seam against counter to reshape; transfer to prepared sheet.

4. Cover loosely with plastic wrap, place sheet in warmed oven, and let rise for 10 minutes; do not let plastic touch oven rack. Remove sheet from oven and let sit on counter until dough is puffy and has risen by 50 percent, about 20 minutes. Meanwhile, heat oven to 425 degrees. Bring 4 quarts water and baking soda to boil in Dutch oven.

5. Working with 1 bagel at a time, place in boiling water and cook for 10 seconds, flipping them over halfway through cooking. Using wire skimmer,

G-F TESTING LAB

FLOUR SUBSTITUTION	Do not substitute other all-purpose blends for the ATK All-Purpose Gluten-Free Flour Blend; they will not work in this recipe.
OAT FLOUR	Not all brands of oat flour are gluten-free; read the label. Alternatively, 2 ounces (7 tablespoons) of sorghum flour can be substituted for the oat flour.
WATER	Using the correct amount of water is crucial for this recipe; we strongly recommend weighing the water instead of using a liquid measuring cup.
PSYLLIUM HUSK	Psyllium is crucial to the structure of the bagels; see page 26 for more information.
XANTHAN GUM	Xanthan is crucial to the structure of the bagels; see page 22 for more information.

return bagels to sheet, right side up, with flat bottoms against pan.

6. Set sheet with bagels inside second rimmed baking sheet. Bake for 15 minutes. Reduce oven temperature to 350 degrees, rotate sheet, and continue to bake until bagels are evenly golden brown, about 20 minutes.

7. Remove bagels from oven and let cool on sheet for 5 minutes. Transfer bagels to wire rack and cool for at least 20 minutes before serving. (Cooled bagels can be stored in zipper-lock bag at room temperature for up to 3 days. They can also be sliced, wrapped in double layer of plastic wrap, and frozen for up to 1 month.)

VARIATIONS

Dairy-Free Bagels
Substitute Earth Balance Vegan Buttery Sticks for butter and reduce salt to 1 teaspoon.

Everything Bagels
Combine 2 tablespoons poppy seeds, 2 tablespoons sesame seeds, 1 tablespoon onion flakes, 2 teaspoons garlic flakes, 2 teaspoons caraway seeds, and ½ teaspoon coarse or pretzel salt in bowl. After bagels have been boiled, sprinkle seed mixture evenly over bagels.

TEST KITCHEN TIP **Making Bagels**

1. Divide dough into 6 equal pieces. Working with 1 piece of dough at a time, roll into 9-inch-long rope (do not taper ends).

2. Bring ends of rope together to form circle, overlapping ends by 1 inch. Gently pinch ends of dough together to seal.

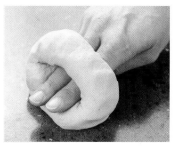

3. Pick up bagel, and using two fingers, gently roll seam against counter to reshape; transfer to prepared sheet.

4. Place 1 bagel at a time in boiling water and cook for 10 seconds, flipping bagels halfway through cooking. Using wire skimmer, return bagels to sheet, right side up with flat bottoms against pan.

5. To provide extra insulation and prevent bagels from getting too dark on bottom during baking, put sheet with bagels inside second rimmed baking sheet.

6. Bake at 425 degrees for 15 minutes. Reduce oven to 350 degrees, rotate sheet, and bake until bagels are evenly golden brown, about 20 minutes.

Whole-Grain Walnut-Cherry Boule

FLOUR SUBSTITUTION	Do not substitute other whole-grain blends for the ATK Whole-Grain Gluten-Free Flour Blend; they will not work in this recipe.
PSYLLIUM HUSK	Psyllium is crucial to the structure of the bread; see page 26 for more information.

WHY THIS RECIPE WORKS

This walnut-cherry boule is a rustic loaf with a thick, burnished crust and a soft but chewy interior crumb flavored with walnuts and dried cherries. While classic boule recipes rely on the gluten bonds for structure, thereby allowing the dough to rise up instead of out, we had to come up with our own tricks. Starting with our whole-grain gluten-free flour blend was a step in the right direction because its high protein content helped give the dough enough structure to rise. And as with our other yeast breads, we added powdered psyllium husk to strengthen the protein network in the whole-grain flour blend. Using more yeast than usual (4 teaspoons) helped with the rise, as did starting the loaf in a hot oven (400 degrees) and then turning down the heat so it could cook through. We further reinforced the rise by increasing the amount of liquid in the batter, which created a lot of steam in the oven, but we wanted the loaf to rise even higher. Switching from whole to low-fat milk made for a higher rise and a moist crumb, as the bread was no longer weighed down with fat. To help make the interior crumb more delicate, we added baking soda. The soda is alkaline, which dissolved a small amount of the rice proteins in the dough and resulted in a more tender crumb. Proofing and baking the loaf in a small skillet prevented the bread from spreading and allowed us to easily transfer the loaf to the baking stone. Finally, a little bit of sugar helped the yeast do its job and added a subtle sweetness that complemented the earthy flavor of our whole-grain flour blend. You will need an 8-inch ovensafe skillet for this recipe.

Whole-Grain Walnut-Cherry Boule

MAKES 1 LOAF

- 16 ounces (2 cups) 1 or 2 percent low-fat milk, heated to 110 degrees
- 4 teaspoons instant or rapid-rise yeast
- 2 tablespoons plus 1 teaspoon sugar
- 2 large eggs
- 15 ounces (3⅓ cups) ATK Whole-Grain Gluten-Free Flour Blend (page 9)
- 2½ tablespoons powdered psyllium husk
- 1½ teaspoons salt
- ¾ teaspoon baking soda
- 1 cup walnuts, toasted and chopped
- ½ cup dried cherries, chopped

1. Adjust oven rack to middle position and heat oven to 200 degrees. As soon as oven reaches 200 degrees, turn it off. (This will be warm proofing box for dough. Do not begin step 2 until oven has been turned off.)

2. Combine warm milk, yeast, and 1 teaspoon sugar in bowl and let sit until bubbly, about 5 minutes. Whisk in eggs. Using stand mixer fitted with paddle, mix flour blend, psyllium, salt, baking soda, and remaining 2 tablespoons sugar together on low speed until combined, about 1 minute. Slowly add yeast mixture and mix until combined, scraping down bowl as needed, about 1 minute. Increase speed to medium and beat until sticky and uniform, about 6 minutes. (Dough will resemble cookie dough.) Reduce speed to low, add walnuts and cherries, and mix until incorporated, 30 to 60 seconds.

3. Spray 18 by 12-inch sheet of parchment paper with vegetable oil spray. Using rubber spatula, transfer dough to prepared parchment. Using wet hands, shape into 6½-inch ball. Transfer dough with parchment to 8-inch ovensafe skillet. Using serrated knife, cut ½-inch-deep X across top of dough. Cover loosely with plastic wrap, place skillet in warmed oven, and let rise for 10 minutes; do not let plastic touch oven rack.

4. Remove skillet from oven and let sit on counter until loaf has risen by 50 percent, about 20 minutes. Meanwhile, place baking stone on rack and heat oven to 400 degrees.

5. Remove plastic and spray loaf with water. Reduce oven temperature to 350 degrees and place skillet on baking stone. Bake until top of bread is well browned, crust is firm, and loaf sounds hollow when tapped, 55 to 75 minutes, rotating skillet half-way through baking.

6. Being careful of hot skillet handle, remove skillet from oven. Transfer bread to wire rack, discarding parchment, and let cool completely, about 3 hours. Serve. (Cooled bread can be wrapped in double layer of plastic wrap and stored at room temperature for up to 3 days or frozen for up to 1 month. See freezing instructions on page 145.)

VARIATION

Dairy-Free Whole-Grain Walnut-Cherry Boule

We prefer the flavor and texture of this boule made with soy milk, but almond milk will also work; do not use rice milk.

Substitute 1 cup unsweetened soy milk and 1 cup water for milk.

TEST KITCHEN TIP **Making Whole-Grain Walnut-Cherry Boule**

1. Using rubber spatula, transfer dough to greased parchment paper and shape with wet hands into 6½-inch ball.

2. Place dough (still on parchment) inside 8-inch ovensafe skillet.

3. Using serrated knife, cut ½-inch-deep X across top of dough. Cover dough with plastic and let rise in turned-off oven.

4. Let dough rise on counter 20 minutes. Meanwhile, heat baking stone in 400-degree oven. After loaf has fully risen, remove plastic and spray loaf with water.

5. Reduce oven temperature to 350 degrees and place skillet with loaf on baking stone.

6. Bake until top of bread is well browned, crust is firm, and loaf sounds hollow when tapped, 55 to 75 minutes, rotating skillet halfway through baking.

Classic Cheese Pan Pizza

✓ WHY THIS RECIPE WORKS

Unlike its thin-crust cousin, pan pizza has a soft, chewy, thicker crust that can stand up to any topping. We wanted to make this pizza with a rich and flavorful crust and began by using our focaccia recipe (page 171) and splitting it between two pans. A generous amount of oil in the dough as well as 4 tablespoons in each pan gave the crust its richness while also crisping the bottom. We decreased the amount of yeast slightly, as the crust did not need as much lift as focaccia. For a final burst of rise before the crust set, also known as oven spring, we preheated the oven to 475 degrees and then lowered it to 350 degrees when we put the pizza in so the crust could bake through without burning. As we had learned during our focaccia recipe testing, using a baking stone in the oven created a more reliable temperature after decreasing the heat. Although we usually add the sauce and toppings before baking pizza, we found that they weighed down our gluten-free crust and made it soggy, so we baked the crust first and let it cool before topping it. For a simple no-bake sauce we simply pureed canned whole tomatoes, garlic, olive oil, red wine vinegar, and spices in the food processor; creamy mozzarella and sharp Parmesan were the perfect toppings. We broiled the topped pizza for a few minutes to melt the cheese and heat the crust through. If you use light-colored cake pans, the crust will not brown as well.

Classic Cheese Pan Pizza

MAKES TWO 9-INCH PIZZAS

- ½ cup plus 3 tablespoons extra-virgin olive oil
- 10.6 ounces (1⅓ cups) warm water (110 degrees)
- 1 tablespoon sugar
- 2¼ teaspoons instant or rapid-rise yeast
- 1 large egg
- 10 ounces (2¼ cups) ATK All-Purpose Gluten-Free Flour Blend (page 7)
- 2 ounces (⅔ cup) oat flour
- 1 tablespoon powdered psyllium husk
- ¾ teaspoon salt
- ½ teaspoon xanthan gum
- 1 cup pizza sauce
- 6 ounces whole-milk mozzarella cheese, shredded (1½ cups)
- 1 ounce Parmesan cheese, grated (½ cup)
- 3 tablespoons chopped fresh basil

1. Adjust oven racks to upper-middle and lower-middle positions and heat oven to 200 degrees. As soon as oven reaches 200 degrees, turn it off. (This will be warm proofing box for dough. Do not begin step 2 until oven has been turned off.) Brush 2 dark 9-inch round cake pans with ¼ cup oil each.

2. Combine warm water, sugar, and yeast in bowl and let sit until bubbly, about 5 minutes. Whisk in remaining 3 tablespoons oil and egg. Using stand mixer fitted with paddle, mix flour blend, oat flour, psyllium, salt, and xanthan gum together on low speed until combined, about 1 minute. Slowly add yeast mixture and mix until combined, scraping down bowl as needed, about 1 minute. Increase speed to medium and beat until sticky and uniform, about 6 minutes. (Dough will resemble cookie dough.)

3. Using rubber spatula, divide dough evenly between prepared pans. Using wet hands, press dough gently into corners and smooth top. Cover loosely with plastic wrap, place on upper rack in warmed oven, and let rise for 10 minutes; do not let plastic touch oven rack.

4. Remove pans from oven and let sit on counter until crusts have risen by 50 percent, about 20 minutes. Meanwhile, place baking stone on lower rack and heat oven to 475 degrees.

5. Reduce oven temperature to 350 degrees. Remove plastic from crusts, place on upper rack (not on stone), and bake until dark golden brown on top and crusts release from pans easily, 45 to 50 minutes, rotating pans halfway through baking.

6. Set wire rack inside rimmed baking sheet. Carefully slide hot crusts out of pans onto prepared rack; let cool for at least 20 minutes or up to 2 hours. (Cooled crusts can be wrapped in double layer of

G-F TESTING LAB

FLOUR SUBSTITUTION	King Arthur Gluten-Free Multi-Purpose Flour 10 ounces = **1½ cups plus ⅓ cup**	Betty Crocker All-Purpose Gluten Free Rice Blend 10 ounces = **2 cups**
	Pizza made with Betty Crocker will have a slightly spongy and chewy texture.	
OAT FLOUR	Not all brands of oat flour are gluten-free; read the label. Alternatively, 2 ounces (7 tablespoons) of sorghum flour can be substituted for the oat flour; we had good luck using Bob's Red Mill "Sweet" White Sorghum Flour.	
PSYLLIUM HUSK	Psyllium is crucial to the structure of the dough; see page 26 for more information.	
XANTHAN GUM	Xanthan is crucial to the structure of the dough; see page 22 for more information.	

plastic wrap and stored at room temperature for up to 1 day or frozen for up to 1 month. If frozen, unwrap and let thaw completely at room temperature before using.)

7. Heat broiler. Spoon ½ cup pizza sauce over top of each crust, leaving ¼-inch border around edge, then sprinkle with mozzarella and Parmesan. Broil pizzas (still on wire rack–lined sheet) on upper rack until cheese is melted, 2 to 3 minutes. Remove pizzas from oven and slide onto cutting board. Sprinkle with basil, slice into quarters, and serve immediately.

VARIATIONS

Pepperoni Pan Pizza
Arrange 2 ounces sliced pepperoni between double layers of coffee filters on plate and microwave until fat begins to render, about 30 seconds. Sprinkle pepperoni on top of cheese before broiling pizzas.

Pan Pizza with Sausage and Peppers
Microwave 4 ounces Italian sausage, casings removed and sausage broken into ½-inch pieces, with ½ green or red bell pepper, cut into ½-inch pieces, and 1 tablespoon water in covered bowl until sausage is no longer pink and bell pepper is crisp-tender, about 4 minutes; drain mixture and transfer to paper towel–lined plate. Sprinkle sausage and pepper mixture over cheese before broiling pizzas.

Easy Pizza Sauce
MAKES 2 CUPS

While it is convenient to use jarred pizza sauce, we think it is almost as easy, and a lot tastier, to whip up your own. Our favorite brand of whole peeled tomatoes is Muir Glen Organic Whole Peeled Tomatoes.

- 1 **(28-ounce) can whole peeled tomatoes, drained with juice reserved**
- 1 **tablespoon extra-virgin olive oil**
- 1 **teaspoon red wine vinegar**
- 2 **garlic cloves, minced**
- 1 **teaspoon dried oregano**
- ½ **teaspoon salt**
- ¼ **teaspoon pepper**

Process drained tomatoes with oil, vinegar, garlic, oregano, salt, and pepper in food processor until smooth, about 30 seconds. Transfer mixture to liquid measuring cup and add reserved tomato juice until sauce measures 2 cups. (Sauce can be refrigerated for up to 1 week or frozen for up to 1 month.)

TEST KITCHEN TIP **Making Pan Pizza**

1. Bake crusts in 350-degree oven, on upper-middle rack (not on stone) until dark golden brown on top and crusts release from pans easily.

2. Using spatula, carefully slide hot crusts out of pans onto wire rack–lined baking sheet. Let crusts cool for at least 20 minutes or up to 2 hours.

3. Spoon ½ cup pizza sauce over top of each cooled crust, leaving ¼-inch border. Sprinkle evenly with cheeses. Broil pizzas until cheese melts, 2 to 3 minutes.

Rosemary Focaccia

G-F TESTING LAB

FLOUR SUBSTITUTION	King Arthur Gluten-Free Multi-Purpose Flour 10 ounces = **1½ cups plus ⅓ cup**	Betty Crocker All-Purpose Gluten Free Rice Blend 10 ounces = **2 cups**
	Focaccia made with Betty Crocker will be very chewy and slightly wet on inside, and the crust will be less crisp.	
OAT FLOUR	Not all brands of oat flour are gluten-free; read the label. Alternatively, 2 ounces (7 tablespoons) of sorghum flour can be substituted for the oat flour; we had good luck using Bob's Red Mill "Sweet" White Sorghum Flour.	
PSYLLIUM HUSK	Psyllium is crucial to the structure of the bread; see page 26 for more information.	
XANTHAN GUM	Xanthan is crucial to the structure of the bread; see page 22 for more information.	

WHY THIS RECIPE WORKS

Focaccia is typically a simple dough containing just flour, yeast, water, salt, and a hefty dose of olive oil for flavor. We decided to tackle hydration first, testing increasing amounts of water and ultimately finding that 1⅓ cups gave us a nice rise without oversaturating the dough. To trap the air bubbles and achieve a good height, we added both psyllium (which helped create an open crumb) and xanthan gum (which gave the bread chew and kept it moist). To achieve the best rise, we had to play with the oven method. Baking the bread at a low temperature for longer led to a flatter bread with a thick, hard crust, while baking the loaf at a high temperature burned the outside before the inside could dry out. We found that preheating the oven to 475 degrees created enough oven spring for a nice rise, while lowering the oven to 350 degrees when adding the bread kept it from burning. During testing our loaves were turning out with inconsistent heights, which we attributed to the fact that we were using different ovens. The speed that oven temperatures drop varies by oven; to ensure a more reliable oven temperature after decreasing the heat, we heated a baking stone on the rack below the bread. Oiling the top of the finished loaf gave the bread a nice shine and prevented the loaf from deflating under the oil's weight during baking. If you don't have a baking stone, you can use a rimmed baking sheet, but your bread will not rise as high and will be slightly wet. We prefer the coarse texture of kosher salt here; if using table salt, reduce all salt amounts by half.

Rosemary Focaccia

MAKES 1 LOAF

- 5   tablespoons extra-virgin olive oil
- 10.6 ounces (1⅓ cups) warm water (110 degrees)
- 1   tablespoon sugar
- 1   tablespoon instant or rapid-rise yeast
- 1   large egg
- 10 ounces (2¼ cups) ATK All-Purpose Gluten-Free Flour Blend (page 7)
- 2   ounces (⅔ cup) oat flour
- 1   tablespoon powdered psyllium husk
-     Kosher salt
- ½   teaspoon xanthan gum
- 1   teaspoon minced fresh rosemary

1. Adjust oven rack to upper-middle and lower-middle positions and heat oven to 200 degrees. As soon as oven reaches 200 degrees, turn it off. (This will be warm proofing box for dough. Do not begin step 2 until oven has been turned off.) Brush 8-inch square baking pan with 1 tablespoon oil.

2. Combine warm water, sugar, and yeast in bowl and let sit until bubbly, about 5 minutes. Whisk in 3 tablespoons oil and egg. Using stand mixer fitted with paddle, mix flour blend, oat flour, psyllium, 1½ teaspoons salt, and xanthan gum together on low speed until combined, about 1 minute. Slowly add yeast mixture and mix until combined, scraping down bowl as needed, about 1 minute. Increase speed to medium and beat until sticky and uniform, about 6 minutes. (Dough will resemble cookie dough.)

3. Using rubber spatula, scrape dough into prepared pan. Using wet hands, press dough gently into corners and smooth top. Cover loosely with plastic wrap, place on upper rack in warmed oven, and let rise for 10 minutes; do not let plastic touch oven rack.

4. Remove pan from oven and let sit on counter until loaf has risen by 50 percent, about 20 minutes. Meanwhile, place baking stone on lower rack and heat oven to 475 degrees.

5. Remove plastic and sprinkle loaf with rosemary and ¼ teaspoon salt. Reduce oven temperature to 350 degrees, place loaf on upper rack (not on stone), and bake until golden brown, 60 to 70 minutes; do not open oven door during baking.

6. Remove bread from oven, brush with remaining 1 tablespoon oil, and let cool in pan for 10 minutes. Unmold bread onto wire rack and let cool completely, about 1 hour. Serve. (Cooled bread can be wrapped in double layer of plastic wrap and stored at room temperature for up to 2 days or frozen for up to 1 month. See freezing instructions on page 145.)

Whole-Grain Dinner Rolls

FLOUR SUBSTITUTION	Do not substitute other whole-grain blends for the ATK Whole-Grain Gluten-Free Flour Blend; they will not work in this recipe.
PSYLLIUM HUSK	Psyllium is crucial to the structure of the rolls; see page 26 for more information.

WHY THIS RECIPE WORKS

Knowing that the wheaty flavor of our whole-grain gluten-free flour blend would taste great in a rich, buttery dinner roll, we took our basic dinner roll recipe and swapped in our whole-grain blend. Finding these rolls a bit too greasy, we reduced the butter to 4 tablespoons and added a few egg yolks to make up for the missing richness. Many of our other yeasted breads require a little baking powder for a tall rise, but we found it wasn't necessary here. The whole-grain blend has a higher protein content than that of the all-purpose blend, which makes the dough stronger. Not only does this strong dough translate into a chewier texture, it's also better at trapping the yeast's gas during rising to produce nice, tall rolls. We did, however, like the addition of baking soda. The soda is alkaline, which dissolves a small amount of the rice proteins in the dough and therefore makes the crumb more delicate. Up until now, we had been baking the rolls in a cake pan to create pull-apart rolls, but that wasn't working because the unsupported center roll always collapsed during baking. To solve this, we switched to a muffin tin so that each roll could have pan support during the rise and the bake. To finish, we sprinkled the rolls with chopped sunflower seeds and kosher salt before baking. If using table salt, reduce all salt amounts by half.

Whole-Grain Dinner Rolls

MAKES 12 ROLLS

12	ounces (1½ cups) 1 or 2 percent low-fat milk, heated to 110 degrees
2¼	teaspoons instant or rapid-rise yeast
5	teaspoons sugar
1	large egg plus 2 large yolks
10	ounces (2¼ cups) ATK Whole-Grain Gluten-Free Flour Blend (page 9)
5	teaspoons powdered psyllium husk Kosher salt
½	teaspoon baking soda
4	tablespoons unsalted butter, cut into 4 pieces and softened
1	tablespoon raw sunflower seeds, chopped

1. Adjust oven rack to middle position and heat oven to 200 degrees. As soon as oven reaches 200 degrees, turn it off. (This will be warm proofing box for dough. Do not begin step 2 until oven has been turned off.) Spray 12-cup muffin tin with vegetable oil spray.

2. Combine warm milk, yeast, and 1 teaspoon sugar in bowl and let sit until bubbly, about 5 minutes. Whisk in egg and yolks. Using stand mixer fitted with paddle, mix flour blend, psyllium, 2 teaspoons salt, baking soda, and remaining 4 teaspoons sugar together on low speed until combined, about 1 minute. Slowly add yeast mixture and mix until combined, scraping down bowl as needed, about 1 minute. Add butter, increase speed to medium, and beat until sticky and uniform, about 6 minutes. (Dough will be very soft and loose.)

3. Working with scant ¼ cup dough at a time, shape into rough rounds using wet hands and place in prepared muffin tin. Cover loosely with plastic wrap, place in warmed oven, and let rise for 10 minutes; do not let plastic touch oven rack.

4. Remove rolls from oven and let sit on counter until dough has doubled in size, about 20 minutes. Meanwhile, heat oven to 350 degrees.

5. Remove plastic, spray rolls with water, then sprinkle with sunflower seeds and ½ teaspoon salt. Bake until deep golden brown, 30 to 35 minutes, rotating muffin tin halfway through baking.

6. Remove rolls from oven and let cool in tin for 10 minutes. Remove rolls from tin and serve warm. (Rolls can be stored in zipper-lock bag for up to 2 days; they cannot be frozen. To refresh, warm rolls in 350-degree oven for 10 minutes.)

VARIATION

Dairy-Free Whole-Grain Dinner Rolls

We prefer the flavor and texture of these rolls made with soy milk, but almond milk will also work; do not use rice milk.

Substitute ¾ cup unsweetened soy milk and ¾ cup water for milk, and Earth Balance Vegan Buttery Sticks for butter. Omit salt in dough.

Hamburger Rolls

FLOUR SUBSTITUTION	King Arthur Gluten-Free Multi-Purpose Flour 12 ounces = **1⅔ cups plus ½ cup**	Betty Crocker All-Purpose Gluten Free Rice Blend 12 ounces = **2¼ cups plus 2 tablespoons**
	Rolls made with Betty Crocker will have a slightly spongy and chewy texture.	
OAT FLOUR	Not all brands of oat flour are gluten-free; read the label. Alternatively, 6 ounces (1⅓ cups) of sorghum flour can be substituted for the oat flour; we had good luck using Bob's Red Mill "Sweet" White Sorghum Flour.	
PSYLLIUM HUSK	Psyllium is crucial to the structure of the rolls; see page 26 for more information.	
BAKING POWDER	Not all brands of baking powder are gluten-free; see page 25 for more information.	

WHY THIS RECIPE WORKS

If you've ever had a store-bought gluten-free hamburger roll, you know how disappointing they can be. Usually dry, crumbly, and stale-tasting, or flat, dense, and tough, these skimpy buns don't have enough structure to stand up to a meaty burger. To start, we employed a handful of tricks we've found to be important to successful gluten-free yeast breads: We added oat flour for a little protein boost, two eggs for structure and richness, psyllium husk powder to create an open crumb and contribute to a sturdy structure, and a combination of yeast and baking powder to encourage the rolls to rise during proofing and baking. These additions made the rolls taste right, but their dry, dense texture still needed work, and they looked more like a dinner roll than a hamburger bun. To fix the dry, dense texture of the rolls, we tested adding more water incrementally beyond the 2 cups in our working recipe. In the end, just ¼ cup additional water made all the difference in opening up the crumb and making the rolls more tender. But the extra water made the dough so slack that the rolls couldn't hold their shape during rising and baking. Even with all the protein boosts and binders we had added to the dough, they just spread out over the pan into pancakes. Rather than tinker with the liquid amount again and wreck the ideal crumb we had created, we decided to think outside of the bun. To help contain the slack dough, we constructed foil collars for each roll so that they could maintain a tall, round shape while proofing and during the first half of baking. Greasing the collars ensured that they released from the partially baked rolls easily. A final spritz of water and a sprinkling of sesame seeds before baking were the final touches for our tender but hearty hamburger rolls.

Hamburger Rolls
MAKES 8 ROLLS

18	ounces (2¼ cups) warm water (110 degrees)
2¼	teaspoons instant or rapid-rise yeast
2	tablespoons plus 1 teaspoon sugar
2	large eggs
2	tablespoons unsalted butter, melted and cooled
12	ounces (2⅔ cups) ATK All-Purpose Gluten-Free Flour Blend (page 7)
6	ounces (2 cups) oat flour
3	tablespoons powdered psyllium husk
2	teaspoons baking powder
1½	teaspoons salt
1	teaspoon sesame seeds

1. Adjust oven rack to middle position and heat oven to 200 degrees. As soon as oven reaches 200 degrees, turn it off. (This will be warm proofing box for dough. Do not begin step 2 until oven has been turned off.) Line rimmed baking sheet with parchment paper and spray with vegetable oil spray. Using double layer of aluminum foil, create eight 13½ by 2-inch strips, then shape each into 4-inch circle and secure with staples. Spray inside of collars with vegetable oil spray and place on prepared sheet.

2. Combine warm water, yeast, and 1 teaspoon sugar in bowl and let sit until bubbly, about 5 minutes. Whisk in eggs and melted butter. Using stand mixer fitted with paddle, mix flour blend, oat flour, psyllium, baking powder, salt, and remaining 2 tablespoons sugar together on low speed until combined, about 1 minute. Slowly add yeast mixture and mix until combined, scraping down bowl as needed, about 1 minute. Increase speed to medium and beat until sticky and uniform, about 6 minutes. (Dough will resemble cookie dough.)

3. Working with ½ cup dough at a time, shape each into rough round using wet hands, and place in foil collar. Cover loosely with plastic wrap, place in warmed oven, and let rise for 10 minutes; do not let plastic touch oven rack.

4. Remove rolls from oven and let sit on counter until dough has doubled in size, about 20 minutes. Meanwhile, heat oven to 400 degrees.

5. Reduce oven temperature to 350 degrees. Remove plastic and adjust foil collars as needed to be flush with pan. Spray rolls with water and sprinkle with sesame seeds. Bake until golden brown and firm, 35 to 40 minutes, rotating sheet and removing foil collars halfway through baking.

6. Transfer rolls to wire rack and let cool completely before serving, about 1 hour. (Split rolls can be wrapped in double layer of plastic wrap and stored at room temperature for up to 2 days, or frozen for up to 1 month. If frozen, microwave at 50 percent power for 1 minute then toast until golden.)

VARIATION

Dairy-Free Hamburger Rolls
Substitute vegetable oil for melted butter.

TEST KITCHEN TIP **Working with Foil Collars**

1. Using double layer of aluminum foil, create eight 13½ by 2-inch strips.

2. Shape each strip into 4-inch circle and secure with staples.

3. Spray inside of collars with vegetable oil spray and place on greased, parchment-lined baking sheet.

4. Working with ½ cup dough at a time, shape into rough rounds using wet hands, and place in foil collars.

5. After rolls have risen, remove plastic wrap and adjust collars as needed to be flush with baking sheet.

6. Remove foil collars halfway through baking time to ensure even browning around edges of rolls.

Hamburger Rolls

Most store-bought gluten-free hamburger rolls are a sad accompaniment to a burger. To create a roll that stood up to even a big pub-style burger, we had to get a little creative in the kitchen.

1. ADD OAT FLOUR: Lower-protein gluten-free flours aren't as effective as all-purpose flour at trapping air or gas bubbles that form from leavening (yeast, baking powder, or baking soda) or steam during baking. Adding a small amount of a higher-protein flour can do wonders to trap those gasses and encourage a tall rise and an open crumb. We turned to oat flour in addition to our all-purpose gluten-free flour blend for our hamburger rolls because it gave them an open crumb and a tall rise without imparting any off-flavors or colors.

2. FAST-TRACK THE YEAST: In order to get tall, fluffy rolls, it's important to get the bread rising quickly once the dough is mixed. This is because the dough starts off loose and wet but becomes more dense and dry as it sits (for even a short time), and the yeast has an easier time doing its job while the dough is loose and malleable. To start, we gave the instant yeast a boost by blooming it in warm water laced with sugar before making the dough. Once the dough was made and the rolls were shaped, we kept the yeast working at a fast pace by starting the rise in a warm (but turned-off) oven.

3. GET CRAFTY WITH COLLARS: Even with the addition of oat flour, our rolls were spreading too much during proofing and baking. We wanted our hamburger rolls to taste and look like the real thing, so using loaf pans or muffin tins were out. We used foil collars with success in some of our sandwich breads to encourage the loaves to rise beyond the loaf pan rim, so we decided to craft free-form collars for the rolls. Not only did the collars encourage the rolls to rise beautifully, they ensured the rolls turned out uniformly.

4. START HOT, THEN TURN DOWN THE HEAT: To get nice browning and a good rise, we found two oven temperatures to be ideal. When the rolls were baked at a moderate heat for an extended amount of time, the bottoms were getting thick and tough, but at a high temperature the rolls were browning too quickly and the crust was getting too hard. Preheating the oven to 400 degrees but dropping the temperature to 350 degrees when putting in the rolls allowed us to achieve good oven spring without overcooking our rolls.

Maple-Sorghum Skillet Bread

G-F TESTING LAB

SORGHUM FLOUR	Sorghum flour and sweet white sorghum flour will both work in this bread. The grind, color, and flavor of the sorghum flour will vary slightly from brand to brand; however, all five of the brands we tried produced decent skillet breads. We had good luck using Bob's Red Mill "Sweet" White Sorghum Flour.
CORNMEAL	The test kitchen's favorite cornmeal is Whole-Grain Arrowhead Mills Cornmeal. This brand has been processed in a gluten-free facility, but not all brands are. Make sure to read the label. See page 27 for more information.
BAKING POWDER	Not all brands of baking powder are gluten-free; see page 25 for more information.
XANTHAN GUM	The xanthan can be omitted, but the bread will be more crumbly.

WHY THIS RECIPE WORKS

We wanted to create a quick and easy gluten-free skillet bread with a tender, dense crumb and a rough-textured, thick crust—a bread that would be great served alongside chili or barbecue. To start, we zeroed in on sorghum flour, which is increasingly popular in gluten-free baking because of its high protein content and its nutty flavor. We began by modeling our bread after a traditional skillet cornbread but using only sorghum flour and a combination of sour cream, milk, eggs, and maple syrup. This produced a fine, moist crumb more similar to a cake than to a quick bread. Since sorghum flour produces such a light and fluffy texture, we added ¾ cup of yellow cornmeal for its familiar coarse texture. The maple syrup had the added benefits of further enhancing the nutty flavor of the sorghum and contributing to a nicely browned, crisp crust. Baking the bread in a greased preheated cast-iron skillet gave it a seriously crunchy, golden crust. Using a combination of oil and butter for greasing the skillet (as well as for mixing into the batter) proved perfect on two fronts: The butter added flavor while the oil raised the smoke point so the butter wouldn't burn. We prefer to use a cast-iron skillet here because it makes the best crust; however, any 10-inch oven-safe skillet will work for this recipe. This bread is best served warm.

Maple-Sorghum Skillet Bread
MAKES 1 LOAF

- ¼ cup vegetable oil
- 6 ounces (1⅓ cups) sorghum flour
- 3¾ ounces (¾ cup) cornmeal
- 1¼ cups sour cream
- ½ cup whole milk
- ½ cup maple syrup
- 4 tablespoons unsalted butter
- 1 teaspoon baking powder
- ½ teaspoon baking soda
- ¾ teaspoon salt
- ¼ teaspoon xanthan gum
- 2 large eggs

1. Adjust oven rack to middle position and heat oven to 450 degrees. When oven has reached 450 degrees, place 10-inch cast-iron skillet on rack and let heat for 10 minutes. Add oil and continue to heat skillet until just smoking, about 5 minutes.

2. Meanwhile, whisk sorghum flour, cornmeal, sour cream, milk, and maple syrup together in bowl. (Batter will be thick.)

3. Being careful of hot skillet handle, remove skillet from oven. Add butter and gently swirl to incorporate. Pour hot oil-butter mixture into sorghum mixture and whisk to incorporate. Whisk in baking powder, baking soda, salt, and xanthan gum, followed by eggs.

4. Quickly scrape batter into hot skillet and smooth top. Bake until top begins to crack, edges are golden brown, and toothpick inserted in center comes out clean, 20 to 24 minutes, rotating skillet halfway through baking.

5. Being careful of hot skillet handle, remove skillet from oven. Let bread cool in skillet for 5 minutes, then transfer to wire rack and let cool for 20 minutes before serving. (Cooled bread can be wrapped in double layer of plastic wrap and stored at room temperature for up to 2 days; it cannot be frozen.)

VARIATION

Dairy-Free Maple-Sorghum Skillet Bread
We prefer the flavor and texture of this bread made with soy milk, but almond milk will also work; do not use rice milk.

Use dairy-free sour cream. Substitute unsweetened soy milk for milk, and Earth Balance Vegan Buttery Sticks for butter. Omit salt.

TEST KITCHEN TIP **Making Skillet Bread**

After whisking hot oil-butter mixture and remaining ingredients into batter, scrape batter into hot skillet and smooth top.

Whole-Grain Crackers

G-F TESTING LAB

FLOUR SUBSTITUTION	Do not substitute other whole-grain blends for the ATK Whole-Grain Gluten-Free Flour Blend; they will not work in this recipe.
BAKING POWDER	Not all brands of baking powder are gluten-free; see page 25 for more information.
XANTHAN GUM	The xanthan can be omitted, but the crackers will be less crisp.

WHY THIS RECIPE WORKS

Gluten-free crackers are difficult to find and they tend to be either in the rice cracker camp or they are really dry and crumbly. For our first batch, we combined our whole-grain flour blend, water, a little sugar, and salt, rolled the mixture into a thin sheet, cut it up into squares, and crossed our fingers. This batch was bland, crumbly, and not at all crisp. Fixing the flavor was fairly simple: We added a good dose of extra-virgin olive oil and sesame seeds, and switched to kosher salt (which we also sprinkled over the top before baking). To fix the texture we added an egg white, which crisped up the crackers significantly, as well as xanthan gum, which helped make the dough easier to work with. To keep things simple, instead of tediously cutting each cracker we found that scoring the dough worked just as well. After baking the crackers, we simply broke apart the sheets along the scored lines.

Whole-Grain Crackers

MAKES 8 DOZEN

- 10 ounces (2¼ cups) ATK Whole-Grain Gluten-Free Flour Blend (page 9)
- ¼ cup sesame seeds
- 1 tablespoon sugar
- 1 teaspoon baking powder
- ¼ teaspoon baking soda
  Kosher salt
- ½ teaspoon xanthan gum
- 5 ounces (½ cup plus 2 tablespoons) water
- 6 tablespoons extra-virgin olive oil
- 1 large egg white

1. Adjust oven racks to upper-middle and lower-middle positions and heat oven to 350 degrees. Whisk flour blend, sesame seeds, sugar, baking powder, baking soda, 1 teaspoon salt, and xanthan together in bowl. In separate bowl, whisk water, oil, and egg white together until well combined. Using rubber spatula, stir water mixture into flour mixture until dough comes together. (Dough will be malleable and easy to shape.)

2. Divide dough into 2 equal pieces, shape each piece into 4-inch square, and cover with plastic wrap. Working with 1 piece of dough at a time, roll dough between 2 large sheets of parchment paper into 12 by 9-inch rectangle (about ⅛ inch thick). Remove top sheet of parchment. Using sharp knife, score dough into 1½-inch squares. Slide each parchment with dough onto rimmed baking sheet and sprinkle each with 1 teaspoon salt.

3. Bake crackers until firm, 30 to 35 minutes, switching and rotating sheets halfway through baking. Let crackers cool completely on sheets, about 20 minutes. Break crackers apart along scored lines. Serve. (Crackers can be stored in zipper-lock bag at room temperature for up to 1 week.)

VARIATIONS

Whole-Grain Poppy Seed–Thyme Crackers
Substitute poppy seeds for sesame seeds and add 4 teaspoons minced fresh thyme to flour mixture.

Whole-Grain Sesame-Rosemary Crackers
Add 1 teaspoon minced fresh rosemary to flour mixture.

TEST KITCHEN TIP
Making Whole-Grain Crackers

1. Roll dough into 12 by 9-inch rectangle between parchment, remove top sheet, and use knife to score dough into 1½-inch squares.

2. Break apart baked and cooled crackers along scored lines.

Cheddar Cheese Coins

G-F TESTING LAB

FLOUR SUBSTITUTION	King Arthur Gluten-Free Multi-Purpose Flour 7½ ounces = **1¼ cups plus 2 tablespoons**	Betty Crocker All-Purpose Gluten Free Rice Blend 7½ ounces = **1½ cups**
	Crackers made with Betty Crocker will have a slightly bitter aftertaste, and the dough will be more difficult to roll into a log in step 2.	

For crisp, cheesy gluten-free crackers, we started with our all-purpose gluten-free flour blend as the base. But in our first tests, the crackers were not crisp enough; we found that adding just 1 tablespoon of cornstarch made a big difference. As for cheese, extra-sharp cheddar turned out to be the right choice: It had a sharp, crowd-pleasing flavor whereas mild or even sharp cheddar cheese didn't deliver. Paprika and cayenne rounded out the flavors in our cracker, while butter and just 3 tablespoons water were enough to bind the dough. Our first batch of crackers tasted great but left our fingers greasy. The culprit turned out to be the gluten-free flour blend. It doesn't absorb fat as readily as wheat flour does, so we looked at our ingredient list for ways to cut back on the fat. Cheese and butter were the only two sources, and we certainly didn't want to lose any cheese flavor. Instead we cut the butter from 8 to 6 tablespoons, still enough to create a flaky texture without leaving our fingers feeling slick.

Cheddar Cheese Coins

MAKES ABOUT 5 DOZEN

   8 **ounces extra-sharp cheddar cheese, shredded (2 cups)**
 7½ **ounces (1⅔ cups) ATK All-Purpose Gluten-Free Flour Blend (page 7)**
   1 **tablespoon cornstarch**
  ½ **teaspoon salt**
  ¼ **teaspoon paprika**
  ⅛ **teaspoon cayenne pepper**
   6 **tablespoons unsalted butter, cut into 6 pieces and chilled**
   3 **tablespoons water**

1. Process cheddar, flour blend, cornstarch, salt, paprika, and cayenne in food processor until combined, about 30 seconds. Scatter butter over top and process until mixture resembles wet sand, about 20 seconds. Add water and process until dough ball forms, about 20 seconds. (Dough will be malleable and easy to shape.)

2. Transfer dough to counter and divide into 2 equal pieces. Roll each half into 10-inch log, wrap in plastic wrap, and refrigerate until firm, at least 1 hour or up to 2 days.

3. Adjust oven racks to upper-middle and lower-middle positions and heat oven to 350 degrees. Line 2 rimmed baking sheets with parchment paper. Unwrap logs and slice into ¼-inch-thick coins, giving dough quarter turn after each slice to keep log round. Place coins on prepared sheets, spaced ½ inch apart.

4. Bake until light golden around edges, 22 to 28 minutes, switching and rotating sheets halfway through baking. Let coins cool completely on sheets before serving, about 20 minutes. (Coins can be stored in airtight container at room temperature for up to 2 days.)

VARIATIONS

Pimento Cheese Coins
Increase paprika to 1 tablespoon and cayenne to ½ teaspoon. Add 1 teaspoon garlic powder to food processor with spices.

Mustard, Gruyère, and Caraway Cheese Coins
Substitute Gruyère for cheddar. Add 1 teaspoon caraway seeds to food processor with spices. Substitute 4 tablespoons whole-grain mustard for water.

Everything Cheese Coins
Substitute Gruyère for cheddar. Add 2 tablespoons poppy seeds, 2 teaspoons sesame seeds, 1 teaspoon granulated garlic, and 1 teaspoon onion flakes to food processor with spices.

TEST KITCHEN TIP **Cutting Cheese Coins**

Unwrap logs and slice into ¼-inch-thick coins, giving dough quarter turn after each slice to keep log round.

COOKIES AND BARS

■ DAIRY FREE OR INCLUDES A DAIRY-FREE VARIATION

Whole-Grain Chocolate Chip Cookies

G-F TESTING LAB

FLOUR SUBSTITUTION	Do not substitute other whole-grain blends for the ATK Whole-Grain Gluten-Free Flour Blend; they will not work in this recipe.
XANTHAN GUM	Xanthan is crucial to the structure of the cookies; see page 22 for more information.
CHOCOLATE	Not all brands of chocolate are processed in a gluten-free facility; read the label.
RESTING TIME	Do not shortchange the dough's 30-minute rest or else the cookies will spread more and taste gritty.

WHY THIS RECIPE WORKS

We wanted a whole-grain cookie or two in our lineup, and although a whole-grain chocolate chip cookie might not seem like a logical choice, we actually found that chocolate and our teff-heavy blend were a winning combination. The teff lent a rich, caramel flavor and in fact created a great base for the chocolate chip cookies, but the cookies did not spread and were overly gritty, and butter leached out. So we added 2 tablespoons of milk and rested the batter for 30 minutes to hydrate the dough just enough to eliminate grittiness. Resting the dough also improved the structure, and with more baking soda we were able to get the cookies to spread. For a chewy center and a slightly crisp outside we used a combination of sugars. Granulated sugar contributed a caramelized, crisp texture and provided structure, while brown sugar added moisture and enhanced the caramel notes. We went up on brown sugar and down on granulated to achieve a perfectly chewy center with crisp edges. Our traditional recipe has 12 tablespoons of butter, but we knew our gluten-free version couldn't handle that much fat. We found that 8 tablespoons of butter provided richness without making the cookies greasy. A little bit of extra salt and vanilla added the perfect balance of salty caramel flavor.

Whole-Grain Chocolate Chip Cookies

MAKES 24 COOKIES

8	ounces (1¾ cups) ATK Whole-Grain Gluten-Free Flour Blend (page 9)
1¼	teaspoons baking soda
¾	teaspoon xanthan gum
¾	teaspoon salt
8	tablespoons unsalted butter, melted and cooled
4⅔	ounces (⅔ cup packed) light brown sugar
2⅓	ounces (⅓ cup) granulated sugar
1	large egg
2	tablespoons milk
1	tablespoon vanilla extract
1¼	cups semisweet chocolate chips

1. Whisk flour blend, baking soda, xanthan gum, and salt together in bowl. In large bowl, whisk melted butter, brown sugar, and granulated sugar together until no lumps remain. Whisk in egg, milk, and vanilla until very smooth. Stir in flour mixture with rubber spatula until dough is completely homogeneous. Fold in chocolate chips. Cover bowl with plastic wrap and let dough rest for 30 minutes. (Dough will be sticky and soft.)

2. Adjust oven rack to middle position and heat oven to 350 degrees. Line 2 baking sheets with parchment paper. Working with 1½ tablespoons of dough at a time, use 2 soupspoons to portion out dough and space 2 inches apart on prepared sheets.

3. Bake cookies, 1 sheet at a time, until golden brown and edges have begun to set but centers are still soft, 12 to 14 minutes, rotating sheet halfway through baking.

4. Let cookies cool on sheet for 5 minutes, then transfer to wire rack. Serve warm or at room temperature. (Cookies can be stored in airtight container at room temperature for up to 1 day.)

VARIATION

Dairy-Free Whole-Grain Chocolate Chip Cookies

We prefer the flavor and texture of these cookies made with soy milk, but almond milk will also work; do not use rice milk.

Reduce salt to ⅛ teaspoon. Substitute Earth Balance Vegan Buttery Sticks for butter, and unsweetened soy milk for milk. Use dairy-free semisweet chocolate chips (or finely chopped chocolate bar).

TEST KITCHEN TIP

Shaping Chocolate Chip Cookies

Working with 1½ tablespoons of dough at a time, use 2 soupspoons to portion out dough and space 2 inches apart on prepared sheets.

White Chocolate–Macadamia Nut Cookies

G-F TESTING LAB

FLOUR SUBSTITUTION	King Arthur Gluten-Free Multi-Purpose Flour 8 ounces = ¾ cup plus ⅔ cup	Betty Crocker All-Purpose Gluten Free Rice Blend 8 ounces = 1½ cups plus 2 tablespoons
	Cookies made with King Arthur will spread more and will be more delicate; cookies made with Betty Crocker will be drier and the dough will be harder to handle.	
XANTHAN GUM	Xanthan is crucial to the structure of the cookies; see page 22 for more information.	
CHOCOLATE	Not all brands of chocolate are processed in a gluten-free facility; read the label.	
RESTING TIME	Do not shortchange the dough's 30-minute rest or else the cookies will spread more and taste gritty.	

WHY THIS RECIPE WORKS

White chocolate–macadamia nut cookies are an exotic rendition of the classic chocolate chip cookie, but without a good base recipe you may as well eat the stir-ins on their own. Gluten-free cookies tend to be unsatisfying because they're often gritty and greasy, and they spread all over the baking sheet. All these problems are related to the characteristics of gluten-free flours—namely, how they absorb liquids and fats, and their low protein content. First we addressed the greasy nature of our cookies. We know that gluten-free flours simply can't absorb as much butter or oil as wheat flour can, so we scaled down the amount of butter in our recipe. Removing some of the butter made the cookies less greasy, but it also made them taste grittier. We weren't surprised by this result because the reduction of butter made the dough drier. To add some moisture back into the dough, we added 2 tablespoons of milk. We also gave the dough a 30-minute rest before scooping and baking to give the flours time to absorb the liquid and soften.

White Chocolate–Macadamia Nut Cookies

MAKES 24 COOKIES

8	ounces (1¾ cups) ATK All-Purpose Gluten-Free Flour Blend (page 7)
1	teaspoon baking soda
¾	teaspoon xanthan gum
½	teaspoon salt
8	tablespoons unsalted butter, melted and cooled
5¼	ounces (¾ cup packed) light brown sugar
2⅓	ounces (⅓ cup) granulated sugar
1	large egg
2	tablespoons milk
1	tablespoon vanilla extract
¾	cup white chocolate chips
½	cup macadamia nuts, chopped

1. Whisk flour blend, baking soda, xanthan gum, and salt together in bowl. In large bowl, whisk melted butter, brown sugar, and granulated sugar together until no lumps remain. Whisk in egg, milk, and vanilla until very smooth. Stir in flour mixture with rubber spatula until dough is completely homogeneous. Fold in white chocolate chips and macadamia nuts. Cover bowl with plastic wrap and let dough rest for 30 minutes. (Dough will be sticky and soft.)

2. Adjust oven rack to middle position and heat oven to 350 degrees. Line 2 baking sheets with parchment paper. Working with 1½ tablespoons of dough at a time, use 2 soupspoons to portion out dough and space 2 inches apart on prepared sheets.

3. Bake cookies, 1 sheet at a time, until golden brown and edges have begun to set but centers are still soft, 12 to 14 minutes, rotating sheet halfway through baking.

4. Let cookies cool on sheet for 5 minutes, then transfer to wire rack. Serve warm or at room temperature. (Cookies can be stored in airtight container at room temperature for up to 1 day.)

VARIATION

Dairy-Free White Chocolate–Macadamia Nut Cookies

We prefer the flavor and texture of these cookies made with soy milk, but almond milk will also work; do not use rice milk.

Substitute vegetable oil for butter, and unsweetened soy milk for milk. Use dairy-free white chocolate chips (or finely chopped chocolate bar).

TEST KITCHEN TIP **Freezing Cookie Dough**

Since most gluten-free cookies turn stale pretty quickly after they've been baked, we've found that freezing the cookie dough for drop cookies can be a great option. Simply freeze portions of the dough on a baking sheet until they're solid, then transfer them to a zipper-lock freezer bag for easy storage; bake the frozen cookies as directed, adding 2 to 3 extra minutes to the baking time. For Rugelach, we found it necessary to thaw the dough for the cookies before baking. We did not have success freezing Oatmeal Cookies with Chocolate Chunks and Dried Cherries or Almond Biscotti.

Oatmeal Cookies with Chocolate Chunks

G-F TESTING LAB

FLOUR SUBSTITUTION	King Arthur Gluten-Free Multi-Purpose Flour 3 ounces = ⅓ **cup plus ¼ cup**	Betty Crocker All-Purpose Gluten Free Rice Blend 3 ounces = ½ **cup plus 2 tablespoons**
	Cookies made with King Arthur and Betty Crocker will be drier.	
OATS	Not all brands of oats are gluten-free; read the label. Do not substitute quick oats.	
BAKING POWDER	Not all brands of baking powder are gluten-free; see page 25 for more information.	
XANTHAN GUM	Xanthan is crucial to the structure of the cookies; see page 22 for more information.	
CHOCOLATE	Not all brands of chocolate are processed in a gluten-free facility; read the label.	
RESTING TIME	Do not shortchange the dough's 30-minute rest or else the cookies will taste gritty.	

WHY THIS RECIPE WORKS

Creating a recipe for chewy, moist, gluten-free oat cookies turned out to be more challenging than we had anticipated. Packing so much oat flavor in our cookies meant using a full 3 cups of oats, and while our cookies had great oat flavor, they were tough and dry as a result. The oats were soaking up all the available liquid, so instead of stirring them into the cookie dough raw, we decided to beat them at their own game: We soaked half of the oats (toasted first to bring out their full flavor) in warm water before adding them to the dough. This succeeded in creating soft cookies, but now they were too cakey. The cakeyness was thanks to our flour blend, as all the starches in it were giving the cookies a tender, delicate crumb. Substituting 4 ounces of almond flour for a portion of the flour blend contributed additional protein and fat, turning our cookies into the chewy, moist version we were after. Chopping the dried cherries and bittersweet chocolate ensured bright flavor in every bite.

Oatmeal Cookies with Chocolate Chunks and Dried Cherries

MAKES 24 COOKIES

9	ounces (3 cups) old-fashioned rolled oats
½	cup warm tap water
4	ounces (1⅓ cups) almond flour
3	ounces (⅔ cup) ATK All-Purpose Gluten-Free Flour Blend (page 7)
½	teaspoon salt
½	teaspoon baking powder
¼	teaspoon xanthan gum
⅛	teaspoon ground nutmeg
8	tablespoons unsalted butter, melted and cooled
7	ounces (1 cup packed) brown sugar
3½	ounces (½ cup) granulated sugar
1	large egg plus 1 large yolk
2	tablespoons vegetable oil
1	teaspoon vanilla extract
3	ounces bittersweet chocolate, chopped coarse
½	cup dried cherries, chopped

1. Adjust oven rack to middle position and heat oven to 375 degrees. Spread oats onto rimmed baking sheet and bake, stirring occasionally, until fragrant and lightly browned, about 10 minutes; let cool completely.

2. Combine warm water and half of cooled oats in bowl, cover with plastic wrap, and let sit until water is absorbed, about 10 minutes. In separate bowl, whisk almond flour, flour blend, salt, baking powder, xanthan gum, and nutmeg together.

3. In large bowl, whisk melted butter, brown sugar, granulated sugar, egg and yolk, oil, and vanilla together until no lumps remain and mixture is very smooth. Stir in oat-water mixture, flour mixture, and remaining toasted oats using rubber spatula until dough is completely homogeneous. Fold in chocolate and dried cherries. Cover bowl with plastic and let dough rest for 30 minutes. (Dough will be sticky and soft.)

4. Adjust oven rack to middle position and heat oven to 325 degrees. Line 2 baking sheets with parchment paper. Working with generous 2 tablespoons of dough at a time, use wet hands to roll dough into balls and space 2 inches apart on prepared sheets. Press dough to ½-inch thickness using bottom of greased measuring cup.

5. Bake cookies, 1 sheet at a time, until edges are set and beginning to brown but centers are still soft and puffy, 22 to 25 minutes, rotating sheet halfway through baking.

6. Let cookies cool on sheet for 10 minutes, then transfer to wire rack. Serve warm or at room temperature. (Cookies can be stored in airtight container at room temperature for up to 2 days.)

VARIATION

Dairy-Free Oatmeal Cookies with Chocolate Chunks and Dried Cherries
Substitute vegetable oil for butter and use dairy-free bittersweet chocolate.

Chocolate Crinkle Cookies

G-F TESTING LAB

FLOUR SUBSTITUTION	King Arthur Gluten-Free Multi-Purpose Flour 5 ounces = ⅔ cup plus ¼ cup	Betty Crocker All-Purpose Gluten Free Rice Blend 5 ounces = **1 cup**
	Cookies made with King Arthur will taste a bit starchy; cookies made with Betty Crocker will be slightly pasty.	
CHOCOLATE	Not all brands of chocolate are processed in a gluten-free facility; read the label.	
BAKING POWDER	Not all brands of baking powder are gluten-free; see page 25 for more information.	
XANTHAN GUM	The xanthan can be omitted, but the cookies will be crumbly and spread more.	
RESTING TIME	Do not shortchange the dough's 30-minute rest or else the dough will be hard to handle.	

✓ WHY THIS RECIPE WORKS

For a gluten-free take on chocolate crinkle cookies that lived up to their name, we used a combination of unsweetened chocolate and cocoa powder (plus a little espresso powder) for a deep, rich chocolate flavor. Using brown sugar instead of granulated lent a more complex, tempered sweetness with a bitter molasses edge that complemented the chocolate. A combination of both baking powder and baking soda was key to achieving the hallmark crinkly look. As the cookies baked, the baking soda created bubbles of carbon dioxide that caused the dough to spread (leaving behind those crackly tops), while the baking powder provided lift without deflating. Although these cookies looked great, they were just a little too delicate and crumbly. We knew that adding xanthan gum would prevent the cookies from crumbling apart, but we also intuited that it would cause the cookies to spread less, creating a cakier, less fudgy texture. To test our instinct we baked up two batches, one with the addition of xanthan gum alone and another with xanthan gum and 2 tablespoons of water. The cookies with just the added xanthan gum were indeed too cakey. The cookies with the xanthan gum and water, on the other hand, held together and maintained their fudgy texture. To ensure these cookies were easy to shape and looked perfect every time (the dough was quite sticky), we rolled the cookies in granulated sugar first, followed by confectioners' sugar.

Chocolate Crinkle Cookies

MAKES 22 COOKIES

- 4 ounces unsweetened chocolate, chopped
- 4 tablespoons unsalted butter, cut into 4 pieces
- 5 ounces (1 cup plus 2 tablespoons) ATK All-Purpose Gluten-Free Flour Blend (page 7)
- 1½ ounces (½ cup) Dutch-processed cocoa powder
- ½ teaspoon salt
- ½ teaspoon baking powder
- ¼ teaspoon baking soda
- ¼ teaspoon xanthan gum
- 10½ ounces (1½ cups packed) brown sugar
- 3 large eggs
- 2 tablespoons water
- 4 teaspoons instant espresso powder (optional)
- 1 teaspoon vanilla extract
- 3½ ounces (½ cup) granulated sugar
- 2 ounces (½ cup) confectioners' sugar

1. Microwave chocolate and butter in bowl at 50 percent power, stirring occasionally, until melted, 2 to 4 minutes; let cool slightly. In separate bowl, whisk flour blend, cocoa, salt, baking powder, baking soda, and xanthan gum together.

2. In large bowl, whisk brown sugar, eggs, water, espresso powder (if using), and vanilla together until no lumps remain and mixture is very smooth. Whisk in cooled chocolate mixture until well combined. Stir in flour mixture with rubber spatula until dough is completely homogeneous. Cover bowl with plastic wrap and let dough rest for 30 minutes. (Dough will be very soft and sticky.)

3. Adjust oven rack to middle position and heat oven to 325 degrees. Line 2 baking sheets with parchment paper. Place granulated sugar and confectioners' sugar in separate shallow dishes. Working in batches, use 2 soupspoons to portion out 2-tablespoon-size pieces of dough and drop into granulated sugar. Coat each piece of dough with sugar, then roll into rough balls. Transfer balls to confectioners' sugar, roll to coat evenly, and space 2 inches apart on prepared sheets.

4. Bake cookies, 1 sheet at a time, until puffed and cracked and edges have begun to set but centers are still soft (cookies will look raw between cracks and seem underdone), about 12 minutes, rotating sheet halfway through baking.

5. Let cookies cool completely on sheet before serving. (Cookies can be stored in airtight container at room temperature for up to 3 days.)

VARIATION

Dairy-Free Chocolate Crinkle Cookies
Substitute vegetable oil for butter.

Whole-Grain Brown Sugar Cookies

G-F TESTING LAB

FLOUR SUBSTITUTION	Do not substitute other whole-grain blends for the ATK Whole-Grain Gluten-Free Flour Blend; they will not work in this recipe.
BAKING POWDER	Not all brands of baking powder are gluten-free; see page 25 for more information.
XANTHAN GUM	The xanthan can be omitted, but the cookies will spread more and will be less chewy.
RESTING TIME	Do not shortchange the dough's 30-minute rest or else the cookies will spread more and taste gritty.

WHY THIS RECIPE WORKS

Brown sugar cookies are the grown-up version of classic white sugar cookies, featuring slightly crisp edges, chewy centers, and deep, toffeelike sweetness. To make a sophisticated gluten-free brown sugar cookie, we looked to our whole-grain gluten-free flour blend to start. Our first batch of cookies tasted great, but they were far from chewy; instead tasters described them as gritty, dry, and hard. We knew from previous testing that our whole-grain blend needed more liquid to hydrate fully, so we started by adding a small amount of milk to the dough and incorporating a resting time to prevent grittiness. These changes helped to eliminate grittiness and dryness, but the cookies still weren't chewy enough. So we tried increasing the amount of melted butter, adding it incrementally until we settled on 14 tablespoons. Another key to ensuring good chew in these cookies turned out to be erring on the side of underbaking; the cookies had the best chew when we pulled them out of the oven when the edges were just barely set. To finish we used a combination of granulated sugar and dark brown sugar to coat the dough balls before baking. Brown sugar alone clumped too much, but cutting it with granulated sugar encouraged it to dry out, making it easier to coat the dough balls evenly. Just be sure to combine the sugars early, and break up any sugar clumps before trying to coat the dough balls.

Whole-Grain Brown Sugar Cookies

MAKES 24 COOKIES

ROLLING SUGAR

- ¼ cup packed dark brown sugar
- ¼ cup granulated sugar

COOKIES

- 10½ ounces (2⅓ cups) ATK Whole-Grain Gluten-Free Flour Blend (page 9)
- ½ teaspoon salt
- ½ teaspoon baking soda
- ¼ teaspoon baking powder
- ¼ teaspoon xanthan gum
- 10½ ounces (1½ cups packed) dark brown sugar
- 14 tablespoons unsalted butter, melted and cooled
- 1 large egg plus 1 large yolk
- 1 tablespoon milk
- 1 tablespoon vanilla extract

1. FOR THE ROLLING SUGAR: Combine sugars in shallow dish and crumble with fingers until no large clumps remain; set aside to dry out.

2. FOR THE COOKIES: Whisk flour blend, salt, baking soda, baking powder, and xanthan gum together in medium bowl. In large bowl, whisk sugar and melted butter together until sugar dissolves and no lumps remain. Whisk in egg and yolk, milk, and vanilla until mixture is very smooth and glossy. Stir in flour mixture with rubber spatula until dough is completely homogeneous. Cover bowl with plastic wrap and let dough rest for 30 minutes. (Dough will be sticky and soft.)

3. Adjust oven rack to middle position and heat oven to 350 degrees. Line 3 baking sheets with parchment paper. Working with 2 tablespoons of dough at a time, roll dough into balls and drop into rolling sugar. Coat each dough ball with sugar and space 2½ inches apart on prepared sheets.

4. Bake cookies, 1 sheet at a time, until edges have begun to set but centers are still soft (cookies will look raw between cracks and seem underdone), 12 to 14 minutes, rotating sheet halfway through baking.

5. Let cookies cool on sheet for 5 minutes, then transfer to wire rack. Serve warm or at room temperature. (Cookies can be stored in airtight container at room temperature for up to 1 day.)

VARIATION

Dairy-Free Whole-Grain Brown Sugar Cookies

We prefer the flavor and texture of these cookies made with soy milk, but almond milk will also work; do not use rice milk.

Substitute vegetable oil for butter, and unsweetened soy milk for milk.

Whole-Grain Gingersnaps

G-F TESTING LAB

FLOUR SUBSTITUTION	Do not substitute other whole-grain blends for the ATK Whole-Grain Gluten-Free Flour Blend; they will not work in this recipe.
BAKING POWDER	Not all brands of baking powder are gluten-free; see page 25 for more information.
XANTHAN GUM	The xanthan can be omitted, but the cookies will be crumbly and spread more.
RESTING TIME	Do not shortchange the dough's 30-minute rest or else the cookies will spread more and taste gritty.

WHY THIS RECIPE WORKS

Most gingersnap recipes don't live up to their name. Once you get past their brittle edges, the cookies turn soft and chewy. We wanted freshly baked gluten-free gingersnaps with a crackly top, a crisp texture, and bold ginger flavor and lingering heat. Our whole-grain gluten-free flour blend seemed to be the right choice here, as its earthy flavor paired well with the spices most often associated with gingersnaps, like cinnamon and cloves, not to mention ginger. For ginger flavor we used a good amount of freshly grated ginger, but found it wasn't enough. We discovered a combination of grated fresh and ground ginger was best, while just ⅛ teaspoon of ground black pepper gave the cookies a little heat. For a crisp, not chewy, gingersnap we knew we would have to limit the amount of moisture in our cookie. To do this, we first looked to the 6 tablespoons of butter in our recipe. Butter is roughly 16 to 18 percent water, and this moisture can make the difference between a cookie that bends and a cookie that snaps. We decided to brown the butter, deepening its rich flavor while simultaneously eliminating its moisture. Next, we looked to sugar. Sugar is hygroscopic, meaning it attracts moisture, and different sugars are more hygroscopic than others. Molasses is often used in gingersnap recipes for its complex, slightly bitter flavor, but it turns out that this type of sugar is the most hygroscopic of all. Making the switch from molasses to dark brown sugar made a huge difference in creating a truly snappy cookie, without a considerable flavor compromise. Finally, to achieve the classic craggy top, we found we needed both baking powder and baking soda.

Whole-Grain Gingersnaps
MAKES 30 COOKIES

- 6 tablespoons unsalted butter
- 5¼ ounces (¾ cup packed) dark brown sugar
- 1 tablespoon grated fresh ginger
- 1 tablespoon ground ginger
- ½ teaspoon ground cinnamon
- ⅛ teaspoon ground cloves
- ⅛ teaspoon pepper
- 6 ounces (1⅓ cups) ATK Whole-Grain Gluten-Free Flour Blend (page 9)
- 1 teaspoon baking powder
- ¼ teaspoon baking soda
- ¼ teaspoon xanthan gum
- ¼ teaspoon salt
- 1 large egg
- 3½ ounces (½ cup) granulated sugar

1. Melt butter in 10-inch skillet over medium heat. Reduce heat to medium-low and cook, swirling pan constantly, until foaming subsides and butter is just beginning to brown, 2 to 4 minutes. Transfer to large bowl and whisk in brown sugar, fresh ginger, ground ginger, cinnamon, cloves, and pepper until smooth. Let cool slightly, about 2 minutes.

2. Whisk flour blend, baking powder, baking soda, xanthan gum, and salt together in bowl. Whisk egg into butter-spice mixture until well combined. Stir in flour mixture with rubber spatula and mix until dough is completely homogeneous. Cover bowl with plastic wrap and let dough rest for 30 minutes. (Dough will be sticky and soft.)

3. Adjust oven rack to middle position and heat oven to 300 degrees. Line 2 baking sheets with parchment paper. Place granulated sugar in shallow dish. Working with 2 teaspoons of dough at a time, roll dough into ball and drop into sugar. Coat each dough ball with sugar and space 1½ inches apart on prepared sheets.

4. Bake cookies, 1 sheet at a time, until cookies are set, 20 to 25 minutes, rotating sheet halfway through baking.

5. Let cookies cool on sheet for 5 minutes, then transfer to wire rack. Cool completely before serving. (Cookies can be stored in airtight container at room temperature for up to 1 week.)

VARIATION
Dairy-Free Whole-Grain Gingersnaps
Substitute vegetable oil for butter; don't heat oil but instead mix it with brown sugar and spices.

Peanut Butter Sandwich Cookies

FLOUR SUBSTITUTION	King Arthur Gluten-Free Multi-Purpose Flour 4 ounces = ¾ **cup**	Betty Crocker All-Purpose Gluten Free Rice Blend 4 ounces = ½ **cup plus** ⅓ **cup**
	Cookies made with Betty Crocker will taste similar, but the dough will be soft, wet, and more difficult to handle.	
XANTHAN GUM	Xanthan is crucial to the structure of the cookies; see page 22 for more information.	
RESTING TIME	Do not shortchange the dough's 30-minute rest or else the cookies will spread more and taste gritty.	

WHY THIS RECIPE WORKS

These easy-to-make sandwich cookies feature crunchy cookies and a smooth filling, both packed with big peanut butter flavor. Since our traditional recipe uses very little flour, developing a gluten-free version was simple. We started by just swapping in our all-purpose gluten-free flour blend for the flour. The cookies turned out pretty close to the original, but tasted a bit gritty and spread out too thin as they baked. Resting the batter helped the cookies taste less gritty, and adding xanthan gum reined in the spreading. Satisfied with the cookies' texture, we focused on flavor. To boost the peanut flavor, we added chopped peanuts to the dough. As for the filling, we found that it was hard to spread over the cookies without breaking them. Softening the peanut butter and butter briefly in the microwave before assembling the sandwich cookies solved this problem easily. To make the filling a bit more sweet and help it stay in place once the cookies were assembled, we added some confectioners' sugar. Using salted peanut butter is important; do not use unsalted peanut butter for this recipe.

Peanut Butter Sandwich Cookies

MAKES 24 SANDWICH COOKIES

COOKIES

1¼	cups dry-roasted, unsalted peanuts
4	ounces (¾ cup plus 2 tablespoons) ATK All-Purpose Gluten-Free Flour Blend (page 7)
1	teaspoon baking soda
½	teaspoon salt
¼	teaspoon xanthan gum
3	tablespoons unsalted butter, melted
½	cup creamy peanut butter
3½	ounces (½ cup) granulated sugar
3½	ounces (½ cup packed) light brown sugar
3	tablespoons whole milk
1	large egg

FILLING

¾	cup creamy peanut butter
3	tablespoons unsalted butter
3	ounces (¾ cup) confectioners' sugar

1. FOR THE COOKIES: Pulse peanuts in food processor until finely chopped, about 8 pulses. Whisk flour blend, baking soda, salt, and xanthan gum together in bowl. In separate bowl, whisk butter, peanut butter, granulated sugar, brown sugar, milk, and egg together. Stir flour mixture into peanut butter mixture with rubber spatula until combined. Stir in peanuts until evenly distributed. Cover bowl with plastic wrap and let dough rest for 30 minutes.

2. Adjust oven racks to upper-middle and lower-middle positions and heat oven to 350 degrees. Line 2 baking sheets with parchment paper. Working with half of dough, keeping other half covered, portion out generous 2 teaspoons of dough, roll into balls, and space 3 inches apart on prepared sheets; dough will be very sticky. Using damp hands, press dough balls into 2-inch cookies. Repeat with remaining dough.

3. Bake cookies until deep golden brown and firm to touch, 12 to 15 minutes, switching and rotating sheets halfway through baking. Let cookies cool on sheets for 5 minutes, then transfer to wire rack and let cool completely before assembling.

4. FOR THE FILLING: Microwave peanut butter and butter until melted and warm, about 40 seconds. Stir in confectioners' sugar until combined.

5. While filling is warm, place 24 cookies upside down on counter. Place 1 tablespoon filling in center of each cookie. Top each with one of remaining cookies, right side up, and press gently until filling spreads to edges. Let filling set for 1 hour before serving. (Assembled cookies can be stored in airtight container for up to 3 days.)

VARIATION

Dairy-Free Peanut Butter Sandwich Cookies
We prefer the flavor and texture of these cookies made with soy milk, but almond milk will also work; do not use rice milk.

Substitute vegetable oil for butter, and unsweetened soy milk for milk.

Linzer Cookies

G-F TESTING LAB

FLOUR SUBSTITUTION	King Arthur Gluten-Free Multi-Purpose Flour We do not recommend using King Arthur in this recipe.	Betty Crocker All-Purpose Gluten Free Rice Blend 10 ounces = **2 cups**
	Cookies made with King Arthur were too delicate and they broke apart during assembly; cookies made with Betty Crocker will be slightly dry.	
XANTHAN GUM	Xanthan is crucial to the structure of the cookies; see page 22 for more information.	
CHILLING TIME	Do not shortchange the dough's chilling times or else the dough will be difficult to work with and the cookies won't hold their shape.	

WHY THIS RECIPE WORKS

These old-world jam cookies rely on ground almonds for their trademark nutty flavor. For our gluten-free linzer cookies we took advantage of the ground almonds for flavor as well as for structural reasons. We were using our all-purpose gluten-free flour blend, but because of the blend's high amount of starch we wound up with a dough that was too soft and sticky. Substituting some almond flour worked to our advantage, adding both flavor and structure since it is high in protein (and the gluten-free flours in our blend are not). In addition to providing some much-needed structure, the almond flour also helped make the dough easier to work with. To achieve a crisp, short texture for our cookies, we opted to cream the butter (melted butter creates a chewy texture in cookies) and swap superfine sugar for granulated (to create a more fine-textured cookie). To prevent the cookies from spreading in the oven, we chilled the dough before rolling and cutting the cookies (which also made the dough easier to work with), and added ¼ teaspoon of xanthan gum. For the raspberry filling, simply spreading jam in between the cookies wasn't enough; when we took a bite, the jam leaked out. Instead, we added a little gelatin to thicken the filling. If you do not have superfine sugar (which is sold in the baking aisle at most supermarkets), process granulated sugar in a food processor for 30 seconds.

Linzer Cookies

MAKES 24 SANDWICH COOKIES

- ½ teaspoon unflavored gelatin
- 2 teaspoons grated lemon zest plus 2 teaspoons juice
- ½ cup raspberry jam
- 10 ounces (2¼ cups) ATK All-Purpose Gluten-Free Flour Blend (page 7)
- 8 ounces (2⅔ cups) almond flour
- ½ teaspoon salt
- ¼ teaspoon xanthan gum
- 12 tablespoons unsalted butter, cut into 12 pieces and softened
- 7 ounces (1 cup) superfine sugar
- 1 large egg plus 1 large yolk
- 2 teaspoons vanilla extract
- Confectioners' sugar

1. Sprinkle gelatin over lemon juice in bowl and let sit until gelatin softens, about 5 minutes. Microwave jam in separate bowl until hot, whisking occasionally, about 30 seconds. Add softened gelatin mixture to hot jam and whisk to dissolve. Cover and refrigerate until needed.

2. Whisk flour blend, almond flour, salt, and xanthan gum together in medium bowl. Using stand mixer fitted with paddle, beat butter, superfine sugar, and lemon zest on medium-high speed until pale and fluffy, about 3 minutes. Add egg and yolk and vanilla, and beat until well combined, about 2 minutes. Reduce speed to low, add flour mixture, and beat until completely incorporated and dough is homogeneous, 2 to 4 minutes, scraping down bowl as needed.

3. Divide dough into 4 equal pieces. Press each piece into 4-inch disk, wrap in plastic wrap, and refrigerate until firm, at least 1 hour or up to 2 days. (Dough can also be frozen for up to 2 weeks; let thaw completely in refrigerator, about 12 hours, before rolling.)

4. Working with 1 piece of dough at a time, roll into 10-inch circle (⅛ inch thick) between 2 large sheets of parchment paper. Slide dough, still between parchment, onto baking sheet and refrigerate until firm, about 30 minutes.

5. Adjust oven rack to middle position and heat oven to 325 degrees. Line 2 baking sheets with parchment paper. Working in batches (keeping remaining dough chilled), use 2½-inch cookie cutter to cut out rounds, and space ¼ inch apart on prepared sheets. Using 1-inch cookie cutter, cut out centers from half of cookies. Scraps should be combined and rerolled once.

6. Bake cookies, 1 sheet at a time, until firm to touch and edges are just beginning to brown, 12 to 15 minutes, rotating sheet halfway through baking. Let cookies cool on sheet for 5 minutes, then transfer to wire rack and let cool completely before assembling. (Unassembled cookies can be stored in airtight container at room temperature for up to 5 days.)

7. Spread 1 teaspoon jam mixture on cookies without cutouts, and top with cut-out cookies to form sandwiches. Dust cookies with confectioners' sugar before serving.

VARIATION

Dairy-Free Linzer Cookies
Substitute Earth Balance Vegan Buttery Sticks for butter.

TEST KITCHEN TIP **Making Linzer Cookies**

1. Soften gelatin in lemon juice. Whisk softened gelatin into hot jam to dissolve. Cover and refrigerate until needed.

2. Divide dough into 4 equal pieces. Press each piece into 4-inch disk, wrap in plastic wrap, and refrigerate until firm, at least 1 hour or up to 2 days.

3. Working with 1 piece of dough at a time, roll into 10-inch circle (⅛ inch thick) between 2 large sheets of parchment paper. Slide dough, still between parchment, onto baking sheet and refrigerate until firm, about 30 minutes.

4. Working in batches (keeping remaining dough chilled), use 2½-inch cookie cutter to cut out rounds, and space ¼ inch apart on prepared sheets.

5. Using 1-inch cookie cutter, cut out centers from half of cookies. These will be tops of cookies.

6. Spread 1 teaspoon jam mixture over cookie bottoms, top with cookie tops, and press lightly. Dust cookies with confectioners' sugar before serving.

Almond Biscotti

✔ WHY THIS RECIPE WORKS

Despite their elegant appearance, these twice-baked cookies are easy to make. Italians like their biscotti dry and hard, while American versions tend to be buttery and more tender. We wanted something in between: a crisp but not tooth-shattering cookie. We began our testing by substituting our all-purpose gluten-free flour blend in a variety of traditional recipes from our archives, and found that just 4 tablespoons of butter gave us rich flavor and a cookielike texture, while two eggs helped with structure and binding. To avoid crumbly cookies, we added ¾ teaspoon xanthan gum. Adding 2 tablespoons of water and letting the dough rest for 30 minutes before baking eliminated any grittiness. Baking biscotti twice (first as a log, then again as individual cookies) is the traditional method, and it worked well for our gluten-free version. For the second baking, we found that placing the cookies on a wire rack helped them bake through more evenly because the rack allowed air to circulate around the cookies. To punch up the almond flavor, we used both almond and vanilla extracts. A combination of hazelnuts and almonds also works well.

Almond Biscotti
MAKES 24 COOKIES

- 10 ounces (2¼ cups) ATK All-Purpose Gluten-Free Flour Blend (page 7)
- 1 teaspoon baking powder
- ¾ teaspoon xanthan gum
- ½ teaspoon salt
- 7 ounces (1 cup) sugar
- 4 tablespoons unsalted butter, cut into 4 pieces and softened
- 2 large eggs
- 2 tablespoons water
- ½ teaspoon vanilla extract
- ½ teaspoon almond extract
- ¾ cup whole almonds, toasted and chopped coarse

1. Whisk flour blend, baking powder, xanthan gum, and salt together in medium bowl. Using stand mixer fitted with paddle, beat sugar and butter on medium-high speed until pale and fluffy, about 3 minutes. Add eggs, water, vanilla, and almond extract and beat until well combined, about 2 minutes. Reduce speed to low, add flour mixture, and beat until completely incorporated and dough is homogeneous, 2 to 4 minutes, scraping down bowl as needed. (Dough will be sticky and loose.) Add almonds and beat until combined, about 30 seconds. Cover bowl with plastic wrap and let dough rest for 30 minutes.

2. Adjust oven rack to middle position and heat oven to 350 degrees. Line baking sheet with parchment paper. Using rubber spatula, transfer dough to prepared sheet. Using wet hands, shape dough into 12 by 3½-inch-long rectangle. Bake until golden and just beginning to crack on edges, about 35 minutes, rotating pan halfway through baking.

3. Remove biscotti loaf from oven and let cool for 10 minutes. Reduce oven temperature to 325 degrees. Transfer cooled loaf to cutting board and slice on bias into ½-inch-thick slices using serrated knife. Arrange slices, cut side down, on wire rack set in rimmed baking sheet, spaced ¼ inch apart.

4. Bake biscotti until crisp and lightly golden brown on both sides, about 35 minutes, flipping cookies halfway through baking. Let cool completely before serving. (Cookies can be stored in airtight container at room temperature for up to 3 weeks.)

VARIATIONS
Dairy-Free Almond Biscotti
Omit salt. Substitute Earth Balance Vegan Buttery Sticks for butter.

Anise Biscotti
Substitute 1 teaspoon anise-flavored liqueur (such as ouzo or anisette) for almond extract. Add 1½ teaspoons anise seeds to dough with almonds in step 1.

G-F TESTING LAB

FLOUR SUBSTITUTION	King Arthur Gluten-Free Multi-Purpose Flour 10 ounces = **1½ cups plus ⅓ cup**	Betty Crocker All-Purpose Gluten Free Rice Blend 10 ounces = **2 cups**
	Biscotti made with King Arthur will be fragile and will spread more; biscotti made with Betty Crocker be more crumbly and the dough will be difficult to handle.	
BAKING POWDER	Not all brands of baking powder are gluten-free; see page 25 for more information.	
XANTHAN GUM	Xanthan is crucial to the structure of the biscotti; see page 22 for more information.	
RESTING TIME	Do not shortchange the dough's 30-minute rest or else the cookies won't hold their shape.	

Pistachio Spice Biscotti

Substitute pistachios for almonds. Add 1 teaspoon ground cardamom, ½ teaspoon ground cloves, ½ teaspoon pepper, ¼ teaspoon ground cinnamon, and ¼ teaspoon ground ginger to flour mixture in step 1.

Chocolate-Dipped Biscotti

Microwave 12 ounces bittersweet chocolate in bowl at 50 percent power, stirring occasionally, until melted, 2 to 4 minutes. Dip bottom third of cooled biscotti in chocolate, letting excess chocolate drip back into bowl; transfer to greased wire rack set over parchment paper to catch drips. Let cookies cool until chocolate is set, about 1 hour.

TEST KITCHEN TIP **Making Biscotti**

1. Using rubber spatula, transfer dough to parchment-lined baking sheet.

2. Using wet hands (dough will be very sticky), shape dough into 12 by 3½-inch-long rectangle.

3. Bake until golden and just beginning to crack on edges, about 35 minutes, rotating pan halfway through baking.

4. Reduce oven temperature. After loaf has cooled slightly, transfer to cutting board and slice on bias into ½-inch-thick slices using serrated knife.

5. Arrange slices, cut side down, on wire rack set in rimmed baking sheet, spaced ¼ inch apart.

6. Bake biscotti until crisp and lightly golden brown on both sides, about 35 minutes, flipping cookies halfway through baking. Let cool completely before serving.

Rugelach

G-F TESTING LAB

FLOUR SUBSTITUTION	King Arthur Gluten-Free Multi-Purpose Flour 5½ ounces= **1 cup**	Betty Crocker All-Purpose Gluten Free Rice Blend 5½ ounces= **1 cup plus 2 tablespoons**
	Rugelach made with King Arthur will be difficult to work with; rugelach made with Betty Crocker will be drier.	
XANTHAN GUM	Xanthan is crucial to the structure of the rugelach; see page 22 for more information.	

✓ WHY THIS RECIPE WORKS

Rugelach are a traditional Jewish treat, part pastry and part cookie, that can be filled with a variety of nuts, jams, and dried fruit. Its dough is similar to that of a standard butter cookie but usually includes some cream cheese for structure, richness, and chew. Our first attempt at making these cookies was a disaster, as the filling melted all over the tray and the cookies lost their shape completely. Reducing the amount of butter from 8 to 6 tablespoons and adding a little xanthan gum helped the cookies hold their shape better. Chilling the dough for 30 minutes before rolling firmed it up and made it easier to work with while also giving the flour blend time to hydrate so that the cookies tasted less gritty. But our rugelach were still a little too tough. To make them more delicate, we added baking soda, which not only tenderized the cookies but also helped them brown better during baking. Finally, we turned our attention to the filling, made of apricot jam, golden raisins, and walnuts, which consistently leaked out during baking. To solve this issue, we used less filling, changed the shape of the cookies from crescents to rolled-and-cut slices, and insulated the bottom of the cookies by baking them on top of two stacked baking sheets. Be sure to sprinkle the cookies with the cinnamon sugar before you transfer them to the baking sheet, or the sugar will burn onto the pan.

Rugelach

MAKES ABOUT 30 COOKIES

DOUGH

- 5½ ounces (1¼ cups) ATK All-Purpose Gluten-Free Flour Blend (page 7)
- 1 tablespoon sugar
- ¾ teaspoon xanthan gum
- ½ teaspoon salt
- ¼ teaspoon baking soda
- 4 ounces cream cheese, cut into ½-inch pieces and chilled
- 6 tablespoons unsalted butter, cut into ½-inch pieces and chilled
- 1 teaspoon vanilla extract

FILLING AND EGG WASH

- 3 tablespoons sugar
- 1½ teaspoons ground cinnamon
- 1 large egg, lightly beaten
- 1 teaspoon water
- 6 tablespoons apricot jam
- ⅓ cup walnuts, toasted and chopped fine
- 3 tablespoons golden raisins, chopped fine

1. FOR THE DOUGH: Process flour blend, sugar, xanthan gum, salt, and baking soda together in food processor until combined, about 3 seconds. Add cream cheese, butter, and vanilla and process until dough comes together, about 20 seconds.

2. Divide dough into 3 equal pieces and shape each into 7 by 2-inch rectangle. Wrap each tightly in plastic wrap and refrigerate for at least 30 minutes or up to 2 days. (If dough is too firm after chilling, let soften at room temperature for 15 minutes before rolling.)

3. Working with 1 piece of dough at a time, roll dough between 2 sheets of parchment paper into 12 by 5-inch rectangle (⅛ inch thick). Slide dough, still between parchment, onto baking sheet and refrigerate until sheet of dough is stiff, about 10 minutes.

4. FOR THE FILLING AND EGG WASH: Mix sugar and cinnamon together in bowl. In separate bowl, mix egg with water.

5. Adjust oven rack to middle position and heat oven to 375 degrees. Line rimmed baking sheet with parchment paper, spray with vegetable oil spray, and place inside second baking sheet.

6. Slide 1 sheet of dough, still between parchment, onto counter. Loosen parchment on top, then flip dough over and remove second piece of parchment. Spread 2 tablespoons jam over dough, leaving 1-inch border around edge. Sprinkle with 2 tablespoons walnuts, 1 tablespoon raisins, and 1½ teaspoons cinnamon sugar.

7. With long side facing you, use loosened parchment to roll dough tightly into log. Roll log seam-side down, trim ends, and slice into 1-inch cookies. Brush cookies with egg wash, sprinkle with 1½ teaspoons cinnamon sugar, and transfer to prepared sheet, spaced about 1 inch apart. Repeat with remaining dough and filling; all cookies should fit on 1 sheet. (Unbaked cookies can be frozen for up to 1 month; place on prepared baking sheet and let thaw completely at room temperature, about 1½ hours, before baking.)

8. Bake cookies until golden and slightly puffy, about 20 minutes, rotating sheet halfway through baking. Let cookies cool on sheet for 5 minutes, then transfer to wire rack and let cool completely

before serving. (Cookies can be stored in airtight container at room temperature for up to 1 day.)

VARIATIONS

Dairy-Free Rugelach
Omit salt, use dairy-free cream cheese, and substitute Earth Balance Vegan Buttery Sticks for butter.

Blackberry-Almond Rugelach
Omit raisins. Substitute blackberry jam for apricot jam, and toasted, chopped almonds for walnuts.

TEST KITCHEN TIP **Forming Rugelach**

1. Working with 1 piece of dough at a time, roll dough between 2 sheets of parchment paper into 12 by 5-inch rectangle (⅛ inch thick). Refrigerate dough for 10 minutes before filling and rolling cookies.

2. Loosen parchment on top, then flip dough over and remove second piece of parchment.

3. Spread 2 tablespoons jam over dough, leaving 1-inch border around edge. Sprinkle with 2 tablespoons walnuts, 1 tablespoon raisins, and 1½ teaspoons cinnamon sugar.

4. With long side facing you, use loosened parchment to roll dough tightly into log.

5. With log seam-side down, trim ends and slice into 1-inch cookies.

6. Brush cookies with egg wash, sprinkle evenly with 1½ teaspoons cinnamon sugar, and transfer to prepared sheet.

Rugelach

Making a gluten-free version of rugelach posed many challenges: collapsing, melting cookies; leaking, burning filling; and charred bottoms. Here's how we made gluten-free rugelach with a tangy, flaky dough rolled with the perfect amount of sweet, jammy filling.

1. USE LESS BUTTER AND ADD XANTHAN GUM: Cutting back on the butter helped to minimize greasiness and prevent the rugelach from melting all over the baking sheet. Because starches are liquid when hot and don't set up until cool, and because the protein structures made from our all-purpose gluten-free flour blend are weaker, these cookies don't hold their shape the way that traditional cookies do. To further prevent the cookies from spreading too much, we added a small amount of xanthan gum.

2. CHILL THE DOUGH TWICE: We relied on cream cheese and butter in order to make a tender dough with just the right richness, tang, and chew. But this composition made for a soft, delicate dough. Refrigerating the dough for 30 minutes before rolling it out gave the starches time to fully hydrate and allowed the dough to firm up, which made it easier to roll out. We found that with so much butter and cream cheese, this dough softened again during the rolling process. Chilling it for another 10 minutes after rolling allowed us to fill and cut our cookies easily.

3. USE LESS FILLING: These cookies, stuffed with apricot jam, golden raisins, and toasted walnuts, were consistently leaking during baking. The sugary filling would then burn and glue our cookies to the baking sheet. Because our gluten-free cookies lacked the structure of regular rugelach, they weren't able to support and contain the usual amount of filling. Reducing the amount of filling and finely chopping the golden raisins and walnuts to ensure even distribution solved the problem.

4. USE TWO SHEET PANS: Rugelach typically has a high sugar content in the form of jam, raisins, and cinnamon sugar. Combined with the fact that our flour blend is higher in starch than all-purpose flour (and therefore higher in sugar), this meant that our gluten-free rugelach were constantly burning on the bottom, becoming bitter and overcaramelized. We set the baking sheet in a second baking sheet to insulate the pan and prevent the bottoms of the cookies from burning.

Lime-Glazed Coconut-Cardamom Cookies

G-F TESTING LAB

FLOUR SUBSTITUTION	King Arthur Gluten-Free Multi-Purpose Flour 12 ounces = **1⅔ cups plus ½ cup**	Betty Crocker All-Purpose Gluten Free Rice Blend 12 ounces = **2¼ cups plus 2 tablespoons**
	Cookies made with King Arthur will be very sandy; cookies made with Betty Crocker will be dry and crumbly, and the dough will be wet and difficult to handle.	
XANTHAN GUM	Xanthan is crucial to the structure of the cookies; see page 22 for more information.	
RESTING TIME	Do not shortchange the dough's 30-minute rest or else the cookies will spread more and taste gritty.	

WHY THIS RECIPE WORKS

These rich, buttery cookies are flavored with cardamom and lime and topped with a zesty cream cheese glaze and toasted coconut. Using the test kitchen's simple butter cookie recipe as our starting point, we swapped in our gluten-free all-purpose flour blend and added a small amount of xanthan gum for structure. Using one whole egg and one yolk added both richness and tenderness without the binding properties of the extra egg white, which made the cookies tough. A hefty 12 tablespoons of butter provided rich flavor and gave the cookies their signature short texture. To get rid of the sandy texture that plagues most gluten-free baked goods, we added a small amount of milk (just ¼ cup) and let the batter rest for 30 minutes to hydrate. For more flavor, we whipped the lime zest and cardamom with the sugar and butter to bloom them and cut any harshness. A simple glaze of cream cheese, lime juice, and confectioners' sugar added the perfect amount of tartness to these cookies, while a toasted coconut topping added crunch.

Lime-Glazed Coconut-Cardamom Cookies
MAKES 40 COOKIES

COOKIES

- 12 ounces (2⅔ cups) ATK All-Purpose Gluten-Free Flour Blend (page 7)
- ½ teaspoon salt
- ½ teaspoon xanthan gum
- 7 ounces (1 cup) granulated sugar
- 12 tablespoons unsalted butter, cut into 12 pieces and softened
- 1 teaspoon ground cardamom
- ½ teaspoon grated lime zest
- ¼ cup milk
- 1 large egg plus 1 large yolk
- 2 teaspoons vanilla extract

TOPPING

- 1½ cups sweetened shredded coconut, chopped fine and toasted
- 3 tablespoons lime juice (2 limes)

- 1 tablespoon cream cheese, softened
- 6 ounces (1½ cups) confectioners' sugar

1. FOR THE COOKIES: Whisk flour blend, salt, and xanthan gum together in medium bowl. Using stand mixer fitted with paddle, beat sugar, butter, cardamom, and lime zest on medium-high speed until pale and fluffy, about 3 minutes. Add milk, egg and yolk, and vanilla and beat until well combined, about 2 minutes. Reduce speed to low, add flour mixture, and beat until completely incorporated and dough is homogeneous, 2 to 4 minutes, scraping down bowl as needed. Cover bowl with plastic wrap and let dough rest for 30 minutes.

2. Adjust oven rack to middle position and heat oven to 325 degrees. Line 2 baking sheets with parchment paper. Working with 1 heaping tablespoon of dough at a time, roll into balls using wet hands, and space 1 inch apart on prepared sheets.

3. Bake cookies, 1 sheet at a time, until firm to touch and lightly golden around edges, 12 to 16 minutes, rotating sheet halfway through baking. Let cookies cool on sheet for 5 minutes, then transfer to wire rack and cool completely before glazing.

4. FOR THE TOPPING: Place coconut in shallow dish. Whisk 2 tablespoons lime juice and cream cheese together in bowl until smooth, then whisk in sugar until smooth. Add remaining 1 tablespoon lime juice as needed until glaze is easy to spread. Dip tops of cooled cookies into glaze, allowing excess to drip back into bowl, then coat with coconut. Let glaze dry completely before serving, about 30 minutes. (Cookies can be stored in airtight container at room temperature for up to 2 days.)

VARIATION

Dairy-Free Lime-Glazed Coconut-Cardamom Cookies

We prefer the flavor and texture of these cookies made with soy milk, but almond milk will also work; do not use rice milk.

Substitute ½ cup vegetable oil for butter, and unsweetened soy milk for milk. Use dairy-free cream cheese.

Whole-Grain Graham Crackers

G-F TESTING LAB

FLOUR SUBSTITUTION	Do not substitute other whole-grain blends for the ATK Whole-Grain Gluten-Free Flour Blend; they will not work in this recipe.
BAKING POWDER	Not all brands of baking powder are gluten-free; see page 25 for more information.
XANTHAN GUM	Xanthan is crucial to the structure of the crackers; see page 22 for more information.
RESTING TIME	Do not shortchange the dough's 30-minute rest or else the dough will be too soft to roll out and cut.

WHY THIS RECIPE WORKS

We wanted to create gluten-free graham crackers with the characteristic crunch, sweet layers, and nutty flavor of the original, but without using graham flour, which is not gluten-free. Using our whole-grain gluten-free flour blend seemed like a natural starting point because its molasses-like flavor and coarse texture are very similar to graham flour. To soften the whole-grain flour blend and prevent the cookies from tasting sandy, we added ¼ cup of milk and let the batter rest on the counter for 30 minutes to hydrate the flours. We also added a little xanthan gum to prevent the cookies from spreading during baking. For a nice rise without making the cookies puffy, a combination of baking powder and baking soda was key. Following the traditional method for making graham crackers, we incorporated 8 tablespoons of chilled butter into the dough, which helped us achieve the signature flaky, tender layers inside the cookie. To add additional depth of flavor, we stirred in a little cinnamon and a combination of sugar, molasses, and a full tablespoon of vanilla. Increasing the amount of sugar slightly, from ½ cup to ⅔ cup, gave us the crisp crunch that is the hallmark of a good graham cracker. Poking the dough with holes before baking helped keep the cookies flat, and scoring the dough made it easy to snap the cookies apart after they baked and cooled. Finally, we found it necessary to bake the cookies on a double sheet pan to prevent them from overbrowning.

Whole-Grain Graham Crackers

MAKES 32 COOKIES

- 12 ounces (2⅔ cups) ATK Whole-Grain Gluten-Free Flour Blend (page 9)
- 4⅔ ounces (⅔ cup) sugar
- 1 teaspoon baking powder
- ½ teaspoon baking soda
- ½ teaspoon salt
- ½ teaspoon xanthan gum
- ¼ teaspoon ground cinnamon
- 8 tablespoons unsalted butter, cut into ½-inch pieces and chilled
- ¼ cup milk
- 2 tablespoons molasses
- 1 tablespoon vanilla extract

1. Process flour blend, sugar, baking powder, baking soda, salt, xanthan gum, and cinnamon together in food processor until combined, about 5 seconds. Add butter and process until mixture resembles coarse cornmeal, about 15 seconds. Add milk, molasses, and vanilla, and process until dough comes together, about 20 seconds.

2. Transfer dough to bowl, cover with plastic wrap, and let rest for at least 30 minutes. (Dough can be wrapped in plastic wrap and refrigerated for up to 2 days or frozen for up to 2 weeks. Let refrigerated dough soften at room temperature before rolling. Let frozen dough thaw for 12 hours in refrigerator, then soften at room temperature.)

3. Adjust oven rack to middle position and heat oven to 375 degrees. Set rimmed baking sheet in second baking sheet. Divide dough into 2 equal pieces. Roll 1 piece of dough into rough 17 by 10-inch rectangle (⅛ inch thick) between 2 large sheets of parchment paper. (Keep other dough piece refrigerated.)

4. Discard top sheet parchment. Using knife, trim dough into 14 by 8-inch rectangle. Score dough lightly into sixteen 3½ by 2-inch rectangles. Using tines of fork, prick each rectangle several times.

5. Slide parchment with dough onto prepared sheet. Bake until lightly browned on edges, 12 to 16 minutes, rotating sheet halfway through baking. Let cool on sheet for 5 minutes, then transfer to wire rack and let cool completely. Let baking sheets cool before repeating with remaining dough.

6. Break cookies apart along scored lines and serve. (Cookies can be stored in airtight container at room temperature for up to 3 days.)

VARIATION

Dairy-Free Whole-Grain Graham Crackers
Do not use rice milk.

Omit salt. Substitute Earth Balance Vegan Buttery Sticks for butter, and unsweetened almond or soy milk for milk.

Lemon Madeleines

G-F TESTING LAB

FLOUR SUBSTITUTION	King Arthur Gluten-Free Multi-Purpose Flour 2½ ounces = **7 tablespoons**	Betty Crocker All-Purpose Gluten Free Rice Blend 2½ ounces = **½ cup**
	Madeleines made with King Arthur will have a coarse crumb; madeleines made with Betty Crocker will be slightly dry and dome dramatically in the center.	
BAKING POWDER	Not all brands of baking powder are gluten-free; see page 25 for more information.	
RESTING TIME	Do not shortchange the batter's 30-minute rest or else the madeleines will taste gritty.	

WHY THIS RECIPE WORKS

Madeleines can be found at nearly every corner coffee shop these days, but those dense, flavorless, prepackaged cookies are a far cry from the buttery, rich tea cakes that originated in France. For gluten-free madeleines that were light and tender, we started by taking our favorite test kitchen recipe and swapping in our all-purpose gluten-free flour blend. Although they tasted delicious, they were also tough and dense. To fix this, we started by adding baking powder, which created rise by producing air bubbles during baking. These air bubbles interrupted the structure of the baked madeleines, giving them a more tender, cakelike crumb. Even with the addition of baking powder, however, our madeleines were still a little tough. Eggs stood out to us as a possible source of this toughness, and after exhaustive testing we found that one whole egg and two yolks got us the closest to our ideal texture, though it still wasn't the light, tender treat we were after. In addition to leaveners, fat and sugar can have a tenderizing effect on baked goods. We didn't notice any change when we adjusted the amount of melted butter we were using, but noticed a significant change when we increased the amount of sugar. Eventually we settled on a full 6 tablespoons of sugar (more sugar than flour blend by weight) for a tender, cakey texture.

Lemon Madeleines
MAKES 12 MADELEINES

2½   ounces (⅓ cup plus ¼ cup) ATK All-Purpose
       Gluten-Free Flour Blend (page 7)
¼   teaspoon baking powder
⅛   teaspoon salt
1   large egg plus 2 large yolks
2⅔   ounces (6 tablespoons) granulated sugar
4   tablespoons unsalted butter,
       melted and cooled
1   tablespoon grated lemon zest
1½   teaspoons vanilla extract
       Confectioners' sugar

1. Whisk flour blend, baking powder, and salt together in medium bowl. Whisk egg and yolks, granulated sugar, melted butter, lemon zest, and vanilla together in large bowl until well combined and very smooth. Stir in flour mixture with rubber spatula and mix until flour is completely incorporated and dough is homogeneous, about 1 minute. Cover bowl with plastic wrap and let batter rest for 30 minutes.

2. Adjust oven rack to middle position and heat oven to 375 degrees. Spray madeleine pan thoroughly with vegetable oil spray. Working with generous 2 teaspoons batter at a time, portion batter into molds. Bake madeleines until edges just begin to brown and spring back when pressed lightly, 8 to 10 minutes, rotating pan halfway through baking.

3. Let madeleines cool in pan for 5 minutes. Run thin knife around edges of molds to loosen, then transfer madeleines, ridged side up, to clean dish towel. Let madeleines cool completely.

4. Dust madeleines with confectioners' sugar before serving. (Madeleines can be stored in airtight container at room temperature for up to 2 days.)

VARIATIONS
Dairy-Free Lemon Madeleines
Substitute vegetable oil for butter.

Almond Madeleines
Omit lemon zest. Substitute ½ teaspoon almond extract for vanilla extract.

Orange-Cardamom Madeleines
Omit vanilla. Substitute orange zest for lemon zest, and add ½ teaspoon ground cardamom to sugar mixture in step 1.

Blondies

FLOUR SUBSTITUTION	King Arthur Gluten-Free Multi-Purpose Flour 8 ounces = ¾ **cup plus** ⅔ **cup**	Betty Crocker All-Purpose Gluten Free Rice Blend 8 ounces = 1½ **cups plus 2 tablespoons**
	Blondies made with King Arthur will taste a bit starchy and have very crisp edges; blondies made with Betty Crocker will be a bit dry and crumbly.	
CHOCOLATE	Not all brands of chocolate are processed in a gluten-free facility; read the label.	
BAKING POWDER	Not all brands of baking powder are gluten-free; see page 25 for more information.	
XANTHAN GUM	Xanthan is crucial to the structure of the blondies; see page 22 for more information.	

✓ WHY THIS RECIPE WORKS

Chewy but crisp around the edges, blondies are simply butterscotch-flavored brownies that rely on brown sugar and butter to give them their signature flavor. We began our testing by swapping in our all-purpose gluten-free flour blend in our traditional blondie recipe. It was no surprise that these blondies had problems: They were flat, sandy, and greasy. To start, we scaled way back on the butter, from 12 tablespoons to 7 tablespoons, to eliminate the greasiness. The reduced amount of butter also lightened the batter so that the blondies now had a nice rise. Next we tested mixing methods and found that the key to getting that hallmark blondie "chew" was to use melted butter, rather than creaming the butter with sugar. To fix the sandiness, we added a couple tablespoons of milk, which helped to hydrate and soften the flours. For sweetening, we used a combination of light brown sugar (for its toffeelike flavor) and granulated sugar (for structure). To further enhance the flavor we used a substantial amount of vanilla extract (4 teaspoons), and a little salt to sharpen the sweetness. To add texture and flavor to the bars, we included both semisweet and white chocolate chips. The blondies required a longer than usual baking time to dry them out or else they tasted mushy.

Blondies
MAKES 16 BARS

    8 ounces (1¾ cups) ATK All-Purpose
       Gluten-Free Flour Blend (page 7)
    ¾ teaspoon salt
    ½ teaspoon baking powder
    ½ teaspoon xanthan gum
    7 tablespoons unsalted butter,
       melted and cooled
    7 ounces (1 cup packed) light brown sugar
  3½ ounces (½ cup) granulated sugar
    2 large eggs
    2 tablespoons milk
    4 teaspoons vanilla extract
    ½ cup white chocolate chips
    ½ cup semisweet chocolate chips

1. Adjust oven rack to middle position and heat oven to 325 degrees. Make foil sling for 8-inch square baking pan by folding 2 long sheets of aluminum foil so each is 8 inches wide. Lay sheets of foil in pan perpendicular to each other, with extra foil hanging over edges. Push foil into corners and up sides of pan, smoothing foil flush to pan; spray with vegetable oil spray.

2. Whisk flour blend, salt, baking powder, and xanthan gum together in bowl. In large bowl, whisk melted butter, brown sugar, and granulated sugar together until no lumps remain. Whisk in eggs, milk, and vanilla until very smooth. Stir in flour mixture with rubber spatula until flour is completely incorporated and batter is homogeneous, about 1 minute. Fold in white chocolate and semisweet chocolate chips. Scrape batter into prepared pan and smooth top with spatula.

3. Bake until deep golden brown and toothpick inserted in center comes out clean, 50 to 60 minutes, rotating pan halfway through baking.

4. Let blondies cool completely in pan, about 2 hours. Using foil sling, remove blondies from pan. Cut into squares and serve. (Blondies can be stored in airtight container at room temperature for up to 2 days.)

TEST KITCHEN TIP **Making a Foil Sling**

Fold 2 long sheets of aluminum foil so each is 8 inches wide. Lay sheets in pan perpendicular to each other, with extra foil hanging over edges. Push foil into corners and smooth flush to pan.

Lunchbox Brownies

G-F TESTING LAB

FLOUR SUBSTITUTION	King Arthur Gluten-Free Multi-Purpose Flour 7½ ounces = **1¼ cups plus 2 tablespoons**	Betty Crocker All-Purpose Gluten Free Rice Blend 7½ ounces = **1½ cups**
	Brownies made with King Arthur will be slightly starchy and dry; brownies made with Betty Crocker will slightly dry and spongy.	
BAKING POWDER	Not all brands of baking powder are gluten-free; see page 25 for more information.	
XANTHAN GUM	Xanthan is crucial to the structure of the brownies; see page 22 for more information.	
RESTING TIME	Do not shortchange the batter's 30-minute rest or else the brownies will taste gritty.	

WHY THIS RECIPE WORKS

Chewy, chocolaty brownies should be simple and satisfying, but too often the gluten-free versions are dense and remarkably low on chocolate flavor. For simple old-fashioned brownies without a lot of fuss, we used plenty of Dutch-processed cocoa powder for the chocolate flavor and ditched the bar chocolate. We didn't miss the flavor of the bar chocolate and loved the ease of not having to prep it. To bring out the best flavor from the cocoa, we found it important to bloom it with melted butter and oil in the microwave. The real key to our success with this simple brownie, however, was discovering the perfect ratio of oil to butter. We worked to get the right balance of saturated fat (butter) and unsaturated fat (oil) for maximum chew and found that equal parts worked best. We then added an egg yolk in addition to two whole eggs, whose emulsifiers prevented fat from separating and leaking out during baking. A little milk gave the brownies the right amount of moisture, while adding a rest allowed the milk to hydrate the gluten-free flours, eliminating grittiness. A modest amount of all-purpose gluten-free flour blend, plus baking powder and xanthan gum, gave the brownies a structure that was partway between fudgy and chewy. Nailing the baking time was essential—too little time in the oven and the brownies were gummy and underbaked; too much time and they were dry. Thirty minutes in the oven provided the right balance. A tablespoon of vanilla rounded out the flavor of this quick and easy brownie. See page 217 for details on how to make a foil sling.

Lunchbox Brownies

MAKES 16 BARS

- 7½ ounces (1⅔ cups) ATK All-Purpose Gluten-Free Flour Blend (page 7)
- ½ teaspoon baking powder
- ½ teaspoon xanthan gum
- ½ teaspoon salt
- 2 ounces (⅔ cup) Dutch-processed cocoa powder
- 4 tablespoons unsalted butter, cut into 4 pieces
- ¼ cup vegetable oil
- 10½ ounces (1½ cups) sugar
- 2 large eggs plus 1 large yolk
- 3 tablespoons milk
- 1 tablespoon vanilla extract

1. Make foil sling for 8-inch square baking pan by folding 2 long sheets of aluminum foil so each is 8 inches wide. Lay sheets of foil in pan perpendicular to each other, with extra foil hanging over edges. Push foil into corners and up sides of pan, smoothing foil flush to pan; spray with vegetable oil spray.

2. Whisk flour blend, baking powder, xanthan gum, and salt together in bowl. In large bowl, microwave cocoa, butter, and oil together at 50 percent power until butter has melted and cocoa has dissolved, about 1 minute; let cool slightly. Whisk in sugar, eggs and yolk, milk, and vanilla until very smooth. Stir in flour mixture with rubber spatula until flour is completely incorporated and dough is homogeneous, about 1 minute. Cover bowl with plastic wrap and let dough rest for 30 minutes.

3. Adjust oven rack to middle position and heat oven to 325 degrees. Scrape batter into prepared pan and smooth top with spatula. Bake until toothpick inserted in center comes out with few moist crumbs attached, 30 to 35 minutes, rotating pan halfway through baking.

4. Let brownies cool completely in pan, about 2 hours. Using foil sling, remove brownies from pan. Cut into squares and serve. (Brownies can be stored in airtight container at room temperature for up to 2 days.)

VARIATION

Dairy-Free Lunchbox Brownies

We prefer the flavor and texture of these brownies made with almond milk, but soy milk will also work; do not use rice milk.

Omit salt. Substitute Earth Balance Vegan Buttery Sticks for butter, and unsweetened almond milk for milk. Increase baking time to 35 to 40 minutes.

Whole-Grain Pecan Bars

FLOUR SUBSTITUTION	Do not substitute other whole-grain blends for the ATK Whole-Grain Gluten-Free Flour Blend; they will not work in this recipe.

✓ WHY THIS RECIPE WORKS

To create a gluten-free version of this classic with a buttery crust, gooey filling, and nutty topping, we began our testing by swapping in our whole-grain gluten-free flour blend in the test kitchen's pecan bar recipe. To no surprise, we ran into a couple of problems during our first round of testing. The bars were much too tough as well as sandy and greasy. We started by scaling back the amount of butter in the crust to eliminate the greasiness, because gluten-free flours don't absorb fat well. Still, we were left with a tough, crumbly crust that didn't stand up to the gooey filling. In the next round of testing we found that omitting the baking powder from the crust of our original pecan bar recipe gave us the more tender, cookielike crust that we had been looking for. Baking powder is normally used in baked goods to provide rise; however, we were trying to get away from a cakelike texture in this particular crust. To fix the sandiness of the crust, we added 2 tablespoons of water to hydrate our flour blend. We also baked the crust before adding the filling so that it could set up and wouldn't turn soggy. Since the ratio of filling to crust is less in bars than in pie, our filling needed to be intensely flavored. To enhance the flavor and cut through the sweetness of these bars, we added a small amount of vanilla and ½ teaspoon of salt. See page 217 for details on how to make a foil sling.

Whole-Grain Pecan Bars

MAKES 16 BARS

CRUST

- 5 ounces (1 cup plus 2 tablespoons) ATK Whole-Grain Gluten-Free Flour Blend (page 9)
- 2⅓ ounces (⅓ cup packed) light brown sugar
- ¼ cup pecans, toasted and chopped coarse
- ½ teaspoon salt
- 4 tablespoons unsalted butter, cut into ¼-inch pieces and chilled
- 2 tablespoons water

FILLING

- 3½ ounces (½ cup packed) light brown sugar
- ⅓ cup light corn syrup
- 4 tablespoons unsalted butter, melted and cooled
- 2 teaspoons vanilla extract
- ½ teaspoon salt
- 1 large egg, lightly beaten
- 1¾ cups pecans, toasted and chopped coarse

1. Adjust oven rack to middle position and heat oven to 350 degrees. Make foil sling for 8-inch square baking pan by folding 2 long sheets of aluminum foil so each is 8 inches wide. Lay sheets of foil in pan perpendicular to each other, with extra foil hanging over edges. Push foil into corners and up sides of pan, smoothing foil flush to pan; spray with vegetable oil spray.

2. FOR THE CRUST: Pulse flour blend, sugar, pecans, and salt in food processor until mixture resembles coarse cornmeal, about 5 pulses. Sprinkle butter and water over top and pulse until mixture again resembles coarse cornmeal, about 8 pulses.

3. Transfer mixture to prepared pan and press firmly into even layer using bottom of measuring cup. Bake until beginning to brown, 20 to 24 minutes, rotating pan halfway through baking.

4. FOR THE FILLING: As soon as crust finishes baking, whisk sugar, corn syrup, melted butter, vanilla, and salt together in bowl until well combined. Whisk in egg until very smooth. Pour mixture over hot crust and sprinkle evenly with pecans. Bake until edges begin to bubble, 25 to 30 minutes.

5. Let bars cool completely in pan, about 2 hours. Using foil sling, remove bars from pan. Cut into squares and serve. (Bars can be stored in airtight container at room temperature for up to 2 days.)

VARIATION

Dairy-Free Whole-Grain Pecan Bars
Omit salt. Substitute Earth Balance Vegan Buttery Sticks for butter.

Key Lime Bars

G-F TESTING LAB

FLOUR SUBSTITUTION	King Arthur Gluten-Free Multi-Purpose Flour 6 ounces = ¾ **cup plus** ⅓ **cup**	Betty Crocker All-Purpose Gluten Free Rice Blend 6 ounces = ⅔ **cup plus** ½ **cup**
	Lime bars made with King Arthur will taste somewhat pasty; lime bars made with Betty Crocker will have a softer, more delicate crust.	
XANTHAN GUM	Xanthan is crucial to the structure of the crust; see page 22 for more information.	

WHY THIS RECIPE WORKS

We wanted to bring all the essence of Key lime pie to a Key lime bar, creating a bar that balanced a tart and creamy topping and a buttery rich base. For the base, we wanted something similar to shortbread: a crisp, buttery crust that could support the topping yet slice neatly and easily. We started with a classic shortbread recipe by mixing pieces of softened butter into our all-purpose gluten-free flour blend, along with sugar and salt, using a stand mixer to ensure a fine crumb. The flavor was exactly what we wanted, but without gluten this base couldn't support the topping. Adding just ¼ teaspoon of xanthan gum gave the crust the structure it needed to hold up and slice neatly without crumbling. As for the filling, it also had to be sturdy and sliceable. By adding cream cheese and an egg yolk to the usual sweetened condensed milk and lime juice and zest, we created a rich and firm filling. Letting the bars cool for a full 2 hours and then refrigerating them for an additional 2 hours were key to ensuring the custard topping set up. You can use either Key limes or regular limes here; Key limes have a delicate flavor, while regular limes have a stronger, more tart flavor. In order to yield ½ cup of juice, you'll need about 20 Key limes or 4 regular limes; do not substitute bottled lime juice. Be sure to zest the limes before juicing them. See page 217 for details on how to make a foil sling.

Key Lime Bars

MAKES 16 BARS

CRUST

- 6 ounces (1⅓ cups) ATK All-Purpose Gluten-Free Flour Blend (page 7)
- 2⅓ ounces (⅓ cup) sugar
- ¼ teaspoon salt
- ¼ teaspoon xanthan gum
- 8 tablespoons unsalted butter, cut into ½-inch pieces and softened
- 1–2 tablespoons water

FILLING

- 2 ounces cream cheese, softened
- 1 tablespoon grated lime zest plus ½ cup juice (4 limes)
  Pinch salt
- 1 (14-ounce) can sweetened condensed milk
- 1 large egg yolk
- ¾ cup sweetened shredded coconut, toasted (optional)

1. Adjust oven rack to middle position and heat oven to 350 degrees. Make foil sling for 8-inch square baking pan by folding 2 long sheets of aluminum foil so each is 8 inches wide. Lay sheets of foil in pan perpendicular to each other, with extra foil hanging over edges. Push foil into corners and up sides of pan, smoothing foil flush to pan; spray with vegetable oil spray.

2. FOR THE CRUST: Using stand mixer fitted with paddle, mix flour blend, sugar, salt, and xanthan gum on low speed until combined. Add butter, 1 piece at a time, and continue to mix until dough forms and pulls away from sides of bowl, 2 to 3 minutes. (Add 1 to 2 tablespoons of water as needed if dough appears dry.)

3. Transfer mixture to prepared pan and press firmly into even layer using bottom of measuring cup. Bake crust until fragrant and beginning to brown, 25 to 30 minutes, rotating pan halfway through baking. Let crust cool for about 30 minutes.

4. FOR THE FILLING: Stir cream cheese, lime zest, and salt together in bowl until well combined and no lumps remain. Whisk in condensed milk until well combined. Whisk in lime juice and egg yolk until very smooth. Pour filling evenly over cooled crust. Bake until bars are set and edges begin to pull away slightly from sides of pan, 15 to 20 minutes, rotating pan halfway through baking.

5. Let bars cool completely in pan, about 2 hours. Cover with foil and refrigerate bars until thoroughly chilled, about 2 hours. Using foil sling, remove bars from pan. Sprinkle with toasted coconut, if using. Cut into squares and serve. (Bars can be refrigerated for up to 2 days; crust will soften.)

Ginger-Fig Streusel Bars

G-F TESTING LAB

FLOUR SUBSTITUTION	King Arthur Gluten-Free Multi-Purpose Flour 6 ounces = ¾ **cup plus** ⅓ **cup**	Betty Crocker All-Purpose Gluten Free Rice Blend 6 ounces = ⅔ **cup plus** ½ **cup**
	Fig bars made with King Arthur will taste slightly pasty; fig bars made with Betty Crocker will have a softer, more delicate crust.	
XANTHAN GUM	Xanthan is crucial to the structure of the crust; see page 22 for more information.	
OATS	Not all brands of old-fashioned rolled oats are gluten-free; read the label. Do not substitute quick oats; they will not work in this recipe.	

WHY THIS RECIPE WORKS

For a novel approach to a classic fig bar, we introduced the bright, slightly spicy flavor of ginger and a crisp streusel topping. A streusel bar should have a sturdy, buttery, shortbreadlike base and a rich crumble topping that lends texture and stays in place. For the base, we started with butter, our all-purpose gluten-free flour blend, and sugar (plus salt for a little flavor). By mixing pieces of softened butter into the dry ingredients using a stand mixer, a method called reverse creaming, we developed the ideal delicate, short crumb. The buttery flavor was exactly what we wanted, but without gluten this base couldn't support the weight of a filling and topping. Adding just ¼ teaspoon of xanthan gum gave the crust the structure it needed to hold up and slice neatly without crumbling. We also baked the crust before adding the fruit and streusel so that it could set up and wouldn't turn soggy from the moisture in the fig filling. For the streusel topping, we simply took a portion of our shortbread base mixture and added light brown sugar, walnuts, and oats. The last component on our list was the fruit filling. Fig preserves or spread with the addition of lemon juice, lemon zest, and zippy crystallized ginger provided just the right jammy consistency as well as bright flavors we were seeking. After baking the base, all we had to do was spread on the filling, crumble our streusel over the top, and return the pan to the oven for a short stint. See page 217 for details on how to make a foil sling.

Ginger-Fig Streusel Bars
MAKES 16 BARS

- 6 ounces (1⅓ cups) ATK All-Purpose Gluten-Free Flour Blend (page 7)
- 2⅓ ounces (⅓ cup) granulated sugar
- ½ teaspoon ground ginger
- ¼ teaspoon salt
- ¼ teaspoon xanthan gum
- 8 tablespoons unsalted butter, cut into ½-inch pieces and softened
- 2 tablespoons packed light brown sugar
- ⅓ cup walnuts, toasted and chopped fine
- ¼ cup old-fashioned rolled oats
- 9 ounces (¾ cup) fig preserves
- 1 tablespoon minced crystallized ginger
- ½ teaspoon grated lemon zest plus 2 teaspoons juice

1. Adjust oven rack to middle position and heat oven to 375 degrees. Make foil sling for 8-inch square baking pan by folding 2 long sheets of aluminum foil so each is 8 inches wide. Lay sheets of foil in pan perpendicular to each other, with extra foil hanging over edges. Push foil into corners and up sides of pan, smoothing foil flush to pan; spray with vegetable oil spray.

2. Using stand mixer fitted with paddle, mix flour blend, granulated sugar, ground ginger, salt, and xanthan gum on low speed until combined, about 5 seconds. Add butter, 1 piece at a time, and beat until well combined, 2 to 3 minutes.

3. Measure ½ cup dough into medium bowl; set aside for topping. Press remaining mixture evenly into prepared pan using bottom of measuring cup. Bake crust until edges begin to brown, 14 to 18 minutes, rotating pan halfway through baking.

4. Meanwhile, mix brown sugar, walnuts, and oats into reserved dough until well incorporated. In separate bowl, combine preserves, crystallized ginger, and lemon zest and juice.

5. Spread fig preserve mixture evenly over hot crust, then sprinkle with hazelnut-size clumps of oat topping. Bake until topping is golden brown and filling is bubbling, 22 to 25 minutes.

6. Let bars cool completely in pan, 1 to 2 hours. Using foil sling, remove bars from pan. Cut into squares and serve. (Bars can be refrigerated for up to 2 days; crust and streusel will soften.)

FRUIT DESSERTS, PIES, AND TARTS

■ DAIRY FREE OR INCLUDES A DAIRY-FREE VARIATION

Whole-Grain Cherry Crisp

G-F TESTING LAB

FLOUR SUBSTITUTION	Do not substitute other whole-grain blends for the ATK Whole-Grain Gluten-Free Flour Blend; they will not work in this recipe.
CHERRIES	Make sure to use cherries packed in syrup. Cherries packed in water do not work in this recipe. The cherries in syrup should weigh 4½ pounds before draining.
OATS	Do not use quick oats; they have a dusty texture that doesn't work in this recipe. Make sure to buy old-fashioned rolled oats that have been processed in a gluten-free facility. See page 27 for more information.

WHY THIS RECIPE WORKS

For a satisfyingly rich gluten-free cherry crisp, we decided to pair our cherry filling with a crumble topping made with our whole-grain flour blend. Since fresh sour cherries are available only for one short month of the year, we decided to proceed with jarred or canned cherries, packed in either water or syrup. When testing each type, we drained off all the liquid and added in our own flavorings. Red wine gave us depth and highlighted the rich cherry flavor. A bit of almond extract helped enhance the almonds in the topping. Thickening the cherries was our major hurdle. We tried varying amounts of cornstarch with a wide range of results; 2 tablespoons seemed to work beautifully sometimes but not always. It was clear that these differences were related to whether the cherries were packed in water or syrup. Cherries in syrup thickened up nicely, while cherries in water always seemed, well, watery. Cherries packed in water were out. Moving on, a mixture of toasted oats and almonds paired well with our flour blend for a hearty topping. For just the right consistency, we pulsed in some of the almonds and oats at the end. We parbaked the filling to soften the cherries before adding our topping and popping the assembled crisp back into the oven to finish baking. The result was a sweet, crunchy, perfect crisp.

Whole-Grain Cherry Crisp

SERVES 6

TOPPING

- ¾ cup old-fashioned rolled oats
- ¾ cup sliced almonds
- 1½ ounces (⅓ cup) ATK Whole-Grain Gluten-Free Flour Blend (page 9)
- 1¾ ounces (¼ cup packed) brown sugar
- 2 tablespoons granulated sugar
- 2 teaspoons vanilla extract
- 1 teaspoon water
- ⅛ teaspoon salt
- 6 tablespoons unsalted butter, cut into 6 pieces and softened

FILLING

- 5¼ ounces (¾ cup) granulated sugar
- 2 tablespoons cornstarch
- 4½ pounds pitted sour cherries in syrup, drained (6½ cups)
- 2 tablespoons red wine
- ¼ teaspoon almond extract

1. FOR THE TOPPING: Adjust oven rack to middle position and heat oven to 400 degrees. Place oats and almonds on separate sides of parchment paper–lined baking sheet. Bake until lightly toasted, 3 to 5 minutes; let cool completely on baking sheet.

2. Pulse ½ cup toasted oats, flour blend, brown sugar, granulated sugar, vanilla, water, and salt in food processor until combined, about 5 pulses. Sprinkle butter and ½ cup toasted almonds over top and process until mixture clumps together into large, crumbly balls, about 30 seconds, stopping halfway through to scrape down bowl. Sprinkle remaining ¼ cup almonds and remaining ¼ cup oats over top and pulse to just combine, about 2 pulses; transfer to bowl.

3. FOR THE FILLING: Whisk granulated sugar and cornstarch together in large bowl. Stir in cherries, wine, and almond extract until combined. Transfer fruit mixture to 8-inch square baking dish and cover with aluminum foil. Place on foil-lined rimmed baking sheet and bake until fruit has released its juices, about 20 minutes.

4. Remove baking dish from oven, uncover, and stir gently. Pinch topping into ½-inch pieces (with some smaller loose bits) and sprinkle over fruit. Bake uncovered until topping is well browned and firm and juices are bubbling around edges, 25 to 35 minutes, rotating dish halfway through baking. Let cool on wire rack until warm, about 15 minutes. Serve.

VARIATION

Dairy-Free Whole-Grain Cherry Crisp
In topping, omit salt and substitute Earth Balance Vegan Buttery Sticks for butter.

Blueberry Cobbler with Cornmeal Biscuits

G-F TESTING LAB

FLOUR SUBSTITUTION	King Arthur Gluten-Free Multi-Purpose Flour 4½ ounces = ½ **cup plus** ⅓ **cup**	Betty Crocker All-Purpose Gluten Free Rice Blend 4½ ounces = ¾ **cup plus 2 tablespoons**
	Biscuits made with King Arthur will be a bit pasty; biscuits made with Betty Crocker will be drier and a bit pasty.	
CORNMEAL	The test kitchen's favorite cornmeal is Whole-Grain Arrowhead Mills Cornmeal. This brand has been processed in a gluten-free facility, but not all brands are. Make sure to read the label. See page 27 for more information.	
BAKING POWDER	Not all brands of baking powder are gluten-free; see page 25 for more information.	
XANTHAN GUM	Xanthan is crucial to the structure of the biscuits; see page 22 for more information.	

WHY THIS RECIPE WORKS

Because blueberry and corn are such a classic and winning combination, for our gluten-free cobbler we settled on rustic cornmeal drop biscuits instead of traditional biscuits. Equal cup amounts of cornmeal and our all-purpose flour blend proved to be the best starting point, as this combination created a sturdy biscuit that would hold up to our fruit filling. For leaveners, we used both baking soda and baking powder to give us the lift and sturdiness we needed for the biscuits to hold their shape, as well as to keep them from being too dense. As with our traditional cobblers, we found that baking the filling and biscuits separately, then combining them just before serving, gave us a perfectly cooked filling and tender biscuits. Be ready to serve the cobbler as soon as it comes out of the oven; the bottom of the biscuits will become quite soggy if allowed to sit on top of the warm fruit for too long.

Blueberry Cobbler with Cornmeal Biscuits
SERVES 8

BISCUITS

5	ounces (1 cup) cornmeal
4½	ounces (1 cup) ATK All-Purpose Gluten-Free Flour Blend (page 7)
3	tablespoons sugar
2	teaspoons baking powder
¼	teaspoon baking soda
½	teaspoon salt
¼	teaspoon xanthan gum
8	tablespoons unsalted butter, cut into ¼-inch pieces and chilled
¾	cup buttermilk, chilled

FILLING

2⅓	ounces (⅓ cup) sugar
4	teaspoons cornstarch
¼	teaspoon salt
30	ounces (6 cups) blueberries
1½	teaspoons grated lemon zest plus 1 tablespoon juice

1. FOR THE BISCUITS: Adjust oven rack to upper-middle and lower-middle positions and heat oven to 375 degrees. Line baking sheet with parchment paper. Pulse cornmeal, flour blend, 2 tablespoons sugar, baking powder, baking soda, salt, and xanthan gum in food processor until combined, about 5 pulses. Scatter butter pieces over top and pulse until mixture resembles coarse cornmeal with few slightly larger butter lumps, about 10 pulses.

2. Transfer cornmeal mixture to medium bowl, add buttermilk, and stir with fork until dough gathers into moist clumps. Using greased ¼-cup dry measure, scoop out and drop eight 2¼-inch-wide mounds of dough onto prepared sheet, spaced about 1 inch apart. (Do not make biscuits wider or they won't all fit in pie plate when baked.)

3. Sprinkle remaining 1 tablespoon sugar over biscuits and bake on upper rack until biscuits are puffed and lightly browned, 25 to 30 minutes, rotating sheet halfway through baking. Let biscuits cool on wire rack. (Cooled biscuits can be held at room temperature in zipper-lock bag for up to 2 hours.)

4. FOR THE FILLING: Stir sugar, cornstarch, and salt together in large bowl. Gently stir in blueberries and lemon zest and juice until evenly combined. Transfer to 9-inch deep-dish pie plate, cover with aluminum foil, and place on rimmed baking sheet. Bake on lower rack until blueberries are beginning to burst and juices are bubbling around edge, 40 to 50 minutes, stirring halfway through baking.

5. Uncover blueberries and stir gently. Arrange biscuits on top of fruit and continue to bake until biscuits have warmed through, about 5 minutes. Serve immediately.

VARIATION
Dairy-Free Blueberry Cobbler with Cornmeal Biscuits
Do not use soy milk or rice milk in this recipe.

In biscuits, omit salt, substitute Earth Balance Vegan Buttery Sticks for butter, and ¾ cup almond milk mixed with 2 teaspoons lemon juice for buttermilk.

Strawberry Shortcakes

G-F TESTING LAB

FLOUR SUBSTITUTION	King Arthur Gluten-Free Multi-Purpose Flour 9 ounces = **1½ cups plus 2 tablespoons**	Betty Crocker All-Purpose Gluten Free Rice Blend 9 ounces = **1½ cups plus ⅓ cup**
	Shortcakes made with King Arthur will be slightly sandy and will spread more; shortcakes made with Betty Crocker will be drier and slightly rubbery.	
BAKING POWDER	Not all brands of baking powder are gluten-free; see page 25 for more information.	
PSYLLIUM HUSK	Psyllium is crucial to the structure of the shortcakes; see page 26 for more information.	
RESTING TIME	Do not shortchange the shortcake dough's 30-minute rest or else the shortcakes will taste gritty and mushy.	

✔ WHY THIS RECIPE WORKS

Our idea of the perfect strawberry shortcake is one with a juicy, chunky strawberry filling sandwiched between two halves of a sweet, tender biscuit and served with a dollop of whipped cream. Since the filling isn't cooked, getting the right texture for the strawberries was key. So we quartered the berries and mashed some of them for a filling that had bites of sweet strawberries and plenty of juice. With our filling settled, we moved on to developing a gluten-free biscuit that met our standards. We wanted a drop biscuit that would be easy to make yet offer the same tender texture and buttery flavor as a traditional rolled and cut biscuit. In order to achieve this, we had to tweak the traditional ingredients (flour, baking powder, baking soda, sugar, salt, butter, and buttermilk) quite a bit. We added psyllium husk powder and an egg for the structure and elasticity normally provided by gluten development. We tried making the biscuits with buttermilk but found the dough very liquid-y, and it spread too much in the oven. This is because our flour blend does not absorb liquid to the same degree that all-purpose flour does. We switched to whole-milk yogurt, which, as a thicker liquid, produced a dough with the right consistency. It also helped us achieve a richness and tenderness previously lacking in our biscuits. Since we weren't using buttermilk, we added a squirt of lemon juice to add a little extra tanginess. Our gluten-free flour blend also does not absorb fat well, but we wanted to keep the biscuits buttery. To this end, we used a combination of butter (for flavor) and oil. This kept the fat from leaching out of the biscuit. As with other chemically leavened gluten-free quick breads, we found that a 30-minute rest greatly improved the texture of these biscuits. It not only helped us work with the dough but left enough time for the starches to fully hydrate, giving us biscuits that were tender and sweet instead of gritty and starchy. Once the biscuits were fully cooled, we split them and filled them with our macerated berries and a dollop of slightly sweetened whipped cream.

Strawberry Shortcakes

SERVES 6

STRAWBERRIES

- 2 pounds strawberries, hulled and quartered (6 cups)
- 6 tablespoons granulated sugar

SHORTCAKES

- 9 ounces (2 cups) ATK All-Purpose Gluten-Free Flour Blend (page 7)
- 2 tablespoons granulated sugar
- 4 teaspoons baking powder
- ¼ teaspoon baking soda
- 1½ teaspoons powdered psyllium husk
- ½ teaspoon salt
- 3 tablespoons unsalted butter, cut into ¼-inch pieces and chilled
- ¾ cup plain whole-milk yogurt
- 1 large egg, lightly beaten
- 2 tablespoons vegetable oil
- 2 teaspoons lemon juice
- 1 tablespoon turbinado sugar

WHIPPED CREAM

- 1 cup heavy cream, chilled
- 1 tablespoon granulated sugar
- 1 teaspoon vanilla extract

1. FOR THE STRAWBERRIES: Using potato masher, crush one-third of strawberries with sugar in bowl. Stir in remaining strawberries, cover, and let sit at room temperature while making biscuits, or up to 2 hours.

2. FOR THE SHORTCAKES: Whisk flour blend, granulated sugar, baking powder, baking soda, psyllium, and salt together in large bowl. Using fingers, rub butter into flour mixture until only small pea-size pieces remain. In separate bowl, whisk yogurt, egg, oil, and lemon juice together. Using rubber spatula, stir yogurt mixture into flour mixture until well combined and no flour pockets remain, about 1 minute. Cover with plastic wrap and let rest at room temperature for 30 minutes.

3. Adjust oven rack to middle position and heat oven to 450 degrees. Line rimmed baking sheet with parchment paper and place inside second baking sheet. Using greased ⅓-cup dry measure, scoop out and drop six 2½-inch-wide mounds of dough onto prepared sheet, spaced about 1½ inches apart. Sprinkle with turbinado sugar.

4. Bake biscuits until golden and crisp, about 15 minutes, rotating sheet halfway through baking. Let biscuits cool completely on wire rack, about 30 minutes.

5. FOR THE WHIPPED CREAM: Using stand mixer fitted with whisk, whip cream, sugar, and vanilla on medium-low speed until foamy, about 1 minute. Increase speed to high and whip until stiff peaks form, 1 to 3 minutes.

6. Split each biscuit open through middle. Using slotted spoon, portion strawberries over biscuit bottom. Dollop with whipped cream, cap with biscuit top, and serve immediately.

VARIATION
Peach Shortcakes
Substitute 2 pounds peaches, peeled, pitted, and cut into ¼-inch wedges, for strawberries, and skip step 1. Gently toss three-quarters of peaches with ¼ cup granulated sugar in large bowl and let stand 30 minutes. Toss remaining peaches with 2 tablespoons granulated sugar and 2 tablespoons peach schnapps in separate bowl and microwave, stirring occasionally, until peaches are bubbling, about 1 to 1½ minutes. Using potato masher, crush microwaved peaches and let stand 30 minutes. Add sliced peaches to mashed peaches and combine before assembling shortcakes.

TEST KITCHEN TIP **Making Strawberry Shortcakes**

1. Crush one-third of berries with sugar in bowl with potato masher. Stir in remaining berries, cover, and let sit at room temperature for up to 2 hours.

2. After shortcakes have cooled, split each one open through middle.

3. Using slotted spoon, portion berries over biscuit bottom. Dollop with whipped cream, cap with biscuit top, and serve immediately.

Shortcakes

We wanted a sweet drop biscuit that would offer an easy and quick alternative to a traditional rolled biscuit, but with the same tender texture and buttery flavor. The classic recipe is nothing more than flour, baking powder, baking soda, sugar, and salt mixed with butter and buttermilk. In order to produce an equally tender biscuit with a light, fluffy crumb, we had to rework the ingredient list quite extensively.

1. ADD PSYLLIUM AND EGG FOR STRUCTURE: While traditional biscuits rely on gluten for structure, we had to find another solution. Adding powdered psyllium husk (as we had done in bread recipes) helped strengthen the proteins in gluten-free flours so they could do a better job of trapping gas and steam during baking. However, using too much psyllium imparted an earthy flavor that was out of place in biscuits. An egg provided additional structure along with moisture and elasticity.

2. USE TWO FATS: Butter plays an important role in making biscuits tender and tasty. A batch of fluffy drop biscuits typically relies on at least a stick of butter. We found that our biscuit dough could absorb only 3 tablespoons of butter (the rest just leached out and made the biscuits greasy). With so little fat in the dough, the biscuits were very tough and dry. Two tablespoons of vegetable oil added back some richness, as did replacing the usual buttermilk with thicker, richer whole-milk yogurt.

3. THICKER DAIRY PLEASE: Biscuits are traditionally made with buttermilk. Because gluten-free flours don't absorb liquid well, we found the dough was very liquid-y and spread too much in the oven. Using less milk didn't work—the starches in the flour never hydrated, and they imparted a gritty texture to the baked biscuits. Switching to thicker yogurt (spiked with a little lemon juice for extra tang) produced a dough with the right consistency, and letting the dough rest for 30 minutes (as we had done with muffins and other chemically leavened bread) allowed the starches to hydrate before baking.

4. DOUBLE UP ON SHEET PANS: A biscuit is typically baked at a high temperature for a short time to achieve a golden crust and a nice rise. We struggled to get a nice color on the tops of the biscuits without burning the bottoms. Lowering the oven temperature seemed like a natural solution, but we needed to bake them so long that the insides dried out. We had better luck staying with the high temperature but using a second baking sheet as insulation to keep the bottoms from burning.

Pie Dough

G-F TESTING LAB

FLOUR SUBSTITUTION	King Arthur Gluten-Free Multi-Purpose Flour 13 ounces (for double crust) = **2¼ cups plus 2 tablespoons** 6½ ounces (for single crust) = **⅔ cup plus ½ cup**	Betty Crocker All-Purpose Gluten Free Rice Blend 13 ounces (for double crust) = **2½ cups plus 2 tablespoons** 6½ ounces (for single crust) = **1⅓ cups**
	Pie dough made with King Arthur will be less sturdy.	
XANTHAN GUM	Xanthan is crucial to the structure of the pie dough; see page 22 for more information.	

WHY THIS RECIPE WORKS

Perfect pie dough has just the right balance of tenderness and structure. The former comes from fat, the latter from the long protein chains, called gluten, that form when flour mixes with water. Too little gluten and the dough won't stick together; too much and the crust turns tough. So presumably we would face mostly a structural issue with a gluten-free dough, since gluten-free flours are naturally low in protein. As our first step, we swapped in our gluten-free flour blend for the wheat flour in all the pie dough recipes the test kitchen has developed over the years. We produced workable doughs in every case, but an all-butter dough (which includes sour cream for tenderness) had the necessary richness to stand up to the starchiness of the gluten-free flour blend and was clearly the best starting point. Although we weren't surprised to find that the dough was still too soft and lacked structure, we were taken aback by how tough it was; on its own, the sour cream was not sufficient to tenderize a gluten-free dough. We solved the structural problem easily with the addition of a modest amount of xanthan gum, but flakiness and tenderness were still elusive. In an effort to further tenderize our dough, we tested ingredients that are known to tenderize: baking soda, lemon juice, and vinegar. Vinegar was the clear winner, producing a pie crust that was not only tender, but also light and flaky. Like conventional recipes, this pie dough can be prepared in advance and refrigerated for 2 days; however, it is not sturdy enough to withstand freezing.

Double-Crust Pie Dough
MAKES ENOUGH FOR ONE 9-INCH PIE

- 6 tablespoons ice water
- 3 tablespoons sour cream
- 1 tablespoon rice vinegar
- 13 ounces (2¾ cups plus 2 tablespoons) ATK All-Purpose Gluten-Free Flour Blend (page 7)
- 1 tablespoon sugar
- 1 teaspoon salt
- ½ teaspoon xanthan gum
- 16 tablespoons unsalted butter, cut into ¼-inch pieces and frozen for 10 to 15 minutes

1. Combine ice water, sour cream, and vinegar together in bowl. Process flour blend, sugar, salt, and xanthan gum together in food processor until combined, about 5 seconds. Scatter butter over top and pulse until crumbs look uniform and distinct pieces of butter are no longer visible, 20 to 30 pulses.

2. Pour half of sour cream mixture over flour mixture and pulse to incorporate, about 3 pulses. Add remaining sour cream mixture and pulse until dough comes together in large pieces around blade, about 20 pulses.

3. Divide dough into 2 even pieces. Turn each piece of dough onto sheet of plastic wrap and flatten each into 5-inch disk. Wrap each piece tightly in plastic and refrigerate for at least 1 hour or up to 2 days. Before rolling out dough, let it sit on counter to soften slightly, about 30 minutes. (Dough cannot be frozen.)

Prebaked Pie Shell
MAKES ONE 9-INCH PIE CRUST

- 3 tablespoons ice water
- 1½ tablespoons sour cream
- 1½ teaspoons rice vinegar
- 6½ ounces (¾ cup plus ⅔ cup) ATK All-Purpose Gluten-Free Flour Blend (page 7)
- 1½ teaspoons sugar
- ½ teaspoon salt
- ¼ teaspoon xanthan gum
- 8 tablespoons unsalted butter, cut into ¼-inch pieces and frozen for 10 to 15 minutes

1. Combine ice water, sour cream, and vinegar together in bowl. Process flour blend, sugar, salt, and xanthan gum together in food processor until combined, about 5 seconds. Scatter butter over top and pulse until crumbs look uniform and distinct pieces of butter are no longer visible, 20 to 30 pulses.

2. Pour sour cream mixture over flour mixture and pulse until dough comes together in large pieces around blade, about 20 pulses.

3. Turn dough onto sheet of plastic wrap and flatten into 5-inch disk. Wrap tightly in plastic and refrigerate for at least 1 hour or up to 2 days. Before rolling out dough, let it sit on counter to soften slightly, about 30 minutes. (Dough cannot be frozen.)

4. Roll dough into 12-inch circle between 2 large sheets of plastic wrap. Remove top plastic, gently invert dough over 9-inch pie plate, and ease dough into plate. Remove remaining plastic and trim dough ½ inch beyond lip of pie plate. Tuck overhanging dough under itself to be flush with edge of pie plate. Crimp dough evenly around edge using your fingers. Cover loosely with plastic and freeze until chilled, about 15 minutes.

5. Adjust oven rack to lower-middle position and heat oven to 375 degrees. Bake crust until crisp and golden, 25 to 35 minutes, rotating pie plate halfway through baking. Remove crust from oven and let cool slightly. (Crust can be held at room temperature for up to 1 day before filling.)

TEST KITCHEN TIP **Making a Single-Crust Pie**

1. Roll dough into 12-inch circle between 2 large sheets of plastic wrap.

2. Remove top plastic and gently invert dough over 9-inch pie plate.

3. Working around circumference, ease dough into plate by gently lifting plastic wrap with 1 hand while pressing dough into plate bottom with other hand.

4. Remove plastic wrap. Trim excess dough with kitchen shears, leaving ½-inch overhang beyond lip of pie plate.

5. Tuck overhang underneath itself to form tidy, even edge that sits on lip of pie plate.

6. Using index finger of 1 hand and thumb and index finger of other hand, create fluted ridges perpendicular to edge of pie plate.

Strawberry-Rhubarb Pie

✓ WHY THIS RECIPE WORKS

Since the filling for this summery pie is naturally gluten-free, we started by following our traditional recipe but using our flaky double-crust gluten-free pie dough. But the top crust essentially melted into the filling and the vents collapsed, trapping so much steam and moisture that the top crust slid off to the side while the bottom crust sogged out. The starches in our gluten-free flour blend were the likely culprit because they absorb excess moisture so readily. Next we tried making a lattice top but it busted around the perimeter and collapsed into the juicy filling. Reducing the filling on the stovetop wasn't the answer either: The filling became sticky and jammy, and our crust was still soggy. So we considered an entirely new approach. We rolled out our top and bottom crusts and cut out numerous star cookies from the top crust. We parbaked the bottom crust, and fully baked the star cookies. Then we filled the parbaked crust and baked the pie topless. After taking the pie out of the oven, we shingled the baked stars over the top of the pie for a playful finishing touch. Don't let the second piece of pie dough sit on the counter for too long, or it will be too soft to work with. This pie is best served the day it is made.

Strawberry-Rhubarb Pie

SERVES 8

1¼	pounds rhubarb, sliced into ½-inch pieces (6 cups)
7	ounces (1 cup) plus 1 tablespoon sugar
1	pound strawberries, hulled and halved if smaller than 1 inch or quartered if larger than 1 inch (3 cups)
1	recipe Double-Crust Pie Dough (page 237)
1	large egg white, lightly beaten
3	tablespoons low-sugar or no-sugar-needed fruit pectin
2	teaspoons cornstarch
	Pinch salt

1. Toss rhubarb with ¾ cup sugar in bowl and microwave until sugar is mostly dissolved, 2½ minutes, stirring mixture halfway through. Stir in 1 cup strawberries and let sit at room temperature, stirring occasionally, for 1 hour.

2. Adjust oven racks to upper-middle and lower-middle positions and heat oven to 375 degrees. Roll 1 disk of dough into 12-inch circle between 2 large sheets of plastic wrap. Remove top plastic, gently invert dough over 9-inch pie plate, and ease dough into plate. Remove remaining plastic and trim dough ½ inch beyond lip of pie plate. Tuck overhanging dough under itself to be flush with edge of pie plate. Crimp dough evenly around edge using your fingers. Cover loosely with plastic and freeze until chilled, about 15 minutes.

3. Line baking sheet with parchment paper. Roll second disk of dough into 12-inch circle between 2 large sheets of plastic wrap. Remove top plastic. Using 3-inch star cookie cutter, cut 14 stars from dough and transfer to prepared baking sheet, spaced ½ inch apart. Brush cookies with egg white and sprinkle with 1 tablespoon sugar.

4. Bake star cookies on upper rack and chilled crust on lower rack until both are crisp and golden, 15 to 20 minutes for stars and 25 to 30 minutes for crust, rotating both halfway through baking. Remove both from oven and let cool slightly. Increase oven temperature to 425 degrees. (Cookies can be held at room temperature for up to 6 hours before turning stale.)

5. Drain rhubarb mixture through fine-mesh strainer into large saucepan, then return mixture to bowl. Add remaining 2 cups strawberries to saucepan and bring to simmer over medium-high heat. Reduce heat to medium-low and simmer until mixture measures 1½ cups, 15 to 25 minutes.

6. Combine remaining ¼ cup sugar, pectin, cornstarch, and salt in bowl, then stir into saucepan. Stir in rhubarb mixture and bring to boil over medium-high heat. Cook, stirring constantly, until

G-F TESTING LAB

FLOUR SUBSTITUTION	See page 236 for information about using various brands of gluten-free flour in the pie dough.

filling is thickened and slightly darkened, about 2 minutes. Immediately pour filling into partially baked pie crust.

7. Place pie on aluminum foil–lined baking sheet and bake on lower rack until crust is deep golden brown and filling is bubbling, about 15 minutes. Transfer pie to wire rack. Shingle star cookies attractively over filling and press gently to adhere. Let pie cool at room temperature until juices have thickened, 2 to 3 hours. Serve.

TEST KITCHEN TIP **Making Strawberry-Rhubarb Pie**

1. Microwave rhubarb and sugar until sugar dissolves, 2½ minutes. Stir in 1 cup of strawberries and let fruit sit for 1 hour to draw out liquid.

2. Using 3-inch star cookie cutter, cut 14 stars from dough. Transfer cookies to parchment-lined baking sheet, then brush with egg white and sprinkle with sugar.

3. Bake star cookies on upper rack and chilled crust on lower rack until both are golden, 15 to 20 minutes for stars and 25 to 30 minutes for crust.

4. After simmering drained rhubarb liquid and remaining strawberries together to thicken and reduce, add pectin–cornstarch mixture and drained rhubarb mixture and cook until thickened.

5. Pour filling immediately into pie crust and bake on foil-lined baking sheet until crust is deep golden brown and filling is bubbling, about 15 minutes.

6. Shingle star cookies attractively over filling and press gently to adhere. Let pie cool at room temperature until juices have thickened, 2 to 3 hours, before serving.

Dutch Apple Pie

G-F TESTING LAB

FLOUR SUBSTITUTION	King Arthur Gluten-Free Multi-Purpose Flour 4½ ounces = ½ **cup plus** ⅓ **cup**	Betty Crocker All-Purpose Gluten Free Rice Blend 4½ ounces = ¾ **cup plus 2 tablespoons**
	See page 236 for information about using various brands of gluten-free flour in the prebaked pie shell. Topping made with King Arthur will melt together; topping made with Betty Crocker taste slightly pasty.	
RESTING TIME	Do not shortchange the topping's 30-minute rest or else the topping will be gritty.	

WHY THIS RECIPE WORKS

A Dutch apple pie is known for its rich, cream-thickened filling and sweet streusel topping. For the filling, we followed the standard procedure for our classic deep-dish apple pie: We sautéed the apples to cook off excess moisture and avoid a soggy crust and soupy filling. Once they were softened, we removed them from the pan and added the heavy cream to the pan, allowing it to cook until thickened. We combined the apples and cream mixture, chilled them (so they wouldn't melt the streusel topping that would soon be mounded on top), loaded them into our gluten-free prebaked pie crust, and topped the filling with a basic streusel dough we'd developed for our New York–Style Crumb Cake. But the steam released from the apples turned the topping dense and soggy. The solution was cranking up the oven temperature from 375 to 425 degrees, which helped the topping set up before it could absorb excess moisture. For a finished look, dust the pie with confectioners' sugar just before serving, if desired.

Dutch Apple Pie

SERVES 8

FILLING
- 2 tablespoons unsalted butter
- 2½ pounds Granny Smith apples, peeled, quartered, cored, and sliced crosswise into ¼-inch-thick pieces
- 2 pounds McIntosh apples, peeled, quartered, cored, and sliced crosswise into ¼-inch-thick pieces
- 1¾ ounces (¼ cup) granulated sugar
- ½ teaspoon ground cinnamon
- ⅛ teaspoon salt
- ¾ cup golden raisins
- ½ cup heavy cream

TOPPING
- 4 tablespoons unsalted butter, melted and still warm
- 1¾ ounces (¼ cup) granulated sugar
- 1¾ ounces (¼ cup packed) light brown sugar
- 1 large egg yolk
- 2 teaspoons water
- ½ teaspoon ground cinnamon
- Pinch salt
- 4½ ounces (1 cup) ATK All-Purpose Gluten-Free Flour Blend (page 7)

- 1 recipe Prebaked Pie Shell (page 237), slightly cooled

1. FOR THE FILLING: Melt butter in Dutch oven over medium heat. Stir in apples, sugar, cinnamon, and salt, cover, and cook, stirring occasionally, until apples are softened, 5 to 7 minutes. Add raisins and cook, covered, until some apples have begun to break down, 5 to 7 minutes; transfer to large bowl.

2. Set large colander over now-empty Dutch oven. Transfer cooked apples to colander, let drain for 2 to 3 minutes; return apples to bowl. Stir cream into pot and boil over high heat, stirring occasionally, until thickened and wooden spoon leaves trail in mixture, about 5 minutes. Pour cream mixture over apples and gently combine. Spread apples onto rimmed baking sheet and refrigerate until cold, about 30 minutes.

3. FOR THE TOPPING: While apples cool, whisk melted butter, granulated sugar, brown sugar, egg yolk, water, cinnamon, and salt in bowl to combine. Stir in flour blend with rubber spatula until cohesive dough forms. Cover and let topping rest at room temperature for at least 30 minutes.

4. Adjust oven rack to middle position and heat oven to 425 degrees. Transfer apple mixture to slightly cooled pie shell and press into even layer. Pinch topping into ¼- to ½-inch pieces and sprinkle over top. Place pie on aluminum foil–lined rimmed baking sheet and bake until topping is golden and crisp, 25 to 30 minutes, rotating pie halfway through baking.

5. Let pie cool on wire rack to room temperature, 2 to 3 hours. Serve.

Pecan Pie

G-F TESTING LAB

FLOUR SUBSTITUTION	See page 236 for information about using various brands of gluten-free flour in the prebaked pie shell.

WHY THIS RECIPE WORKS

Pecan pie filling is naturally gluten-free, so we weren't too worried about adapting this recipe given that we had a recipe for gluten-free pie dough. Unfortunately, when we baked our favorite pecan pie filling in our gluten-free crust, the filling made the bottom crust soggy, and the crimped edges lacked the golden-brown color of a perfectly baked pie crust. Our original recipe starts with the pie crust parbaked at 375 degrees, and the filling is started on the stovetop over gentle heat to prevent curdling. The filling is then poured into the warm parbaked crust, and the pie is baked in a low 275-degree oven for about an hour. Jump starting the cooking of the filling on the stovetop ensures even cooking so that it doesn't harden at the edges while the center is still baking into its thick, silky texture. Assembling the pie while both the filling and crust are still hot helps the custard to begin firming up immediately, preventing it from soaking into the pastry. But during the pie's long baking time, the starches of our gluten-free pie dough still absorbed moisture from the filling before having the chance to crisp. We found that the crust would need to be fully baked into a flaky shell before the filling could be added, so we baked the empty pie crust to the desired golden-brown color at 375 degrees. We then reduced the oven temperature to 275 degrees, poured the warm pecan filling into the warm crust, and returned the pie to the oven. The sweet, custardy filling still needed close to an hour to set, but we found that the crust didn't overbake at such a low temperature during this time. This pie is best served the day it is made.

Pecan Pie

SERVES 8

- 6 tablespoons unsalted butter, cut into 6 pieces
- 7 ounces (1 cup packed) dark brown sugar
- ½ teaspoon salt
- 3 large eggs
- ¾ cup light corn syrup
- 1 tablespoon vanilla extract
- 8 ounces (2 cups) pecans, toasted and chopped fine

- 1 recipe Prebaked Pie Shell (page 237), slightly cooled

1. Adjust oven rack to lower-middle position and heat oven to 275 degrees.

2. Melt butter in heatproof bowl set in skillet of water maintained at just below simmer. Remove bowl from skillet and stir in sugar and salt until butter is absorbed. Whisk in eggs, then corn syrup and vanilla, until smooth. Return bowl to hot water and stir until mixture is shiny and hot to touch and registers 130 degrees. Off heat, stir in pecans.

3. Pour pecan mixture into slightly cooled pie shell and bake until filling looks set but yields like Jell-O when gently pressed with back of spoon, 50 to 60 minutes.

4. Let pie cool on wire rack until filling has set, about 2 hours. Serve slightly warm or at room temperature.

TEST KITCHEN TIP Making Pecan Pie Filling

Cook the butter, sugar, and egg mixture in a heatproof bowl set in a skillet of barely simmering water until the mixture is shiny and hot to the touch before adding the pecans.

Lemon Meringue Pie

G-F TESTING LAB

FLOUR SUBSTITUTION   See page 236 for information about using various brands of gluten-free flour in the prebaked pie shell.

✓ WHY THIS RECIPE WORKS

A lemon meringue pie worthy of its name features a tart, bracing filling that is firm but not gelatinous, and a tall meringue that doesn't break down. For our gluten-free version, we stuck closely to the test kitchen's classic method, swapping in our gluten-free pie crust for the usual pie dough or cookie crust. We wanted a meringue that didn't puddle on the bottom or "weep" on the top. We discovered that if the filling is piping hot when the meringue is applied, the underside of the meringue will not undercook; if the oven temperature is relatively low, the top of the meringue won't overcook. Baking the pie in a relatively cool oven also produced the best-looking, most evenly baked meringue. To further stabilize the meringue and keep it from weeping, we beat in a small amount of cornstarch. Make the pie crust, let it cool, and then begin work on the filling. As soon as the filling is made, cover it with plastic wrap to keep it hot and then start working on the meringue topping. You want to add hot filling to the cooled crust and then apply the meringue topping and quickly get the pie into the oven.

Lemon Meringue Pie

SERVES 8

FILLING

1½   cups water
 7   ounces (1 cup) sugar
 ¼   cup cornstarch
 ⅛   teaspoon salt
 6   large egg yolks
 1   tablespoon grated lemon zest plus
     ½ cup juice (3 lemons)
 2   tablespoons unsalted butter,
     cut into 2 pieces

MERINGUE

 ⅓   cup water
 1   tablespoon cornstarch
 4   large egg whites

 ½   teaspoon vanilla extract
 ¼   teaspoon cream of tartar
 ½   cup (3½ ounces) sugar

 1   recipe Prebaked Pie Shell (page 237),
     slightly cooled

1. FOR THE FILLING: Adjust oven rack to middle position and heat oven to 325 degrees. Bring water, sugar, cornstarch, and salt to simmer in large saucepan, whisking constantly. When mixture starts to turn translucent, whisk in egg yolks, 2 at a time. Whisk in lemon zest and juice and butter. Return mixture to brief simmer, then remove from heat. Lay sheet of plastic wrap directly on surface of filling to keep warm and prevent skin from forming.

2. FOR THE MERINGUE: Bring water and cornstarch to simmer in small saucepan and cook, whisking occasionally, until thickened and translucent, 1 to 2 minutes. Remove from heat and let cool slightly.

3. Using stand mixer fitted with whisk, whip egg whites, vanilla, and cream of tartar on medium-low speed until foamy, about 1 minute. Increase speed to medium-high and beat in sugar, 1 tablespoon at a time, until incorporated and mixture forms soft, billowy mounds. Add cornstarch mixture, 1 tablespoon at a time, and continue to beat to glossy, stiff peaks, 2 to 3 minutes.

4. Meanwhile, remove plastic from filling and return to very low heat during last minute or so of beating meringue (to ensure filling is hot).

5. Pour lemon filling into slightly cooled pie shell. Using rubber spatula, immediately distribute meringue evenly around edge and then center of pie, attaching meringue to pie crust to prevent shrinking. Using back of spoon, create attractive swirls and peaks in meringue. Bake until meringue is light golden brown, about 20 minutes, rotating pie halfway through baking. Let pie cool on wire rack until filling has set, about 2 hours. Serve.

Coconut Cream Pie

G-F TESTING LAB

FLOUR SUBSTITUTION	See page 236 for information about using various brands of gluten-free flour in the prebaked pie shell.

WHY THIS RECIPE WORKS

A great coconut cream pie should be rich and creamy and full of deep, tropical coconut flavor, and it should have a delicate crust. For the filling, we tried using 2 cups of coconut milk as the base of our lush custard, simmering it until thickened on the stovetop. While it boasted a concentrated coconut flavor, it turned out fat-laden and unappealing. We substituted light coconut milk, but it was seriously lacking in flavor. Instead, a combination of coconut milk and whole milk gave us just the right silky, stable custard. The filling now had more coconut flavor, but still not quite enough. The solution was simple: stirring unsweetened shredded coconut into the finished filling. But it contributed an unpleasant stringiness to our once-smooth filling. Simmering the shredded coconut along with the coconut milk and milk softened it perfectly. With our luxurious custard in hand, we chose to use our gluten-free prebaked pie shell as the base. Its buttery yet neutral flavor was the perfect medium for our velvety custard of paradise. Do not use low-fat coconut milk here because it doesn't have enough flavor. Also, don't confuse coconut milk with cream of coconut. The filling should be warm—neither piping hot nor room temperature—when poured into the slightly cooled pie crust.

Coconut Cream Pie

SERVES 8

PIE

- 1 (13.5-ounce) can coconut milk
- 1 cup whole milk
- 4⅔ ounces (⅔ cup) sugar
- 1½ ounces (½ cup) unsweetened shredded coconut
- ¼ teaspoon salt
- 5 large egg yolks
- ¼ cup cornstarch
- 2 tablespoons unsalted butter, cut into 2 pieces
- 1½ teaspoons vanilla extract
- 1 recipe Prebaked Pie Shell (page 237), completely cooled

TOPPING

- 1½ cups heavy cream, chilled
- 1½ tablespoons sugar
- 1½ teaspoons dark rum (optional)
- ½ teaspoon vanilla extract
- 1 tablespoon unsweetened shredded coconut, toasted

1. FOR THE PIE: Bring coconut milk, whole milk, ⅓ cup sugar, shredded coconut, and salt to simmer in medium saucepan over medium-high heat, stirring occasionally.

2. As coconut milk mixture begins to simmer, whisk egg yolks, cornstarch, and remaining ⅓ cup sugar together in medium bowl until smooth. Slowly whisk 1 cup simmering coconut milk mixture into yolk mixture to temper, then slowly whisk tempered yolk mixture into saucepan. Reduce heat to medium and cook, whisking vigorously, until mixture is thickened and few bubbles burst on surface, about 30 seconds. Off heat, whisk in butter and vanilla. Let mixture cool, stirring often, until just warm, about 5 minutes.

3. Pour coconut filling into completely cooled pie shell. Lay sheet of plastic wrap directly on surface of filling to prevent skin from forming. Refrigerate pie until filling is chilled and set, at least 4 hours or up to 24 hours.

4. FOR THE TOPPING: Before serving, use stand mixer fitted with whisk to whip cream, sugar, rum, if using, and vanilla on medium-low speed until foamy, about 1 minute. Increase speed to high and whip until soft peaks form, 1 to 3 minutes. Spread whipped cream attractively over top of pie, sprinkle with shredded toasted coconut, and serve.

Chocolate Angel Pie

✓ WHY THIS RECIPE WORKS

Having devoted so much time and energy to developing gluten-free versions of our favorite pies and tarts, we were delighted to discover that a delicious classic, chocolate angel pie, is naturally gluten-free (meringue crust and all). The ideal chocolate angel pie should have a light, crisp meringue crust, a filling so chocolaty and satiny it could put a truffle to shame, and plenty of whipped cream to top it off. For an ultracrisp and sliceable meringue, we whipped egg whites with sugar, cornstarch, and vanilla, along with cream of tartar for stability. We baked the meringue at 275 degrees for 1½ hours and then dropped the temperature to 200 degrees for an additional hour in order to cook off excess moisture while preventing the sugars from burning into a dark, tacky meringue. To prevent the crust from sticking to the pan, we relied on a dose of cornstarch to coat the greased pie plate. Next, we needed to boost the chocolate flavor. By making a cooked custard with egg yolks to stabilize our creamy filling, we were able to load nearly a pound of chocolate into the filling. A delicate balance of 9 ounces milk chocolate and 5 ounces bittersweet chocolate lent depth and complexity. To finish, we slathered on lightly sweetened whipped cream and sprinkled a dusting of cocoa powder over the top. With the airy, crisp meringue serving as the perfect gluten-free crust, this heavenly pie is like chocolate sitting on a cloud. Serve the assembled pie within 3 hours of chilling.

Chocolate Angel Pie
SERVES 8 TO 10

FILLING
- 9 ounces milk chocolate, chopped fine
- 5 ounces bittersweet chocolate, chopped fine
- 3 large egg yolks (reserve egg whites for meringue)
- 1½ tablespoons granulated sugar
- ½ teaspoon salt
- ½ cup half-and-half
- 1¼ cups heavy cream, chilled

MERINGUE CRUST
- 1 tablespoon cornstarch, plus extra for pie plate
- 3½ ounces (½ cup) granulated sugar
- 3 large egg whites
- Pinch cream of tartar
- ½ teaspoon vanilla extract

TOPPING
- 1⅓ cups heavy cream, chilled
- 2 tablespoons confectioners' sugar
- Unsweetened cocoa powder

1. FOR THE FILLING: Microwave milk chocolate and bittersweet chocolate in large bowl at 50 percent power, stirring occasionally, until melted, 2 to 4 minutes. Meanwhile, whisk egg yolks, sugar, and salt together in medium bowl. Bring half-and-half to simmer in small saucepan over medium heat. Whisking constantly, slowly add hot half-and-half to egg yolk mixture in 2 additions until incorporated.

2. Return half-and-half mixture to now-empty saucepan and cook over low heat, whisking constantly, until thickened slightly, 30 seconds to 1 minute. Stir half-and-half mixture into melted chocolate until combined. Let cool slightly, about 8 minutes.

3. Using stand mixer fitted with whisk, whip cream on medium-low speed until foamy, about 1 minute. Increase speed to high and whip until soft peaks form, 1 to 3 minutes. Gently whisk one-third of whipped cream into cooled chocolate mixture. Fold in remaining whipped cream until no white streaks remain. Cover and refrigerate at least 3 hours or up to 24 hours.

4. FOR THE MERINGUE CRUST: Adjust oven rack to lower-middle position and heat oven to 275 degrees. Grease 9-inch pie plate and dust well with extra cornstarch, using pastry brush to distribute evenly. Combine sugar and 1 tablespoon cornstarch in bowl. Using stand mixer fitted with whisk, whip egg whites and cream of tartar on medium-low speed until foamy, about 1 minute. Increase speed to medium-high and whip whites to soft, billowy mounds, 1 to 3 minutes. Gradually add sugar mixture and whip until glossy, stiff peaks form, 3 to 5 minutes. Add vanilla to meringue and whip until incorporated.

5. Spread meringue into prepared pie plate, following contours of plate to cover bottom, sides, and edges. Bake for 1½ hours.

6. Rotate pie plate, reduce oven temperature to 200 degrees, and continue to bake until completely dried out, about 1 hour. (Shell will rise above rim

of pie plate; some cracking is OK.) Let crust cool completely, about 30 minutes.

7. FOR THE TOPPING: Spread cooled chocolate filling into pie crust. Using stand mixer fitted with whisk, whip cream and sugar on medium-low speed until foamy, about 1 minute. Increase speed to high and whip until stiff peaks form, 1 to 3 minutes. Spread whipped cream evenly over chocolate. Refrigerate until filling is set, about 1 hour. Dust with cocoa before serving.

TEST KITCHEN TIP **Making Chocolate Angel Pie**

1. Cook half-and-half, egg yolks, sugar, and salt together to make custard, then stir custard into bowl of melted chocolate. Let filling cool slightly, about 8 minutes.

2. Whisk some of whipped cream into filling to lighten, then fold in remaining whipped cream until no streaks remain. Cover and refrigerate filling for 3 hours.

3. Using stand mixer fitted with whisk, make meringue by whipping egg whites, cream of tartar, sugar, cornstarch, and vanilla together until glossy, stiff peaks form.

4. Spread meringue into pie plate that has been greased and coated with cornstarch, following contours of plate to cover bottom, sides, and edges.

5. Bake meringue crust for 2½ hours, reducing oven temperature from 275 to 200 degrees after 1½ hours. Let crust cool completely before filling.

6. Spread cooled chocolate filling into pie crust, then top with whipped cream and refrigerate for 1 hour before serving.

Tart Shell

✓ WHY THIS RECIPE WORKS

While pie crust is tender and flaky, classic tart crust should be fine-textured, buttery-rich, crisp, and crumbly—it is often described as being similar to shortbread. We began experimenting with our classic recipe (which combines flour, confectioners' sugar, an egg yolk, heavy cream, and a stick of butter), substituting our gluten-free flour blend for the all-purpose flour, but found the crust too sweet and fragile. Adding xanthan gum helped reinforce the structure, but our tart shell was still too crumbly and too sweet (since rice flours, unlike all-purpose flour, have a distinct sweetness). Our next step was to go down on sugar and test adding another egg, egg yolks, and more cream. But still the crust was sandy and overly sweet. Our traditional tart crust uses confectioners' sugar to make the crust more shortbreadlike, but since our working recipe was leaning too far in the shortbread direction, so much so that the crust was almost powdery, we decided to try granulated sugar. Unfortunately, the granulated sugar produced a hard, candied shell. In the end we found that reducing the amount of sugar and using a mix of confectioners' sugar and brown sugar did the trick. We also learned that we didn't need the cream at all—just a very small amount of water was all that was required to bind the dough together. Refer to pages 254–255 when making this recipe.

Tart Shell

MAKES ONE 9-INCH TART SHELL

- 1 **large egg yolk**
- ½ **teaspoon vanilla extract**
- 7 **ounces (1⅓ cups plus ¼ cup) ATK All-Purpose Gluten-Free Flour Blend (page 7)**
- 2⅓ **ounces (⅓ cup packed) light brown sugar**
- 1 **ounce (¼ cup) confectioners' sugar**
- 1 **teaspoon xanthan gum**
- ¼ **teaspoon salt**
- 8 **tablespoons unsalted butter, cut into ¼-inch pieces and chilled**
- 2 **teaspoons ice water**

1. Whisk egg yolk and vanilla together in bowl. Process flour blend, brown sugar, confectioners' sugar, xanthan gum, and salt together in food processor until combined, about 5 seconds. Scatter butter over top and pulse until mixture resembles coarse cornmeal, about 10 pulses.

2. With processor running, add egg yolk mixture and continue to process until dough just comes together around processor blade, about 15 seconds. Add 1 teaspoon ice water and pulse until dough comes together. If dough does not come together, add remaining 1 teaspoon ice water and pulse until dough comes together.

3. Turn dough onto sheet of plastic wrap and flatten into 6-inch disk. Wrap dough tightly in plastic and refrigerate for at least 1 hour or up to 2 days. (Dough can also be frozen for up to 2 months; let thaw completely on counter before rolling out.)

4. Let dough sit on counter to soften slightly, about 10 minutes. Spray 9-inch tart pan with removable bottom with vegetable oil spray. Roll dough into 12-inch circle between 2 large sheets plastic wrap. Slide it onto baking sheet and remove top plastic. Place tart pan upside down in center of dough. Holding tart pan and baking sheet firmly, flip over sheet pan, dough, and tart pan and set back on counter. Remove sheet pan and remaining plastic.

5. Run rolling pin over edges of tart pan to cut dough. Gently press dough into bottom of tart pan. Roll dough scraps into ½-inch rope. Line pan edge with rope and gently press into fluted sides. Line pan with plastic and, using measuring cup, gently smooth dough to even thickness. Trim away excess dough above rim of tart pan with paring knife. Cover loosely with plastic wrap and freeze until chilled and firm, about 15 minutes.

6. Adjust oven rack to middle position and heat oven to 375 degrees. Set chilled tart pan on rimmed baking sheet. Press greased heavy-duty aluminum foil into tart shell, covering edges to prevent burning, and fill with 1 cup of pie weights. Bake until tart shell is just set, about 25 minutes, rotating

G-F TESTING LAB

FLOUR SUBSTITUTION	King Arthur Gluten-Free Multi-Purpose Flour 7 ounces = **1¼ cups**	Betty Crocker All-Purpose Gluten Free Rice Blend We do not recommend using Betty Crocker in this recipe
	The tart shell made with King Arthur will be more crumbly and grainy; the tart shell made with Betty Crocker was too delicate and it crumbled apart during baking.	
XANTHAN GUM	Xanthan is crucial to the structure of the tart dough; see page 22 for more information.	

sheet halfway through baking. Carefully remove weights and foil and continue to bake tart shell until lightly golden, about 10 minutes. Let tart shell cool in pan.

VARIATION

Dairy-Free Tart Shell
Omit salt and substitute Earth Balance Vegan Buttery Sticks for butter.

TEST KITCHEN TIP **Making a Tart Shell**

Because our gluten-free tart dough is softer than traditional dough, you need to roll it out between sheets of plastic wrap. We also discovered a supereasy method for getting this dough into the pan: We pressed the tart pan into the dough to cut it, and then inverted the baking sheet along with the tart pan so that the dough fell right into the pan. Make sure to chill the dough before starting this process. If at any point the dough becomes too soft to work with, slip the dough onto a baking sheet and refrigerate it until workable. Note that this dough needs to be lined with greased foil and weighted with pie weights before baking, or else it will puff up in the oven and the sides will shrink down.

1. Roll dough into 12-inch circle between 2 sheets of plastic wrap. Slide onto baking sheet, then carefully remove top sheet of plastic.

2. Place tart pan, bottom side up, in center of dough and press gently so that sharp edge of tart pan cuts dough.

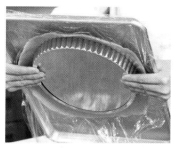

3. Holding tart pan in place, pick up baking sheet and carefully flip it over so that tart pan is right side up on counter. Remove baking sheet and peel off remaining plastic.

4. Run rolling pin over edges of tart pan to cut dough completely. Gently ease and press dough into bottom of pan, reserving scraps.

5. Roll dough scraps into ½-inch rope, line edge of tart pan with rope, and gently press into fluted sides.

6. Line tart pan with plastic wrap and, using measuring cup, gently press and smooth dough to even thickness (sides should be ¼ inch thick). Trim any excess dough with paring knife.

French Apple Tart

G-F TESTING LAB

FLOUR SUBSTITUTION	See page 254 for information about using various brands of gluten-free flour in the tart shell.

✓ WHY THIS RECIPE WORKS

This stunning tart features a luxurious apple puree topped with a showstopping spiral fan of apple slices. We wanted a filling that was more distinctive than just a straight apple puree. So we added butter and apricot preserves to our filling for a rich concentrated puree that reinforced the bright flavor of the fresh apples. To make the tart easier to assemble, we sautéed the apple slices briefly so they were pliable. After baking, we brushed the tart with a quick glaze made by straining the apricot preserves we were already using in the filling. We briefly ran the tart under the broiler to get the burnished finish that characterizes this French classic. You may have extra apple slices after arranging the apples in step 4. If you don't have a potato masher, you can puree the apples in a food processor. To ensure that the outer ring of the pan releases easily from the tart, avoid getting apple puree and apricot glaze on the crust. The tart is best served the day it is made.

French Apple Tart

SERVES 8

½   cup apricot preserves
10   Golden Delicious apples (8 ounces each), peeled and cored
3   tablespoons unsalted butter
1   tablespoon water
¼   teaspoon salt
1   recipe Tart Shell (page 253)

1. Microwave apricot preserves until fluid, about 30 seconds. Strain preserves through fine-mesh strainer into small bowl, reserving solids. Measure out and reserve 3 tablespoons strained preserves for brushing tart.

2. Cut 5 apples lengthwise into quarters, and cut each quarter lengthwise into 4 slices. Melt 1 tablespoon butter in 12-inch skillet over medium heat.

Add apple slices and water and toss to combine. Cover and cook, stirring occasionally, until apples begin to turn translucent and are slightly pliable, 3 to 5 minutes. Spread apples out onto large plate and let cool. Do not clean skillet.

3. Cut remaining 5 apples into ½-inch-thick wedges. Melt remaining 2 tablespoons butter in now-empty skillet over medium heat. Add apple wedges, reserved apricot solids and strained apricot preserves, and salt. Cover and cook, stirring occasionally, until apples are very soft, about 10 minutes. Mash apples to puree with potato masher. Continue to cook, stirring occasionally, until puree is reduced to 2 cups, about 5 minutes.

4. Adjust 1 oven rack to lowest position and second rack 5 to 6 inches from broiler element, and heat oven to 375 degrees. Spread apple puree into cooled tart shell and smooth surface. Select 5 thinnest apple slices and set aside for center. Starting at outer edge of tart, arrange remaining slices, tightly overlapping, in concentric circles. Bend reserved slices to fit in center. Bake tart on baking sheet on lower rack for 30 minutes.

5. Remove tart from oven and heat broiler. While broiler heats, warm reserved preserves in microwave until fluid, about 20 seconds, and brush evenly over apples, avoiding crust. Broil tart, checking every 30 seconds and turning as necessary, until apples are attractively caramelized, 1 to 3 minutes.

6. Transfer baking sheet with tart to wire rack and let cool to room temperature, about 1½ hours. Remove outer metal ring of tart pan, slide thin metal spatula between tart and pan bottom, and carefully slide tart onto serving platter. Cut into wedges and serve.

VARIATION

Dairy-Free French Apple Tart
Use Dairy-Free Tart Shell (page 255) and substitute Earth Balance Vegan Buttery Sticks for butter.

Baked Raspberry Tart

G-F TESTING LAB

FLOUR SUBSTITUTION   You can substitute 2½ tablespoons of King Arthur Gluten-Free Multi-Purpose Flour or Betty Crocker All-Purpose Gluten Free Rice Blend; neither will affect the flavor or texture of the filling. See page 254 for information about using various brands of gluten-free flour in the tart shell.

WHY THIS RECIPE WORKS

This rustic raspberry tart mixes fresh berries right into a buttery custard filling before baking. The heat of the oven gently brings together the crisp tart shell, custard, and tangy raspberries into a rich-tasting but simple and beautiful tart. We started by baking our gluten-free tart shell until it was lightly golden brown. We then arranged the raspberries in the base of the cooled shell before pouring our custard mixture on top. Our first attempt at the custard filling was a simple mixture of butter, egg, and sugar. We turned to cornstarch for its gluten-free thickening power. The resulting tart was starchy, coarse, and bland. After replacing the cornstarch with our all-purpose gluten-free flour blend the custard had a smooth, silky texture. But it was still lacking in flavor, so we turned to browning our butter to give it a nutty richness. This gave us a richer, fuller, and more complex tart. We rounded out the overall profile of the filling with heavy cream for richness, a bit of lemon zest and juice for brightness, as well as a moderate amount of vanilla extract and framboise to reinforce the sweet berry flavor. Do not substitute frozen raspberries here. This tart is best served the day it is made.

Baked Raspberry Tart

SERVES 8

6	tablespoons unsalted butter, cut into 6 pieces
1	large egg, plus 1 large white
3½	ounces (½ cup) sugar
¼	teaspoon salt
1	teaspoon vanilla extract
1	teaspoon framboise or kirsch (optional)
¼	teaspoon grated lemon zest plus 1½ teaspoons juice
2½	tablespoons ATK All-Purpose Gluten-Free Flour Blend (page 7)
2	tablespoons heavy cream
10	ounces (2 cups) raspberries
1	recipe Tart Shell (page 253)

1. Adjust oven rack to middle position and heat oven to 375 degrees. Melt butter in small saucepan over medium heat, stirring occasionally, until butter smells nutty and milk solids are golden brown, about 7 minutes; transfer to bowl and let cool to room temperature.

2. Whisk egg and white together in large bowl until combined. Whisk in sugar and salt until light in color, about 1 minute. Whisk in browned butter, vanilla, framboise (if using), and lemon zest and juice. Whisk in flour blend, followed by cream, until well combined.

3. Put tart pan on rimmed baking sheet. Arrange raspberries in single layer in bottom of cooled tart shell. Pour filling mixture evenly over raspberries. Bake tart on baking sheet until filling is set (center should not jiggle when shaken) and surface is puffed and deep golden brown, about 35 minutes, rotating baking sheet halfway through baking.

4. Transfer baking sheet with tart to wire rack and let cool to room temperature, about 1½ hours. Remove outer metal ring of tart pan, slide thin metal spatula between tart and pan bottom, and carefully slide tart onto serving platter. Cut into wedges and serve.

TEST KITCHEN TIP **Making a Raspberry Tart**

Arrange raspberries in single layer in bottom of cooled tart shell. Pour filling mixture evenly over raspberries.

Whole-Grain Free-Form Pear Tart

FLOUR SUBSTITUTION	Do not substitute other whole-grain blends for the ATK Whole-Grain Gluten-Free Flour Blend; they will not work in this recipe.
XANTHAN GUM	Xanthan is crucial to the structure of the tart dough; see page 22 for more information.
PEARS	The pears should be ripe but firm, which means the flesh at the base of the stem should give slightly when gently pressed with a finger. The test kitchen prefers to use Bartlett pears in this recipe, but Bosc pears can also work. Be sure to let the pears drain for 20 minutes, or else the tart will be wet and may leak.

WHY THIS RECIPE WORKS

The problem with free-form tarts is making a dough sturdy enough to hold the fruit without leaking. We thought we would have a fighting chance using our whole-grain gluten-free flour blend because it is so high in protein. Our first step was to test our blend in tart recipes developed by the test kitchen. But most of the tarts suffered from filling that leached out of the crust and scorched in the oven. Structural issues aside, our favorite crust contained a bit of sour cream for tenderness. By increasing the amount of sour cream from ¼ cup to ¾ cup, our dough became even more tender and that much closer to tasting like real tart dough. Adding a bit of xanthan gum made the dough even easier to handle and helped prevent cracking during shaping and folding. Our traditional recipes for free-form tarts call for chilling the dough after rolling, before filling and baking. But as we folded our chilled gluten-free dough, we could see cracking and tearing. By topping and shaping the more tender gluten-free crust without chilling, we were able to protect the integrity of our tart. As for the fruit, we microwaved our pears with half of the sugar to pull excess moisture out of the fruit so it wouldn't sog out the dough. Like conventional recipes, this tart dough can be prepared in advance and refrigerated for 2 days or frozen for up to 1 month.

Whole-Grain Free-Form Pear Tart

MAKES ONE 9-INCH TART, SERVES 6

TART DOUGH

- ¾ cup sour cream
- 1 tablespoon ice water
- 1 teaspoon rice vinegar
- ½ teaspoon vanilla extract
- 7½ ounces (1⅔ cups) ATK Whole-Grain Gluten-Free Flour Blend (page 9)
- 2 tablespoons granulated sugar
- ¾ teaspoon xanthan gum
- ¾ teaspoon salt
- 8 tablespoons unsalted butter, cut into ½-inch pieces and frozen for 10 to 15 minutes

FILLING

- 3 pounds ripe but firm Bartlett or Bosc pears, peeled, halved lengthwise, cored, and each half cut lengthwise into 4 slices
- 3½ ounces (½ cup) granulated sugar
- ¼ cup dried cranberries, chopped coarse
- 1½ tablespoons lemon juice
- ¼ teaspoon ground cinnamon
- Pinch salt
- 1 egg white, lightly beaten
- 1 tablespoon turbinado sugar

1. FOR THE TART DOUGH: Whisk sour cream, ice water, vinegar, and vanilla together in bowl. Process flour blend, sugar, xanthan gum, and salt together in food processor until combined, about 5 seconds. Scatter butter over top and pulse until mixture resembles coarse cornmeal, about 10 pulses.

2. Pour half of sour cream mixture over flour mixture and pulse until incorporated, about 3 pulses. Pour remaining sour cream mixture over flour mixture and pulse until dough comes together, about 6 pulses.

3. Turn dough onto sheet of plastic wrap and flatten into 6-inch disk. Wrap dough tightly and refrigerate for at least 1 hour or up to 2 days. (Dough can also be frozen for up to 1 month; let thaw completely on counter before rolling out.)

4. FOR THE FILLING: Combine pears and ¼ cup granulated sugar in bowl, cover, and microwave, stirring occasionally, until pears are translucent and slightly pliable, 7 to 10 minutes. Transfer to colander and let pears drain for about 20 minutes.

5. Adjust oven rack to upper-middle position and heat oven to 350 degrees. Roll dough into 15-inch circle between 2 large sheets greased parchment paper. Slide onto baking sheet and remove top parchment. If necessary, trim parchment paper to fit sheet.

6. Gently combine cooled pears, remaining ¼ cup sugar, cranberries, lemon juice, cinnamon, and salt in bowl. Mound pear mixture in center of dough, leaving 3-inch border around edge. Using parchment to help, fold outer 3 inches dough over filling, pleating dough every 2 to 3 inches as needed. Brush tart crust with egg white and sprinkle with turbinado sugar.

7. Bake tart until dark brown and crust feels firm, 60 to 70 minutes. Let tart cool slightly on baking sheet,

about 5 minutes. Slide onto wire rack using parchment, then use spatula to loosen tart from parchment and remove parchment. Let tart cool until juices have thickened, about 25 minutes. Serve warm or at room temperature.

TEST KITCHEN TIP **Making a Whole-Grain Free-Form Tart**

1. Make tart dough in food processor, then refrigerate for at least 1 hour before rolling out.

2. Microwave pears and ¼ cup granulated sugar until pears are translucent and slightly pliable, 7 to 10 minutes. Transfer to colander and let drain.

3. Roll dough into 15-inch circle between 2 large sheets of greased parchment paper. Slide onto baking sheet and remove top parchment.

4. Gently combine cooled pears, remaining ¼ cup granulated sugar, cranberries, lemon juice, cinnamon, and salt in bowl. Mound pear mixture in center of dough, leaving 3-inch border around edge.

5. Using parchment to help, fold outer 3 inches dough over filling, pleating dough every 2 to 3 inches as needed.

6. Brush tart crust with egg white and sprinkle with turbinado sugar.

Whole-Grain Free-Form Tart Dough

Our higher-protein whole-grain flour blend was essential in developing a free-form tart dough since more protein means less chance of the dough cracking when forming the characteristic folds of the rustic tart. That said, we still needed to strike a balance between using a structured dough that could keep the filling contained and creating flaky layers of pastry that are the hallmark of a great tart crust. Here is what we learned.

1. ADD XANTHAN GUM FOR STRUCTURE: In traditional tart dough, you do not want a lot of gluten development because it makes the dough tough. Although our whole-grain gluten-free flour blend has more protein than that in our all-purpose blend, the proteins still form weaker bonds when compared with traditional wheat flour. The resulting tart dough, therefore, had a hard time holding together, was difficult to shape, and leaked around the edges during baking. To give the dough some extra structure and elasticity, we added a small amount of xanthan gum to bind the proteins into a sturdier network.

2. ADD SOUR CREAM FOR WORKABILITY: The test kitchen's traditional free-form tart dough includes cream cheese for tenderizing and workability. In our testing we explored alternatives to the cream cheese to see if they would make any difference. We tried adding yogurt and sour cream. Yogurt added a tang that tasters didn't like, but sour cream resulted in richness and tenderness that tasters preferred over the dough made with cream cheese. As a result, the new dough was even easier to roll out and more readily held together when shaping the tart.

3. ADD VINEGAR FOR FLAKINESS AND TENDERNESS: In our quest for a flaky and tender free-form tart crust, we tested ingredients that are known to tenderize dough, namely baking soda, lemon juice, and vinegar. Baking soda produced a crust that was too crumbly and overly browned. Lemon juice and vinegar produced crusts that were indeed tender, but the crust made with vinegar was also light and flaky. Adding vinegar lowered the pH of the dough, which weakened the bonds just enough to produce a tart that was tender with flaky layers.

4. ROLL BETWEEN SHEETS OF PARCHMENT PAPER: Our whole-grain gluten-free dough is a lot softer than regular tart dough, but we knew that using extra flour blend to roll it out would work against us; this additional flour would have no opportunity to hydrate, which meant, as we had learned from our testing of muffins and other baked goods, that we'd end up with a gritty texture. Instead, we simply rolled out the dough between two sheets of greased parchment paper to prevent sticking and allow for easy transfer to the baking sheet.

CAKES

■ DAIRY FREE OR INCLUDES A DAIRY-FREE VARIATION

Rainbow Sprinkle Cupcakes

G-F TESTING LAB

FLOUR SUBSTITUTION	King Arthur Gluten-Free Multi-Purpose Flour 6½ ounces = ⅔ cup plus ½ cup	Betty Crocker All-Purpose Gluten Free Rice Blend 6½ ounces = 1⅓ cups
	Cupcakes made with King Arthur will not rise as well and will taste slightly pasty; cupcakes made with Betty Crocker will be slightly drier and pasty.	
WHITE CHOCOLATE	Not all brands of white chocolate are processed in a gluten-free facility; read the label.	
BAKING POWDER	Not all brands of baking powder are gluten-free; see page 25 for more information.	
XANTHAN GUM	Xanthan is crucial to the structure of the cupcakes; see page 22 for more information.	
SPRINKLES	Not all brands of sprinkles are processed in a gluten-free facility; read the label.	

WHY THIS RECIPE WORKS

Rainbow (or confetti) cupcakes are festive and especially popular with children, so we wanted to develop an easy-to-make gluten-free version that would deliver on flavor and looks alike. We began with our recipe for light, fluffy yellow cake. While that recipe calls for whipping egg whites to create lift and a lightweight crumb, we found that we didn't need to whip the egg whites, as this created a huge dome (which made frosting the cupcakes a challenge). These cupcakes were so fluffy that they fell apart in our hands. Instead, we switched to an easier mixing method that combined everything in a bowl. The cupcakes were more compact and less crumbly, but they were still doming too much. We needed baking soda (it helps with browning and tenderness) but found we could really reduce the amount of baking powder. This solved the structural problems, but the change in mixing method meant that the butter wasn't getting emulsified and was leaching out. Swapping in oil for the butter fixed the greasiness, but we missed the rich flavor of the butter. The addition of sour cream and white chocolate added flavor plus kept the cupcakes rich and moist. To achieve confetti throughout the cakes, we simply mixed rainbow sprinkles into the batter. As the cupcakes baked, the sprinkles dissolved, forming colorful spots suspended in every bite. Mixing more sprinkles into the frosting completed the festive look and added a nice, crunchy texture. See our favorite recipe for Vanilla Frosting (page 270).

Rainbow Sprinkle Cupcakes
MAKES 12 CUPCAKES

CUPCAKES
- 4 ounces white chocolate, chopped coarse
- 6 tablespoons vegetable oil
- 6½ ounces (¾ cup plus ⅔ cup) ATK All-Purpose Gluten-Free Flour Blend (page 7)
- 1 teaspoon baking powder
- ⅛ teaspoon baking soda
- ½ teaspoon xanthan gum
- ½ teaspoon salt
- 2 large eggs
- 2 teaspoons vanilla extract
- 3½ ounces (½ cup) sugar
- ⅓ cup sour cream
- ¼ cup rainbow sprinkles

FROSTING
- 2 cups vanilla frosting
- 2 tablespoons rainbow sprinkles

1. FOR THE CUPCAKES: Adjust oven rack to middle position and heat oven to 325 degrees. Line 12-cup muffin tin with paper liners. Microwave chocolate and oil together in bowl at 50 percent power, stirring often, until chocolate is melted, about 2 minutes; whisk smooth and let cool slightly. In separate bowl, whisk flour blend, baking powder, baking soda, xanthan gum, and salt together.

2. In large bowl, whisk eggs and vanilla together. Whisk in sugar until well combined. Whisk in cooled chocolate mixture and sour cream until combined. Whisk in flour blend mixture until batter is thoroughly combined and smooth. Gently whisk in sprinkles until thoroughly incorporated.

3. Portion batter evenly into prepared muffin tin. Bake until cupcakes are set on top and toothpick inserted into center of cupcakes comes out clean, 19 to 22 minutes, rotating muffin tin halfway through baking.

4. Let cupcakes cool in muffin tin for 10 minutes, then transfer to wire rack and let cool completely, about 1 hour. (Unfrosted cupcakes can be stored in airtight container at room temperature for up to 1 day.)

5. FOR THE FROSTING: Stir sprinkles into frosting. Spread or pipe frosting onto cupcakes before serving.

VARIATION
Dairy-Free Rainbow Sprinkle Cupcakes
We had good luck using Milkless Polar Dream White chocolate bar.

Use dairy-free white chocolate and dairy-free sour cream. Substitute Dairy-Free Cream Cheese Frosting (page 270) for frosting.

Whole-Grain Carrot Cupcakes

G-F TESTING LAB

FLOUR SUBSTITUTION	Do not substitute other whole-grain blends for the ATK Whole-Grain Gluten-Free Flour Blend; they will not work in this recipe.
BAKING POWDER	Not all brands of baking powder are gluten-free; see page 25 for more information.
XANTHAN GUM	The xanthan can be omitted, but the cupcakes will be more crumbly.
RESTING TIME	Do not shortchange the batter's 30-minute rest or else the cupcakes will taste wet and mushy.

WHY THIS RECIPE WORKS

We set out to transform an old-time favorite, classic carrot cake, into a gluten-free cupcake. We were after a tender, open crumb and slightly domed tops—which can be quite challenging in gluten-free baked goods. We started with our whole-grain gluten-free flour blend because we thought that its earthy flavor would pair well with the natural sweetness of carrots. We began our testing using the test kitchen's favorite carrot cake recipe, swapping in our whole-grain blend and portioning the batter out into cupcake liners. Unfortunately, this first batch was not successful and produced cupcakes that were overly sweet, dense, and gummy with flat, crystallized tops. Thinking that the sugars were partly to blame here, we focused on them first. The original recipe had equal amounts of granulated and brown sugar, and after testing various amounts and ratios of them both we found that going down on the brown sugar got us heading in the right direction. Looking next to the carrots, we found that they released their moisture during baking, which caused the cupcakes to taste wet and mushy. To encourage the carrots to release this moisture before baking, we stirred them into the batter and then let the batter rest for 30 minutes. Giving the batter a good stir after this rest helped to reincorporate this moisture evenly. In addition to the natural moisture from the carrots, we added a few tablespoons of milk to loosen up the batter, which made the cupcakes taller and more tender. We prefer these cupcakes with Cream Cheese Frosting (page 270), but Vanilla Frosting (page 270) will also work here.

Whole-Grain Carrot Cupcakes

MAKES 12 CUPCAKES

- 7½ ounces (1⅔ cups) ATK Whole-Grain Gluten-Free Flour Blend (page 9)
- 1 teaspoon baking powder
- ½ teaspoon baking soda
- ¼ teaspoon ground nutmeg
- ¼ teaspoon salt
- ⅛ teaspoon xanthan gum
- ⅛ teaspoon ground cinnamon
   Pinch ground cloves
- 3½ ounces (½ cup) granulated sugar
- 1¾ ounces (¼ cup packed) light brown sugar
- 2 large eggs
- 3 tablespoons 1 or 2 percent low-fat milk
- ⅓ cup vegetable oil
- 8 ounces carrots, peeled and shredded (1½ cups)
- 2 cups cream cheese frosting

1. Whisk flour blend, baking powder, baking soda, nutmeg, salt, xanthan gum, cinnamon, and cloves together in bowl.

2. In separate bowl, whisk granulated sugar, brown sugar, eggs, milk, and oil together until thoroughly combined. Using rubber spatula, stir in shredded carrots and flour blend mixture until thoroughly incorporated. Cover bowl with plastic wrap and let batter rest at room temperature for 30 minutes.

3. Adjust oven rack to middle position and heat oven to 350 degrees. Line 12-cup muffin tin with paper liners. Stir batter to recombine, and portion evenly into prepared muffin tin. Bake until toothpick inserted into center of cupcakes comes out clean, 18 to 22 minutes, rotating muffin tin halfway through baking.

4. Let cupcakes cool in muffin tin for 10 minutes, then transfer to wire rack and let cool completely, about 1 hour. (Unfrosted cupcakes can be stored in airtight container at room temperature for up to 1 day.) Spread or pipe frosting onto cupcakes before serving.

VARIATION

Dairy-Free Whole-Grain Carrot Cupcakes

We prefer the flavor and texture of these cupcakes made with soy milk, but almond milk will also work; do not use rice milk.

Substitute unsweetened soy milk for milk. Substitute Dairy-Free Cream Cheese Frosting (page 270) for frosting.

Frostings

Vanilla Frosting

MAKES ABOUT 2 CUPS

Do not use salted butter in this recipe; even if you omit the salt, it will ruin this frosting. Do not omit the heavy cream; it is essential for a smooth frosting. To make a vanilla bean frosting (with specks of vanilla), substitute seeds from 1 small vanilla bean for vanilla extract.

12	tablespoons unsalted butter, softened
1½	tablespoons heavy cream
1¼	teaspoons vanilla extract
⅛	teaspoon salt
6	ounces (1½ cups) confectioners' sugar

Using stand mixer fitted with whisk, whip butter, cream, vanilla, and salt together on medium-high speed until smooth, 1 to 2 minutes. Reduce mixer speed to medium-low, slowly add sugar, and whip until incorporated and smooth, 1 to 2 minutes. Increase speed to medium-high and whip frosting until light and fluffy, 3 to 5 minutes.

VARIATION

Double-Batch Vanilla Frosting

To make a vanilla bean frosting (with specks of vanilla), substitute seeds from 1 large vanilla bean for vanilla extract.

To make 4 cups of frosting (enough for a layer cake), double all ingredients; mixing times will not change.

TEST KITCHEN TIP

Piping Frosting onto Cupcakes

Fit pastry bag with large star tip and fill with frosting. Starting at outer edge of cupcake and working toward center, pipe frosting evenly onto cupcake.

Cream Cheese Frosting

MAKES ABOUT 2 CUPS

Do not substitute low-fat or nonfat cream cheese in this recipe; they will make the frosting soupy. If the frosting becomes too soft to work with, refrigerate it until firm. To make a vanilla bean frosting (with specks of vanilla), substitute seeds from 1 small vanilla bean for vanilla extract.

8	ounces cream cheese, softened
5	tablespoons unsalted butter, softened
1	tablespoon sour cream
¾	teaspoon vanilla extract
⅛	teaspoon salt
4	ounces (1 cup) confectioners' sugar

Using stand mixer fitted with whisk, whip cream cheese, butter, sour cream, vanilla, and salt together on medium-high speed until smooth, 1 to 2 minutes. Reduce mixer speed to medium-low, slowly add sugar, and whip until incorporated and smooth, 1 to 2 minutes. Increase speed to medium-high and whip frosting until light and fluffy, 3 to 5 minutes.

VARIATIONS

Dairy-Free Cream Cheese Frosting

Use dairy-free cream cheese and dairy-free sour cream; substitute Earth Balance Vegan Buttery Sticks for butter.

Double-Batch Cream Cheese Frosting

To make a vanilla bean frosting (with specks of vanilla), substitute seeds from 1 large vanilla bean for vanilla extract.

To make 4 cups of frosting (enough for a layer cake), double all ingredients; mixing times will not change.

Chocolate Cream Cupcakes

WHY THIS RECIPE WORKS

Hostess CupCakes were a childhood favorite for most of us here in the test kitchen, so we wanted to develop a gluten-free version that would live up to our fond memories of the original. First, we focused on creating a tender, moist cupcake with deep chocolate flavor. A combination of cocoa powder and melted bittersweet chocolate provided the best chocolaty flavor, but we were faced with an overly delicate and greasy texture. Suspecting that butter was the culprit, we swapped it out for oil, which coats the gluten-free flour particles more consistently; this is because the water in butter weakens the bonds between the fat and the protein of the flour, creating pools of grease. To make a stronger cake that could support the cream filling, we added an extra egg. Content with the rich chocolate flavor and tender yet sturdy crumb of our cupcake, we turned our attention to developing a sweet, creamy filling that wouldn't dribble out. Combining marshmallow crème and the right amount of gelatin gave us the base for a perfect creamy filling. We tried to inject the filling into the center of the baked cupcakes with a pastry bag, but the cakes cracked open and spilled filling out the sides. Instead, we used a paring knife to cut inverted cones from the tops of the cupcakes, added the filling, and plugged the holes with the top rounds. For a shiny, fudgy glaze to finish the cupcakes, we melted semisweet chocolate chips with butter. To finish the look of these cakes, we couldn't resist piping some curlicues across the top of each cupcake using some extra filling.

Chocolate Cream Cupcakes

MAKES 12 CUPCAKES

CUPCAKES

- ½ cup vegetable oil
- 3 ounces bittersweet chocolate, chopped
- 1 ounce (⅓ cup) Dutch-processed cocoa powder
- 3½ ounces (¾ cup) ATK All-Purpose Gluten-Free Flour Blend (page 7)
- ¾ teaspoon baking powder
- ½ teaspoon baking soda
- ½ teaspoon xanthan gum
- ½ teaspoon salt
- 3 large eggs
- 1 teaspoon vanilla extract
- 5¼ ounces (¾ cup) sugar
- ⅓ cup whole milk

FILLING AND GLAZE

- 1 teaspoon unflavored gelatin
- 3 tablespoons water
- 4 tablespoons unsalted butter, softened, plus 3 tablespoons unsalted butter
- 1 teaspoon vanilla extract
  Pinch salt
- 1¼ cups marshmallow crème
- ½ cup semisweet chocolate chips

1. FOR THE CUPCAKES: Adjust oven rack to lower-middle position and heat oven to 350 degrees. Line 12-cup muffin tin with paper liners.

2. Microwave oil, chocolate, and cocoa together in bowl at 50 percent power, stirring often, until chocolate is melted, about 2 minutes; whisk smooth and let cool slightly. In separate bowl, whisk flour blend, baking powder, baking soda, xanthan gum, and salt together.

3. In large bowl, whisk eggs and vanilla together. Whisk in sugar until well combined. Whisk in cooled chocolate mixture and milk until combined. Whisk in flour blend mixture until batter is thoroughly combined and smooth.

4. Portion batter evenly into prepared muffin tin. Bake until toothpick inserted into center of cupcakes comes out clean, 16 to 18 minutes, rotating muffin tin halfway through baking. Let cupcakes cool in muffin tin for 10 minutes, then transfer to wire rack and let cool completely, about 1 hour. (Unfilled and unglazed cupcakes can be stored in airtight container at room temperature for up to 1 day.)

5. FOR THE FILLING AND GLAZE: Sprinkle gelatin over water in large bowl and let sit until gelatin is softened, about 5 minutes. Microwave until mixture

G-F TESTING LAB

FLOUR SUBSTITUTION	King Arthur Gluten-Free Multi-Purpose Flour 3½ ounces = ½ **cup plus 2 tablespoons**	Betty Crocker All-Purpose Gluten Free Rice Blend 3½ ounces = ⅔ **cup**
	Cupcakes made with King Arthur will be slightly drier and crumbly; cupcakes made with Betty Crocker will be slightly drier and spongy.	
CHOCOLATE	Not all brands of chocolate are processed in a gluten-free facility; read the label.	
BAKING POWDER	Not all brands of baking powder are gluten-free; see page 25 for more information.	
XANTHAN GUM	Xanthan is crucial to the structure of the cupcakes; see page 22 for more information.	
MARSHMALLOW CRÈME	Not all brands of marshmallow crème are processed in a gluten-free facility; read the label.	

is bubbling around edges and gelatin dissolves, about 30 seconds. Whisk in softened butter, vanilla, and salt until combined. Let mixture cool until just warm to touch, about 5 minutes, then whisk in marshmallow crème until smooth; refrigerate until set, about 30 minutes.

6. Transfer ⅓ cup filling into pastry bag fitted with small plain tip for garnishing finished cupcakes (or zipper-lock bag; trim corner of bag before piping). Reserve remaining mixture for filling cupcakes. Microwave chocolate and 3 tablespoons butter in bowl at 50 percent power, stirring often, until melted, about 30 seconds. Let glaze cool to room temperature, about 10 minutes.

7. Cut cone-shaped piece from center of each cupcake and fill with 1 tablespoon filling. Cut off tip of cone, then replace on cupcakes and press lightly to adhere. Frost each cupcake with 2 teaspoons cooled glaze and let sit for 10 minutes. Pipe curlicues across top of cupcakes with filling in pastry bag, and serve.

TEST KITCHEN TIP **Making Chocolate Cream Cupcakes**

1. Using paring knife, cut cone-shaped piece from center of each cupcake.

2. Cut off all but top ¼ inch of cone, leaving circular disk of cake.

3. Fill each cupcake with 1 tablespoon filling.

4. Replace disk of cake and press lightly to adhere.

5. Frost each cupcake with 2 teaspoons cooled glaze and let sit for 10 minutes.

6. Pipe curlicues across top of cupcakes with filling in pastry bag, and serve.

Lemon Layer Cake

G-F TESTING LAB

FLOUR SUBSTITUTION	King Arthur Gluten-Free Multi-Purpose Flour 9 ounces = **1½ cups plus 2 tablespoons**	Betty Crocker All-Purpose Gluten Free Rice Blend 9 ounces = **1½ cups plus ⅓ cup**
	Cake made with Betty Crocker will be slightly spongy and rubbery.	
BAKING POWDER	Not all brands of baking powder are gluten-free; see page 25 for more information.	
XANTHAN GUM	Xanthan is crucial to the structure of the cake; see page 22 for more information.	

WHY THIS RECIPE WORKS

For an exceptional gluten-free dessert, nothing fits the bill like a sophisticated lemon layer cake. We wanted to produce a delicate dessert, with creamy lemon curd dividing layers of tender cake, all draped in swirls of meringuelike frosting. For our base, we started with the test kitchen's recipe for an airy egg white–based butter cake, swapping in our all-purpose gluten-free flour blend. Using a reverse creaming method (softened butter is added piece by piece to the dry ingredients, typically done to prevent gluten development) gave this cake a fine crumb and a tender texture. But it turned out too tender; the cake started to collapse under the weight of the lemon curd. The edges were tough and chewy, and the bottom of the cake had a sticky, greasy layer of separated butter and eggs. First, we modified the mixing method because we weren't worried about overdeveloping gluten. We melted the butter and incorporated it with the other wet ingredients; this helped the starches of the gluten-free flour best absorb the fat so that it wouldn't leach out. Next, the addition of xanthan gum helped to build a stronger cake without compromising the airy, light texture, while baking soda helped produce a fluffier yet strong crumb. Looking to eliminate the tough edges of the cake layers, we noted that the bottom of the cake didn't have this chewy quality because of the parchment paper lining the bottom of the pan. Lining the sides of the pan with parchment as well helped resolve this issue. For instructions on how to line the sides of a cake pan with parchment, see page 280.

Lemon Layer Cake
SERVES 10 TO 12

FILLING
- ¾ cup lemon juice (4 lemons)
- ¾ teaspoon unflavored gelatin
- 7¾ ounces (1 cup plus 2 tablespoons) sugar
  Pinch salt
- 3 large eggs plus 4 large yolks
- 6 tablespoons unsalted butter, cut into ½-inch cubes and frozen

CAKE
- 1 cup whole milk
- 8 tablespoons unsalted butter, melted
- 5 large egg whites
- 2 teaspoons vanilla extract
- 9 ounces (2 cups) ATK All-Purpose Gluten-Free Flour Blend (page 7)
- 8¾ ounces (1¼ cups) sugar
- 1 tablespoon baking powder
- ½ teaspoon baking soda
- 1 teaspoon salt
- ¾ teaspoon xanthan gum

ICING
- 2 large egg whites
- 7 ounces (1 cup) sugar
- ¼ cup water
- 1 tablespoon lemon juice
- 1 tablespoon corn syrup

1. FOR THE FILLING: Measure 1 tablespoon lemon juice into bowl, sprinkle gelatin over top, and let sit until gelatin softens, about 5 minutes. Heat remaining lemon juice, sugar, and salt in medium saucepan over medium-high heat, stirring occasionally, until sugar dissolves and mixture is hot but not boiling, about 1 minute.

2. Whisk eggs and yolks together in medium bowl until combined, then slowly whisk in hot lemon-sugar mixture. Return mixture to saucepan and cook over medium-low heat, stirring constantly, until mixture is thickened and registers 170 degrees, and spatula scraped along bottom of pan leaves trail, 4 to 6 minutes.

3. Off heat, stir in gelatin mixture until dissolved. Stir in frozen butter until incorporated. Strain mixture through fine-mesh strainer into bowl (you should have 2 cups). Press plastic wrap directly onto surface of mixture and refrigerate until firm and spreadable, at least 4 hours. (Filling can be refrigerated for up to 1 day; fold with rubber spatula to loosen before using.)

4. FOR THE CAKE: Adjust oven rack to middle position and heat oven to 350 degrees. Grease two

9-inch round cake pans. Line bottoms with parchment paper, and line sides with strips of parchment, then grease parchment.

5. Whisk milk, melted butter, egg whites, and vanilla together in bowl. Using stand mixer fitted with paddle, mix flour blend, sugar, baking powder, baking soda, salt, and xanthan gum on low speed until combined, about 1 minute. Add all but ½ cup milk mixture, increase speed to medium, and beat until pale and fluffy, scraping down bowl as needed, about 1½ minutes. Reduce speed to medium-low, add remaining ½ cup milk mixture, and beat until incorporated, about 1 minute. Give batter final stir by hand. Divide batter evenly between prepared pans, and smooth tops.

6. Bake until cakes are light golden and spring back when pressed lightly, 30 to 35 minutes, switching and rotating pans halfway through baking. Let cakes cool in pans for 10 minutes. Remove cakes from pans, discard parchment, transfer to wire rack, and let cool completely, about 1½ hours. (Unfrosted cakes can be wrapped tightly with plastic wrap and stored at room temperature for up to 1 day.)

7. Using long serrated knife, cut each layer in half evenly into 2 thin layers. Line edges of cake platter with 4 strips of parchment to keep platter clean. Place 1 bottom cake layer on platter and spread ⅔ cup filling evenly over top, leaving ½-inch border at edge. Repeat with 2 more cake layers and remaining 1⅓ cups filling. Top with remaining cake layer, cut side down, and press gently to adhere. Smooth out any filling that has leaked out sides.

8. FOR THE ICING: Combine all ingredients in clean mixer bowl. Set bowl over saucepan filled with 1 inch of barely simmering water (do not let bottom of bowl touch water). Cook, whisking constantly, until mixture registers 160 degrees, 5 to 10 minutes.

9. Remove bowl from heat. Using stand mixer fitted with whisk, whip warm egg white mixture on medium speed until soft peaks form, about 5 minutes. Increase speed to medium-high and continue to whip until mixture has cooled to room temperature and stiff, glossy peaks form, 5 to 7 minutes. Frost cake with icing using back of spoon to create billowy swirls. Remove parchment strips and serve.

VARIATION

Dairy-Free Lemon Layer Cake

We prefer the flavor and texture of this cake made with almond milk, but soy milk will also work; do not use rice milk.

Omit salt. Substitute Earth Balance Vegan Buttery Sticks for butter, and unsweetened almond milk for milk.

TEST KITCHEN TIP **Cutting and Stacking a Layer Cake**

1. Measure height of cake and use paring knife to mark midpoint at several places around sides of cake.

2. Using marks as guide, score entire circumference of cake with long serrated knife.

3. Following scored line, run knife around cake several times, slowly cutting inward, to slice layers apart.

Lemon Layer Cake

The trick to a good lemon layer cake is making layers that are strong enough to support the heavy curd while maintaining a light and airy crumb.

1. LINE THE SIDES AND BOTTOMS OF THE CAKE PANS: Throughout much of our testing, we noticed a tough, candylike texture around the sides of the cake. We figured that it would disappear as we tinkered with the recipe, but it didn't. Finding this crust unappealing, even underneath all of the billowy frosting, we realized that the bottom of the cake didn't possess this chewy quality thanks to the parchment paper lining the pan bottom. Adding a lining of parchment paper around the edge of the cake pan to protect the sides of the cake solved this problem.

2. ADD XANTHAN GUM AND BAKING SODA: In order for the thin layers of cake to support the heavy curd, they need to be very strong. Adding a substantial amount of xanthan gum gave the cake necessary structure and support. To help prevent this sturdy cake from tasting overly dense, we added some baking soda in addition to the baking powder to help with lift and to help tenderize the crumb.

3. MELT THE BUTTER: Rather than start the mixing method by creaming the butter with the sugar or the dry ingredients, we found it better to melt the butter and add it to the liquid ingredients. We then simply beat the liquid and dry ingredients together, which encouraged the flour to absorb the butter so that the cake didn't taste greasy.

4. BEAT THE CAKE BATTER VIGOROUSLY: To help build as much structure and incorporate as much air as possible into the cake batter (which translates to a sturdy but airy cake) we whipped the wet ingredients into the dry ingredients for a total of 2½ minutes. This extra whipping also ensured that the cake batter was well mixed and emulsified. We added most of the liquid at the outset, leaving just a small amount to be added at the end, in order to prevent the batter from splattering out of the bowl during mixing.

Whole-Grain Brown Sugar Layer Cake

G-F TESTING LAB

FLOUR SUBSTITUTION	Do not substitute other whole-grain blends for the ATK Whole-Grain Gluten-Free Flour Blend; they will not work in this recipe.
BAKING POWDER	Not all brands of baking powder are gluten-free; see page 25 for more information.
XANTHAN GUM	Xanthan is crucial to the structure of the cake; see page 22 for more information.

✔ WHY THIS RECIPE WORKS

Sweet and buttery, brown sugar cake makes delicious use of our whole-grain gluten-free flour blend. Although we thought that a brown sugar cake should solely feature its namesake for sweetness, we found that using all brown sugar in the batter made the cake overly heavy and dense. Swapping in some granulated sugar for the brown sugar solved this problem without sacrificing the caramel flavor brown sugar imparts. Because both our whole-grain blend and butter are heavy ingredients, we had to devise ways to make our cake light and fluffy. We turned to low-fat milk to lighten the batter without sacrificing the richness that milk provided. We bolstered that with a little sour cream, a bound fat that we have found usually helps the structure of our gluten-free baked goods without leaching fat. Another way we lightened the cake was to use a whole tablespoon of baking powder plus a little baking soda. Fully hydrated, our whole-grain blend needed all this leavener to give the cake lift. Finally, the mixing method played a huge role in this cake, in both incorporating the brown sugar evenly and keeping the cake airy. We found that we needed an electric mixer to keep the brown sugar fully dissolved in the batter. It also incorporated lots of air into the batter, helping to keep our cake light. And extra baking time ensured the cake wasn't gummy. Tangy cream cheese frosting nicely complemented the cake's whole-grain flavor. It is important to use fresh brown sugar that is soft so that it incorporates well. We prefer the flavor of Cream Cheese Frosting (page 270, Double-Batch variation) on this cake, but Vanilla Frosting (page 270, also Double-Batch variation) will also work well.

Whole-Grain Brown Sugar Layer Cake

SERVES 10 TO 12

12½ ounces (2¾ cups) ATK Whole-Grain
     Gluten-Free Flour Blend (page 9)
  1 tablespoon baking powder
  ¼ teaspoon baking soda
1½ teaspoons salt
  ½ teaspoon ground cinnamon
  ½ teaspoon xanthan gum
  ¾ cup 1 or 2 percent low-fat milk
  ½ cup sour cream
  2 tablespoons vanilla extract
10½ ounces (1½ cups packed) dark brown sugar
1¾ ounces (¼ cup) granulated sugar
10 tablespoons unsalted butter, melted
  4 large eggs
  4 cups cream cheese frosting

1. Adjust oven rack to middle position and heat oven to 325 degrees. Grease two 9-inch round cake pans, line bottoms with parchment paper, and line sides with strips of parchment.

2. Combine flour blend, baking powder, baking soda, salt, cinnamon, and xanthan gum together in bowl. In separate bowl, whisk milk, sour cream, and vanilla together until combined. Using stand mixer fitted with whisk, whip brown sugar, granulated sugar, and melted butter at medium speed until smooth, about 1 minute. Add eggs, 1 at a time, and whip until combined, scraping down bowl as needed.

3. Reduce speed to low and add flour blend mixture in 3 additions, alternating with milk mixture in 2 additions. Scrape down bowl thoroughly. Increase speed to medium-high and whip batter until light and fluffy and no clumps of brown sugar remain, about 4 minutes. Give batter final stir by hand.

4. Scrape batter into prepared pans and smooth tops. Bake until toothpick inserted in centers comes out clean, about 30 minutes, then continue to bake for 15 minutes longer, rotating pans halfway through baking.

5. Let cakes cool in pans for 10 minutes. Remove cakes from pans, discard parchment, transfer to wire rack, and let cool completely, about 2 hours. (Unfrosted cakes can be wrapped tightly with plastic wrap and stored at room temperature for up to 1 day.)

6. Line edges of cake platter with 4 strips of parchment to keep platter clean, and place dab of frosting in center to anchor cake. Place 1 cake layer on platter and spread 1½ cups frosting evenly over top. Top with second cake layer, press lightly to adhere, then spread 1 cup frosting evenly over top. Spread remaining 1½ cups frosting evenly over sides of cake. To smooth frosting, run edge of offset spatula around cake sides and over top. Carefully remove parchment strips and serve.

VARIATION

Dairy-Free Whole-Grain Brown Sugar Layer Cake

We prefer the flavor and texture of this cake made with soy milk, but almond milk will also work; do not use rice milk.

Use dairy-free sour cream. Substitute unsweetened soy milk for milk, vegetable oil for butter, and Dairy-Free Cream Cheese Frosting (page 270) for frosting.

TEST KITCHEN TIP **Preparing a Cake Pan**

Gluten-free cakes tend to stick to the pan more than traditional cakes, and often require an extra step of lining the sides of the cake pan with parchment paper in addition to the bottom.

1. Grease pan with oil spray, butter, or shortening. The grease helps parchment paper stay in place, especially on sides of pan.

2. Trim piece of parchment to fit nicely inside cake pan, then lay flat into pan bottom.

3. Cut strips of parchment to match height of cake pan, then lay flat against pan sides.

TEST KITCHEN TIP **Frosting a Layer Cake**

1. Line edges of cake platter with 4 strips of parchment paper to keep platter clean. Place small dab of frosting in center of platter to anchor cake.

2. Place 1 cake layer on platter and spread 1½ cups frosting evenly over top. Top with second cake layer, press lightly to adhere, then spread 1 cup frosting evenly over top.

3. Spread remaining 1½ cups frosting evenly over sides of cake. To smooth frosting, run edge of offset spatula around cake sides and over top. Carefully remove parchment strips before serving.

New York–Style Cheesecake

✓ WHY THIS RECIPE WORKS

Classic New York cheesecake owes its distinctive browned top, puffed perimeter, and luxurious texture to a risky baking technique. It typically spends the first 10 minutes in a 500-degree oven, after which the oven is turned down to 200 degrees for the remainder of the baking time. Success with this method is dependent on the oven temperature falling at a very specific rate—too fast and the cheesecake will be soupy; too slow and it will be burned, cracked, and grainy. For success every time, we turned the conventional method on its head: We baked the cheesecake for about 3 hours at the lower temperature and then removed it from the oven while we heated the oven to 500 degrees. Finishing the cake at the higher temperature produced the proper appearance and texture—but without the risk. Having discovered the secret to a perfectly velvety cheesecake, we were ready to build a simple gluten-free graham cracker crust. We ordered every brand of gluten-free graham crackers and cookies we could get our hands on and plugged them into our favorite crust recipe. Theoretically, any and all of these options would be an easy substitution for a classic crust. Instead, each brand performed catastrophically: One melted into a brittle toffee, another became chewy and greasy, while another never bound together at all, resulting in a dusty pile of crumbs in the pan. It was clear that we couldn't create a consistent graham cracker crust relying on the widely inconsistent gluten-free products on the market. Next, we tried using ground Rice Chex cereal as our "cookie" crumb. While we had better luck developing an appropriate texture for our crust, we couldn't get past the iconic cereal flavor. Instead, we decided to make a press-in dough for a buttery cookie crust using our whole-grain gluten-free flour blend. It gave our cheesecake a base with a firm texture and rich, wheaty flavor as well as a sturdy yet short crumb able to withstand prolonged contact with the wet filling without turning soggy. This cheesecake takes at least 12 hours to make (including chilling), so we recommend making it the day before serving. An accurate oven thermometer and instant-read thermometer are essential. To ensure proper baking, check that the oven thermometer is holding steady at 200 degrees and refrain from frequently taking the temperature of the cheesecake (unless it is within a few degrees of 165, allow 20 minutes between checking). Keep a close eye on the cheesecake in step 6 to prevent overbrowning.

New York–Style Cheesecake

SERVES 12 TO 16

WHOLE-GRAIN CRUST

6	tablespoons unsalted butter, melted
4	ounces (¾ cup plus 2 tablespoons) ATK Whole-Grain Gluten-Free Flour Blend (page 9)
2⅓	ounces (⅓ cup) sugar
⅛	teaspoon salt
⅛	teaspoon xanthan gum

FILLING

2½	pounds cream cheese, softened
10½	ounces (1½ cups) sugar
⅛	teaspoon salt
⅓	cup sour cream
2	teaspoons lemon juice
2	teaspoons vanilla extract
6	large eggs plus 2 large yolks

1. FOR THE WHOLE-GRAIN CRUST: Adjust oven racks to upper-middle and lower-middle positions and heat oven to 325 degrees. Brush bottom of 9-inch springform pan with ½ tablespoon butter.

2. In large bowl, whisk flour blend, sugar, salt, and xanthan gum together until combined. Whisk in 5 tablespoons butter until fully incorporated and mixture resembles wet sand. Using your hands, press crumb mixture evenly into pan bottom. Using bottom of dry measuring cup, firmly pack crust into pan. Bake on lower rack until edges begin to

G-F TESTING LAB

FLOUR SUBSTITUTION	Do not substitute other whole-grain blends for the ATK Whole-Grain Gluten-Free Flour Blend; they will not work in this recipe.
XANTHAN GUM	The xanthan can be omitted, but the crust will be much less crisp.

darken and crust is firm on top, 22 to 25 minutes; let cool completely. Reduce oven temperature to 200 degrees.

3. FOR THE FILLING: Using stand mixer fitted with paddle, beat cream cheese, ¾ cup sugar, and salt at medium-low speed until combined, about 1 minute. Beat in remaining ¾ cup sugar until combined, about 1 minute. Scrape beater and bowl well. Add sour cream, lemon juice, and vanilla and beat at low speed until combined, about 1 minute. Add egg yolks and beat at medium-low speed until thoroughly combined, about 1 minute. Scrape beater and bowl. Add whole eggs, 2 at a time, beating until thoroughly combined, about 30 seconds after each addition.

4. Strain filling through fine-mesh strainer into bowl, using rubber spatula to help batter pass through strainer. Brush sides of springform pan with remaining ½ tablespoon melted butter. Pour filling into crust and set aside for 10 minutes to allow air bubbles to rise to top. Gently draw tines of fork across surface of cake to pop air bubbles that have risen to surface.

5. When oven thermometer reads 200 degrees, bake cheesecake on lower rack for 45 minutes. After 45 minutes, remove cake from oven and use toothpick to pierce any bubbles that have risen to surface. Return to oven and continue to bake until center registers 165 degrees, 2¼ to 2¾ hours longer.

6. Remove cake from oven and increase oven temperature to 500 degrees. When oven is 500 degrees, bake cheesecake on upper rack until top is evenly browned, 4 to 12 minutes. Let cool for 5 minutes, then run thin knife between cheesecake and side of pan. Let cheesecake cool until barely warm, 2½ to 3 hours. Wrap tightly in plastic wrap and refrigerate until cold and firmly set, at least 6 hours. (Cake can be refrigerated for up to 2 days.)

7. To unmold cheesecake, remove sides of pan. Slide thin metal spatula between crust and pan bottom to loosen, then slide cheesecake onto serving plate. Let cheesecake stand at room temperature for about 30 minutes. Serve.

TEST KITCHEN TIP **Making New York–Style Cheesecake**

1. Pour filling into crust and set aside for 10 minutes to allow air bubbles to rise to top. Gently draw tines of fork across surface of cake to pop air bubbles that have risen to surface.

2. After 45 minutes, remove cake from oven and use toothpick to pierce any bubbles that have risen to surface. Return to oven and continue to bake until center registers 165 degrees, 2¼ to 2¾ hours longer.

3. Remove cake from oven and increase oven temperature to 500 degrees. When oven is 500 degrees, bake cheesecake on upper rack until top is evenly browned, 4 to 12 minutes.

Whole-Grain Apple Upside-Down Cake

G-F TESTING LAB

FLOUR SUBSTITUTION	Do not substitute other whole-grain blends for the ATK Whole-Grain Gluten-Free Flour Blend; they will not work in this recipe.
BAKING POWDER	Not all brands of baking powder are gluten-free; see page 25 for more information.
XANTHAN GUM	Xanthan is crucial to the structure of the cake; see page 22 for more information.

WHY THIS RECIPE WORKS

Our gluten-free upside-down cake pairs sweet apples with a rich whole-grain cake. We knew we'd need a cake sturdy enough to stand up to the thick fruit topping. To start, we precooked the apples to thicken their juices and to make a thick caramel glaze. Then we turned to the cake. Although gluten-free flours are generally highly absorbent, they do have trouble absorbing fat, so we made some changes to avoid a greasy, dense cake. We went down on the amount of butter in the traditional recipe and added xanthan gum. This helped, but the cake was still dense and heavy so we tried swapping out some of the sour cream for low-fat milk. This lightened up the cake, opened up the crumb, and helped the cake to rise while keeping it sturdy yet tender. Be sure to let the cake cool fully in the pan.

Whole-Grain Apple Upside-Down Cake

SERVES 8

TOPPING

4	tablespoons unsalted butter, cut into 4 pieces
3½	ounces (½ cup packed) light brown sugar
1½	pounds Granny Smith apples, peeled, cored, and cut into ½-inch-thick wedges
⅛	teaspoon salt

CAKE

5	tablespoons 1 or 2 percent low-fat milk
¼	cup sour cream
1	large egg plus 1 large yolk
½	teaspoon vanilla extract
6	ounces (1⅓ cups) ATK Whole-Grain Gluten-Free Flour Blend (page 9)
5¼	ounces (¾ cup) granulated sugar
½	teaspoon ground cinnamon
½	teaspoon baking powder
¼	teaspoon baking soda
¼	teaspoon xanthan gum
¼	teaspoon salt
6	tablespoons unsalted butter, cut into 6 pieces and softened

1. Adjust oven rack to middle position and heat oven to 350 degrees. Grease 9-inch round cake pan.

2. FOR THE TOPPING: Melt butter in 12-inch skillet over medium-high heat. Stir in sugar and cook, swirling pan occasionally, until sugar is dark brown, about 2 minutes. Stir in apples and salt and cook, stirring often, until apples have softened slightly and juices are thickened and syrupy, 5 to 7 minutes. Scrape apple mixture into prepared pan and lightly press into even layer.

3. FOR THE CAKE: Whisk milk, sour cream, egg and yolk, and vanilla together in bowl. Using stand mixer fitted with paddle, mix flour blend, sugar, cinnamon, baking powder, baking soda, xanthan gum, and salt on low speed until combined, about 1 minute. Add butter, 1 piece at a time, and mix until mixture resembles moist crumbs, about 2 minutes.

4. Add half of milk mixture, increase speed to medium, and beat until light and fluffy, about 1 minute. Reduce speed to medium-low, add remaining milk mixture, and beat until incorporated, about 30 seconds. Give batter final stir by hand.

5. Spoon batter over apples and gently spread into even layer. Bake until toothpick inserted into center comes out clean, 35 to 40 minutes, rotating pan halfway through baking, then continue to bake 10 minutes longer.

6. Let cake cool in pan, about 2 hours. Run thin knife around edge of cake to loosen. Place serving platter over top of cake pan, invert cake, and let sit until cake releases from pan, about 1 minute. Gently remove cake pan and serve.

VARIATION

Dairy-Free Whole-Grain Apple Upside-Down Cake

We prefer the flavor and texture of this cake made with almond milk. Do not substitute soy or rice milk in this recipe.

In topping and cake, substitute Earth Balance Vegan Buttery Sticks for butter and omit salt. In cake, substitute unsweetened almond milk for milk and use dairy-free sour cream.

Lemon Bundt Cake

✔ WHY THIS RECIPE WORKS

To develop a sturdy yet tender lemon Bundt cake we had to attack our traditional recipe on all fronts. Since many of our gluten-free cakes were more successful using melted butter and a simple bowl method, we started there. The resulting cake was greasy and heavy, even when we went down on the amount of butter. The traditional creaming method helped this issue and got us closer to a light and even crumb, but the cake was too crumbly. To create better structure, we added a bit of xanthan gum and another egg. Our all-purpose gluten-free flour blend is mostly white rice flour, which is naturally sweeter than all-purpose flour, so we needed to reduce the amount of sugar in the cake. A healthy dose of lemon juice and zest cut the sweetness even more and amplified the lemon flavor. And finally, because we were using so much lemon juice, whole milk, rather than buttermilk, provided the best texture and cleanest flavor. A simple glaze gave the cake an extra burst of lemony flavor.

Lemon Bundt Cake

SERVES 12

CAKE RELEASE

- 2 tablespoons unsalted butter, melted
- 1 tablespoon ATK All-Purpose Gluten-Free Flour Blend (page 7)

CAKE

- 15 ounces (3⅓ cups) ATK All-Purpose Gluten-Free Flour Blend (page 7)
- 1 teaspoon salt
- 1 teaspoon baking powder
- ½ teaspoon baking soda
- ¼ teaspoon xanthan gum
- ¾ cup whole milk
- 3 tablespoons lemon zest plus ⅓ cup juice (3 lemons)
- 2 teaspoons vanilla extract
- 12 tablespoons unsalted butter, softened
- 10½ ounces (1½ cups) granulated sugar
- 4 large eggs

GLAZE

- 4 ounces (1 cup) confectioners' sugar
- 4–6 teaspoons lemon juice

1. FOR THE CAKE RELEASE: Adjust oven rack to lower-middle position and heat oven to 350 degrees. Whisk melted butter and flour blend together in bowl to make paste. Brush paste thoroughly into 12-cup nonstick Bundt pan, without leaving clumps.

2. FOR THE CAKE: Whisk flour blend, salt, baking powder, baking soda, and xanthan gum together in bowl. In separate bowl, whisk milk, lemon zest and juice, and vanilla together.

3. Using stand mixer fitted with paddle, beat softened butter and sugar on medium-high speed until pale and fluffy, about 3 minutes. Add eggs, 1 at a time, and beat until combined. Reduce speed to low and add flour blend mixture in 3 additions, alternating with milk mixture in 2 additions, scraping down bowl as needed. Give batter final stir by hand.

4. Scrape batter into prepared pan, smooth top, and gently tap pan on counter to settle batter. Bake cake until wooden skewer inserted in center comes out with few crumbs attached, 45 to 55 minutes, rotating pan halfway through baking.

5. Let cake cool in pan for 10 minutes. Run thin knife around edges of cake to loosen. Gently turn cake out onto wire rack and let cool completely, about 2 hours. (Cake can be wrapped tightly with plastic wrap and stored at room temperature for up to 2 days.)

6. FOR THE GLAZE: Whisk sugar and 4 teaspoons lemon juice together in bowl until smooth. Gradually add remaining 2 teaspoons lemon juice until glaze is thick but pourable. Drizzle glaze over cake, letting it drip down sides, and let set for 10 minutes. Serve.

VARIATION

Dairy-Free Lemon Bundt Cake

We prefer the flavor and texture of this cake made with soy milk, but almond milk will also work; do not use rice milk.

In cake release, substitute vegetable oil for melted butter. In cake, substitute unsweetened soy milk for milk, and ½ cup vegetable oil for butter.

Rosemary Polenta Cake with Clementines

FLOUR SUBSTITUTION	King Arthur Gluten-Free Multi-Purpose Flour 5½ ounces = **1 cup**	Betty Crocker All-Purpose Gluten Free Rice Blend 5½ ounces = **1 cup plus 2 tablespoons**
	Cake made with King Arthur will be dense and will taste starchy; cake made with Betty Crocker will be slightly dry and crumbly.	
INSTANT POLENTA	Not all brands of instant polenta are processed in a gluten-free facility; read the label.	
BAKING POWDER	Not all brands of baking powder are gluten-free; see page 25 for more information.	
XANTHAN GUM	Xanthan is crucial to the structure of the cake; see page 22 for more information.	

WHY THIS RECIPE WORKS

Topping this rustic polenta cake with a crown of honey whipped cream and clementines transforms it to special occasion status. Because the cake is usually made with more polenta than flour, we thought it would be easy to make it gluten-free. We were wrong. Simply swapping in our all-purpose gluten-free flour blend produced a cake that was overly heavy and crumbly—more like cornbread, less like cake. Our flour blend did not stand up well to the weight of the polenta. Adding more flour blend and reducing the amount of polenta helped to lighten up the texture a bit, but the cake was still pretty dry and dense. So we increased the amount of liquid (rosemary-steeped milk, for flavor) used to make the polenta. This worked well, and the looser batter translated into a moister cake. We also moved to a creaming method where the butter and sugar are first beaten together until fluffy, which helped transform the heavy batter into a lovely cake.

Rosemary Polenta Cake with Clementines

SERVES 8

CAKE

- 1¼ cups whole milk
- 2 sprigs fresh rosemary
- 7 ounces (1¼ cups) instant polenta
- 2 large eggs
- ¼ cup honey
- 2 teaspoons vanilla extract
- 5½ ounces (1¼ cups) ATK All-Purpose Gluten-Free Flour Blend (page 7)
- 1 teaspoon baking powder
- ½ teaspoon salt
- ¼ teaspoon xanthan gum
- 8 tablespoons unsalted butter, softened
- 5¼ ounces (¾ cup) sugar

WHIPPED CREAM AND CLEMENTINES

- ½ cup heavy cream
- 1 tablespoon honey
- 4 clementines, peeled and sliced ⅛ inch thick

1. FOR THE CAKE: Adjust oven rack to middle position and heat oven to 350 degrees. Grease 9-inch round cake pan, then line bottom with parchment paper.

2. Bring milk and rosemary sprigs to simmer in medium saucepan, then steep off heat for 10 minutes; discard rosemary. Toast polenta on rimmed baking sheet in oven until fragrant, about 10 minutes. Whisk polenta into milk until combined.

3. Whisk eggs, honey, and vanilla together in bowl. In separate bowl, whisk flour blend, baking powder, salt, and xanthan gum together. Using stand mixer fitted with paddle, beat butter and sugar on medium-high speed until pale and fluffy, about 3 minutes. Reduce speed to low and add egg mixture, scraping down bowl as needed. Add flour blend mixture and beat until combined, about 1 minute. Break up any large clumps of polenta, then beat into batter until combined, about 30 seconds. Increase speed to medium and beat until smooth, about 2 minutes.

4. Scrape batter into prepared pan. Bake until toothpick inserted into center comes out clean, 30 to 35 minutes, rotating pan halfway through baking.

5. Let cake cool in pan for 10 minutes. Remove cake from pan, discard parchment, transfer to wire rack, and let cool completely, about 2 hours. (Unfrosted cake can be wrapped tightly with plastic wrap and stored at room temperature for up to 2 days.)

6. FOR THE WHIPPED CREAM AND CLEMENTINES: Using stand mixer fitted with whisk, whip cream and honey on medium-low speed until foamy, about 1 minute. Increase speed to high and whip until soft peaks form, 1 to 3 minutes. Spread over top of cake, leaving ¼-inch border at edge. Shingle clementines over top. Use serrated knife to cut slices for serving.

VARIATION

Dairy-Free Rosemary Polenta Cake

We prefer the flavor and texture of this cake made with soy milk, but almond milk will also work; do not use rice milk.

Substitute unsweetened soy milk for milk, Earth Balance Vegan Buttery Sticks for butter, and dairy-free whipped topping for whipped cream with honey. Omit salt.

Chocolate-Hazelnut Torte

G-F TESTING LAB

FLOUR SUBSTITUTION	King Arthur Gluten-Free Multi-Purpose Flour **2 tablespoons**	Betty Crocker All-Purpose Gluten Free Rice Blend **2 tablespoons**
CHOCOLATE	Not all brands of chocolate are processed in a gluten-free facility; read the label.	

✓ WHY THIS RECIPE WORKS

This decadent chocolate-hazelnut torte has a crackly, meringuelike top and a dense, moist interior. It is based on a delicate balance of eggs, butter, sugar, chocolate, and ground nuts, with just a small amount of flour to create a structure slightly cakier and lighter than a flourless chocolate cake. We substituted our all-purpose gluten-free flour blend for the all-purpose flour in our standard recipe and were pleasantly surprised to find that our blend provided the structural support the cake needed. The key to this cake's texture is really determined by the quantity and texture of the nuts. We preferred the more refined texture of a cake made with toasted, finely ground nuts; we ground them in a food processor along with some sugar to prevent them from clumping. For lift, this cake relies solely on beaten eggs—it contains no other leaveners. To maximize the lift, we separated the eggs. We beat the egg yolks into the batter to provide body and richness and then whipped the whites separately to stiff peaks and folded them into the batter for lightness. Baking this cake in a springform pan made for easy removal. To toast and skin hazelnuts easily, combine the hazelnuts, 3 cups water, and ¼ cup baking soda in a small saucepan and boil for 4 minutes; drain, rinse, and rub the nuts in a dish towel to remove the skins before toasting for 15 minutes in a 350-degree oven. For neat, professional-looking pieces of cake, clean the knife thoroughly between slices.

Chocolate-Hazelnut Torte

SERVES 8

6	ounces bittersweet chocolate, chopped coarse
1⅓	cups hazelnuts, skinned and toasted
7	ounces (1 cup) granulated sugar
2	tablespoons ATK All-Purpose Gluten-Free Flour Blend (page 7)
¼	teaspoon salt
8	tablespoons unsalted butter, softened
5	large eggs, separated, plus 1 large yolk
⅛	teaspoon cream of tartar
	Confectioners' sugar

1. Adjust oven rack to middle position and heat oven to 350 degrees. Grease 9-inch springform pan, line bottom with parchment paper, and grease parchment. Melt chocolate in microwave at 50 percent power, stirring often, about 2 minutes; let cool.

2. Process hazelnuts, ¼ cup granulated sugar, flour blend, and salt together in food processor until nuts are very finely ground, about 15 seconds.

3. Using stand mixer fitted with paddle, beat butter and remaining ¾ cup granulated sugar together at medium-high speed until light and fluffy, about 3 minutes. Beat in yolks, 1 at a time, until combined, about 30 seconds. Reduce mixer speed to low and beat in melted chocolate, followed by ground hazelnut mixture, until incorporated, about 1 minute.

4. In clean mixer bowl fitted with whisk, whip egg whites and cream of tartar at medium-low speed until frothy, about 1 minute. Increase speed to medium-high and whip until stiff peaks form, 3 to 4 minutes.

5. Gently fold one-third of whipped egg whites into chocolate batter until only few streaks remain. Repeat twice more with remaining egg whites, and continue to fold batter until no streaks remain.

6. Scrape batter into prepared pan, smooth top, and gently tap pan on counter to settle batter. Bake until toothpick inserted into center comes out clean, about 40 minutes, rotating pan halfway through baking.

7. Immediately run thin knife around edge of cake and let cake cool completely in pan, about 3 hours. (Cooled cake can be wrapped with plastic wrap and stored at room temperature for up to 2 days.) Remove sides of pan, gently slide thin metal spatula between parchment and pan bottom to loosen, then slide torte onto platter and remove parchment. Before serving, dust with confectioners' sugar.

VARIATION

Dairy-Free Chocolate-Hazelnut Torte
We had good luck using Scharffen Berger bittersweet chocolate.

Use dairy-free chocolate. Omit salt and substitute Earth Balance Vegan Buttery Sticks for butter.

Molten Chocolate Cakes

G-F TESTING LAB

FLOUR SUBSTITUTION	King Arthur Gluten-Free Multi-Purpose Flour **2 tablespoons**	Betty Crocker All-Purpose Gluten Free Rice Blend **2 tablespoons**
CHOCOLATE	Not all brands of chocolate are processed in a gluten-free facility; read the label.	

WHY THIS RECIPE WORKS

Molten chocolate cakes are a classic restaurant show-stopper. We set out to develop a practical gluten-free recipe for these elegant cakes that home cooks could easily master. To create a decadent yet light cake, we started by beating whole eggs and sugar together to create a thick foam before adding the melted butter and chocolate. This delivered the rich, moist texture we were looking for without weighing it down. While many molten chocolate cakes contain no flour, we found that a modest 2 tablespoons of our all-purpose gluten-free flour blend provided just enough structure for our cakes to walk the line between a soufflé and a fudgy cake. To create the perfect lava center, we found that many recipes simply underbake the cakes, leaving the center as partially raw batter. Not only was the thought of consuming partially raw eggs unsettling to some, but achieving the ideal gooeyness hinged on the exact cooking time and temperature of these cakes (leaving little room for oven variations or error). Other recipes call for inserting a spoonful of chocolate ganache into the middle of each cake before baking, but this required making a separate ganache. To keep this recipe simple, we just pressed a piece of bittersweet chocolate into the center of each cake before placing them in the oven, where the chocolate melted into the ideal oozing molten center. As a bonus, we found that the batter can be made ahead and poured into ramekins and refrigerated, then baked just before serving. Serve with lightly sweetened whipped cream and fresh berries.

Molten Chocolate Cakes

SERVES 8

CAKE RELEASE

- 1 tablespoon unsalted butter, softened
- 1 tablespoon Dutch-processed cocoa powder

CAKES

- 10 ounces bittersweet chocolate, chopped coarse, plus 4 ounces, broken into 8 equal pieces
- 8 tablespoons unsalted butter
- 5 large eggs plus 1 large yolk
- 3½ ounces (½ cup) granulated sugar
- 1 teaspoon vanilla extract
- ½ teaspoon salt
- 2 tablespoons ATK All-Purpose Gluten-Free Flour Blend (page 7)
    Confectioners' sugar

1. FOR THE CAKE RELEASE: Adjust oven rack to middle position and heat oven to 400 degrees. Mix softened butter and cocoa together to make paste. Brush paste evenly inside eight 6-ounce ramekins.

2. FOR THE CAKES: Microwave 10 ounces chopped chocolate and butter in bowl at 50 percent power, stirring often, until melted, about 2 minutes; whisk smooth and let cool slightly.

3. Using stand mixer fitted with whisk, whip eggs and yolk, granulated sugar, vanilla, and salt together at high speed until volume nearly triples, color is very light, and mixture drops from whisk in smooth, thick ribbon, 5 to 7 minutes. Reduce speed to low, add melted chocolate mixture and flour blend, and mix until incorporated, about 1 minute, stopping to scrape bottom of bowl halfway through mixing.

4. Give batter final stir by hand. Portion batter evenly into prepared ramekins. Gently press broken chocolate piece into center of each ramekin to submerge, breaking up any large pieces as needed. (Ramekins can be covered with plastic wrap and refrigerated for up to 8 hours.)

5. Place ramekins on rimmed baking sheet and bake until cakes have puffed above rims of ramekins, have thin crust on top, and jiggle slightly in center when gently shaken, 11 to 14 minutes (for refrigerated cakes, increase baking time to 15 to 20 minutes). Dust with confectioners' sugar and serve immediately.

VARIATION

Dairy-Free Molten Chocolate Cakes

We had good luck using Scharffen Berger bittersweet chocolate.

In cake release, substitute vegetable oil for butter. In cakes, substitute ⅓ cup vegetable oil for butter and use dairy-free chocolate.

Lavender Tea Cakes

G-F TESTING LAB

FLOUR SUBSTITUTION	King Arthur Gluten-Free Multi-Purpose Flour 3½ ounces = ½ **cup plus 2 tablespoons**	Betty Crocker All-Purpose Gluten Free Rice Blend 3½ ounces = ⅔ **cup**
	Cakes made with King Arthur will be denser and slightly pasty; cakes made with Betty Crocker will be drier and more chewy.	
BAKING POWDER	Not all brands of baking powder are gluten-free; see page 25 for more information.	
XANTHAN GUM	Xanthan is crucial to the structure of the cakes; see page 22 for more information.	

WHY THIS RECIPE WORKS

With their buttery crumb, these lavender-infused glazed tea cakes are a perfect tea time treat. We started with our gluten-free pound cake, simply portioning the batter into a muffin tin—which did not work. First, the leavening needed adjustment. The original recipe contained baking powder only, so we reduced the amount for a more modest rise and added baking soda for a more tender crumb. For a boost of elegant flavor, we pulsed dried lavender blossoms with sugar, then we continued to use the food processor to mix a well-emulsified batter. The cakes were really sticking to the muffin tin, no matter how well we greased it; we had better luck brushing the pan with a mixture of butter and sugar. This both made the pan nonstick and created a crisp exterior on the cakes. We then draped each cake in a simple glaze. For a sophisticated final touch, decorate the cakes with candied violets.

Lavender Tea Cakes with Vanilla Bean Glaze

MAKES 12 TEA CAKES

CAKE RELEASE

- 2 tablespoons granulated sugar
- 2 tablespoons unsalted butter, melted

CAKES

- 3½ ounces (¾ cup) ATK All-Purpose Gluten-Free Flour Blend (page 7)
- ¼ teaspoon baking powder
- ¼ teaspoon baking soda
- ¼ teaspoon salt
- ⅛ teaspoon xanthan gum
- 4⅓ ounces (½ cup plus 2 tablespoons) granulated sugar
- 1 teaspoon dried lavender
- 2 large eggs
- 2 ounces cream cheese
- 1½ teaspoons water
- ¾ teaspoon vanilla extract
- 4 tablespoons unsalted butter, melted

GLAZE

- 1 vanilla bean
- 7 ounces (1¾ cups) confectioners' sugar
- 2–4 tablespoons milk

1. FOR THE CAKE RELEASE: Adjust oven rack to middle position and heat oven to 325 degrees. Whisk sugar and melted butter together in bowl. Brush 12-cup muffin tin with butter-sugar mixture.

2. FOR THE CAKES: Combine flour blend, baking powder, baking soda, salt, and xanthan gum in bowl.

3. Process sugar and lavender together in food processor for 30 seconds. Add eggs, cream cheese, water, and vanilla and process to combine, about 15 seconds. With processor running, add melted butter, about 20 seconds. Scrape down sides of bowl, add flour blend mixture, and process until batter is smooth, about 15 seconds.

4. Portion batter evenly into prepared muffin tin. Bake until cakes are golden brown and toothpick inserted into center of cakes comes out clean, about 15 minutes, rotating pan halfway through baking.

5. Let cakes cool in muffin tin for 10 minutes. Invert muffin tin over wire rack and gently tap pan several times to help cakes release. Let cakes cool completely on rack, flat side up, about 30 minutes. (Unfrosted cakes can be stored in airtight container at room temperature for up to 1 day.)

6. FOR THE GLAZE: Cut vanilla bean in half lengthwise. Using tip of paring knife, scrape out seeds. Whisk vanilla seeds, sugar, and 2 tablespoons milk together in bowl until smooth. Gradually add remaining 2 tablespoons milk as needed until glaze is thick but still pourable. Spoon glaze over flat side of each cooled cake, letting some drip down sides. Let glaze set for 10 minutes before serving.

VARIATION

Dairy-Free Lavender Tea Cakes with Glaze

We prefer the flavor of these cakes made with soy milk, but almond milk will also work; do not use rice milk.

In cake release and cakes, substitute vegetable oil for butter. In cakes, use dairy-free cream cheese. In glaze, substitute unsweetened soy milk for milk.

Whole-Grain Sticky Toffee Pudding Cakes

G-F TESTING LAB

FLOUR SUBSTITUTION	Do not substitute other whole-grain blends for the ATK Whole-Grain Gluten-Free Flour Blend; they will not work in this recipe.
BAKING POWDER	Not all brands of baking powder are gluten-free; see page 25 for more information.
RESTING TIME	Do not shortchange the batter's 30-minute rest or else the cakes will taste gritty.

WHY THIS RECIPE WORKS

Sticky toffee pudding is a richly flavored sponge cake full of dates in a sweet toffee sauce. We thought that the earthy, molasses-like flavors of our whole-grain gluten-free flour blend would work well in these cakes. Our existing recipe for sticky toffee pudding cakes achieves its moist crumb by baking the filled ramekins in a water bath, covered with aluminum foil to seal in the steam. The additional moisture made our gluten-free cakes mushy and wet because the flours in our blend absorb more moisture than wheat flour does. Minus the water bath, our cakes turned out tender and delicate but were now gritty. The starches in our blend needed time to soften, so we rested the batter. For fruity date flavor, we used the soaking liquid from the dates in the batter and pulsed half of the dates so that every bite of cake had both bits and chunks of sticky dates.

Whole-Grain Sticky Toffee Pudding Cakes

SERVES 8

PUDDING CAKES

- 8 ounces (1¾ cups) ATK Whole-Grain Gluten-Free Flour Blend (page 9)
- ½ teaspoon baking powder
- ½ teaspoon salt
- ¾ cup warm water
- ½ teaspoon baking soda
- 1⅓ cups pitted whole dates, sliced ¼ inch thick
- 5¼ ounces (¾ cup packed) light brown sugar
- 2 large eggs
- 1½ teaspoons vanilla extract
- 4 tablespoons unsalted butter, melted

TOFFEE SAUCE

- 8 tablespoons unsalted butter
- 7 ounces (1 cup packed) light brown sugar
- ⅔ cup heavy cream
- 1 tablespoon rum

1. FOR THE PUDDING CAKES: Whisk flour blend, baking powder, and salt together in bowl. Whisk warm water and baking soda together in small bowl,

add ⅔ cup dates, and soak for 5 minutes. Drain dates and reserve soaking liquid.

2. Pulse remaining ⅔ cup dates and sugar in food processor to combine, about 5 pulses. Add eggs, vanilla, and date soaking liquid and process to combine, about 5 seconds. With processor running, slowly add melted butter until incorporated. Add flour blend mixture and pulse to combine, about 5 pulses. Transfer batter to bowl, stir in softened dates, cover, and let rest for 30 minutes.

3. Adjust oven rack to middle position and heat oven to 350 degrees. Grease eight 6-ounce ramekins and place on wire rack set in rimmed baking sheet. Portion batter evenly among prepared ramekins. (Ramekins can be covered individually with plastic wrap and refrigerated for up to 8 hours.)

4. Place sheet in oven and bake until tops of cakes are set and toothpick inserted into center of each cake comes out clean, 30 to 35 minutes, rotating pan halfway through baking (for refrigerated cakes, increase baking time to 35 to 40 minutes).

5. FOR THE TOFFEE SAUCE: Meanwhile, melt butter in medium saucepan over medium heat. Whisk in sugar and cook, stirring occasionally, until sugar is dissolved and mixture looks puffy, 3 to 4 minutes. Slowly whisk in cream and rum, reduce heat to medium-low, and simmer until frothy, about 3 minutes. Remove from heat and cover to keep warm. (Sauce can be refrigerated in airtight container for up to 2 days; reheat in microwave, about 3 minutes.)

6. Let cakes cool in ramekins for 10 minutes. Run thin knife around edges of ramekins to loosen cakes, then flip out onto individual plates or bowls. Drizzle with warm toffee sauce and serve.

VARIATION

Dairy-Free Whole-Grain Sticky Toffee Pudding Cakes

We had good luck using Silk Soy Creamer.

In cakes and toffee sauce, substitute Earth Balance Vegan Buttery Sticks for butter. In toffee sauce, substitute plain soy creamer for heavy cream.

Nutritional Information for Our Recipes

Analyzing recipes for their nutritional values is a tricky business, and we did our best to be as realistic and accurate as possible throughout this book. We were absolutely strict about measuring when cooking and never resorted to guessing or estimating. And we never made the portion sizes unreasonably small to make the nutritional numbers appear lower. We also didn't play games when analyzing the recipes in the nutritional program to make the numbers look better. To calculate the nutritional values of our recipes per serving, we used The Food Processor SQL by ESHA Research. When using this program, we entered all the ingredients, including optional ones, using weights for important ingredients such as meat, cheese, and most vegetables. We also used all of our preferred brands in these analyses. Yet there are two tricky ingredients to be mindful of when analyzing a recipe—salt and fat—they require some special rules of their own.

When the recipe called for seasoning with an unspecified amount of salt and pepper (often raw meat), we added ½ teaspoon salt and ¼ teaspoon pepper to the analysis. We did not, however, include additional salt or pepper in our analysis when the food was "seasoned to taste" at the end of cooking. As for fat, it can be difficult to accurately predict the amount of oil absorbed during frying. We compared our recipes, without any added cooking fat, to similar foods in The Food Processor SQL to estimate how much fat was absorbed during cooking. We found a good rule of thumb is that most foods absorb 10 percent of their weight in oil on average. (The exception to this rule is our recipe for Polenta Fries, which are shallow fried and not deep fried. For this recipe we used 5 percent of the recipe's weight to account for the oil absorption.) We then added the estimated amount of fat back into our nutritional analysis to calculate our final numbers.

Note: Unless otherwise indicated, information applies to a single serving. If there is a range in the serving size in the recipe, we used the highest number of servings to calculate the nutritional values.

	Cal	Fat	Sat Fat	Chol	Sodium	Carb	Fiber	Protein
GLUTEN-FREE BASICS								
America's Test Kitchen All-Purpose Gluten-Free Flour Blend (one ounce)	100	0g	0g	0mg	10mg	23g	1g	1g
America's Test Kitchen Whole-Grain Gluten-Free Flour Blend (one ounce)	110	2.5g	0g	0mg	0mg	19g	4g	4g
A GOOD START								
Whole-Grain Pancakes (per pancake)	140	6g	1.5g	25mg	180mg	17g	3g	4g
Dairy-Free Whole-Grain Pancakes (per pancake)	130	6g	0.5g	20mg	170mg	16g	3g	4g
Fluffy Oat Pancakes (per pancake)	120	4.5g	1.5g	30mg	190mg	14g	2g	4g
Dairy-Free Fluffy Oat Pancakes (per pancake)	120	5g	0.5g	25mg	190mg	13g	2g	4g
Johnnycakes (per johnnycake)	80	4.5g	1.5g	5mg	150mg	10g	1g	1g
Dairy-Free Johnnycakes (per johnnycake)	70	3.5g	0.5g	0mg	160mg	10g	1g	1g
Maple Butter (per tablespoon)	90	9g	6g	25mg	115mg	3g	0g	0g
Whole-Grain Waffles (per waffle)	590	25g	6g	160mg	520mg	76g	11g	20g
Dairy-Free Whole-Grain Waffles (per waffle)	580	27g	2.5g	140mg	530mg	71g	12g	17g
Whole-Grain Blueberry Muffins	320	16g	8g	80mg	400mg	41g	4g	6g
Dairy-Free Whole-Grain Blueberry Muffins	300	14g	1.5g	45mg	440mg	41g	5g	5g
Coconut-Cashew Muffins	350	19g	10g	70mg	270mg	41g	2g	5g
Dairy-Free Coconut-Cashew Muffins	360	21g	6g	45mg	280mg	41g	2g	5g
Corn Muffins	310	15g	9g	70mg	290mg	40g	2g	4g
Dairy-Free Corn Muffins	340	18g	3.5g	30mg	380mg	43g	2g	5g
Currant Scones	330	16g	10g	70mg	350mg	43g	1g	3g
Dairy-Free Currant Scones	350	17g	7g	30mg	470mg	46g	1g	4g
Date-Nut Bread (per ⅔" slice)	300	12g	4.5g	45mg	330mg	43g	2g	5g

	Cal	Fat	Sat Fat	Chol	Sodium	Carb	Fiber	Protein
Dairy-Free Date-Nut Bread (per ⅔" slice)	310	14g	1.5g	30mg	320mg	43g	2g	4g
Whole-Grain Chai Spice Bread (per ⅔" slice)	300	14g	6g	55mg	460mg	39g	4g	6g
Dairy-Free Whole-Grain Chai Spice Bread (per ⅔" slice)	310	16g	1.5g	30mg	460mg	38g	4g	6g
Whole-Grain Gingerbread Coffee Cake	300	12g	6g	60mg	500mg	44g	3g	5g
Dairy-Free Whole-Grain Gingerbread Coffee Cake	290	11g	3.5g	35mg	530mg	44g	3g	5g
New York–Style Crumb Cake	500	24g	14g	150mg	230mg	64g	1g	5g
Dairy-Free New York–Style Crumb Cake	500	25g	10g	95mg	390mg	64g	1g	5g
Yeasted Doughnuts	380	17g	4.5g	50mg	190mg	54g	2g	4g
Dairy-Free Yeasted Doughnuts	380	17g	3g	35mg	210mg	54g	2g	4g
Cinnamon Sugar–Glazed Doughnuts	390	17g	4g	50mg	190mg	56g	2g	4g
Vanilla-Glazed Doughnuts	390	17g	4g	50mg	190mg	56g	2g	4g
Chocolate-Glazed Doughnuts	480	21g	7g	55mg	200mg	69g	3g	5g
Popovers	200	8g	3.5g	135mg	270mg	23g	1g	7g
Three-Grain Breakfast Porridge	370	5g	1.5g	5mg	340mg	73g	7g	10g
Dairy-Free Three-Grain Breakfast Porridge	370	5g	1.5g	5mg	340mg	73g	7g	10g
Three-Grain Breakfast Porridge with Blueberries and Maple	410	5g	1.5g	5mg	340mg	83g	9g	11g
Three-Grain Breakfast Porridge with Tahini and Apricots	590	15g	2.5g	5mg	350mg	104g	11g	15g
Quinoa Granola with Sunflower Seeds and Almonds (per ½ cup)	345	19g	8g	0mg	70mg	36g	5g	8g
Quinoa Granola with Pecans, Espresso, and Chocolate (per ½ cup)	400	26g	12.5g	0mg	70mg	39g	5g	6.5g
Quinoa Granola with Pepitas, Cayenne, and Golden Raisins (per ½ cup)	355	20g	8g	0mg	75mg	37.5g	5g	8.5g

GRAINS

	Cal	Fat	Sat Fat	Chol	Sodium	Carb	Fiber	Protein
Coconut Rice with Bok Choy and Lime	230	8g	5g	0mg	800mg	36g	2g	4g
Indonesian-Style Fried Rice	480	17g	2g	125mg	1380mg	67g	4g	14g
Black Rice Salad with Snap Peas and Ginger-Sesame Vinaigrette	310	14g	2g	0mg	450mg	44g	5g	6g
Brown Rice Bowls with Roasted Carrots, Kale, and Fried Eggs	480	25g	4.5g	185mg	590mg	51g	6g	13g
Miso Brown Rice Cakes	440	17g	2g	95mg	880mg	60g	3g	11g
Sriracha Mayonnaise (per tablespoon)	70	7g	1g	5mg	110mg	1g	0g	0g
Buckwheat Bowls with Lemon-Yogurt Sauce	510	26g	4g	5mg	620mg	60g	10g	13g
Dairy-Free Buckwheat Bowls with Lemon-Yogurt Sauce	520	26g	3.5g	0mg	610mg	61g	11g	13g
Oat Berry and Mushroom Risotto	130	4.5g	0g	0mg	440mg	24g	4g	7g
Rainbow Quinoa Pilaf with Swiss Chard and Carrots	240	7g	0g	0mg	500mg	36g	4g	6g
Rainbow Quinoa Pilaf with Bell Pepper, Lime, and Cilantro	230	7g	0g	0mg	410mg	35g	3g	6g
Quinoa, Black Bean, and Mango Salad with Lime Dressing	450	27g	3.5g	0mg	350mg	45g	8g	9g
Millet Salad with Corn and Queso Fresco	230	9g	1.5g	0mg	320mg	31g	3g	5g
Millet Salad with Oranges, Olives, and Almonds	260	12g	1.5g	0mg	420mg	33g	5g	5g
Millet Salad with Endive, Blueberries, and Goat Cheese	310	17g	4.5g	10mg	380mg	34g	5g	8g
Millet Cakes with Spinach and Carrots	350	15g	2g	50mg	410mg	46g	8g	10g
Dairy-Free Millet Cakes with Spinach and Carrots	360	14g	1.5g	45mg	400mg	47g	8g	10g
Cucumber-Yogurt Sauce (per tablespoon)	10	1g	0g	0mg	0mg	0g	0g	1g
Polenta Fries	270	16g	1g	0mg	590mg	27g	2g	3g
Herb Mayonnaise (per tablespoon)	80	9g	1g	5mg	70mg	0g	0g	0g

	Cal	Fat	Sat Fat	Chol	Sodium	Carb	Fiber	Protein
COMFORT FOODS								
Buffalo Chicken Wings	380	27g	10g	185mg	1520mg	3g	0g	28g
Chicken Wings with Sweet and Spicy Thai Sauce	400	22g	6g	165mg	1080mg	20g	0g	28g
New England Clam Chowder	430	20g	11g	110mg	1180mg	37g	3g	23g
Quicker New England Clam Chowder	380	19g	10g	85mg	1260mg	38g	3g	14g
Pecan-Crusted Chicken	550	32g	9g	115mg	450mg	27g	4g	38g
Orange-Flavored Chicken	900	53g	10g	160mg	1420mg	65g	1g	40g
Chicken Parmesan	620	41g	9g	125mg	1150mg	25g	4g	36g
Chicken and Dumplings	520	20g	6g	160mg	1080mg	46g	4g	36g
Dairy-Free Chicken and Dumplings	520	20g	4.5g	140mg	1140mg	46g	4g	36g
Batter-Fried Fish	420	27g	3g	75mg	670mg	15g	0g	32g
Tartar Sauce (per tablespoon)	310	33g	4.5g	15mg	430mg	3g	0g	0g
Breaded Pork Cutlets	430	29g	4.5g	105mg	310mg	16g	0g	28g
Lemon-Thyme Breaded Pork Cutlets	430	29g	4.5g	105mg	310mg	16g	0g	28g
Cheesy Southwestern Meatloaf	490	25g	11g	220mg	1140mg	23g	2g	41g
Vegetable Pot Pie with Crumble Topping	680	37g	22g	115mg	1330mg	71g	11g	15g
Beef Pot Pie	630	30g	13g	150mg	1110mg	41g	3g	43g
Vegetable Lasagna	500	25g	11g	75mg	1130mg	43g	5g	23g
Chicken Enchiladas (per enchilada)	290	18g	8g	65mg	690mg	17g	3g	16g
Strata with Spinach and Gruyère	400	24g	10g	200mg	600mg	26g	2g	18g
Strata with Sausage, Mushrooms, and Monterey Jack Cheese	460	30g	11g	260mg	750mg	26g	1g	20g
BREAD, PIZZA, AND CRACKERS								
Whole-Grain Sandwich Bread (per ½" slice)	180	5g	1g	40mg	290mg	28g	6g	6g
Dairy-Free Whole-Grain Sandwich Bread (per ½" slice)	180	6g	0g	35mg	290mg	28g	6g	6g
Honey-Millet Sandwich Bread (per ½" slice)	200	5g	0g	35mg	290mg	33g	7g	6g
Honey Butter (per tablespoon)	120	11g	7g	30mg	150mg	4g	0g	0g
Flourless Nut and Seed Loaf (per ½" slice)	180	12g	3.5g	0mg	110mg	14g	4g	5g
Brioche (per ½" slice)	220	8g	4g	75mg	310mg	31g	3g	5g
Dairy-Free Brioche (per ½" slice)	280	12g	5g	60mg	360mg	39g	4g	5g
Whole-Grain Sprouted Bread (per ½" slice)	180	4.5g	0g	0mg	250mg	32g	6g	7g
Baguettes (per 1" slice)	50	0.5g	0g	15mg	85mg	10g	1g	1g
Rustic Bread with Sesame Seeds (per 1" slice)	130	1.5g	0g	25mg	240mg	26g	4g	3g
Bagels	340	7g	3.5g	15mg	1360mg	62g	5g	5g
Dairy-Free Bagels	340	7g	2.5g	0mg	1230mg	62g	5g	5g
Everything Bagels	380	10g	4g	15mg	1540mg	65g	6g	7g
Whole-Grain Walnut-Cherry Boule (per ⅔" slice)	260	10g	1g	35mg	400mg	36g	8g	9g
Dairy-Free Whole-Grain Walnut-Cherry Boule (per ⅔" slice)	250	10g	1g	30mg	390mg	34g	8g	8g
Classic Cheese Pan Pizza (per slice)	430	27g	7g	40mg	440mg	37g	3g	9g
Pepperoni Pan Pizza (per slice)	470	30g	8g	50mg	570mg	37g	3g	11g
Pan Pizza with Sausage and Peppers (per slice)	460	28g	7g	45mg	520mg	37g	3g	12g
Rosemary Focaccia (per 2" square)	130	5g	0.5g	10mg	135mg	18g	1g	2g
Whole-Grain Dinner Rolls	170	7g	3g	60mg	310mg	21g	4g	6g
Dairy-Free Whole-Grain Dinner Rolls	170	8g	2g	45mg	350mg	20g	4g	5g
Hamburger Rolls	310	6g	2g	55mg	590mg	54g	6g	7g
Dairy-Free Hamburger Rolls	310	7g	0.5g	45mg	590mg	54g	6g	7g

	Cal	Fat	Sat Fat	Chol	Sodium	Carb	Fiber	Protein
Maple-Sorghum Skillet Bread (per 2" piece)	180	10g	4g	40mg	190mg	21g	1g	3g
Dairy-Free Maple-Sorghum Skillet Bread (per 2" piece)	150	7g	1.5g	25mg	220mg	20g	1g	3g
Whole-Grain Crackers (six crackers)	130	8g	0.5g	0mg	125mg	13g	3g	3g
Whole-Grain Poppy Seed–Thyme Crackers (six crackers)	130	8g	1g	0mg	120mg	13g	3g	3g
Whole-Grain Sesame-Rosemary Crackers (six crackers)	130	8g	0.5g	0mg	125mg	13g	3g	3g
Cheddar Cheese Coins (six crackers)	230	14g	9g	40mg	270mg	18g	0g	7g
Pimento Cheese Coins (six crackers)	230	14g	9g	40mg	270mg	18g	1g	7g
Mustard, Gruyère, and Caraway Cheese Coins (six crackers)	250	15g	8g	45mg	410mg	18g	1g	8g
Everything Cheese Coins (six crackers)	250	15g	9g	45mg	290mg	19g	1g	8g

COOKIES AND BARS (Nutritional information based on one cookie or bar)

	Cal	Fat	Sat Fat	Chol	Sodium	Carb	Fiber	Protein
Whole-Grain Chocolate Chip Cookies	150	7g	4g	20mg	140mg	21g	2g	2g
Dairy-Free Whole-Grain Chocolate Chip Cookies	150	7g	3g	10mg	120mg	21g	2g	2g
White Chocolate–Macadamia Nut Cookies	160	8g	4g	20mg	115mg	20g	0g	1g
Dairy-Free White Chocolate–Macadamia Nut Cookies	160	9g	2g	10mg	115mg	20g	1g	1g
Oatmeal Cookies with Chocolate Chunks and Dried Cherries	200	9g	3.5g	25mg	65mg	28g	2g	3g
Dairy-Free Oatmeal Cookies with Chocolate Chunks	170	6g	1g	15mg	65mg	28g	2g	3g
Chocolate Crinkle Cookies	160	6g	3.5g	30mg	95mg	28g	1g	2g
Dairy-Free Chocolate Crinkle Cookies	170	6g	2.5g	25mg	95mg	28g	1g	2g
Whole-Grain Brown Sugar Cookies	180	8g	4g	35mg	85mg	25g	2g	2g
Dairy-Free Whole-Grain Brown Sugar Cookies	170	10g	0.5g	15mg	85mg	21g	2g	2g
Whole-Grain Gingersnaps	80	3g	1.5g	10mg	50mg	12g	1g	1g
Dairy-Free Whole-Grain Gingersnaps	80	3.5g	0g	5mg	50mg	12g	1g	1g
Peanut Butter Sandwich Cookies	210	14g	4g	15mg	160mg	20g	1g	5g
Dairy-Free Peanut Butter Sandwich Cookies	220	14g	2.5g	10mg	160mg	20g	1g	5g
Linzer Cookies	200	11g	4g	30mg	60mg	24g	1g	3g
Dairy-Free Linzer Cookies	200	11g	2.5g	15mg	120mg	24g	1g	3g
Almond Biscotti	120	4.5g	1.5g	20mg	55mg	19g	1g	2g
Dairy-Free Almond Biscotti	120	4.5g	1g	15mg	75mg	19g	1g	2g
Anise Biscotti	120	4.5g	1.5g	20mg	55mg	19g	1g	2g
Pistachio Spice Biscotti	120	4g	1.5g	20mg	55mg	19g	1g	2g
Chocolate-Dipped Biscotti	190	10g	4.5g	20mg	55mg	26g	2g	3g
Rugelach	90	5g	2g	15mg	65mg	9g	0g	1g
Dairy-Free Rugelach	100	7g	2.5g	10mg	45mg	9g	0g	1g
Blackberry-Almond Rugelach	90	5g	2g	15mg	65mg	10g	1g	1g
Lime-Glazed Coconut-Cardamom Cookies	120	5g	3.5g	20mg	45mg	18g	0g	1g
Dairy-Free Lime-Glazed Coconut-Cardamom Cookies	110	4.5g	1.5g	10mg	45mg	18g	0g	1g
Whole-Grain Graham Crackers	90	3.5g	2g	10mg	70mg	12g	1g	1g
Dairy-Free Whole-Grain Graham Crackers	90	3.5g	1g	0mg	65mg	12g	1g	1g
Lemon Madeleines	100	5g	2.5g	55mg	45mg	11g	0g	1g
Dairy-Free Lemon Madeleines	100	6g	0.5g	45mg	45mg	11g	0g	1g
Almond Madeleines	90	5g	2.5g	55mg	45mg	11g	0g	1g
Orange-Cardamom Madeleines	90	5g	2.5g	55mg	45mg	11g	0g	1g
Blondies	230	9g	5g	40mg	150mg	37g	1g	2g
Lunchbox Brownies	200	8g	3g	45mg	105mg	31g	1g	2g
Dairy-Free Lunchbox Brownies	200	8g	2g	35mg	60mg	31g	1g	2g

	Cal	Fat	Sat Fat	Chol	Sodium	Carb	Fiber	Protein
Whole-Grain Pecan Bars	230	15g	4.5g	25mg	160mg	23g	2g	3g
Dairy-Free Whole-Grain Pecan Bars	220	14g	2.5g	10mg	60mg	23g	2g	3g
Key Lime Bars	220	11g	7g	40mg	105mg	29g	0g	3g
Ginger-Fig Streusel Bars	190	7g	3.5g	15mg	60mg	29g	1g	1g

FRUIT DESSERTS, PIES, AND TARTS

	Cal	Fat	Sat Fat	Chol	Sodium	Carb	Fiber	Protein
Whole-Grain Cherry Crisp	390	14g	6g	25mg	45mg	62g	5g	6g
Dairy-Free Whole-Grain Cherry Crisp	390	14g	4g	0mg	100mg	62g	5g	6g
Blueberry Cobbler with Cornmeal Biscuits	350	12g	7g	30mg	400mg	58g	5g	4g
Dairy-Free Blueberry Cobbler with Cornmeal Biscuits	340	12g	4.5g	0mg	370mg	57g	5g	3g
Strawberry Shortcakes	540	28g	14g	105mg	600mg	69g	4g	6g
Peach Shortcakes	550	28g	14g	105mg	600mg	72g	4g	6g
Strawberry-Rhubarb Pie	510	24g	15g	60mg	400mg	72g	3g	4g
Dutch Apple Pie	620	26g	16g	95mg	230mg	96g	7g	4g
Pecan Pie	680	42g	15g	125mg	360mg	73g	3g	6g
Lemon Meringue Pie	430	18g	10g	175mg	230mg	63g	1g	5g
Coconut Cream Pie	630	47g	32g	220mg	270mg	47g	2g	6g
Chocolate Angel Pie	510	38g	23g	150mg	190mg	41g	2g	6g
French Apple Tart	450	16g	10g	65mg	170mg	76g	6g	2g
Baked Raspberry Tart	420	22g	14g	105mg	180mg	51g	3g	3g
Whole-Grain Free-Form Pear Tart	550	23g	12g	50mg	340mg	87g	12g	7g

CAKES

	Cal	Fat	Sat Fat	Chol	Sodium	Carb	Fiber	Protein
Rainbow Sprinkle Cupcakes	420	25g	11g	70mg	180mg	45g	0g	3g
Dairy-Free Rainbow Sprinkle Cupcakes	420	25g	11g	65mg	200mg	45g	0g	3g
Whole-Grain Carrot Cupcakes	350	21g	8g	65mg	300mg	37g	3g	5g
Dairy-Free Whole-Grain Carrot Cupcakes	350	21g	8g	65mg	300mg	37g	3g	5g
Chocolate Cream Cupcakes	360	23g	9g	65mg	210mg	40g	2g	4g
Lemon Layer Cake	480	17g	9g	145mg	450mg	77g	1g	6g
Dairy-Free Lemon Layer Cake	470	16g	6g	110mg	600mg	76g	1g	6g
Whole-Grain Brown Sugar Layer Cake	660	38g	22g	160mg	640mg	70g	4g	10g
Dairy-Free Whole-Grain Brown Sugar Layer Cake	680	41g	17g	130mg	680mg	70g	4g	10g
New York–Style Cheesecake	450	33g	19g	185mg	290mg	30g	1g	9g
Whole-Grain Apple Upside-Down Cake	400	18g	10g	85mg	200mg	57g	5g	5g
Dairy-Free Whole-Grain Apple Upside-Down Cake	400	18g	7g	45mg	270mg	57g	5g	5g
Lemon Bundt Cake	400	14g	8g	95mg	330mg	64g	1g	4g
Dairy-Free Lemon Bundt Cake	380	12g	1g	60mg	330mg	64g	1g	4g
Rosemary Polenta Cake with Clementines	390	15g	9g	80mg	200mg	58g	3g	5g
Dairy-Free Rosemary Polenta Cake with Clementines	340	10g	4g	35mg	290mg	56g	3g	5g
Chocolate-Hazelnut Torte	370	25g	10g	135mg	95mg	36g	4g	7g
Dairy-Free Chocolate-Hazelnut Torte	380	27g	9g	110mg	190mg	33g	4g	8g
Molten Chocolate Cakes	440	31g	17g	175mg	190mg	46g	5g	7g
Dairy-Free Chocolate Molten Cakes	470	37g	19g	140mg	330mg	37g	6g	10g
Lavender Tea Cakes with Vanilla Bean Glaze	220	8g	5g	50mg	115mg	36g	0g	2g
Dairy-Free Lavender Tea Cakes with Vanilla Bean Glaze	230	9g	1.5g	30mg	120mg	36g	0g	2g
Whole-Grain Sticky Toffee Pudding Cakes	580	28g	15g	120mg	290mg	78g	5g	6g
Dairy-Free Whole-Grain Sticky Toffee Pudding Cakes	530	21g	7g	45mg	470mg	79g	5g	6g

Weight-to-Volume Equivalents for G-F Flours

Different brands of wheat flour all contain the same ingredients so they measure out the same. However, different gluten-free flour brands contain different ingredients, which will pack differently. For this reason, weight-to-volume equivalents vary from brand to brand, as you can see from the information below.

You can avoid this problem if you simply weigh your flour (this is how our recipes are written). Ten ounces of gluten-free flour blend is the same, no matter the brand. If you decide to measure flour by volume, the G-F Testing Lab feature gives you relevant conversion information.

Note that these flour blends are not always interchangeable in our recipes. For details, see the G-F Testing Lab notes for each recipe.

OUNCES	ATK Whole-Grain Flour Blend / ATK All-Purpose Flour Blend	Betty Crocker All-Purpose Gluten Free Rice Blend / Bob's Red Mill GF All-Purpose Baking Flour	King Arthur Gluten-Free Multi-Purpose Flour
1	3½ tablespoons	3 tablespoons	3 tablespoons
1.5	⅓ cup	5 tablespoons	¼ cup
2	7 tablespoons	6 tablespoons	6 tablespoons
2.5	⅓ cup plus ¼ cup	½ cup	7 tablespoons
3	⅔ cup	½ cup plus 2 tablespoons	⅓ cup plus ¼ cup
3.5	¾ cup	⅔ cup	½ cup plus 2 tablespoons
4	¾ cup plus 2 tablespoons	½ cup plus ⅓ cup	¾ cup
4.5	**1 cup**	¾ cup plus 2 tablespoons	½ cup plus ⅓ cup
5	1 cup plus 2 tablespoons	**1 cup**	⅔ cup plus ¼ cup
5.5	1¼ cups	1 cup plus 2 tablespoons	**1 cup**
6	1⅓ cups	⅔ cup plus ½ cup	¾ cup plus ⅓ cup
6.5	¾ cup plus ⅔ cup	1⅓ cups	⅔ cup plus ½ cup
7	1⅓ cups plus ¼ cup	1¼ cups plus 2 tablespoons	1¼ cups
7.5	1⅔ cups	1½ cups	1¼ cups plus 2 tablespoons
8	1¾ cups	1½ cups plus 2 tablespoons	¾ cup plus ⅔ cup
8.5	1¾ cups plus 2 tablespoons	1⅔ cups	1⅓ cups plus ¼ cup
9	**2 cups**	1½ cups plus ⅓ cup	1½ cups plus 2 tablespoons
9.5	2 cups plus 2 tablespoons	1¾ cups plus 2 tablespoons	1¾ cups
10	2¼ cups	**2 cups**	1½ cups plus ⅓ cup
10.5	2⅓ cups	2 cups plus 2 tablespoons	1⅔ cups plus ¼ cup
11	1¾ cups plus ⅔ cup	1⅔ cups plus ½ cup	**2 cups**
11.5	2⅓ cups plus ¼ cup	2⅓ cups	1¾ cups plus ⅓ cup
12	2⅔ cups	2¼ cups plus 2 tablespoons	1⅔ cups plus ½ cup
12.5	2¾ cups	2½ cups	2¼ cups
13	2¾ cups plus 2 tablespoons	2½ cups plus 2 tablespoons	2¼ cups plus 2 tablespoons
13.5	**3 cups**	2⅔ cups	1¾ cups plus ⅔ cup
14	3 cups plus 2 tablespoons	2½ cups plus ⅓ cup	2⅓ cups plus ¼ cup
14.5	3¼ cups	2¾ cups plus 2 tablespoons	2½ cups plus 2 tablespoons
15	3⅓ cups	**3 cups**	2¾ cups
15.5	2¾ cups plus ⅔ cup	3 cups plus 2 tablespoons	2½ cups plus ⅓ cup
16	3⅓ cups plus ¼ cup	2⅔ cups plus ½ cup	2⅔ cups plus ¼ cup
16.5	3⅔ cups	3⅓ cups	**3 cups**

Conversions and Equivalents

The recipes in this book were developed using standard U.S. measures following U.S. government guidelines. The charts below offer equivalents for U.S. and metric measures. All conversions are approximate and have been rounded up or down to the nearest whole number.

EXAMPLE:

> 1 teaspoon = 4.9292 milliliters, rounded up to 5 milliliters
> 1 ounce = 28.3495 grams, rounded down to 28 grams

VOLUME CONVERSIONS

U.S.	METRIC
1 teaspoon	5 milliliters
2 teaspoons	10 milliliters
1 tablespoon	15 milliliters
2 tablespoons	30 milliliters
¼ cup	59 milliliters
⅓ cup	79 milliliters
½ cup	118 milliliters
¾ cup	177 milliliters
1 cup	237 milliliters
1¼ cups	296 milliliters
1½ cups	355 milliliters
2 cups (1 pint)	473 milliliters
2½ cups	591 milliliters
3 cups	710 milliliters
4 cups (1 quart)	0.946 liter
1.06 quarts	1 liter
4 quarts (1 gallon)	3.8 liters

WEIGHT CONVERSIONS

OUNCES	GRAMS
½	14
¾	21
1	28
1½	43
2	57
2½	71
3	85
3½	99
4	113
4½	128
5	142
6	170
7	198
8	227
9	255
10	283
12	340
16 (1 pound)	454

CONVERSIONS FOR INGREDIENTS COMMONLY USED IN BAKING

Baking is an exacting science. Because measuring by weight is far more accurate than measuring by volume, and thus more likely to achieve reliable results, in our recipes we provide ounce measures in addition to cup measures for many ingredients. Refer to the chart below to convert these measures into grams.

INGREDIENT	OUNCES	GRAMS
1 cup granulated (white) sugar	7	198
1 cup packed brown sugar (light or dark)	7	198
1 cup confectioners' sugar	4	113
1 cup cocoa powder	3	85
4 tablespoons butter* (½ stick, or ¼ cup)	2	57
8 tablespoons butter* (1 stick, or ½ cup)	4	113
16 tablespoons butter* (2 sticks, or 1 cup)	8	227

* In the United States, butter is sold both salted and unsalted. We generally recommend unsalted butter. If you are using salted butter, take this into consideration before adding salt to a recipe.

OVEN TEMPERATURES

FAHRENHEIT	CELSIUS	GAS MARK
225	105	¼
250	120	½
275	135	1
300	150	2
325	165	3
350	180	4
375	190	5
400	200	6
425	220	7
450	230	8
475	245	9

CONVERTING TEMPERATURES FROM AN INSTANT-READ THERMOMETER

We include doneness temperatures in many of the recipes in this book. We recommend an instant-read thermometer for the job. Refer to the above table to convert Fahrenheit degrees to Celsius. Or, for temperatures not represented in the chart, use this simple formula:

Subtract 32 degrees from the Fahrenheit reading, then divide the result by 1.8 to find the Celsius reading.

EXAMPLE:

"Roast chicken until thighs register 175 degrees."
To convert:
$175°F - 32 = 143°$
$143° \div 1.8 = 79.44°C$, rounded down to $79°C$

Index

Flour (cont.)

    sorghum, 24

    sweet white rice, 24

    teff, 25

    wheat, 4–5

    white rice, 24

    see also Gluten-Free Flour Blends

Flourless Nut and Seed Loaf, *146,* 147

Fluffy Oat Pancakes, *40,* 41

Focaccia, Rosemary, *170,* 171

Foil sling, for bar cookies, 217

French Apple Tart, *256,* 257

Frostings

    Cream Cheese, 270

    Cream Cheese, Double-Batch, 270

    piping onto cupcakes, 270

    spreading onto layer cakes, 280

    Vanilla, 270

    Vanilla, Double-Batch, 270

Fruit

    See Berries; *specific fruits*

G

Ginger

    -Fig Streusel Bars, *224,* 225

    -Sesame Vinaigrette and Snap Peas, Black Rice
        Salad with, *82,* 83

    Whole-Grain Gingerbread Coffee Cake, *60,* 61

    Whole-Grain Gingersnaps, *196,* 197

Gluten

    defined, 3

    development of, 3

    -free diet, key challenges, 5

    science of, 3

Gluten-Free Flour Blends

    All-Purpose, ATK, nutritional information, 300

    All-Purpose, ATK, recipe for, *6,* 7

    all-purpose, store-bought, tests on, 10–12

    measuring techniques, 15

    weight-to-volume equivalents, 304

    Whole-Grain, ATK, nutritional information, 300

Gluten-Free Flour Blends (cont.)

    Whole-Grain, ATK, recipe for, *8,* 9

    whole-grain, store-bought, taste tests on, 13

Gluten-free recipes

    baking tips, 14–18

    binders and leaveners for, 25–26

    flours and starches for, 23–25

    grains and seeds for, 26–28

    making dairy-free, 20–21

    pasta and noodles for, 30

    replacing wheat flour in, 4–5

    rice for, 28–29

    troubleshooting, 19

Graham Crackers, Whole-Grain, *212,* 213

Grain(s) (gluten-free)

    Buckwheat Bowls with Lemon-Yogurt Sauce,
        88, 89

    Oat Berry and Mushroom Risotto, *90,* 91

    Polenta Fries, *100,* 101

    for recipes, 26–28

    rinsing, 79

    Rosemary Polenta Cake with Clementines,
        288, 289

    sprouting, 153

    storing, 27

    Three-, Breakfast Porridge, 73

        with Blueberries and Maple, *72,* 73

        with Tahini and Apricots, 73

    see also Cornmeal; Millet; Oats; Quinoa; Rice;
        Whole-Grain

Granola, Quinoa

    with Pecans, Espresso, and Chocolate, 75

    with Pepitas, Cayenne, and Golden Raisins, 75

    with Sunflower Seeds and Almonds, *74,* 75

Greens

    Brown Rice Bowls with Roasted Carrots, Kale,
        and Fried Eggs, *84,* 85

    Millet Cakes with Spinach and Carrots, *98,* 99

    Rainbow Quinoa Pilaf with Swiss Chard and
        Carrots, *92,* 93

    Strata with Spinach and Gruyère, *136,* 137

    Swiss chard, preparing, 93

Guar gum, 22, 25